Cambridge

IGCSE®

ICT

Second Edition

Graham Brown
Brian Sargent
David Watson

HODDER
EDUCATION
AN HACHETTE UK COMPANY

Acknowledgements

The Publishers would like to thank the following for permission to reproduce copyright material:

p.1 © Cifotart – Fotolia.com; **p.6** *t* © Mykola Mazuryk – Fotolia, *tcl* © Devyatkin – Fotolia, *tcr* © vetkit – Fotolia, *bcl* © Devyatkin – Fotolia, *bcr* © anmalkov – Fotolia, *br* © rocksunderwater/istockphoto.com, *bl* © peno – Fotolia; **p.10** *t* © karammiri – Fotolia, *b* © Gjermund Alsos – Fotolia; **p.11** © bloomua – Fotolia; **p.12** © alexey_boldin – Fotolia; **p.13** © bloomua – Fotolia; **p.14** © Oleksiy Mark – Fotolia; **p.19** *t* © Ingram Publishing, *b* © Dmitriy Melnikov – Fotolia. com; **p.20** *t* © Cindy England/istockphoto.com, *c* © George Clerk/istockphoto.com, *b* www.purestockx.com; **p.21** © Dmitry Vinogradov/istockphoto.com; **p.22** *t* © Mariano Ruiz/istockphoto.com, *c* © Drive Images/Alamy, *b* © kmit – Fotolia.com; **p.23** *t* © jerges/istockphoto.com, *c* © George Dolgikh – Fotolia.com, *b* © Thinkstock/Jupiterimages/Getty Images; **p.24** © Martin Firus/istockphoto.com; **p.25** © 216Photo/iStockphoto.com; **p.26** *t* © HP_Photo – Fotolia. com, *b* © Photodisc/Getty Images; **p.28** *t* © fotoIE /istockphoto.com, *b* © Michal Mrozek/iStockphoto.com; **p.29** *t* © asterix0597/istockphoto.com, *c* © Brand X/Getty Images; **p.30** *t* © Piotr Adamowicz – Fotolia.com, *b* © Jostein Hauge/istockphoto.com; **p.32** *t* © Access IS, UK, *c* © eaconstox/Alamy, *b* © THINKX/Alamy; **p.33** © Access IS, UK; **p.34** *t* © Royalty-Free/Corbis, *c* © thumb/istockphoto.com; **p.35** © Ingram Publishing; **p.36** © LoopAll – Fotolia. com; **p.37** © jamdesign – Fotolia.com; **p.38** © Andrey Turchaninov/istockphoto.com; **p.39** *t* © Konstantin Shevtsov – Fotolia.com, *b* © Murat BAYSAN – Fotolia.com; **p.40** *t* © Ted Foxx/Alamy, *c* © Miguel Navarro/Getty Images, *b* © Piero Cruciatti/Alamy; **p.42** © Ronen/iStockphoto.com; **p.43** *t* ©Tomasz Zachariasz /istockphoto.com, *ct* © Andrew Lambert Photography/Science Photo Library, *cb* © Yury Kosourov/istockphoto.com, *b* © oliver leedham/Alamy; **p.48** *t* © rocksunderwater/istockphoto.com, *b* © Long Ha/istockphoto.com; **p.49** © fotoIE/istockphoto.com; **p.53** © imagebroker/Alamy; **p.54** © Brennan; **p.56** © Tatiana Popova/istockphoto.com; **p.57** © scubabartek/istockphoto.com; **p.58** © sambrogio/istockphoto.com; **p.59** *t* © hadkhanong – Fotolia.com, *c* © Savone/Alamy, *b* © Alexandr Malyshev – iStock via Thinkstock; **p.60** © Sheval/Alamy; **p.65** © alexey_boldin – Fotolia; **p.66** *t* © Gjermund Alsos – Fotolia, *b* © karammiri – Fotolia; **p.71** © Supertrooper – Fotolia.com; **p.72** (Figure 4.11) *l and r* © karammiri – Fotolia, *b* © Supertrooper – Fotolia.com; **p.73** © ONOKY – Photononstop/Alamy; **p.79** © supergenijalac – iStock via Thinkstock; **p.85** *t and c* © Hodder & Stoughton Ltd, *b* © Laurence Dutton/Getty Images; **p.88** © Angela Jones – Fotolia.com; **p.91** © THINKX/Alamy; **p.105** © Baloncici – iStock via Thinkstock; **p.119** © filipfoto – iStock via Thinkstock; **p.121** © Piero Cruciatti/Alamy; **p.126** © tournee – Fotolia.com; **p.127** © Andrew Aitchison/In Pictures/Corbis; **p.129** © Patryk Kosmider – Fotolia.com; **p.158** *t* © A. T. Willett/Alamy, *b* © Tim Mainiero/Alamy; **p.183** © Oleksiy Mark – Fotolia.

t = top, *b* = bottom, *l* = left, *r* = right, *c* = centre

The questions, example answers, marks awarded and/or comments that appear in this book/CD were written by the authors. In examination, the way marks would be awarded to answers like these may be different.

Computer hardware and software brand names mentioned in this book are protected by their respective trademarks and are acknowledged.

Every effort has been made to trace all copyright holders, but if any have been inadvertently overlooked the publishers will be pleased to make the necessary arrangements at the first opportunity.

Although every effort has been made to ensure that website addresses are correct at time of going to press, Hodder Education cannot be held responsible for the content of any website mentioned in this book. It is sometimes possible to find a relocated web page by typing in the address of the home page for a website in the URL window of your browser.

The authors would like to thank the following for their assistance, patience, understanding and proofreading: Tracy Brown, Philippa Brown, Laura Brown, Jenna Brown, Karla Brown, John Reeves, Brian Sargent and Stuart Morris.

On the CD: Images © Graham Brown – Remora, SnowAngel, Dog, Snowball, Trees, Turtle; Video © Graham Brown – Wreck, Presvideo.

Hachette UK's policy is to use papers that are natural, renewable and recyclable products and made from wood grown in sustainable forests. The logging and manufacturing processes are expected to conform to the environmental regulations of the country of origin.

Orders: please contact Bookpoint Ltd, 130 Milton Park, Abingdon, Oxon OX14 4SB. Telephone: (44) 01235 827720. Fax: (44) 01235 400454. Lines are open 9.00–5.00, Monday to Saturday, with a 24-hour message answering service. Visit our website at www.hoddereducation.com.

® IGCSE is the registered trademark of Cambridge International Examinations

© Graham Brown, Brian Sargent and David Watson 2015

First published in 2010 by

Hodder Education

An Hachette UK Company

Carmelite House, 50 Victoria Embankment, London EC4Y 0DZ

This second edition published 2015

Impression number 5

Year   2019   2018   2017   2016

Cover photo © Oleksiy Mark – Fotolia

This edition typeset in 11/13pt ITC Galliard by Aptara, Inc.

Printed in Italy

A catalogue record for this title is available from the British Library

ISBN 978 1471 807213

Contents

Introduction

Aims

This book has been written to provide the knowledge, understanding and practical skills that you'll learn through studying the Cambridge International Level 1/Level 2 course in Information and Communication Technology, also known as Cambridge IGCSE ICT. This book, together with the accompanying CD provides:

- practice tasks which offer guidance on how to answer questions for the practical parts of the course
- activities which allow students practice in answering questions for the practical parts of the course
- source data files for the tasks and activities
- advice for the practical parts of the course
- suggestions for possible teaching methods.

Although it has been written with the Cambridge syllabus in mind, it can also be used as reference text for other practical ICT qualifications at GCSE and other equivalent Level 2 courses.

Using the book

The text is in 21 chapters. Although some elements of the practical chapters may be examined in the theory question papers, and vice versa, the sections for the theory work are in Chapters 1–10 and the sections for the practical work in Chapters 11–21. Answers on the Teacher's CD include some marking guidance.

Examination questions

The practical section contains examination-style questions.

Colour codes and symbols used

Throughout the book there are a number of colours and symbols used. Key presses are shown as <Enter>, but be careful with Chapter 21, where html codes are also shown in angled brackets, like this <html>. Different sections of text are in the following styles.

> ### Tasks
> These are examination-style questions in the practical section (which often include the use of source files from the CD for the practical tasks) that are answered within the chapter. The text demonstrates the techniques used to solve the task and gives some example answers. These provide easy-to-follow step-by-step instructions, so that practical skills are developed alongside the knowledge and understanding.

> ### Activities
> These are examination-style questions in the practical section, usually at the end of a chapter or section for the students to answer. These often include the use of source files from the CD.

> ## Exercises
>
> In the theory section, these are short exercises for the students to complete in order to confirm their understanding of the concepts covered in a section or chapter.

HTML markup

```
All html markup appears in a blue proportionally spaced font
with a blue dotted border.
```

Cascading stylesheets

```
All cascading stylesheets appear in a cerise proportionally
spaced font with a cerise dotted border.
```

Advice

These give advice and shortcuts for improving your ICT skills.

Text colours

Some words or phrases within the text are printed in red. Definitions of these terms can be found in the glossary on the CD.

In the practical section, words that appear in blue indicate an action or location found within the software package, for example 'Select the HOME tab.'

In the database sections of the book, words in orange show fieldnames.

Words in green show the functions or formulae entered into the cell of a spreadsheet, for example a cell may contain the function =SUM(B2:B12).

Hardware and software used

The practical elements of the examinations can be undertaken on any hardware platform and using any appropriate software packages. For the purposes of this book, we have needed to choose specific software packages, but the functionality of many other packages is very similar. Many of the skills demonstrated in Chapters 11 to 21 are transferable and can be adapted for other hardware and software platforms.

All the tasks and activities within the practical chapters have therefore been created using a PC platform with *Microsoft Windows 8.1* operating system and include the use of *Notepad*. Independent packages used for the practical sections include packages from *Microsoft Office Professional Edition 2013*, including *Word*, *Excel*, *Access* and *PowerPoint. Internet Explorer* has been used as the web browser, although we would recommend testing all web pages in at least three different web browsers.

For the website authoring section of the book (Chapter 21), all work has been produced in html code without the use of a WYSIWYG package. Although you may have a WYSIWYG package, it is important to realise that you are expected to have knowledge of underlying HTML and cascading stylesheet code. All html written within this chapter is written in HTML version 5, and is W3C validated (at the time of going to print). All cascading stylesheets used have been W3C validated.

Using source files

Source files can be found on the CD and will need to be copied onto your local machine or network drive in order to use them. Copy them and give them read/write access. This is essential to ensure that you can use some of the file types included on the CD. For example, you cannot create queries or reports in *Access* when working from the CD. The CD will contain all source files in a series of sub-folders, one for each of the practical chapters.

PC users

On the keyboard press <Windows> and <E>. The Windows Explorer window opens for This PC. Locate the CD or DVD drive, which may be called drive D: or E:

For the purposes of this section, we will assume that it is called drive E:. If your machine has a different drive for the CD letter, adapt these instructions accordingly. Locate the Chapter source files folder, which can be found at E:\Resources\Chapter source files. To locate an individual file, such as the image snowball.jpg used in Chapter 12, use the path E:\Resources\Chapter source files\Chapter 12\snowball.jpg.

It may be better to copy the contents of this folder into a new folder on your local machine or network drive. To copy an entire folder, drag its contents from the source CD into a new folder. To copy a single file, open the file that you wish to use. Select the VIEW tab, then Edit Document to change the document from Read only and allow you to save it. Select FILE and then Save As to save a new copy with an amended filename. You may need to change the file permissions of these files to read/write to enable you work on them; however, check with your network administrator before attempting to make these changes.

MAC users

Double-click on the CD icon on the desktop. Use Finder to navigate to the location for the new folder, then create a new folder (<Apple>+<Shift> +<N>). With Finder, choose the CD and select all files (<Apple>+<A>) and copy them (<Apple>+<C>). Go to the new folder using Finder and paste the files (<Apple>+<V>).

Changing the source files to match your regional settings

Before attempting any of these processes, back up all source files. The source .csv (comma separated value) files supplied on the CD have commas as separators between fields and full stops within currency values. If your regional settings for these values are different to these (for example, if you use commas within currency values rather than full stops and your software settings require you to use semicolons for separators between fields), then the source data files will need to be edited for use with the regional settings for your software. This process may be required to convert the source data files before the start of the practical examinations. You can do this process in many packages, but the easiest (at this level) is *Word*. Open the .csv file in *Word* using FILE and Open. Select the file from the list to open the file, which will look similar to this.

```
Who manufactured the car?,Model,Colour,Price that we bought the car
for,Price that we will sell the car for,Year,Extras,Does the car need
cleaning?
TVR,Tuscan,Black,18000,20305,2006,Alloy Wheels   Air Conditioning,N
Mercedes,C200,Silver,4995,5995,2003,Air Conditioning,N
Toyota,MR2 roadster,Electric blue,13995,15895,2005,Leather Seats   Air
Conditioning,N
```

Select the VIEW tab, then Edit Document to change the document from Read only. Select the HOME tab, then the Editing section followed by the Replace icon.

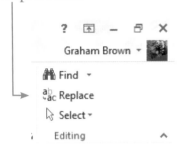

Enter a , (comma) into the Find what: box and a ; (semicolon) into the Replace with: box, then click on Replace All.

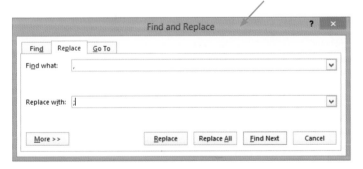

Repeat this process, replacing a . (full stop) with a , (comma). All the characters will have been replaced within the file like this.

```
Who manufactured the car?;Model;Colour;Price that we bought the car
for;Price that we will sell the car for;Year;Extras;Does the car need
cleaning?
TVR;Tuscan;Black;18000;20305;2006;Alloy Wheels   Air Conditioning;N
Mercedes;C200;Silver;4995;5995;2003;Air Conditioning;N
Toyota;MR2 roadster;Electric blue;13995;15895;2005;Leather Seats   Air
Conditioning;N
```

Save the file with the same file name using the HOME tab and Save. This will ensure that the file is saved in .csv format.

Section 1 · ICT Theory

Chapters

1   Types and components of a computer system

Computer systems are now commonplace in every part of our daily life. This first chapter introduces the basic components that make up these computer systems, most of which will be described in much greater depth in later chapters. Basic components, including hardware (both external and internal) and software (both application and system) are all briefly introduced in the following sections.

A good analogy is to compare computers with books: the actual pages and ink used on the pages of a book are equivalent to the hardware used to make up computers; the words written on the pages are equivalent to the software. Without the words, the book is useless. Similarly, without software, computers would be of little use to any of us.

1.1 Hardware and software

Hardware is a general term for the physical components that make up a computer system: the keyboard, mouse, monitor, printer and so on. Hardware can be either external or internal.

Software is a general term for the programs that control the computer system. There are two types of software: application and system. Examples of each are shown on the following pages.

Figures 1.1 and 1.2 on pages 3–4 describe some of the features of both application and system software. Further details about software can be found in the later chapters of this book.

Hardware falls into two categories: external and internal. External hardware (input, output and storage devices) is covered extensively in the following chapters of this book.

Figure 1.3 on page 5 considers the following internal hardware devices:

- the motherboard
- random access memory (RAM)
- read-only memory (ROM)
- video cards
- sound cards
- internal storage devices: hard disk drive (HDD) and solid state drive (SSD).

Since it isn't always possible to see the internal hardware devices, the photographs in Figure 1.4 on page 6 give you some idea of the physical appearance of the components described in Figure 1.3.

Word processor
Word processing software is used to manipulate text documents, such as an essay or a report. Text is entered using a keyboard and the software provides tools for copying, deleting and various types of formatting. Some of the functions include:
- creating, editing, saving and manipulating text
- copy and paste functions
- spell checkers and thesaurus
- importing photos/images into a structured page format
- translation into other languages.

Spreadsheet
Spreadsheet software is used to organise and manipulate numerical data (in the form of integer, real, date, and so on). Numbers are organised on a grid of lettered columns and numbered rows. The grid itself is made up of cells, and each cell is identified using a unique combination of columns and rows (for example, B6). Some of the functions include:
- use of formulas to carry out calculations
- ability to produce graphs
- ability to do modelling and 'what if' calculations.

Database
Database software is used to organise, manipulate and analyse data. A typical database is made up of one or more tables. Tables consist of rows and columns. Each row is called a 'record' and each column is called a 'field'. This provides the basic structure for the organisation of the data within the database. Some of the functions include:
- ability to carry out queries on database data and produce a report (dbms)
- add, delete and modify data in a table.

Control and measuring software
Control and measuring software is designed to allow a computer or microprocessor to interface with sensors so that it is possible to:
- measure physical quantities in the real world (such as temperatures)
- control applications (such as a chemical process) by comparing sensor data with stored data and sending out signals to alter process parameters (for example, open a valve to add acid and change the pH).

APPLICATION SOFTWARE
Programs that allow the user to do specific tasks

Apps
Apps (short for Applications) normally refers to the type of software that runs on mobile phones or tablets. They are usually downloaded from an 'App Store' and range from games to sophisticated software such as phone banking. Common examples include:
- video and music streaming
- GPS (global positioning systems which, together with satellite navigation, help you find your way to a chosen location)
- camera facilities (taking photos and storing/manipulating the images taken).

Photo editing software
Photo editing software allows a user to manipulate digital photographs stored on a computer; for example, change brightness, change contrast, alter colour saturation or remove 'red eye'. These applications also allow for very complex manipulation of photos (for example, change the features of a face, combine photos, alter images to give interesting effects and so on). They allow a photographer to remove unwanted items and generally 'touch up' a photo to make it as perfect as possible.

Video editing software
Video editing software allows a user to manipulate videos to produce an edited video. It enables the addition of titles, colour correction and altering/adding sound to the original video. Essentially it includes:
- rearranging, adding and/or removing sections of video clips and/or audio clips
- applying colour correction, filters and other video enhancements
- creating transitions between clips in the video footage.

Graphics manipulation software
Graphics manipulation software allows bitmap and vector images to be changed. Bitmap images are made up of pixels that contain information about image brightness and colour. Bitmap graphics editors can change the pixels to produce a different image. Vector graphic editors operate in a different way and don't use pixels. This type of software manipulates lines, curves and text to alter the stored image as required. The type of editing software used depends on the format of the original image.

Figure 1.1 Application software

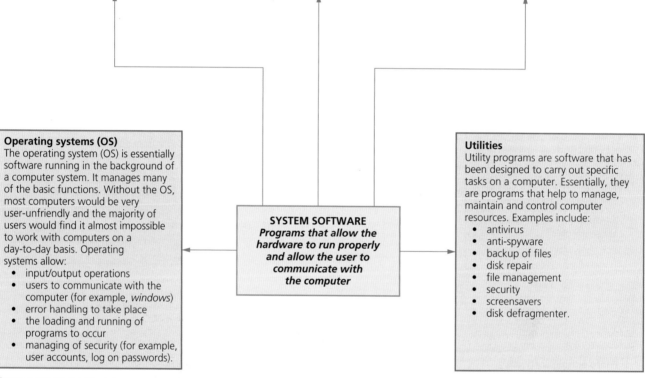

Compiler
A compiler is a computer program that translates a program written in a high-level language (HLL) into machine code (code that is understood by the computer) so that it can be directly used by a computer to perform a required task. The original program is called the **source code** and the code after compilation is called the **object code**. Once a program is compiled, the machine code can be used again and again to perform the same task without recompilation. Examples of high-level languages include Java, Python, Visual Basic, Fortran, C++ and Algol.

Linkers
A linker (or link editor) is a computer program that takes one or more object files produced by a compiler and combines them into a single program that can be run on a computer. For example, many programming languages allow programmers to write different pieces of code, called modules, separately. This simplifies the programming task since it allows the program to be broken up into small, more manageable sub-tasks. However, at some point, it will be necessary to put all the modules together to form the final program. This is the job of the linker.

Device driver
A device driver is the name given to software that enables one or more hardware devices to communicate with the computer's operating system. Without drivers, a hardware device (for example, a printer) would be unable to work with the computer. All hardware devices connected to a computer have associated drivers. As soon as a device is plugged into the USB port of a computer, the operating system looks for the appropriate driver. An error message will be produced if it can't be found. Examples of drivers include printers, memory sticks, mouse, CD drivers, and so on.

Operating systems (OS)
The operating system (OS) is essentially software running in the background of a computer system. It manages many of the basic functions. Without the OS, most computers would be very user-unfriendly and the majority of users would find it almost impossible to work with computers on a day-to-day basis. Operating systems allow:
- input/output operations
- users to communicate with the computer (for example, *windows*)
- error handling to take place
- the loading and running of programs to occur
- managing of security (for example, user accounts, log on passwords).

SYSTEM SOFTWARE
Programs that allow the hardware to run properly and allow the user to communicate with the computer

Utilities
Utility programs are software that has been designed to carry out specific tasks on a computer. Essentially, they are programs that help to manage, maintain and control computer resources. Examples include:
- antivirus
- anti-spyware
- backup of files
- disk repair
- file management
- security
- screensavers
- disk defragmenter.

Figure 1.2 System software

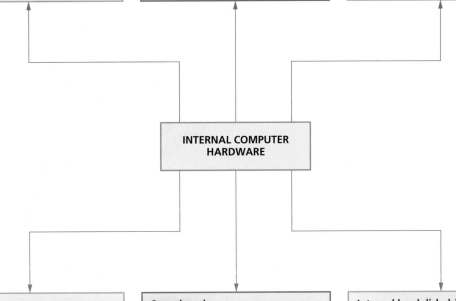

Motherboard
The motherboard is a printed circuit board found in all computers. It allows the processor and other computer hardware to function and communicate with each other. One of the major functions of a typical motherboard is to act as a kind of 'hub' that other computer devices connect to. A typical motherboard consists of a sheet of non-conductive material, such as hard plastic. Thin layers of copper or aluminium are printed onto this sheet. These form the circuits between the various components. In addition to circuits, a motherboard contains several sockets and slots to connect the other components.

Random access memory (RAM)
Random access memory (RAM) is an internal chip where data is temporarily stored when running applications. This memory can be written to and read from. Since its contents are lost when power to the computer is turned off, it is often referred to as a volatile or temporary memory.
RAM stores the data, files or part of the operating system currently in use.

Read-only memory (ROM)
Read-only memory (ROM) is a memory used to store information that needs to be permanent. It is often used to contain, for example, configuration data for a computer system. These chips cannot be altered and can only be read from (hence their name). One of the main advantages is that the information stored on the ROM chip is not lost even when power is turned off to the computer. They are often referred to as non-volatile memories.

INTERNAL COMPUTER HARDWARE

Video card
A video card allows the computer to send graphical information to a video display device such as a monitor, television or projector. It usually connects to the motherboard (see above). Video cards are usually made up of:
- a processing unit
- memory unit (usually RAM)
- a cooling mechanism (often in the form of a heat sink since these cards generate much heat)
- connections to a display unit (monitor, television or projector).

Sound card
A sound card is an integrated circuit board that provides a computer with the ability to produce sounds. These sounds can be heard by the user either through speakers or headphones. Sound cards also allow a user to record sound input from a microphone connected to the computer, and to manipulate sounds stored on a disk. Sound cards use two basic methods to translate digital data into analogue signals (needed for speakers):
- **FM synthesis** mimics different musical instruments according to built-in formulas
- **wavetable synthesis** relies on recordings of actual instruments to produce sound.

Internal hard disk drive/solid state drive (HDD/SSD)
These two devices are covered in considerably more depth in later chapters of this book. Basically, hard disk drives (HDD) are magnetic in nature and are one of the main methods for storing data, files (text, photos and music) and most of the system and application software. More modern computers (and all tablets) use newer storage systems that make use of solid state drive (SSD) technology and are replacing HDD in many cases. Their function is the same as HDD.

Figure 1.3 Internal computer hardware

RAM

ROM

Video card

Sound card

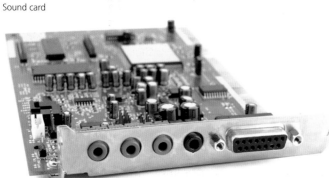

SSD

Motherboard

HDD

Figure 1.4 Internal hardware images

1.2 Main components of a computer system

As already mentioned in Section 1.1, a typical computer system is made up of hardware and software. Figure 1.5 shows an example of a computer system consisting of input devices, output devices and secondary storage. These will be discussed in more detail in Chapter 2, but examples are given in Table 1.1.

Table 1.1 Examples of input, output and secondary storage devices

Device	Examples
Input devices	keyboard, mouse
Output devices	monitor, printer
Secondary storage devices	DVD R/W drive, removable hard disk drive

Internal hardware devices were discussed in Figure 1.3 – these consist of four key components:

- the **central processing unit (CPU)**, contained on the motherboard
- **internal hard disk drive**
- **random access memory (RAM)**
- **read-only memory (ROM)**.

The **central processing unit (CPU)** is the part of the computer that interprets and executes the commands from the computer hardware and software. It is normally part of the computer motherboard.

CPUs used to be made up of discrete components and numerous small integrated circuits; these were combined together on one or more circuit board(s). However, due to modern manufacturing techniques, the CPU is now referred to as a **microprocessor**. This is a single integrated circuit which is at the heart of most PCs and is also found in many household devices and equipment where some control or monitoring is needed (for example, the engine management system in a car).

The CPU is made up of a control unit, which controls the input and output devices; an arithmetic and logic unit (ALU), which carries out calculations and makes logical decisions; and the immediate access store (RAM).

The **internal hard disk drive (HDD)** or **solid state drive (SSD)** is the computer's main internal storage; this is where the applications software, disk operating system and files (for example, text, photos or music) are stored. The main advantage of these storage devices is the fast data transfer/access times and their large capacity to store data (see Chapter 3 for further discussion).

Random access memory (RAM) is an internal chip where data is temporarily stored when running applications. This memory can be written to and read from. Since its contents are lost when power to the computer is turned off, it is often referred to as a volatile or temporary memory. This was fully defined in Figure 1.3.

Read-only memory (ROM) is a memory used to store information that needs to be permanent. It is often used to contain, for example, configuration data for a computer system. These chips cannot be altered and can only be read from (hence their name). One of the main advantages is that the information stored on

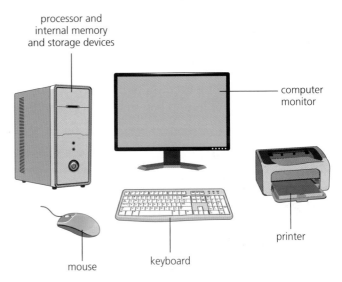

processor and internal memory and storage devices

computer monitor

printer

mouse

keyboard

Figure 1.5 A typical computer system

the ROM chip is not lost even when power to the computer is turned off. It is often referred to as non-volatile memory. This was fully defined in Figure 1.3.

It is worth noting that ROM also contains some coding known as the boot file. This code tells the computer what to do when it first starts up; it is often referred to as the BIOS (basic input/output system).

When the computer is turned on, the BIOS carries out a hardware check to find out if all the devices are present and whether they are functional. Then it loads the operating system into the RAM.

The BIOS stores the date, time and system configuration in a non-volatile chip called a CMOS (complementary metal oxide semiconductor) – this is usually battery powered.

1.3 Operating systems

Operating systems have already been referred to earlier on in this chapter (see Figure 1.2).

To enable computer systems to function and to allow users to communicate with computer systems, special software known as operating systems (OS) has been developed. The general tasks for a typical operating system include:

- control of the operation of the input, output and backing storage devices
- supervising the loading, running and storage of applications programs
- dealing with errors that occur in application programs
- maintaining security of the whole computer system
- maintaining a computer log (which details computer usage)
- allowing communication between the user and the computer system (user interface).

1.3.1 User interfaces

Command line interface (CLI)

Command line interface (CLI) requires a user to type in instructions to choose options from menus, open software and so on. There are often a number of commands that need to be typed in, for example, to save or load a file. The user therefore has to learn a number of commands just to carry out basic operations. Having to key in these commands every time an operation has to be carried out is also slow. However, the advantage of CLI is that the user is in direct communication with the computer and is not restricted to a number of predetermined options.

The section of CLI shown in Figure 1.6 imports data from table A into table B.

The statements in Figure 1.6 show how complex it is just to carry out a fairly straightforward operation using CLI.

```
1.  SQLPrepare(hStmt,

2.  ? (SQLCHAR *) "INSERT INTO tableB SELECT * FROM
    tableA",

3.  ? SQL_NTS):

4.  ? SQLExecute(hStmt);
```

Figure 1.6 CLI code

Graphical user interface (GUI)

Graphical user interface (GUI) allows the user to interact with a computer (or MP3 player, gaming device, mobile phone, and so on) using pictures or *icons* (symbols) rather than having to type in a number of commands. For example, the whole of the CLI code in Figure 1.6 could have been replaced by a single icon.

Simply selecting this icon would automatically execute all of the steps shown in Figure 1.6 without the need to type them in each time.

Table update

GUIs use various technologies and devices to provide the user interface. One of the most common is **WIMP (windows icons menu and pointing device)**, which was developed for use on personal computers (PCs). Here a mouse is used to control a cursor and icons are selected to open/run windows. Each window contains an application, and modern computer systems allow several windows to be open at the same time. An example is shown in Figure 1.7 (here a number of icons can be seen on the left-hand side and at the bottom of the screen).

A windows manager looks after the interaction between windows, the applications and windowing system (which handles the pointing devices and the cursor's position).

In recent years, devices such as **touch-screen** phones use **post-WIMP** interaction, where fingers are in contact with the screen allowing actions such as *pinching* and *rotating*, which would be difficult to do using a single pointer and device such as a mouse.

Figure 1.7 Windows screen showing icons

Summary of the main differences between CLI and GUI

Table 1.2 The main differences between CLI and GUI

Interface	Advantages	Disadvantages
Command line interface (CLI)	• The user is in direct communication with the computer. • The user is not restricted to a number of predetermined options. • It is possible to alter computer configuration settings.	• The user needs to learn a number of commands to carry out basic operations. • All commands need to be typed in, which takes time and can be error-prone. • Each command must be typed in using the correct format, spelling, and so on. • It is more difficult to edit once commands are entered.
Graphical user interface (GUI)	• The user doesn't need to learn any commands. • It is more user-friendly; icons are used to represent applications. • A pointing device (such as a mouse) is used to click on an icon to launch the application – this is simpler than typing in commands.	• It uses up considerably more computer memory than a CLI interface. • The user is limited to the icons provided on the screen. • It needs an operating system, such as *Windows*, to operate, which uses up considerable memory.

Who would use each type of interface?

- CLI: a programmer, analyst or technician; basically somebody who needs to have direct communication with a computer to develop new software, locate errors and remove them, initiate memory dumps (contents of the computer memory at some moment in time), and so on.
- GUI: the end-user who doesn't have (or doesn't need) any great knowledge of how the computer works; a person who uses the computer to run software or play games or store/manipulate photographs, for example.

1.4 Types of computer

There are many types of computer systems in existence. The following sections summarise some of the more common types currently available.

1.4.1 PC/desktop computers

PC/desktop usually refers to a general-purpose computer that is made up of a separate monitor, keyboard, mouse and processor unit.

The term PC (personal computer) usually refers to computer systems that are IBM-compatible, thus distinguishing them from, for example, Macintosh/Apple systems.

It is worth making a comparison here with laptop computers.

The advantages of desktop computers over laptop computers are as follows.

- Spare parts and connections tend to be standardised, which usually results in lower costs.
- The desktop tends to have a better specification (for example, a faster processor) for a given price (often due to size and construction constraints in laptops).
- Power consumption is not critical since they usually plug straight into a wall socket and the larger casings allow a better dissipation of any heat build-up.
- Because they are usually fixed in one location, there is less likelihood of them being damaged.
- Internet access is also more stable since they are not moved around (the user will always have the same data transfer rate).

They do also have disadvantages when compared to laptop computers.

- The most obvious is that they are not particularly portable since they are made up of separate components.
- Because they are not particularly portable, it is necessary to copy files, etc. when you want to do some work elsewhere (for example, at home) – with a laptop you simply take the whole computer with you.
- They tend to be more complicated since all the components (for example, keyboard, mouse) need to be carried round with you and then connected to the computer by wires or wireless connections, which also clutters up the desk space.

1.4.2 Laptop computers

Laptop (or **notebook**) refers to a type of computer where the monitor, keyboard, pointing device and processor are all together in one single unit. This makes them extremely portable.

Key features you would expect to find in a laptop:

- lightweight (to aid portability)
- low power consumption (and also long battery life)
- the processor shouldn't generate too much heat (cooling is very important).

The advantages of laptop computers compared to desktop computers:

- the most obvious is their portability; they can be taken anywhere since the monitor, pointing device, keyboard, processor and backing store units are all together in one single unit
- because everything is in one single unit, there are no trailing wires, etc.
- they can take full advantage of Wi-Fi
- since they are portable, they can link into any multimedia system.

Laptop computers do have disadvantages when compared to desktop computers, however:

- since they are easily portable, they are also easier to steal
- they have limited battery life, so the user may need to carry a heavy adaptor
- the keyboards and pointing devices can sometimes be awkward to use.

1.4.3 Tablets

Tablets are a relatively new internet-enabled portable computer. They work in a similar way to a smartphone. Tablets use touch-screen technology and don't usually have a conventional keyboard (although some tablets that are a cross between tablet and laptop do exist). The keyboard is part of the touch screen and keys are simply touched by the finger or a stylus. Internet access is usually through Wi-Fi or 3G/4G/5G (mobile phone) connectivity. Tablets are equipped with a series of sensors including cameras, microphones, accelerometers and touch screens.

Some of the typical features of tablets include:

- high-definition, anti-glare displays
- front- and back-facing cameras (which are used to take photos and videos, or act as a webcam when doing video calls over the internet)
- lower weight and longer battery life than laptops
- Bluetooth connection to printers and other devices
- flash (solid state) memory and cloud storage facilities to back up and synchronise (often just referred to as 'sync') data sources
- sensors to carry out the following functions:
  - proximity sensors to detect if the device is close to, for example, the ear (which allows it to block unintended 'touches')
  - accelerometer, which detects movement and orientation of the device (for example, moving the display from portrait to landscape to view videos, or to allow it to be used as a 'steering wheel' in car-racing games)
  - can use sophisticated speech-recognitions systems (such as *Siri*) to enable the user to ask the device to look for things (for example, search the address book).

Some of the latest tablet devices have been designed as a hybrid between tablet and smartphone – sometimes referred to as a phablet – which have slightly smaller screens than tablets (typically between 12 cm and 15 cm display size). All of the features of a normal phone are available with some of the features of a tablet (notably they have a larger screen size than a phone; larger memories – typically 32 GB (or more) memory as standard; use quad core processors; allow multiple windows to be open and so on).

Advantages of tablets compared to laptops:

- very fast to switch on (no time delay waiting for the 'windows' system to load up)
- fully portable – they are so lightweight that they can be carried anywhere
- touch-screen technology means they are simple to use and don't need any other input devices
- can use several Apps as standard (such as built-in camera, MP3/4 players and so on)
- don't generate any heat – they use solid state technology
- battery life of a tablet is a lot longer
- when the power button is pressed it goes into standby but remains connected to the internet, so the user still hears alerts when emails or other 'events' are received.

Disadvantages of tablets compared to laptops:

- they often have limited memory or storage compared to a laptop
- they can be expensive to run if the internet is being accessed frequently via 3G/4G/5G mobile phone networks
- typing on a touch screen can be slow and error-prone compared to a standard keyboard
- transferring of files often has to be done through an 'Apps store'; the lack of an App 'drag and drop' facility can prove irritating for users
- laptops tend to support more types of file format than tablets, and are also better equipped to run different types of software.

1.4.4 Smartphones

Smartphones allow normal phone calls to be made but also have an operating system (such as iOS, Android or Windows), allowing them to run a number of computer applications. They allow users to send/receive emails, use a number of Apps, use a camera feature (to take photos or videos), MP3/4 players (for music and videos), and so on.

Smartphones communicate with the internet either by using Wi-Fi hot spots or by using 3G/4G/5G mobile phone networks. They make use of a number of Apps that allow the following functions, among many others:

- send/receive emails
- surf the net (for example, so you can order goods on the move)
- global positioning system (use of maps to navigate to a location)
- calendar functions
- telephone banking (send and receive money using banking Apps)
- Voice over Internet Protocol (VoIP) – telephone network using the internet, which also allows video calling
- streaming of videos
- streaming of music (from radio stations, for example)
- instant access to social networks (social contact with friends no matter where you are in the world)
- instant messaging.

The next generation of smartphones will use touch screens with OLED (organic light-emitting diode) technology. The touch screens are coated with a crystalline layer that allows the phones to be partially solar powered, but this also allows them to use Li-Fi (similar to Wi-Fi except communication uses visible light rather than radio waves). Communication using Li-Fi is considerably faster than Wi-Fi (it has a much higher data transfer rate); it is also more secure (it stops internet 'piggybacking', unauthorised use of the internet connection) and can also be used on flights since it doesn't use radio waves.

The technology works by switching LED bulbs off and on in nanoseconds (10^{-9} of a second) which is too quick for the human eye to detect. Light on represents the binary value 1, while light off represents the value 0. This is the basis behind the method used for communication.

Advantages of smartphones:

- they are very small in size and lightweight – therefore very easy to carry round and have on your person at all times (this is more difficult with laptops since they are much bulkier and also much heavier)
- can use them to make phone calls as well as connect to the internet while on the move
- because they use Wi-Fi and mobile phone networks, they can be used almost anywhere (this is not the case with laptops or PCs, although tablets also use the same technology)
- they have hundreds of Apps (such as camera facility, MP3/4 players, and so on) – again this is similar to tablets, but it is an advantage compared to laptops
- they have a reasonable battery life compared to laptops.

Disadvantages of smartphones:

- the small screens make pages difficult to read and small keyboards make typing things in more difficult and slower (laptops and PCs have much bigger screens and much larger keyboards) – this disadvantage is becoming less of a problem as smartphone screens get larger on newer phablets
- web browsing and photography can drain the battery quickly
- memory size in most phones isn't very large when compared to laptops and PCs – although it is comparable with tablets
- not all website features are compatible with smartphone operating systems
- because of their small size, it is much easier to lose a smartphone (or for it to be stolen) than laptops or PCs
- the data transfer rate using mobile phone networks is slower than with Wi-Fi – this makes streaming of video or music, for example, less than satisfactory at times.

1.4.5 Smartwatches

Smartwatches essentially allow users to wear a mini-computer on their wrists. They offer the same functions as a smartphone and make use of OLED technology (see Chapter 2). As with smartphones, they use touch-screen technology but also have the ability to link to smartphones using Bluetooth technology.

Smartwatches have the following functions:

- internet connectivity (browsing, searches, sending emails and so on)
- ability to make and take phone calls
- messaging via text or video
- weather forecasts
- fitness and health-monitoring capability
- GPS (finding your location and, using satnav, directions to other locations).

These are just a few of the functions; essentially whatever is available on a smartphone is available on a smartwatch. Many of the advantages and disadvantages of smartphones also apply to smartwatches, but the following are additional points to be considered.

Additional advantages:

- they are even more convenient than smartphones since the technology delivers notifications straight to the user's wrist
- they are very easy to use for monitoring fitness and health regimes.

Additional disadvantages:

- smartwatches are relatively large and bulky (so that the display can show the Apps clearly and also permit the use of a battery, which gives an acceptable usage time before recharging), which can make them uncomfortable to wear
- they tend to be rather unattractive in design, which means there is still some reluctance for the technology to be adopted.

1.4.6 Mainframe computers

Mainframe computer is a term used for a large, very powerful, computer system. The name comes from the days when the individual components were housed in large (often room-sized) frames.

Their main purpose is to run commercial applications, such as banking and insurance, where huge amounts of data need to be processed every day.

The main features of mainframe computers are:

- they can have several CPUs
- they have very fast processor speeds
- they can support multiple operating systems
- they have huge amounts of storage capacity
- they have huge internal memories (for example, several hundred gigabytes of RAM)
- they often operate using time sharing or batch processing.

1.5 Impact of emerging technologies

Some of the latest technologies were mentioned in Section 1.4. This section reviews briefly the impact of the following new technologies:

- artificial intelligence (AI) biometrics
- vision enhancement
- robotics
- quantum cryptography
- computer-assisted translation (CAT)
- 3-D and holographic imaging
- virtual reality.

New technologies are being developed at a remarkable rate, so the reader is advised that the above list could be out of date very quickly. A quick review on the internet is advised every six months or so to ensure that the reader is up to date with all the latest technologies.

1.5.1 Artificial intelligence (AI) biometrics

A known problem with biometric technology is that many fingerprint identification systems falsely reject a person's fingerprints – when the scanned fingerprints are checked against the database no matches are found.

Artificial intelligence (AI) biometrics overcomes this problem using dynamic profiling – the system learns by using AI about a person's fingerprints on every scan. This means a person doesn't have to worry about getting their finger in exactly the right place every time on the scanner. The system learns from the different alignments and is therefore still able to match the fingerprints to those stored on a database.

Facial-recognition systems have the same problem. A human being is still able to recognise a face even if the person has grown facial hair, now wears glasses or has aged. Computerised facial-recognition systems are confused by such soft biometric changes. New systems use AI to learn from scanning a number of faces and can pick out these soft biometric features. This means the system can still recognise faces and cross-reference these attributes with corresponding images stored on the database.

Other AI biometric technologies are being developed, so these security systems become increasingly more reliable.

1.5.2 Vision enhancement

Low-vision enhancement systems (LVES) use video technology through a headset connected to a computer. The system allows images to be projected inside the headset in front of the eyes. This effectively brings the objects closer for examination by the user of the system.

Night vision enhancement (NVE) amplifies infrared light and visible light so that an image can still be seen in apparent darkness. For example, the military use this technology to carry out surveillance at night. The dim light source is captured and passed through an **image intensifier tube**, which converts the light into electrons. These electrons pass through another tube where they are amplified to produce several times the original number of electrons. A screen at the end of the tube is coated in phosphor dots that glow when electrons collide with them – this results in an image that is considerably clearer than the original.

1.5.3 Robotics

Robotics has been around for many years, mostly in the manufacturing industry. They are used in car factories to weld car bodies, spray body panels and fit items such as windscreens. No human intervention is required. However, there are areas outside manufacturing where robotics is evolving rapidly, and we could see robots appearing in many areas of our lives in a relatively short space of time.

One application is the use of **drones**. These are unmanned flying devices that are used by both the military and civilians. The military have used drones in reconnaissance missions for a number of years. Civilian uses include surveying the landscape in 3-D for use with GPS, investigating weather phenomena (for example, flying into hurricanes or other weather conditions that would be dangerous for manned surveillance), or search and rescue/fire fighting in natural disasters. All of these are currently under evaluation and many more applications could evolve over the coming years.

Another application is the use of robots in surgical procedures. Robotic surgery allows surgeons to perform complex procedures with more precision, flexibility and control than standard surgical techniques. With this technique, surgeons use robotics equipped with a camera arm and several interactive mechanical arms – these have joints that work like a human's wrist.

1.5.4 Quantum cryptography

Cryptography is the science of making a message unintelligible to any unauthorised user (a hacker). This technique is often referred to as **encryption**. There are many methods of cryptography in existence but all of them have a limited life as computers become faster and faster at number crunching. A consequence of this is that, over the next few years, a hacker is increasingly likely to decipher encrypted messages unless computer designers can further strengthen security systems.

Quantum cryptography is based on the use of photons (light) and their physical quantum properties to produce a virtually unbreakable cryptography system. This helps protect the security of data being transmitted over fibre-optic cables. The technology relies on the fact that photons oscillate in various directions and produce a sequence of random bits (0s and 1s) across the optical network. It is based on the laws of physics rather than mathematics (which is how current cryptography methods work). How this works in detail is beyond the scope of this book.

1.5.5 Computer-assisted translation (CAT)

Existing online language translators have a very limited use.

Consider the insect called a fruit fly, which particularly enjoys eating bananas. What if we typed in the phrase: 'fruit flies like a banana'. This could be translated into German using a free online translator as '*fruchtfliegen wie eine banane*'. The statement in German only refers to the banana-shaped flight path of a piece of fruit thrown through the air! Imagine a whole page being translated that is full of such double meanings of words and phrases.

Computer-assisted translation (CAT) goes some way to overcome these issues. CAT is a type of language translator that uses specific software to help in the translation process. In particular, CAT uses two tools:

- terminology databases – linguistic databases that grow and 'learn' from translations being carried out
- translation memories – these automatically insert known translations for certain words, phrases or sentences.

All CAT software needs some post-editing by the user to remove errors from the translation process. While not perfect, they are certainly more accurate than existing free online translators.

1.5.6 3-D and holographic imaging

Holography is a technology that allows 3-D images (known as holograms) to be produced. The technology involves the use of:

- a source of laser light
- interference of light
- light diffraction, and
- light intensity recording.

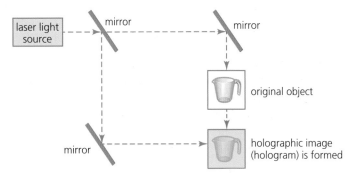

Figure 1.8 Formation of a hologram

As a holographic image is rotated, it appears to move in the same way as the original object, thus appearing to be in three dimensions (3-D). The hologram is produced by first splitting a laser beam. Half of the light (known as the object beam) is reflected off the object on to a photographic plate. The other half of the light (known as the reference beam) is reflected off a mirror and on to the same photographic plate. The holographic image is produced where the two light beams meet on the photographic plate.

Holograms have the following applications:

- engineering design (CAD)
- architecture (ability to rotate design through 360 degrees)
- simulations
- medical imaging (see inside organs in 3-D – links into tomography, which is the same technology behind 3-D printers)
- cinema (special effects)
- gaming (special effects)
- advertising
- holographic televisions (expected by around 2025, these should give a full 3-D experience without the need for special glasses)
- holographic computer memories (a new type of optical storage – a crystal the size of a sugar cube can hold up to 1 TB of data)
- optical computers (these will operate at speeds that are trillions of times faster than-current technology computers).

1.5.7 Virtual reality

Virtual reality is an artificial environment created by software. The user makes use of data goggles, sensor suits, data gloves or helmets to get a feeling of reality (that is, the feeling of 'being there'). The technology is used in training (for example, in a nuclear reactor where the user can see all the walls, pipes, vessels and valves as if they were inside the reactor, so that they can be trained safely to deal with certain events), education (for example, to explore the inside of a building such as a castle in a history lesson) or in games (where the user can interact as if they were there, such as a driving simulator where the road ahead is output on to a visor in a helmet strapped to the user's head).

Virtual reality is used in all of the following areas:

- military applications (for example, training to use a new tank)
- education (for example, looking inside an ancient building as part of a history lesson)
- healthcare (for example, as a diagnostic tool)
- entertainment (for example, games where gloves, goggles or helmets are worn to give realism to the scenario and even to give images or sound to make it seem very real)
- fashion (for example, to do fashion shows before doing the real thing to see the clothes on people, check out the venue and so on)
- heritage (for example, showing monuments such as Stonehenge)
- business (for example, training courses and role-playing scenarios for staff)
- real estate (for example, allowing people to 'look around' houses that are for sale)
- engineering (for example, seeing how new designs will look)
- sport (for example, a golfer trying to improve their swing can use this technology and get feedback to improve their game)
- media (for example, special effects in films such as *The Matrix*)
- scientific visualisation (for example, looking at molecular structures in chemistry).

2 Input and output devices

> In this chapter you will learn about:
>
> - input devices
>   - uses of each device
>   - advantages of each device
>   - disadvantages of each device
> - direct data entry (DDE) devices
> - output devices
>   - uses of each device
>   - advantages of each device
>   - disadvantages of each device.

2.1 Input devices and their uses

As the name suggests, these are hardware devices that allow data to be input into a computer. Many such devices exist, ranging from the more common ones, such as the keyboard, through to the more specialist devices, such as barcode readers. A number are described in this section.

2.1.1 Keyboards

These are the most common input devices and are used to input text, numbers and instructions into the computer. Most use the QWERTY layout (this name comes from the keys on the top row, which spell out 'QWERTY').

Ergonomic keyboards are designed to reduce the health-related problems associated with standard keyboards, such as carpal tunnel syndrome and repetitive strain injury (RSI).

Uses

- Input of data into applications software (for example, text into word processors, numbers into spreadsheets, etc.).
- Typing in commands to the computer (for example, Prnt Scrn, Ctrl+P to print out etc.).

Advantages

- Fast entry of new text into a document.
- Easy to use for most people.
- Easier to do verification checks as the data is entered (can immediately compare the source document with typed data on the screen).

Disadvantages

- Can be difficult to use if the user has limited arm/wrist use.
- Slow method when compared to direct data entry (for example, optical mark recognition).
- Fairly large device that uses up valuable desk space.

> ### Exercise 2a
> Find out about a number of applications that use input/output devices and discuss the reasons why they were chosen (that is, their advantages and disadvantages).

Concept keyboard

The **concept keyboard** uses icons or phrases instead of standard letters. These are often used in fast-food restaurants, where a single key represents one item, for example an ice cream. The person serving only needs to touch this key to order the ice cream and bring up its price on a screen.

- This allows for fast data entry (no need to type in whole commands).
- The keyboards are waterproof (useful in a restaurant environment).
- Also, in certain applications (for example, at unmanned airport information kiosks), these keyboards are tamper resistant, preventing people from keying in information that could potentially corrupt the computer system.

Numeric keypads

A **numeric keypad** is used to enter numbers only (although some have a function key to allow alphabetic characters to be input).

Uses

- **Automatic teller machines (ATMs)**, where the customer can key in their PIN, amount of money, etc.
- Mobile phones, to allow phone numbers, etc., to be keyed in.
- **Point-of-sale (POS) terminals** in case the barcode reader fails to read the barcode – the number has to be keyed in manually by the operator.
- Chip and PIN devices when paying by credit/debit cards (key in PIN, amount of money, etc.).
- Fast entry of numeric data into a spreadsheet.

Advantages

- Faster than standard keyboards when entering numeric data.
- Since many are small devices (for example, mobile phones) they are very easy to carry around.

Disadvantages

- Sometimes have small keys which can make input more difficult.
- Sometimes the order of the numbers on the keypad isn't intuitive.

2.1.2 Pointing devices

Mouse

The **mouse** is an example of a **pointing device**. The user controls the position of a pointer on the screen by moving the mouse around. There are usually two buttons, which have different functions: the left button is usually used to select items by double clicking, while the right button brings up drop-down menus.

Many also have a scroll button, which speeds up the process of moving through a document.

Recent developments have produced the **optical mouse** (where movement is detected by reflected light rather than the position of a moving ball) and the **cordless** or **wireless mouse** (which transmits signals to a USB wireless receiver plugged into the computer). The advantage of an optical mouse is it has no

Figure 2.1 Example of a drop-down menu

moving parts and it also doesn't pick up any dirt. This makes it more robust and improves its performance since the older type of mouse can 'skid' on certain surfaces, reducing the control of the pointer.

Uses

- Opening, closing and minimising software.
- Grouping, moving and deleting files.
- Image editing, for example controlling the size and position of a drawing pasted into a document.
- Controlling the position of a pointer on the screen to allow selection from a menu or selecting an icon, and for scrolling up and down/left and right.

Advantages

- Faster way to choose an option than using a keyboard.
- Very quick way to navigate through applications and the internet.
- Doesn't need a large desk area when compared to a keyboard.

Disadvantages

- Can be more difficult for people with restricted hand/wrist movement than using a keyboard data entry.
- Easy to damage, and the older type of mouse quickly becomes clogged up with dirt.
- Difficult to use if no flat surface is readily available (for example, on an aeroplane).

Exercise 2b

Try out as many input devices as possible and write down your own views on their ease of use, advantages and disadvantages.

Touchpad

Touchpads are used as a pointing device in many laptop computers. The pointer is controlled by the user moving their finger on the touchpad and then gently tapping it to simulate the left button of a mouse (i.e. selection). They also have buttons under the touchpad which serve the same function as the left and right buttons on a mouse. Their uses are the same as those of a mouse.

Advantages

- Same as the mouse (faster than a keyboard for choosing options, used to navigate applications and the internet, etc.).
- Since the touchpad is integrated into the laptop computer there is no need for a separate mouse – this aids the portability and is also a big advantage if there are no flat surfaces available.

Disadvantages

- People with limited hand/wrist movement find the device difficult to use.
- Can be more difficult to control the pointer when compared to a mouse.
- More difficult to use when doing certain operations such as *drag and drop*.

Trackerball

Trackerballs are similar to a mouse except that the ball is on the top or the side of the device; the user controls the pointer on the screen by rotating the ball with their hand. It is easier to use for people with limited hand/wrist movement. Some trackerballs have two buttons, which have the same function as the left and right mouse buttons. If they have a third button, it is the equivalent to a *double click*. Since trackerballs don't physically move, there is no need for desk space.

Uses

- Used in applications where the user has a disability (such as RSI).
- Used in a control room environment where it is faster than a mouse to navigate through process screens.
- Used in some luxury cars to select functions such as radio, telephone, music, satnav and so on.

Advantages

- Doesn't need the same fine control as a mouse.
- Easier to use than a mouse if the operator is disabled.
- More accurate positioning of the pointer on screen than a mouse.
- They are more robust than a mouse.
- Needs less desk space than a mouse or a keyboard.

Figure 2.2 Trackerballs are used in some luxury cars to select functions such as radio, telephone, music and satnav

Disadvantages

- Not supplied with computers as standard, therefore more costly.
- User may need training since it isn't standard equipment.

2.1.3 Remote control

A **remote control** is used to control the operation of other devices remotely using infrared signals. The buttons on the keypad are used to select options (such as television channels, sound levels on a hi-fi, timings on a DVD recorder, etc.)

Uses

- Televisions, satellite systems, DVD players and hi-fi systems all use remote controls to alter functions such as sound volume, on/off, change channels open the disc drawer, and so on.
- Used to control multimedia systems.
- Used in industrial applications to remotely control processes, stop and start machinery, etc.

Advantages

- Can be operated from any reasonable distance, unlike, for example, a corded mouse which is restricted by the length of cord (useful for disabled people).
- Some chemical processes are hazardous, so it is a big advantage to be able to select operations from a distance.

Disadvantages

- Difficult to use if the operator has limited hand/wrist movement.
- It is easier to block the signal if, for example, the walls in the building are very thick.

2.1.4 Joysticks

Joysticks have similar functions to a mouse and a trackerball. By gripping the stick, a pointer on the screen can be controlled. Buttons are used to make selections. Often they have another button on the top of the stick that is used for gaming purposes, for example to fire a weapon.

Uses

- Used in video/computer games.
- Used in **simulators** (for example, flight simulators) to mimic actual controls.

Advantages

- Easier than a keyboard to navigate the screen.
- Control is more realistic than using a mouse, for example.

Disadvantages

- More difficult to control the on-screen pointer than with other devices, such as a mouse.

Driving wheel

A **driving** (steering) **wheel** is an example of an input device that is similar to a joystick in many ways. It connects to a computer (or games machine), usually through a USB port. The wheel allows you to simulate the turning of a steering wheel, and there are associated devices (such as buttons or pedals) which allow you to accelerate and brake. Sensors are used to pick up left/right movement so that the user gets the sensation of steering a car around a circuit or on the road.

Uses

- Used in video/computer games (for example, car-racing games).
- Used in **simulators** (for example, car-driving simulators) to mimic actual vehicle controls.

Advantages

- Easier than a keyboard or joystick to control steering movements; it is more natural.
- The 'driving experience' is nearer to how an actual steering wheel and other controls operate in real life.

Disadvantages

- It can be a rather expensive input device compared to mouse or joystick.
- Movements in the steering can be too sensitive, giving an unrealistic 'feel'.
- Unless it is an expensive simulator, feedback to the driving wheel is non-existent.

2.1.5 Touch screens

With a **touch screen** the user can choose an option by simply touching a button/icon on the screen. The selection is automatically made without the need for any pointing device.

Uses

- Self-service tills, for example at petrol stations, where the user just touches the screen to select the fuel grade and payment method.
- Automatic teller machines (ATMs) to choose from on-screen options.
- Point-of-sale terminals at, for example, restaurants.
- Public information systems at airports, railway stations, tourist offices, etc.
- Personal digital assistants (PDAs), mobile phones and satellite navigation systems.
- Interactive white boards in education.
- Computer-based training (CBT) where answers are selected during on-screen testing.
- They can obviously also be used as an output device, since they still work as a flat-screen monitor.

Advantages

- Faster entry of options than using keyboard or mouse.
- Very easy method for choosing options.
- User-friendly – no training necessary in its use.

Disadvantages

- Limited number of options available.
- Can lead to problems if an operator has to use the system frequently (straining of arm muscles, RSI, etc., are all possible).
- The screen can get very dirty with constant touching; this can reduce its responsiveness and can also make it more difficult to read in strong light.

2.1.6 Scanners

Scanners are used to enter information from hard copy (for example, text documents, photographs) into a computer. The most common type is the flatbed scanner (shown on the right), which is made up of a glass panel and lid. The hard copy document or photo is scanned by a light source and produces a computer-readable image.

The subsequent image can then be manipulated using a drawing package. Images can also be used with optical character recognition (OCR) software to allow the information to used in a word processor, desktop publishing, presentation software, etc. (see Section 2.2.5). Specialist scanners exist that are designed to carry out a specific task, for example barcode scanners (see later).

Uses

- Scan in documents and convert into a format for use in various software packages.
- Scan in old/valuable documents/books, thus protecting the originals, as well as producing records in case the paper copies are lost/destroyed (this is also known as archiving).
- Scan in photographs (not all cameras are digital, so some photographs are still printed on paper requiring conversion to computer format for storage).
- Scan in barcodes at POS terminals.

Advantages

- Images can be stored for editing at a later date.
- Much faster and more accurate (i.e. no typing errors) than typing in documents again.
- It is possible to recover damaged documents and photographs by scanning in and then using appropriate software to produce an acceptable copy.

Disadvantages

- Quality can be limited depending on how good a resolution the scanner is capable of (since most scanners have a range of resolutions you can choose from).
- They can be fairly slow at scanning, especially if the colour scanning mode is chosen or if the chosen scanning resolution is high.

2.1.7 Digital cameras

Digital cameras have largely replaced traditional film-based cameras. The images are stored on a memory card (solid state memory) and can be transferred to a computer by:

- directly reading the memory card (by slotting it into a card reader attached to a computer or a printer)
- connecting the camera to the computer using a USB port
- using wireless data transfer (Wi-Fi or Bluetooth).

The images are uploaded from the camera and stored in a file on the computer; the user can select which photos to upload and which to ignore. The images are then available for printing out as photos, to be used in a 'slide show', imported into software such as a word processor, or for upoading on to the internet.

Advantages

- Easier to produce better-quality photographs than with a traditional camera.
- Easier and faster to upload photographs to a computer rather than having to scan in hard copies when using traditional methods.
- No need to develop film and print out photographs anymore – this saves money and is also environmentally more acceptable (saves paper and reduces the use of the chemicals used in developing traditional film).
- Memory cards can store several hundred photographs.

Disadvantages

- Need to be computer literate in using the cameras properly; also, the transferring, storing and manipulating of the images via a computer requires some understanding of how computers work.
- There is some artistry lost since clever software now corrects errors in the photographs (for example, incorrect exposure, removal of red eye, etc.).
- The resolution still isn't as good as many expensive traditional cameras (this is improving all the time however; the quality of photographs depends on the number of pixels (many cameras now offer more than 20 mega pixels per image), quality of lens, etc.).
- Images often need to be compressed to reduce the amount of memory used (a single image can use more than 4 MB of memory, for example).

Many smartphones and tablets are now capable of taking photographs of a very high quality. Some of the latest smartphones are essentially making cameras almost obsolete for the casual photographer. Because the quality of the lens is an important feature, professional photographers will continue to use digital cameras for a number of years. However, it is now possible to get special attachments for many smartphones to allow special effects, zooming functions and even light filters.

Video cameras

Although specialist video cameras (as shown in the photo) exist, many digital cameras are capable of taking moving images. Since the video footage is simply a number of still photos 'stitched' together, this allows a digital camera to take reasonable video.

These cameras are often referred to as **DV (digital video) cameras**; they store compressed photo frames at a speed of 25 MB per second – this is known as **Motion jpeg**.

In both digital and video versions, the camera picks up the light from the image and this is turned into an electronic signal using light-sensitive sensors. In the case of the DV cameras, these signals are automatically converted into a compressed digital file format.

The advantages of using DV cameras compared to traditional video cameras (that use film) are:

- it is much easier to manipulate video footage using specialist software (for example, remove all the colour except one colour to give dramatic effects, etc.)
- DV format gives a very high quality of image which lends itself to effective editing.

The only real drawback is cost (it is possible to store 20 minutes of video footage on a 1 GB memory card costing about $20; while a video tape costing only $5 would allow a 60-minute video to be taken). But costs of memory cards will no doubt continue to fall, reducing this drawback with time.

2.1.8 Microphones

Microphones can be connected directly to a computer. Sounds can be inputted and then manipulated. The input sound is converted to an analogue signal and then converted into a digital signal. The computer's sound card usually does this automatically, that is, it acts as an analogue to digital converter (ADC).

Uses

- To input speech/sounds to be used in various applications, for example in presentations, sampling (in films, music, etc.) and special effects (films).
- Input in voice-recognition software:
  - the software converts the speech into text that can be used in, for example, a word processor or to input commands into a computer
  - to recognise commands; for example, some cars now have voice-activated systems to switch on the lights, turn the radio volume up, etc.
- Microphones can also be used as a sensor to pick up sound (for example, in a burglar alarm system).
- Used in video conferencing or Voice over Internet Protocol (VoIP) applications.

Advantages

- Faster to read text than to type it in using a keyboard.
- It is possible to manipulate sound in real time using special software rather than work on a recording done at some earlier stage.
- If used in a voice-activation system, it has the advantage of improving safety (since the car driver, for example, doesn't need to take their hands off the wheel to operate a switch or alter the radio station, etc.).

Disadvantages

- Sound files can use up a lot of computer memory.
- Voice-recognition software isn't as accurate as typing in manually (for example, software can't distinguish the difference between '*their*' and '*there*'.

2.1.9 Sensors

This section deals with analogue sensors. A sensor is a device that inputs data to a computer; the data is a measurement of some physical quantity that is continuously changing (for example, temperature, light, moisture, etc.). These physical quantities are analogue in nature. Since computers only understand digital data (1s and 0s), the information from the sensors needs to be converted; this is done using an analogue to digital converter (ADC).

Sensors are used in both monitoring and control applications – various types of sensors are used depending on the application (see the table below). When monitoring, the data sent to the computer is often transferred directly to a spreadsheet package (for example, taking measurements in a scientific experiment, measuring atmospheric pollution, etc.).

Table 2.1 Uses of sensors

Type of sensor	Applications
Temperature	used in automatic washing machines, central heating systems, automatic glasshouses, ovens
Pressure	used in burglar alarm systems, washing machines, robotics, environmental monitoring
Light	used in automatic glasshouses, automatic doors, burglar alarm systems, street lighting control
Sound/acoustic	used in burglar alarm systems, monitoring liquid and powder flow in pipes
Humidity/moisture	used in automatic glasshouses, environmental monitoring, used in factories where moisture levels are crucial (for example, manufacture of microchips, paint spraying)
pH	used in automatic glasshouses, chemical processes, environmental monitoring

Advantages

- More accurate readings taken when compared to human operators.
- Readings are continuous – no break in the monitoring.
- Because it is a continuous process, any necessary action (control system) or warning (monitoring system) will be initiated immediately.
- Systems can be automatic, removing the need for human intervention (very important if the process is hazardous or needs precise control/monitoring).

Disadvantages

- Faulty sensors can give spurious results (for example, sensors on the rear bumper of a car that monitors obstacles; if these become dirty, they may either not identify an obstacle or give a continuous alarm).

2.1.10 Graphics tablet

A **graphics tablet** is used with a stylus to produce freehand drawings. The images produced can then be stored in a file on a computer.

Uses

- Used to produce drawings, computer graphics, etc.
- In countries where the written language uses complex characters (for example, China and Japan) graphics tablets are used as a form of input as it is faster than typing in the characters with a keyboard.
- Used in computer-aided design (CAD) work.

Advantages

- It is possible to modify drawings before they are input.
- They offer a very accurate method of drawing (better than using a mouse or trackerball).
- They can record levels of pressure, unlike other point-and-click devices.

Disadvantages

- They are more expensive than other pointing devices (such as a mouse).
- It takes longer to produce a drawing using this equipment than doing it with pen and paper.
- Menus are often not very user-friendly.
- Larger drawings (such as A4) are expensive to produce.
- The touch screens are damaged easily.

2.1.11 Webcams

Webcams are similar to digital video cameras; however, they are connected directly to the computer (through a USB port) and they don't have a memory. Whatever information the webcam picks up is transmitted directly to the computer. Many computer systems now have webcams built in to their monitors as standard.

Uses

- Many people use webcams as a more personal way of having a conversation while chatting online.
- They are used to enable video conferencing to take place.

Advantages

- They can be left on constantly, only being activated as required; this means it is possible to have an immediate face-to-face video chat much like instant messageing with images.
- They allow people to keep in contact with each other without the need to travel (very useful for elderly or disabled people).

Disadvantages

- They have very limited features and are often of poor quality.
- They need to be connected to the computer (although this is less of an issue with laptop computers when the webcam is usually built in to the monitor lid).

2.1.12 Light pens

Light pens are used with computers as an input device. They contain sensors that send signals to a computer whenever light changes are detected. The devices only work with CRT monitors (see output devices section) as they rely on the screen image being built up row by row by an electron beam. The screen is refreshed 50 times every second; because of this, the computer is able to determine the pen's position by noting exactly when the device detected the electron beam passing its tip. Systems to allow light pens to operate with LCD monitors are still at the development stage.

Uses

- Selecting objects on CRT screens.
- Drawing on screen (for example, with CAD packages).

Advantages

- Greater accuracy than touch screens.
- Small (can be used where space is an issue).
- Easy-to-use technology.

Disadvantages

- Problems with lag when drawing on screen.
- Only works with CRT monitors (at the moment).
- Not that accurate when drawing.
- Rather dated technology.

2.2 Direct data entry (DDE) devices

2.2.1 Devices for reading information from cards

Magnetic stripe readers

These are used to read information on the magnetic stripe found on, for example, the back of a credit or debit card.

The stripe contains useful information, for example: account number, sort code, expiry date and start date.

Uses

- On credit/debit cards for use at ATMs or EFTPOS (electronic funds transfer at point of sale) terminals.
- Security devices to allow entry to buildings, hotel rooms, etc.

Advantages

- Fast data entry compared with keying in with a keyboard or keypad.
- Error free (since no typing is involved).
- Secure (information not in human readable form and, since there is no typing, removes the risk of somebody observing your key strokes).
- Prevents access to restricted/secure areas.
- Not affected by oil, water, moisture etc.
- No moving parts – so physically very robust.

Magnetic stripe

Disadvantages

- If the magnetic stripe gets damaged (for example, due to exposure to a strong magnetic field) the data is lost.
- Doesn't work at a distance (card needs to be in close contact with the reader).
- Since the information is not human readable, this can be a disadvantage in some applications.

Contactless card readers

Contactless debit or credit cards allow customers to pay for items worth up to $25 without entering their PIN. All contactless cards have a small chip that emits radio waves embedded in them. The card is held within a few centimetres of the payment terminal to pay for an item; the terminal picks up the signal from the chip and allows the transaction to be processed.

The steps taken are:

1 Customers look out for the contactless symbol on the payment terminal.
2 The shop assistant enters the amount for payment.
3 The card reader informs the customer to present their contactless card.
4 The customer holds their card in front of the card reader.
5 The terminal display will indicate that the card has been read.

Advantages

- Faster transaction (typical transaction takes 15 seconds as opposed to 30 seconds using a magnetic stripe reader).
- The system uses 128-bit encryption to protect data.
- Customers do not have to worry about typing errors (such as incorrectly typing in a PIN).
- Retailers no longer have access to the customer's credit/debit card information.
- The chip in the contactless credit card responds to the payment terminal reader with a unique number used for that transaction only; it does not simply transmit the consumer's account number; this number is also encrypted.

Disadvantages

- They are more expensive than normal credit/debit cards.
- A thief with a suitable reader could monitor your contactless card transaction while standing at the counter with you, or just behind you (the third point above reduces this risk considerably however: because you don't have to type in a PIN, somebody standing behind you couldn't steal your PIN and use it).
- Can take money twice if the customer uses it as a chip and PIN card (one is contactless and the other is chip and PIN).
- Transactions are usually limited to a small maximum value (e.g. $25).
- Transactions have been carried out without the card holder being aware of this while they were just standing in the payment queue.

Chip and PIN readers

Chip and PIN readers are similar to smart card readers but are used at EFTPOS terminals. The device has a slot into which the card is placed and the chip is read; the PIN is entered using the keypad. The reader also has a small screen which gives instructions to the operator. They are similar to the contactless system, except for two points:

- the customer has to key in their PIN to make a transaction
- the cards do not make use of RF technology.

Uses

- Where payments are made using cards (restaurants, supermarkets, travel agents, etc.).

Advantages

- More secure system (PIN typed in must match up with PIN stored on chip).
- More robust system than magnetic stripe cards.

Disadvantages

- Fraud – need to be careful to ensure PIN isn't read by somebody else while typing it in.

2.2.2 Radio frequency identification (RFID) readers

This technology has already been mentioned in the description of contactless credit/debit card transactions.

Radio frequency identification (RFID) readers use radio waves to read and capture information stored on a **tag**. The tag can be read from a distance of several metres, which is one of its advantages over the barcode system. The RFID tag is made up of two components:

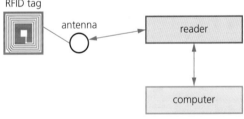

- a microchip that stores and processes information
- an antenna that is used to receive and transmit data/information.

The tags can be passive or battery powered. Passive tags use the reader's radio wave energy to relay the information; battery-powered tags use a small embedded battery to power the RFID.

Figure 2.3 Radio frequency identification readers (RFIDs)

Uses

- Livestock tracking (so that the whereabouts of each animal on a farm is known; it also identifies which farm owns the animal).
- Retail (it is similar to barcodes but doesn't require any scanning; details, such as price, can be stored on the tag and then automatically read at a checkout – a big advantage is that several tags can be read at the same time, thus speeding up the checkout process).
- Admission passes (for example, in theme parks RFID cards eliminate the need to scan or swipe people before 'rides', reducing the waiting time; it also allows the tracking of people in the theme park and certain information, such as height or age, can be stored to prevent entry to certain rides on safety grounds).
- Libraries (books can be tracked in and out automatically by readers at the library entrance; no need to scan barcodes or magnetic stripe cards, making the process quicker and more accurate).

Advantages

- No line-of-sight contact is necessary; the tags can be read from a distance.
- It is a very robust and reliable technology.
- Very fast read rate (typically < 100 milliseconds to respond).
- Bidirectional data transfer (that is, it allows read *and* write operations to take place).
- Bulk detection is possible (i.e., detect several RFID tags at the same time).

Disadvantages

- Tag collision (this is when the signals from two or more tags overlap, interfering with each other).
- Because RFID uses radio waves, they are relatively easy to jam or interrupt.
- It is relatively easy to hack into the data/signal transmitted by the tag.
- RFID is more expensive than a comparable barcode system.

2.2.3 Magnetic ink character recognition/reader (MICR)

Magnetic ink character recognition (MICR) is a system that can read characters printed in a special ink (containing iron particles). Only certain characters written in a standard font can be read.

The system is now used primarily for reading the characters at the bottom of a bank cheque.

These characters are converted into a form that the computer can understand and then stored in a computer file.

Uses

- They are primarily used to process cheques in banking operations. When a cheque is presented its value is first printed on the cheque in the special ink. The cheques are then all gathered together (either at the end of the day or after some specified period) and then read using a batch processing method.

Advantages

- Offer greater security than OCR since the printed characters cannot be altered.
- There is no manual input, so errors are reduced.
- The magnetic ink characters can still be read even if somebody writes over them (for example, a signature).

Disadvantages

- Only certain characters can be read and the number of different characters is very limited.
- More expensive than other methods used in direct data entry.

2.2.4 Optical mark recognition/reader (OMR)

Optical mark recognition (OMR) is a device that can read marks written in pen or pencil. The places where the pen or pencil marks can be made are clearly shown in the image on the right (in this example, the numerical lozenge is shaded in each response using a pen). The position of the mark is stored in the computer's memory after being read by the OMR device.

Uses

- Used to read questionnaires, multiple-choice examination papers and many other types of form where responses are registered in the form of lines or shaded areas.

Advantages

- Very fast way of inputting the results of a survey, etc. The documents are fed in automatically and there is no user input.
- Since there is no typing, they are more accurate than keying in the data.
- They are more accurate than OCR methods.

Disadvantages

- The forms need to be carefully designed to make sure that the marks/shading are correctly positioned to gather accurate information.
- There can be problems if the forms haven't been filled in correctly; sometimes they have to be checked manually before being read, which is both time consuming and expensive.

2.2.5 Optical character recognition/reader (OCR)

Optical character recognition (OCR) is the name given to software that takes scanned text and converts it into a computer-readable form. The text can then be used in various application packages such as word processors, desktop publishing and presentation software.

Uses

- One of the most recent uses is the processing of passports and identity cards.

Advantages

- It is a much faster data-entry system than manually keying in data.
- Since no manual data entry, the number of errors is also reduced.

Disadvantages

- The system still has difficulty reading handwriting.
- Still not a very accurate technique.

Comparison of OCR and OMR

A company has decided to produce a questionnaire to gain information from customers. What features of OCR or OMR need to be considered when designing the data capture form? This comparison is needed before the form is designed and the appropriate input method chosen. The following table summarises the features of both methods.

Table 2.2 Comparison of OCR and OMR

OCR	OMR
Because this method reads handwriting, it is possible for customers to extend their answers to questions	Since this involves shading in lozenges to answer set questions, the information obtained is limited to the choices offered in each question
This method can read handwriting – but poor handwriting may cause reading errors	OMR relies on simply detecting where marks have been made on a page; the position of the marks is compared to a template stored in memory
OCR is used for converting printed documents to an editable electronic format	OMR simply reads the position of marks, so it is ideal for multiple-choice exam papers
OCR requires a complex recognition system	This method requires complex (and expensive) forms to be completed; but the recognition system is simpler than OCR
Fewer 'how to fill in' instructions are needed for forms designed to be completed and then read by OCR	While this method requires more 'how to fill in' instructions, it is easier and faster for customers to complete OMR forms than to complete OCR forms
While OCR is more accurate than data entered into a computer by keyboard, there are still problems recognising all types of handwriting, leading to inaccuracies	OMR is essentially a more accurate method for reading data than OCR

2.2.6 Barcode readers

Barcode readers are used to read information in the form of a barcode.

The readers are usually in the form of a barcode scanner and are often built into POS terminals in supermarkets. **Hand-held scanners or wands** (as shown in the photograph) are also very common for reading barcodes if portability is required (for example, if the barcodes are on large or fixed objects).

Uses

- Used in supermarkets and other shops where the goods are marked with a barcode; the barcodes are used to give information about the product which enables automatic stock control, itemised billing, etc. to take place.
- Used in libraries to keep track of books on loan.
- Used as a safety function in many companies to ensure that electrical equipment is checked on a regular basis (barcodes are placed on an item to identify it and a database holds all the information related to that barcode so it is possible to interrogate the system as part of a safety audit).

Advantages

- Much faster than keying in data manually and fewer mistakes will be made.
- If used as a way of recording data, they can improve safety.
- They allow automatic stock control.
- They are a tried and trusted technology.

Disadvantages

- Relatively expensive system to administer.
- Not foolproof (barcodes can be swapped around on items).
- Can be more easily damaged than RFID tags or magnetic strips.

Quick response (QR) codes

Another type of barcode is the **quick response (QR) code**. This is made up of a matrix of filled in dark squares on a light background. For example, the following QR code contains the message: 'Cambridge IGCSE ICT textbook Chapter 2'.

To make a comparison, normal barcodes (as described on page 34) can hold up to 30 digits; QR codes can hold over 7000 digits. This obviously gives greater scope for the storage of information.

As modern smartphones allow internet access on the move, QR codes can be scanned anywhere. This allows advertising of products on trains, buses, shopping malls and many other places. Using the built-in camera facility on modern phones, and by downloading the appropriate application (or App), it is possible to read the QR code. The code may contain a website link or some form of advertising; for example, the following QR code contains a telephone number and an advertisement for free pizzas if ordered today. On scanning the QR code, the phone number and advertisement will appear on the mobile phone's screen.

Advantages

- There is no need for the user to actually write down or key in a website address; this is done automatically by scanning the QR code.
- QR codes can store website addresses/URLs that appear in magazines, trains, buses or even business cards, providing a very effective method of advertising.

2.3 Output devices and their uses

As the name suggests, these are hardware devices that allow data to be output from a computer. Some devices hold the data temporarily (such as in a printer buffer/memory) whereas others produce permanent output in the form of a hard copy (such as a printer producing output on paper). There is a third type of output device that is used to control processes in conjunction with sensor input devices.

2.3.1 Monitors

CRT monitors

Cathode ray tube (CRT) monitors are the least expensive type of monitor, although they are becoming increasingly rare as TFT monitors are now taking over. They come in various sizes and make use of an electron gun firing against a phosphor screen. The picture is made up of tiny dots that are coloured red, green or blue – the intensity of each coloured dot makes up the vast range of colours interpreted by the eye.

Uses

- They were used as the primary output device for computers so the user can see immediately what they are typing in.
- They are used with light pens, for example, to allow designs to be created on screen.

Advantages

- The angle of viewing is still better than with most TFT monitors.
- They work with light pens in CAD/CAM applications.

Disadvantages

- They tend to be rather heavy and present a safety hazard if not supported properly.
- They run very hot and can cause fires if left unattended (especially as they get older).

- They consume considerably more power than modern TFT monitors.
- They can flicker, which can lead to headaches and eyesight problems with prolonged use.

Thin film transistor (TFT) monitors

Thin film transistor (TFT) monitors are taking over from CRT monitors as the main output device. One of the reasons for the rapid development of laptop computers can be attributed to the advancements made in TFT technology. The screen is made up of thousands of tiny pixels, which are made up of transistors controlled by a microprocessor. Each pixel has three transistors that are coloured red, green or blue – the intensity of each governs the effective colour of the pixel seen by the eye.

Uses

- They are used as the primary output device for computers so the user can see immediately what they are typing in.
- They are an integral part of laptop computers.

Advantages

- They are lightweight and don't pose the same risks as CRT monitors.
- They produce less glare than CRT monitors and also emit less radiation.
- They consume much less power and don't generate as much heat as a CRT monitor.

Disadvantages

- The angle of viewing a TFT is fairly critical otherwise the image isn't very clear (for example, if several people are looking at a screen at the same time).
- Definition is sometimes not as good as a CRT monitor.

LCD and LED monitors

The days of CRT monitors are almost gone. These days, most monitors and television sets are made using liquid crystal display/diode (LCD) technology. These are simply a development of the TFT monitors described above.

The front layer of the monitor is made up of liquid crystal diodes; these tiny diodes are grouped together in threes or fours, which are known as pixels (picture elements). The three colours that are grouped together use red, green and blue diodes. Those systems that use groups of four include a yellow diode – this is said to make the colours more vivid.

Because LCD doesn't emit any light, some form of backlit technology needs to be used. Modern LCD monitors are backlit using light emitting diode (LED) technology. This gives the image better contrast and brightness. Before the use of LEDs, LCD monitors used cold cathode fluorescent lamp (CCFL) as the backlighting method.

Essentially, CCFL uses two fluorescent tubes behind the LCD screen, which supplies the light source. When LEDs are used, a matrix of tiny LEDs is used behind the LCD screen. LEDs have become increasingly more popular due to a number of advantages over older CCFL technology:

- LEDs reach their maximum brightness almost immediately (there is no need to 'warm up' before reaching full efficiency)

- LEDs give a whiter light, which sharpens the image and makes the colours appear more vivid; CCFL had a slightly yellowish tint
- LEDs produce a brighter light, which improves the colour definition
- monitors using LED technology are much thinner than monitors using CCFL technology
- LEDs last almost indefinitely; this makes the technology more reliable and makes for a more consistent product
- LEDs consume very little power, which means they produce less heat as well as using less energy.

What of the future?

Future LED technology will make use of organic light emitting diodes (OLEDs). These use organic materials (made up of carbon compounds) to create semi-conductors that are very flexible.

Organic films are sandwiched between two charged electrodes (one is a metallic cathode and the other a glass anode). When an electric field is applied to the electrodes they give off light. This means that no form of backlighting is required, which allows for very thin screens. It also means that there is no longer a need to use LCD technology, since OLED is a self-contained system.

As can be seen in the photo, OLEDs allow screens to be curved, which ensures a good picture from any angle.

But the important aspect of the technology is how thin this makes the screen. It will be possible, using OLED technology, to bend screens to any shape. If this is adopted by mobile phone manufacturers, it will be possible to develop phones that can wrap around your wrist – much like a watch strap (see smartwatches earlier).

Imagine screens so thin that they can be folded up and placed in your pocket until they are needed. Or how about using folding OLED displays attached to fabrics creating 'smart' clothing (this could be used on outdoor survival clothing where an integrated circuit, mobile phone, GPS receiver and OLED display could all be sewn into the clothing)?

Science fiction becomes science fact – yet again.

Advantages of using OLED compared to existing LED and LCD monitors/ screens:

- the plastic, organic layers of an OLED are thinner, lighter and more flexible than the crystal structures used in LEDs or LCDs
- the light-emitting layers of an OLED are lighter; OLED layers can be made from plastic rather than the glass as used in LED and LCD screens
- OLEDs give a brighter light than LEDs
- OLEDs do not require backlighting like LCD screens – OLEDs generate their own light
- since OLEDs require no backlighting, they use much less power than LCD screens (most of the LCD power is used to do the backlighting); this is very important in battery-operated devices such as mobile phones
- since OLEDs are essentially plastics, they can be made into large, thin sheets (this means they could be used on large advertising boards in airports, subways, and so on)
- OLEDs have a very large field of view, about 170 degrees, which makes them ideal for use in television sets and for advertising screens.

> ### Exercise 2c
>
> Carry out some research into OLED technology (there are numerous internet sites to help you) and answer the following questions:
>
> 1 Why are inkjet printers helping to keep down the cost of OLED screens?
> 2 How are different colours generated using OLED technology?
> 3 How is the brightness of the display controlled?
> 4 OLEDs refresh 1000 times faster than LCDs; why would this be an advantage? Where could it be used to great effect?

LCD/LED screens are used on many hand-held devices, such as mobile phones, tablets and game consoles. The technology behind such screens was discussed at length in Chapter 1.

Modern LCD screens are very thin and very lightweight, and are very responsive to touch. Obviously, the new technologies described above will change the way we use these hand-held devices in the very near future.

2.3.2 Multimedia projectors

Multimedia projectors receive signals that can be either analogue or digital (although most modern projectors only work with digital inputs). The signal source is usually from a computer, television or DVD player. The image from the source is magnified and projected on to a large screen. The devices usually work with a remote control but also use virtual mouse technology, which actually becomes a cordless PC mouse with the same features as a mouse. It is then possible to direct the computer presentation without being tied to the computer. Another feature of the virtual mouse is the laser pointer. Most multimedia projectors take input from various types of video format.

Uses

- Training presentations (to allow the whole audience to see the images from a computer).
- Advertising presentations (large images showing product features, for example a new car, can be shown at exhibitions, shopping malls, etc.).
- Home cinema systems (projecting the images from a DVD or television).

Advantages

- Enables many people to see a presentation rather than crowding round a small computer screen.
- Avoids the need for several networked computers (for example, when looking at a video clip on an internet site – everybody can see the video on the large screen rather than logging on to a number of computers).

Disadvantages

- Images can sometimes be fuzzy.
- Expensive to buy from the outset.
- Setting up projectors can be a little difficult.

2.3.3 Printers

Laser printers

Laser printers produce very high-quality hard-copy output. The print rate per page is very quick if a large number of pages are being printed. They rely on large buffer memories where the data for the whole document is stored before the pages can be printed out.

Uses

- They are used where low noise is required (for example, in an office).
- If fast, high-quality, high-volume printing is required then laser printers are the best option.

Advantages

- Printing is fast (unless only a few pages are to be printed, in which case they are little faster than inkjet printers).
- They can handle very large print jobs.
- The quality is consistently high.
- Toner cartridges last for a long time (and the printers can sometimes be a cost effective option, particularly if colour outputs are not required).

Disadvantages

- Only really fast if several copies are being made.
- Colour laser printers tend to be expensive to run (four colour/black cartridges are needed, as well as diffuser kits, which are expensive to purchase).
- They produce ozone and volatile organic compounds because of their method of printing and type of toner/ink used (these have been linked to health hazards in the office).

Inkjet printers

Inkjet printers are used to produce good quality hard copies. Unlike laser printers, inkjet printers don't have large buffers, therefore printing is done a bit at a time. This is why printing is sometimes paused since the whole page can't be stored in the buffer and it has to wait for the computer to send more data.

Uses

- Used where low output volumes are required (high-volume jobs are difficult to do since the ink cartridges tend to be used up very quickly).
- If high-quality printing is required for single pages (or only a small print job) then these printers are ideal; for example, they are very good at producing photo-quality printouts.
- 3-D inkjet printers are now being used in industry to produce prototypes (see page 40).

Advantages

- High-quality output.
- Cheaper to buy than laser printers.
- Very lightweight and have a small footprint.
- Don't produce ozone and volatile organic compounds, unlike laser printers.

Disadvantages

- Slow output if several copies needed (little buffer capacity to store the pages).
- Can't do large print jobs (ink cartridges run out too quickly).
- Printing can 'smudge' if user is not careful.
- Can be expensive if used a lot (original ink cartridges are expensive to buy).

Dot matrix printers

Dot matrix printers are a type of impact printer where a print head (made up of a matrix of pins) presses against an inked ribbon. They tend to be slow, noisy and the output is not that good. They are still useful, however, where multi-part or continuous stationery is being used.

Uses

- They can be used in noisy environments (for example, garage workshops) and in applications where print quality is not that important.
- They are used in applications where multi-part stationery or the fact that they are an impact printer is of value (for example, producing wage slips).

Advantages

- They can be used in environments that would be a problem to laser or inkjet printers (for example, dusty/dirty or moist atmospheres).
- Carbon copies or multi-part outputs can be produced.
- Very cheap to run and maintain.
- Easy to use if continuous stationery is required (for example, long print jobs such as wages slips).

Disadvantages

- Very noisy – not good in an office environment.
- Actually cost more than an inkjet printer to buy initially.
- Very slow, poor-quality printing.

3-D printers

3-D printers are primarily used in **computer-aided design (CAD)** applications. They are primarily based on inkjet and laser printer technology and can produce solid objects that actually work. The solid object is built up layer by layer using materials such as powdered resin, powdered metal, paper or ceramic.

The alloy wheel shown here was made using an industrial 3-D printer. It was made from many layers of powered metal (0.1 mm thick) using a technology known as **binder 3-D printing**. Other examples are discussed below.

The following information describes some of the features of 3-D printing:

- Various types of 3-D printers exist; they range from the size of a microwave oven up to the size of a small car.
- 3-D printers use **additive** manufacturing (i.e., the object is built up layer by layer); this is in sharp contrast to the more traditional method of **subtractive** manufacturing (i.e., the removal of material to make an object). For example, making a statue using a 3-D printer would involve building it up layer by

layer using powdered stone until the final object was formed. The subtractive method would involve carving the statue out of solid stone (that is, removing the stone not required) until the final item was produced. Similarly, **CNC** (computer controlled machine – a type of lathe) removes metal to form an object; 3-D printing would produce the same item by building up the object from layers of powdered metal.

- **Direct 3-D printing** uses inkjet technology; a print head can move left to right as in a normal printer. However, the print head can also move up and down to build up the layers of an object – each layer being less than a tenth of a millimetre (< 0.1 mm).
- Binder 3-D printing is similar to direct 3-D printing but this method uses two passes for each of the layers: the first pass sprays dry powder then, on the second pass, a binder (a type of glue) is sprayed to form a solid layer.
- Newer technologies are using lasers and UV light to harden liquid polymers; this further increases the diversity of products that can be made.

The steps in the process of producing an object using 3-D printers is summarised in Figure 2.4.

3-D printing is regarded as being possibly the next 'industrial revolution' since it will change the manufacturing methods in many industries. The following list is just a glimpse into what we know can be made using these printers; in the years that follow, this list will probably fill an entire book:

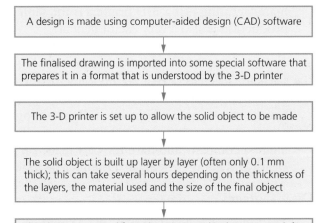

Figure 2.4 Creating a solid object using 3-D printers

- prosthetic limbs can be made to fit exactly on to the injured body part
- making items to allow precision reconstructive surgery (for example, facial reconstruction following an accident); the parts made by this technique are more precise in their design as they can be made from exact scanning of the skull
- in aerospace, manufacturers are looking at making wings and other aeroplane parts using 3-D technology; the bonus will be lightweight, precision parts
- fashion and art – 3-D printing allows new creative ideas to be developed
- making parts for items no longer in production, for example, parts for a vintage car.

These are just a few of the exciting applications that make use of this new technology.

Exercise 2d

Use the internet to research some new and innovative 3-D printing applications.

Advantages

- The manufacturing of items has become much easier than ever before. It is now theoretically possible to manufacture any product a user wants using only a 3-D printer. This has led the way for customised products, as it allows a user to create their own designs in 3-D and have them printed in solid form.

- Because 3-D printers can manufacture items relatively quickly, it allows rapid prototyping. This means that it will take a really short length of time for designs to be converted into working prototypes.
- Even though the cost of 3-D printing is very high, it is still less when compared to labour costs and other costs involved in manufacturing a product in the more conventional way. The fact that the cost of manufacturing using 3-D printers is the same for both small-scale and mass production is also a very useful benefit.
- Medical benefits are emerging, such as producing artificial organs, prosthetics and precision-made items for reconstructive surgery.
- Parts for machinery that are no longer made could now be manufactured using 3-D printers. A car made in the 1930s, for example, will no longer have parts available off-the-shelf. By scanning the broken part (using a 3-D scanner), or by obtaining its blueprint, it will be possible to simply email the file to a company and have the part made on an industrial 3-D printer. This clearly has many benefits in a number of applications.

Disadvantages

- The biggest possible drawback of 3-D printers is the potential to make counterfeit items or items that infringe others' copyright. 3-D printing technology essentially turns every owner of one of these printers into a potential manufacturer. Thus, it could become very difficult to trace the source of fake items; copyright holders would also have great difficulty in protecting their rights.
- All new technologies in the hands of the wrong people can lead to dangerous or illegal activities. With the possibility of creating almost anything with a 3-D printer, this technology could be used to manufacture dangerous items by almost anyone.
- There is the potential for job losses if this technology takes over from some types of manufacturing. Of course, this could also be seen as a benefit by some companies as it could lead to lower manufacturing costs for certain items.

2.3.4 Speakers

(Loud) speakers can be connected directly to a computer or are built into the monitor or casing (as in a laptop computer). Digital data from the computer is converted into analogue form (using a digital to analogue converter – DAC) and the signal amplified through the speakers. A sound card interface is needed in the computer to 'drive' the speakers.

Uses

- Output sound from multimedia presentations.
- Play downloaded sound files.
- Audio output of text on the screen (together with speech-generation software) helps users with disabilities.

2.3.5 Control applications

Actuators

Actuators are transducers* and are used to take signals from a computer and convert them into some form of motion, for example operating motors, pumps, switches and valves.

As part of the control process, digital signals are sent from the computer to an actuator to operate a device – usually conversion of the digital signal to analogue is required first (using a DAC).

*Transducers are devices that change variations in a physical quantity (such as pressure or rotation) into an electrical signal or vice versa.

Motors

The motor is turned on or off by the actuator.

Uses

- Used in automatic washing machines (to make the drum rotate), cookers (to switch on fans), water pumps in central heating systems, and in automatic glasshouses to open windows and switch on fans.
- Control of robot arms in industry.
- In computers to control fans, disk drives and DVD drives.

Buzzers

The buzzers are switched on or off by the actuator.

Uses

- Used in cookers and microwave ovens to tell the operator when the cooking process is complete.
- Used in burglar alarm systems to warn of intruders.

Lights

The actuator is connected to the switch that turns the lights on or off.

Uses

- Security lights.
- In glasshouses to control the lighting conditions.

Heaters

Actuators are connected to switches that turn the heater on or off.

Uses

- Automatic washing machines to heat up the water if necessary.
- Automatically control the temperature in an oven or hot plate.
- Control the heating in a central heating system.
- Temperature control in an automatic glasshouse.

3 Storage devices and media

In this chapter you will learn about:

- backing storage
- why back up data?
- types of access used by secondary storage devices
- types of internal and external secondary storage devices:
  - magnetic
  - optical
  - solid state.

3.1 Backing up of data

This chapter covers many forms of secondary storage and compares the advantages and disadvantages of each type. In Chapter 1 you learnt about the primary memory, known as RAM and ROM. We will consider a number of storage devices later but first it is important to consider why we need to back up data using these devices and also how data is accessed.

3.1.1 What is backing up of data?

Backing up refers to the copying of files/data to a different medium (disk, tape, flash drive, etc.) in case of a problem with the main secondary storage device. Backing up files and data on a regular basis is seen as good computing practice and many computer systems can be set to back up files automatically on a regular basis. An example would be the use of magnetic tapes to back up internet servers on a regular basis, or cloud storage companies using magnetic tape or hard disk drives to back up clients' data on a regular basis.

The backups are often stored in a different place to the main storage. This is in case of fire or some other situation that could lead to irretrievable loss of key data/files.

3.1.2 Why back up data?

There are various reasons why backups are made. Some of the more common reasons are considered below.

- To safegauard against loss of data due to the failure of the original secondary storage device; this could be due to hardware failure (e.g. head crash on a hard drive unit), problems caused by files being overwritten accidentally (or otherwise) or possible corruption of files (for example, caused by power surges).
- To safeguard against damage caused by hackers. This may not be their intention (they may only want to gain access to the information for other purposes, for example to find personal information such as bank account details). However, the very act of hacking in to files could cause problems such as corruption or data loss.
- Backups are also made in case the files need to be used elsewhere; this protects the originals against possible corruption or loss.
- Backups don't necessarily guard against the effect of a virus. The virus could attach itself to the files, which could mean that the backups are also affected. If the computer was 'cleaned' of the virus and then the backup files reloaded, there is a real risk that the virus could infect the computer system again. The best protection is not to get a virus in the first place.

3.2 Types of access

A number of secondary storage devices are discussed in Section 3.3. The way data is stored and read by each of these devices is very different, however.

This section briefly describes the two main methods of accessing data. It is important to understand three new terms here:

- field
- record
- file.

Suppose we are storing data about 20 cars in a car showroom. Data about each car – such as its colour, engine size, type of fuel, number of doors and whether it's new or used – are stored in an allocated space known as a **field**. All of the data about car 1, for example, is known as the **record** for that car. Putting all the data together for all 20 cars produces a **file** like this.

field 1	field 2	field 3	field 4	field 5	field 6	
car 1	red	1.5 litres	petrol	3 doors	new	record 1
car 2	blue	1.3 litres	petrol	5 doors	used	record 2
car 3	green	2.2 litres	diesel	5 doors	used	record 3
...	...	...	...	...	...	
car 20	white	1.6 litres	petrol	2 doors	new	record 20

Figure 3.1 Data for 20 cars in a showroom

3.2.1 Serial access

When using **serial access** it is necessary to start at the beginning of the file and then access each record in turn until the required record is found. In the example above, to find the record for car 15, it is necessary to first read all of the preceding records (that is, 1 to 14) until the required record is located.

It is primarily used on magnetic tape systems and is essentially a very slow form of data access. It is used in applications where speed of access, or where the order in which the data is accessed, isn't important (for example in utility billing, clearing bank cheques or producing pay slips).

When the original magnetic tape (called the **master file**) needs **updating**, an additional tape (called a **transaction file**) is required. The transaction file contains all the new data to allow the master file to be updated (although the transaction file is very often another tape, the new data could in fact be stored on a different medium). The updated tape is referred to as the new master file. When using tapes, it is essential that the records on both master file and transaction file are sorted in the same order (for example, sorted by customer number if it is a billing application – the field used to sort the records is often referred to as a **key field**).

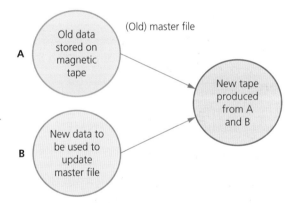

Figure 3.2 Updating a magnetic tape

This is an example of how a master file (MF) can be updated using a Transaction File (TF). The scenario here is a book shop that sells books. All of the books held in stock are stored on the MF in ISBN order – the ISBN acts as the key field for each record (each different book title will have its own record made up of the ISBN, title of book, author, genre, cost price and selling price). All the changes during the day will be stored on the TF – if a book sells, if new books come in, if a book is out of print, and so on. At the end of each day, the

MF is updated using the new data stored on the TF. The basic steps in the update process are shown below:

- at the end of the day, the TF is sorted in the same order as the MF (this will be done using the ISBN which is known here as the key field)
- a new master file (NMF) is created to store the updated records of the books in the shop
- the first record in the TF is then read and the first record in the MF is also read
  - the two records are compared with each other
  - if the key field on the MF < the key field on the TF, then no transactions took place and the MF record is written to the NMF; a new MF record is now read
  - if the key field on the MF = the key field on the TF, then a transaction took place and the new record from the TF is written to the NMF; the next record from both the MF and TF are now read
  - if the transaction file indicates a deletion then the record is simply not written to the NMF and a new record from each file is read
  - if the key field on the MF is greater than the key field on the TF, then the record doesn't yet exist and a new record is created on the NMF and the record is written from the TF to the NMF; a new TF record is now read
- the process is repeated until the end of the MF
- finally, any remaining records on the TF are written to the NMF.

Example

The Master File (MF) contains the following records with key fields shown:

1	2	3	4	6	8	9

The Transaction File (TF) contains the following records with key fields shown:

1	2	4	5	7	8	10

The first record from each file is read. The key fields both match, so the record with key field 1 is written from the TF to the new master file (NMF):

1									

The second record is then read from the MF and TF; again the keys are equal so the record on TF with key field 2 is now written to the NMF:

1	2								

The third record is then read from the MF and TF; this time the key fields are different (3 and 4). The MF key < the TF key, so the MF record with key 3 is now written to the NMF:

1	2	3							

The next record from the MF is read. This time they are both 4 so the record on the TF is written to the NMF:

1	2	3	4						

The next records form both MF and TF are read (6 and 5). The MF key is greater than the TF key, so a new record is created with key field 5. The new record is written to the NMF from the TF:

1	2	3	4	5					

The next record on the TF is read. Again they are different (6 and 7). The MF key < TF key, so the MF record with key 6 is now written to the NMF:

This process continues until all the records have been checked and the final NMF emerges:

> ### Exercise 3a
> Continue the above exercise for the remainder of records to see if you arrive at the above NMF. What would happen if two of the records on the TF (with key fields of 4 and 8) needed deletion to be carried out? What would be the final NMF?

3.2.2 Direct access

Direct access is used with magnetic disks, optical media and solid state media. The computer uses the key field to calculate where data should be stored. It is then able to access the data directly from the calculated position. Consequently, access is much faster than with serial access. When updating files using direct access, the old records/data are simply written over by the new records/data. It is not necessary to sort records into any specific order first.

It is used in applications where data access speed is vital (for example, in real-time operations such as controlling a chemical plant or online systems such as booking air tickets or automatic stock control).

3.3 Secondary storage media

Dating right back to the advent of the personal computer, all systems have come equipped with some form of secondary storage. When a user loads data into a computer, the information is stored temporarily in the RAM – if the computer was turned off, this data would be lost. Secondary storage devices ensure that data is stored permanently so that it can be used again at a later date. This section will consider the various types of secondary storage and the media used.

Throughout the chapter, you will notice that the term **byte** is used to measure the size of memory or storage. Typically, **storage** sizes or file sizes are measured in kilobytes (kB), megabytes (MB), gigabytes (GB) and terabytes (TB) as shown in Table 3.1.

Table 3.1 File sizes

Storage size	Number of bytes	Number of bytes as power of 10
1 KB	1000 bytes	10^3 bytes
1 MB	1 000 000 bytes	10^6 bytes
1 GB	1 000 000 000 bytes	10^9 bytes
1 TB	1 000 000 000 000 bytes	10^{12} bytes

Note that this is different to memory sizes as used internally in the computer, where:
1 KB = 1024 (2^{10}) bytes, 1 MB = 1 048 576 (2^{20}) bytes, 1 GB = 1 073 741 824 (2^{30}) bytes and 1 TB = 1 099 511 627 776 (2^{40}) bytes. These values are all powers of 2.

This section reviews the various types of secondary storage devices available. These are either internal or external (that is, plug-in devices) to the computer.

Devices fall into the three different types of storage media:

- magnetic
- optical
- solid state.

3.3.1 Magnetic storage media

Magnetic storage media depend on the magnetic properties of certain materials (iron and nickel alloys being the most common). Magnetic material is coated on the surface of a disk or tape that can be magnetised in such a way as to represent a 1 or a 0. Many hard disk drives are made up of more than one disk and these disks are known as platters. Each platter is made from glass, ceramic or aluminium coated in a nickel alloy that can be magnetised. In the case of tape, plastic that is coated in a magnetic material is used to store the data.

Fixed/internal hard disk drive (HDD)

Fixed hard disk drives are available on all computers and are the main method used for data storage. On a PC this is usually a fixed hard disk with read/write heads allowing data to be written to or read from the disk surface. The disk surface is coated in a magnetic film that allows data to be stored by altering the magnetic properties to represent binary 1s or 0s (the fundamental units of computer memories). The hard disks usually store the disk operating system (DOS) and other systems software, as well as applications software and files. Applications software (such as spreadsheets and word processors) also needs a hard drive to allow them to quickly retrieve and save data.

Uses

- To store the operating system, systems software and working data/files.
- Storing applications software that needs fast retrieval and storage of data.
- Used in real-time systems (for example, robots, control of a chemical plant where data for the process is stored to allow real-time operations) and in online systems (for example, booking airline tickets or automatic stock control using EFTPOS, which allows immediate updating of the stock files).
- Used in file servers for computer networks.

Advantages

- They have a very fast data transfer rate and fast access times to data.
- They have very large memory capacities.

Disadvantages

- Can be easily damaged if the correct shut down procedure is not carried out; this can lead to a head crash which would result in a loss of data.
- They have many moving parts when compared to, for example solid state drives (SSDs).
- Their read/write operation can be quite noisy compared to SSDs.

Portable hard disk drives

These devices work in much the same way as fixed hard disk drives but are usually connected to the computer via the USB (universal serial bus) port and can be disconnected and used on different computers. The disks are generally capable of storing more data than the equivalent optical disk (CD, DVD and so on).

Uses

- They can be used as backup systems to prevent loss of data.
- They can be used to transfer data/files/software between computers.

Advantages

- The data access time and data transfer rate is very fast.
- They have a large memory capacity.
- They can be used as a method of transferring information between computers.

Disadvantages

- They can be easily damaged if dropped or subjected to a strong magnetic field; as with fixed hard disk drives, an incorrect shut-down procedure could also lead to loss of data.

Magnetic tapes

A **magnetic tape** is a very thin strip of plastic that has been coated in a magnetic layer. They are read and written to by a read/write head. The data is stored in magnetic areas that represent 1s and 0s. Data is read from the tape using serial access (see earlier description). This type of storage is useless in a real-time or online applications (due to the very slow data access speeds) and is best suited to offline or batch processing.

Uses

- In applications where batch processing is used, for example, clearing bank cheques, utility billing (gas, electricity, water) and producing pay slips; in these applications there is no need for any specific processing order and speed of data access is not essential.
- Used as a backup media since all the data needs to be stored.
- Used in long-term archiving of data; magnetic tapes have huge data storage capacities and are known to be very stable, which makes them ideal for long-term storage.

Advantages

- They are generally less expensive (per byte) than the equivalent hard disk.
- It is a very robust technology (they don't deteriorate very much over time).
- They have a huge data storage capacity.
- The **data transfer rate** is actually fast (this should not be confused with data access time, which is very slow for magnetic tapes).

Disadvantages

- Very slow **data access times** (need to read all the earlier records on the tape until the required record is found – see Section 3.2).
- When updating, another tape is needed (see description in Figure 3.2 on page 45) to store the final updated version.
- They are affected by magnetic fields; a strong magnet can corrupt data stored on the tape.

3.3.2 Optical storage media

CD/DVD disks

CDs and DVDS are described as optical storage devices. Laser light is used to read data and to write data on the surface of the disk. Both CDs and DVDs use a thin layer of metal alloy or light-sensitive organic dye to store the data.

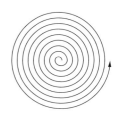

As can be seen from the diagram, they use a single spiral track that runs from the centre of the disk to the edge.

The data is stored in 'pits' and 'bumps' on the spiral track. A red laser is used to read and write the data. CDs and DVDs can be designated as follows:

- R – write once only
- ROM – can only be read
- RW – can be written to or read from many times.

DVD technology is slightly different to that used in CDs. One of the main differences is the use of **dual-layering**, which considerably increases the storage capacity. Basically, this means that there are two individual recording layers. The two layers of a standard DVD are joined together with a transparent (polycarbonate) spacer; a very thin reflector is also sandwiched between the two layers. Reading and writing of the second layer is done by a red laser focusing at a fraction of a millimetre difference compared to the first layer.

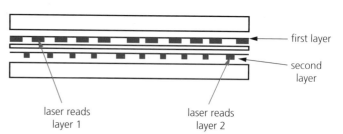

Figure 3.3 Dual-layering in a DVD

Standard, single-layer DVDs still have a larger storage capacity than CDs because the 'pit' size and track width are both smaller. This means that more data can be stored on the DVD surface. DVDs use lasers with a wavelength of 650 nanometres; CDs use lasers with a wavelength of 780 nanometres. The shorter the wavelength of the laser light, the greater the storage capacity of the medium.

CD-ROM and DVD-ROM

These optical disks are read-only memory (ROM), which means they cannot be written over and can only be read. The data is stored as a series of **pits** (equivalent to a binary value of 1) and **lands** (equivalent to the binary value of 0) in the metallic optical layer. The 'pits' are formed by a laser beam etching the surface at the manufacturing stage. Only a single track exists which spirals out from the centre of the disk.

The 'pits' and 'lands' are read by a low-powered laser beam that follows the data stream and reads from the centre outwards in a spiral. The light reflects differently off a 'pit' than it does off a 'land' and this is interpreted as 1s and 0s (that is, data) – hence the term digital media.

Uses

- CD-ROMs are used to store music files, software, computer games and reference software (such as an encyclopaedia).
- DVD-ROMs have much larger storage and are used to store films, computer data and ever-more sophisticated computer/arcade games.
- CD-ROMs and DVD-ROMs are used in applications where there is a real need to prevent the deletion or overwriting of important data.

Advantages

- They hold far more data than floppy disks (one CD/DVD could replace several floppy disks in some applications).
- They are less expensive than hard disk drive systems.

Disadvantages

- The data transfer rate/data access time is slower than for hard disks.

CD-R and DVD-R

The letter R here means the disk is recordable *once* only; it becomes a CD-ROM or DVD-ROM once it has been finalised (this means that the CD/DVD cannot have any additional data written to it). This is the last step in the CD/DVD process; finalising is also used as an alternative word for the 'closing' of a CD-R, in which Table of Contents (TOC) data are written on the disc to enable the computer to read the CD/DVD.

A thin layer of an organic dye (DVDs also use an additional silver alloy or gold reflector) is used as the recording media. A laser beam produces heated spots and unheated spots. On reading the disk, a laser beam is capable of distinguishing between the two types of spots and effectively reads the data stream from the centre outwards in a spiral action. This data is then interpreted as 1s and 0s.

Uses

- Home recordings of music (CD-R) and films (DVD-R).
- Used to store data to be kept for later use or to be transferred to another computer.

Advantages

- Cheaper than RW disks.
- Once burned (and finalised) they are like a ROM.

Disadvantages

- If finalised, the CD-R/DVD-R can only be recorded on once; if an error in the data has occured then the disk has to be discarded since it can no longer be written to.
- Not all CD/DVD players can read CD-R/DVD-R.

CD-RW and DVD-RW

The RW means these disks are a rewritable media and can be written over several times. Unlike CD-R/DVD-R, they don't become ROMs. The recording layer uses a special phase-changing metal alloy (often GeSbTe [Germanium-Antimony-Terbium alloy]; a number of different methods are used to produce these alloys). The alloy can switch between crystalline phase and amorphous phase (non-crystalline), thus changing its reflectivity to light depending on the laser beam power. Spots are produced that can be read by a laser and then interpreted as 1s and 0s. The system allows data to be written, erased and rewritten many times.

Uses

- Used to record television programmes (like a video recorder), which can be recorded over time and time again.
- Not as wasteful as R format as more files/data can be added to at a later stage (with CD-R/DVD-R it is only possible to do a write operation once if you have already finalised the disc).
- Used in CCTV systems.

Advantages

- Can be written over many times.
- Can use different file formats each time it is used.

Disadvantages

- Can be relatively expensive.
- It is possible to accidentally overwrite data.

DVD-RAM

DVD-RAM uses a very different technology to CDs and DVDs. They have the following features:

- instead of a single, spiral track, they use a number of concentric tracks
- the use of concentric tracks allows simultaneous read and write operations to take place
- they allow numerous read and write operations (up to 100 000 times) and have great longevity (over 30 years), which makes them ideal for archiving
- DVD-RAMs can be written to and read from many times.

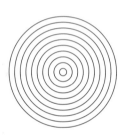

The recording layer is made from a similar phase-changing material as used in RW technology. When writing, a laser heats the phase-changing alloy on the disk to about 500 °C to 700 °C changing the reflective properties from shiny to dull (i.e. pits). If the disk needs to be erased, a laser heats the surface to about 200 °C to return the disk to its original shiny state. A low-power laser is used to read the written marks on the surface. The shiny and dull marks ('pits') represent data to a computer where they are interpreted.

Uses

- In recording devices such as satellite receivers to allow simultaneous recording and playback.
- Used in camcorders to store movies.

Advantages

- They have a long life (estimated 30 years minimum life).
- It is possible to do a rewrite operation over 100 000 times (compare this to the RW format, which only allows about 1000 rewrites).
- Writing on DVD-RAMs is very reliable – they have in-built verification software, so the accuracy of the data is ensured.
- Very fast access if the files are fairly small.
- No need to finalise the disk.
- Very large capacity (about 10 GB if double-sided format I is used).
- They offer the ability to read data at the same time as data is being written.

Disadvantages

- Not as compatible as R or RW format; many systems won't recognise the DVD-RAM format.
- Relatively expensive (about four times the cost of a DVD-RW disk).
- They have been superseded by newer technologies such as solid state memories.

Blu-ray discs

Blu-ray discs are another example of optical storage media. However, they are fundamentally different to DVDs in their construction and in the way they carry out read-write operations. The main differences are:

- a blue laser, rather than a red laser, is used to carry out read and write operations; the wavelength of blue light is only 405 nanometres (compared to 650 nanometres for red light)
- using blue laser light means that the 'pits' and 'bumps' can be much smaller; consequently, Blu-ray can store up to five times more data than a normal DVD
- Blu-ray uses a single 1.1 mm-thick polycarbonate disk; normal DVDs use a sandwich of two 0.6 mm thick disks
- using two sandwiched layers can cause birefringence (light is refracted into two separate beams causing reading errors); because Blu-ray uses only one layer, the disks don't suffer from birefringence
- Blu-ray discs automatically come with a secure encryption system, which helps to prevent piracy and copyright infringement.

Table 3.2 summarises the main differences between CDs, DVDs and Blu-ray.

Table 3.2 Comparison of CDs, DVDs and Blu-ray

Disk type	Laser colour	Wavelength of laser light	Disk construction	Track pitch (distance between tracks)
CD	red	780 nm	single 1.2 mm polycarbonate layer	1.60 μm
DVD	red	650 nm	two 0.6 mm polycarbonate layers	0.74 μm
Blu-ray	blue	405 nm	single 1.1 mm polycarbonate layer	0.30 μm

Note: nm = 10^{-9} metres; μm = 10^{-6} metres.

Uses

- Home video consoles.
- Storing and playing back movies (one high-definition movie of two hours duration uses up 25 GB of memory).
- PCs can use this technology for data storage or backing up hard drives.
- Camcorders can use this media (in cartridge form) to store movie footage.

Advantages

- Very large storage capacity, therefore ideal for storing high-definition movies.
- Very fast data transfer rate.
- The data access speed is also greater than with other optical media.
- Blu-ray discs automatically come with a secure encryption system, which helps to prevent piracy and copyright infringement.

Disadvantages

- Relatively expensive.
- Encryption problems (which are used to stop piracy) when used to store video.
- There are fewer movie titles on Blu-ray format, which is reducing its impact on the home movie market.

All these optical storage media are used as backup systems (for photos, music and multimedia files). This also means that CDs and DVDs can be used to transfer files between computers. Manufacturers often supply their software using CDs and DVDs. When the software is supplied in this way, the disk is usually in a read-only format.

The most common use of DVD and Blu-ray is the supply of movies or games. The memory capacity of CDs isn't big enough to store most movies.

The future of optical media

In recent times both the CD and DVD are showing signs of becoming obsolete. Many computer systems now come with USB connectors only and no DVD or CD drive. The main method of transferring files between devices has become flash memory. Many people now store all their music in the following ways:

- on hard disk drive systems (set up as sound systems, as shown in the photo)
- in MP3 format on:
  - a computer/tablet
  - their mobile/smartphone
  - a portable music player (such as an iPod)
- using the 'cloud' to store all their files so they can access their music from anywhere in the world
- by 'streaming' their music from the internet; provided the user has an internet connection they can access music through a laptop computer, mobile phone, tablet or any other receiving device.

It is a similar story for movies, where streaming is becoming increasingly common. Many television sets are now set up as 'smart' televisions – this means it is now possible to simply stream movies or television programmes on demand without the need for any DVD or Blu-ray players. In effect, the television set has become the central computer with a link to the internet using wireless connection.

Floppy disks met the same fate in the early twenty-first century. How often do you see floppy disks? It is very likely that CDs and DVDs will meet the same fate and be replaced by one of the systems described above or something entirely new.

Exercise 3b

Using this student book and the internet, do some research to find out all the different ways to store music files and movie files.

Draw a table similar to the one shown below to list all the advantages and disadvantages of each of the methods you have identified.

Storage method	Advantages	Disadvantages

3.3.3 Solid state storage media

Solid state drives (SSD)

Solid state drives (SSD) are rapidly taking over from HDDs. They have no moving parts and all data is retrieved at the same rate no matter where it is stored. They don't rely on magnetic properties; the most common type of solid state storage devices store data by controlling the movement of electrons within NAND* chips. The data is stored as 0s and 1s in millions of tiny transistors within the chip. This effectively produces a non-volatile rewritable memory.

*NAND flash memory is a type of non-volatile storage that does not require power to retain data. NAND flash memory stores data in an array of memory cells made from floating-gate transistors which are insulated from each other by an oxide layer. NAND is a type of logic gate and is basically one of the building blocks of many electronic circuits including solid state storage devices.

However, a number of solid state storage devices sometimes use electronically erasable programmable read-only memories (EEPROM) technology. The main difference is the use of NOR* chips rather than NAND. This makes them faster in operation; however, devices using EEPROM are considerably more expensive than those that use NAND technology. EEPROM also allows data to be read or erased in single bytes at a time. Use of NAND only allows blocks of data to be read or erased. This makes EEPROM technology more useful in certain applications where data needs to be accessed or erased in byte-size chunks.

*NOR flash memory is also a type of non-volatile storage; a NOR gate is a type of logic gate that makes up many electronic circuits. NOR gates work in a different way to NAND gates, but the differences are outside the scope of this student book. Essentially, solid state memories made from NOR gates allow faster read/write operations than those made from NAND gates, but the storage devices cost much more to manufacture – consequently, most solid state storage devices use NAND gate technology.

Because of the cost implications, the majority of solid state storage devices use NAND technology. The two are usually distinguished by the terms flash (uses NAND) and EEPROM (uses NOR).

So, what are the main advantages of using SSD rather than HDD? The main advantages of SSDs are summarised below:

- they are more reliable (no moving parts to go wrong)
- they are considerably lighter (which makes them suitable for laptops)
- they don't have to get 'up to speed' before they work properly
- they have a lower power consumption
- they run much cooler than HDDs (both these points again make them very suitable for laptop computers)
- because there are no moving parts, they are very thin
- data access is considerably faster than HDD.

The main drawback of SSD is the questionable longevity of the technology. Most solid state storage devices are conservatively rated at only 20 GB write operations per day over a three-year period – this is known as SSD endurance. For this reason, SSD technology is not used in internet servers, for example, where a huge number of write operations take place every day. However, this issue is being addressed by a number of manufacturers to improve the durability of these solid state systems.

Memory sticks/pen drives

Memory sticks/pen drives can store several gigabytes of data and use the solid state technology described above. They are usually connected to a computer through the USB port and power to operate them is drawn from the host computer. They are extremely small and very portable. Most operating systems recognise these storage media, which means no additional software is needed to operate them.

Some expensive software now uses these storage methods (sometimes referred to as portable flash drives) as a form of security. They plug into the computer using the USB port and are known as dongles. The software installed on a computer sends out a request (in encrypted form) to the dongle asking for an encrypted validation key. Thus a person trying to carry out software piracy would have to break the code on the dongle first before they could use the software. Some systems go one stage further and have key bits of software stored on the dongle in encrypted form. The software looks for these pieces of encrypted code to enable it to run. This gives an added security benefit to the software.

Uses

- Transporting files between computers or used as a backup store.
- Used as a security device to prevent software piracy (known as a dongle).

Advantages

- Very compact and portable media.
- Very robust.
- Doesn't need additional software to work on most computers.
- They are not affected by magnetic fields.

Disadvantages

- Can't write-protect the data/files.
- Easy to lose (due to their small physical size).
- The user needs to be very careful when removing a memory stick from a computer – incorrect removal (for example, while it is still doing a read/write operation) will corrupt the data on the memory stick, rendering it useless.

Flash memory cards

These are a form of electrically **erasable programmable read-only memory (EEPROM)** and are examples of solid state memories.

Uses

- Storing photos on digital cameras.
- Used as mobile phone memory cards.
- Used in **MP3** players to store music files.
- Used as a backup store in hand-held computer devices.

Advantages

- Very compact and can be easily removed and used in another device or for transferring photos directly to a computer or printer.
- Since they are solid state memories, they are very robust.

Disadvantages

- Expensive per gigabyte of memory when compared to hard drive disks.
- Have a finite life regarding the number of times they can be read from or written to.
- Have a lower storage capacity than hard disks.

4 Networks and the effects of using them

In this chapter you will learn about:

- networks
- network devices such as routers, hubs and switches
- IP and MAC addresses
- Wi-Fi and Bluetooth
- how to set up and configure a small network
- intranets and extranets
- LAN, WAN and WLAN
- network security (e.g. policing)
- accessing the internet
- authentication
- viruses
- data protection acts
- faxes and emails
- video, audio and web conferencing.

Most computer systems are now connected together in some way to form what is known as a **network**. This ranges from basic school/home networks of only a few computers (often set up to share resources such as printers or software) to large networks such as the **internet**, which effectively allows any computer connected to it to communicate with any other computer similarly connected.

This chapter considers the types of network that exist and many of the features that are available because of networking. You will learn that devices such as **hubs** and **switches** are needed to distribute data within a network; that local area networks (**LANs**) can be connected together using **bridges**; and that devices such as **modems** and **routers** are needed to connect these LANs or single computers to external networks, such as the internet.

4.1 Networks

4.1.1 Network devices

Modems

Modem means 'modulator demodulator' and is a device that converts (i.e. modulates) a computer's digital signal into an analogue signal for transmission over an existing telephone line. It also does the reverse process, in that it converts analogue signals from a telephone line into digital signals (demodulates), to enable the computer to process the data.

Modems are essentially used to allow computers to connect to networks (for example, the internet) over long distances using the existing telephone networks.

Dial-up modems operate at transmission speeds of about 60 kilobits* per second, which is extremely slow by today's standards.

*60 kilobits = 60 000 bits. 1 bit refers to a **bi**nary dig**it** and has the value 1 or 0.

Modern broadband or **ADSL (asymmetric digital subscriber line)** modems operate at up to 100 Megabits* per second (12.5 Mbytes/second) when using fibre-optic cables (although the old technology copper cables can usually only offer a maximum of 20 Mbits/second). The term 'asymmetric' actually means that the modem is faster at **downloading** data (i.e. receiving data) than it is at **uploading data** (i.e. sending data).

*1 byte = 8 bits; 100 megabits = 100 million bits.

Although ADSL modems still use the existing telephone network, unlike dial-up modems they do **not** tie up the line while accessing the internet – they can always be 'on', so internet access is available 24 hours if necessary, and the landline telephone can be used at the same time. ADSL modems can allow telephone conversations and internet traffic to occur at the same time because of the wide bandwidth signal used (different frequencies are used to transmit internet signals so they don't interfere with normal telephone traffic). Cable modems also exist, which allow cable television providers to offer internet access as well as receiving television signals.

Hubs

Hubs are hardware devices that can have a number of devices or computers connected to them. They are often used to connect together a number of devices to form a LAN – for example, a star network (see later). Its main task is to take any **data packet** (this is a group of data being transmitted) received at one of its ports and broadcast it to **every** computer in the network. This essentially means that using a hub is not a very secure or efficient method of data distribution.

Switches

Switches are similar to hubs but are much more efficient in the way that they distribute data packets. As with hubs, they connect a number of devices or computers together to form a LAN.

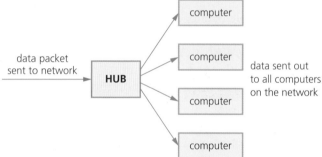

Figure 4.1 How hubs work

However, unlike a hub, the switch checks the data packet received and works out its destination address (or addresses) and sends the data to the appropriate computer(s) *only*. This makes using a switch a more secure way of distributing data.

Each device or computer on a network has a **media access control (MAC)** address that uniquely identifies it. Data packets sent to switches will have a MAC address identifying the source of the data and additional addresses identifying each device that should receive the data (see Section 4.1.2 for more on MAC addresses).

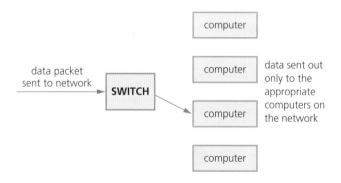

Figure 4.2 How switches work

Bridge

Bridges are devices that connect one LAN to another LAN that uses the same protocol (communication rules). They are often used to connect together different parts of a LAN so that they can function as a single LAN.

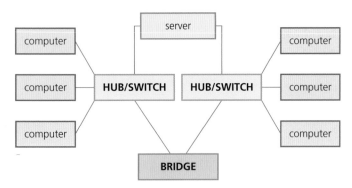

Figure 4.3 How bridges work

Bridges tend to be used to interconnected LANs (or parts of LANs) since sending out every data packet to all possible destinations would quickly flood larger networks with unnecessary traffic. For this reason a router is used to communicate with other networks, such as the internet.

Router

Routers enable data packets to be routed between the different networks, for example to join a LAN to a wide area network (**WAN**). A router would typically have an internet cable plugged into it and several cables connecting to computers and other devices on the LAN.

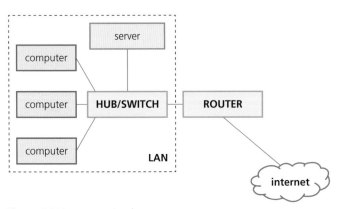

Figure 4.4 How routers work

Broadband routers sit behind a firewall. The firewall protect the computers on a network. The router's main function is to transmit internet and transmission protocols between two networks and also allow private networks to be connected together.

Routers inspect the data packets (see below) sent to it from any computer on any of the networks connected to it. Since every computer on the same network has the same part of an **internet protocol (IP)** address, the router is able to send the data packet to the appropriate switch and it will then be delivered using the MAC destination address (see Section 4.1.2). If the MAC address doesn't match any device on the network, it passes on to another switch on the same network until the appropriate device is found.

Data packets

The data is carried in the packet according to which protocol (set of rules) is used. Packets of data usually contain the following information:

- some form of header to identify the data packets
- the sender's IP address
- the receiver's IP address
- how many data packets make up the whole 'message'
- the identity number of each packet.

This information allows the router to route a packet across a network to its correct destination and allows the data packets to be reassembled in their correct order according to identity number at the receiving station.

When a router receives a packet of data, it checks the destination IP address against the stored routing table. The routing table stores the MAC address of the device, the assigned IP address and the lease time the IP address is assigned for. The bits forming the destination IP address in the data packet are used to point to the correct route. The packet is sent to a number of routers until it reaches its final destination.

Note: MAC addresses and IP addresses are discussed in more detail later.

Other hardware

Gateway

A **gateway** is a network point (or **node**) that acts as an entrance to another network. It is a key point for data on its way to or from other networks. All networks will have boundaries so that all communication within the network is conducted using devices such as switches or routers. If a network node needs to communicate outside its network, it needs to use a gateway.

Network interface card (NIC)

A **network interface card (NIC)** is needed to allow a device to connect to a network (for example, the internet). It is usually part of the device hardware and frequently contains the MAC address generated at the manufacturing stage.

Network cables

Even though many computer systems use Wi-Fi, **network cables** are still used because they have the following advantages over Wi-Fi:

- faster data transfer rates
- can be more secure than wireless networks.

The cables can be either copper or fibre optics – the latter offers higher data transfer rates and also better security (see notes on quantum cryptography).

4.1.2 Internet protocol (IP) and media access control (MAC) addresses

Each device on the internet is given a unique address known as its **internet protocol (IP) address**. This is a 32-bit number that is usually written in the form:

109.108.158.1

A home computer is given an IP address when it connects to the internet. This is assigned by the ISP and is unique for that particular internet session. The only IP addresses that remain fairly unchanged are the web servers. An IP address can be used instead of typing in the full URL; for example, http://109.108.158.1 would take you straight to the device containing web page corresponding to this address.

Differences between IP addresses and MAC addresses

As indicated in Section 4.1.1, a MAC address is a unique number that identifies a device connected to the internet. So what is the difference between an IP address and a MAC address? The IP address gives the *location* of a device on the internet, whereas the MAC address *identifies* the device connected to the internet.

You can think of the IP as the address of the house you live in (it will have some unique way of identifying it, such as a postcode or zone code). Using this example, the MAC address can be thought of as a way of uniquely identifying each person living in that house. It is possible to move house (so your IP address will change) but the same people will be living in the new house (so their MAC address will remain unchanged).

4.1.3 Wi-Fi and Bluetooth

Both Wi-Fi and Bluetooth offer wireless communication between devices. They both use radio frequencies as the carrier of data transmission.

How computers use Wi-Fi and Bluetooth to connect to networks

Wi-Fi

A wireless transmitter (WAP) receives information from a network via its connection (e.g. a broadband connection if the internet is used). This transmitter converts the received information into radio waves and then transmits them.

A device (e.g. a computer) receives the radio waves via an installed wireless adaptor which allows it to download the information from the data source. This, of course, works in reverse when the device wishes to transmit data over the network.

Wi-Fi is best suited to operating full-scale networks since it offers much faster data transfer rates, better range and better security than Bluetooth. A Wi-Fi-enabled device (such as a computer or smartphone) can access, for example, the internet wirelessly at any access point (AP) or hot spot up to 100 m away.

Bluetooth

Bluetooth sends and receives radio waves in a band of 79 different frequencies (known as channels). These are all centred on a 2.45 GHz frequency.

Devices using Bluetooth automatically detect and connect to each other, but they don't interfere with other devices since each communicating pair uses a different channel (from the 79 options).

When a device wants to communicate, it picks one of the 79 channels at random. If the channel is already being used, it randomly picks another channel. This is known as spread-spectrum frequency hopping.

To further minimise the risks of interference with other devices, the communication pairs constantly change the frequencies (channels) they are using (several times a second).

Essentially, Bluetooth is useful:

- when transferring data between two or more devices that are very close together (<30 metres distance)
- when the speed of data transmission is not critical
- for low-bandwidth applications (for example, when sending music files from a mobile phone to a headset).

Bluetooth creates a secure **wireless personal area network (WPAN)** based on key encryption.

Table 4.1 summarises some of the differences between Wi-Fi and Bluetooth.

Table 4.1 Differences between Wi-Fi and Bluetooth

Feature	Bluetooth	Wi-Fi
Transmission frequency used	2.4 GHz	2.4, 3.6, 5.0 GHz
Data transfer rate (maximum)	25 Mbits/second (~3.1 Mbytes/second)	250 Mbits/second (~31 Mbytes/second)
Maximum effective range (metres)	30 m	100 m (but can be obstructed by walls etc., reducing effective range to only a few metres)
Maximum number of devices connected	Up to 7	Depends on the router used (can be one device or many devices)
Type of data transmission security	Key matching encryption	WEP (wireless equivalent privacy) and WPA (Wi-Fi protected access) are the most common security systems

4.1.4 How to set up and configure a small network

Suppose you were asked to set up and configure a small network of 10 computers. You would need to consider the following points:

Apart from all the hardware and software, you would also have to think about doing the following:

Purchase of software and hardware →
- switches, hubs and any other devices needed to link everything together in the network
- network cables to connect devices together
- if a connection to the internet is needed, then a router is required to do this
- a firewall (either hardware or software) is needed to help protect the network against hacking
- servers to manage network security, store common software and files, and so on

- setting up an IP account if internet access is required
- setting up the system (or buying appropriate hardware correctly configured) to allow for wireless connectivity
- configuring all the hardware and software so that they work correctly together
- if internet is required, ensuring that a high-speed broadband connection exists
- putting all the common software onto a server and also making sure that a network licence has been acquired so that all network users can make use of the software
- setting up privileges so that each user can only access their own area or common shared area
- setting up a network-manager-level of privilege do that they can monitor network usage, change passwords, etc.

4.1.5 Internet, intranets and extranets

The main features of the internet, intranets and extranets, and the differences between them, are covered at length in Chapter 10. Read Chapter 10 if you wish to cover this topic in some depth before carrying on with the rest of this chapter.

4.1.6 Local area networks (LANs) and wide area networks (WANs)

Local area networks (LANs)

These systems are usually within one building, or certainly not very far away from each other geographically. A typical LAN will consist of a number of computers and devices (for example, printers) that are connected to **hubs** or **switches**. One of the hubs or switches will usually be connected to a **router** and a **modem**

> **Exercise 4a**
>
> Find out any other hardware or tasks that need to be carried out when setting up a small network. Ask questions such as 'would Wi-Fi or Bluetooth be the best type of connectivity?', 'Should PCs or laptops be used?', and so on.

(usually **broadband**) to allow the LAN to connect to the internet; in doing so it then becomes part of a **WAN**.

Advantages

- The sharing of resources (such as expensive peripherals and applications software).
- Ease of communication between users.
- A network administrator to control and monitor all aspects of the network (for example, changing passwords, monitoring internet use and so on).

Disadvantages

- Easier spread of viruses throughout the whole network.
- Printer queues developing, which can be frustrating.
- Slower access to external networks, such as the internet.
- Increased security risk when compared to stand-alone computers.
- If the main server breaks down, in most cases the network will no longer function.

Wide area networks (WANs)

Wide area networks (WANs) are used where computers or networks are situated a long distance from each other geographically (e.g. in a different city or country). As mentioned earlier, if a number of LANs are joined together using a router or modem, then they can form a WAN. The most common examples of WAN include the internet and the network of ATMs (automated teller machines) used by banks.

Because of the long distances between devices, WANs usually make use of some public communications network (such as telephone lines or satellites) but they can use dedicated or leased communication lines which can be less expensive and also more secure (less risk of hacking).

A typical WAN will consist of end systems and intermediate systems (see diagram).

1, 3, 7 and 10 are known as end systems and the remainder are known as intermediate systems. The distance between each system can be considerable, especially if the WAN is run by a multinational company.

Wireless LANs (WLANs)

Wireless LANs (WLANs) are similar to LANs but there are no wires or cables. In other words, they provide wireless network communications over fairly short distances (a few metres) using radio or infrared signals instead of cables.

Devices, known as **access points (APs)** or wireless nodes, are connected into the wired network at fixed locations. Because of the limited range, most commercial LANs (for example, at a college campus or at an airport) need several APs to permit uninterrupted

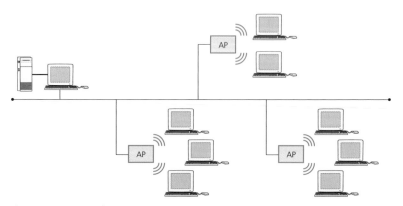

Figure 4.5 A network connecting WLANs

wireless communications. The APs use either **spread spectrum technology** (which is a wideband radio frequency with a range of about 30–50 m) or **infrared** (which has a very short range, about 1–2 m, and is easily blocked; it therefore has a limited use).

The AP receives and transmits data between the WLAN and the wired network structure. End-users access the WLAN through wireless LAN adapters that are built into the devices or are a plug-in module.

Advantages

- All computers can access the same services and resources (such as printers, scanners, internet access) from anywhere within range of the APs.
- As there is no cabling there is a safety improvement and increased flexibility (since the user no longer has to remain at their desk).
- Adding new computers and devices is very easy (all that is required is a WLAN adapter) and the costs are reduced since extra cabling isn't needed.

Disadvantages

- Security can be a big issue since anyone with a WLAN-enabled laptop can access a network if it can pick up a signal; it is therefore necessary to adopt complex data encryption techniques.
- There may be problems of interference, which can affect the signal.
- The data transfer rate is slower than in a wired LAN.

4.1.7 Accessing the internet

The relative advantages and disadvantages of using mobile phones, tablets, laptops and desktop computers were discussed in Chapter 1. Some of the advantages and disadvantages of using these devices to access the internet are summarised below.

Mobile phones and tablets

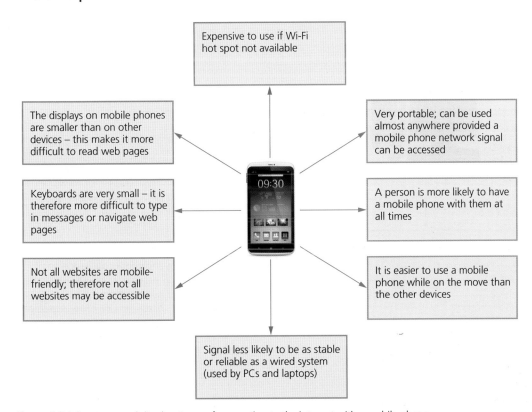

Figure 4.6 Advantages and disadvantages of connecting to the internet with a mobile phone

The same comments also refer to tablets (and phablets) but, as they usually have bigger screens and keyboards, they have an advantage in that respect when compared to mobile phones. The other advantages and disadvantages are similar to mobile phones – it all depends on the screen size of the tablet being used.

Laptops

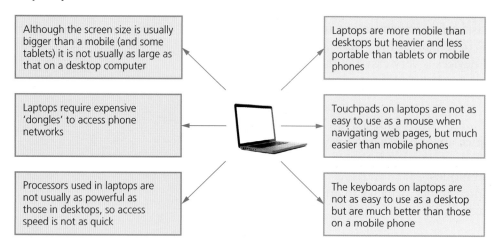

Although the screen size is usually bigger than a mobile (and some tablets) it is not usually as large as that on a desktop computer

Laptops are more mobile than desktops but heavier and less portable than tablets or mobile phones

Laptops require expensive 'dongles' to access phone networks

Touchpads on laptops are not as easy to use as a mouse when navigating web pages, but much easier than mobile phones

Processors used in laptops are not usually as powerful as those in desktops, so access speed is not as quick

The keyboards on laptops are not as easy to use as a desktop but are much better than those on a mobile phone

Figure 4.7 Advantages and disadvantages of connecting to the internet with a laptop

Desktop computers

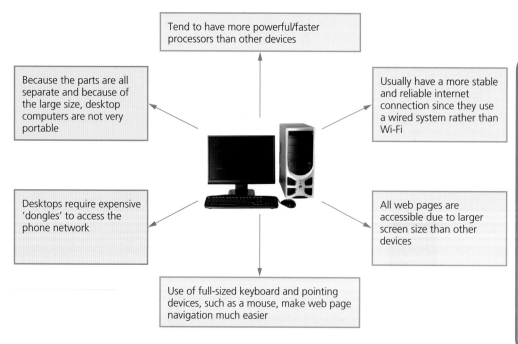

Tend to have more powerful/faster processors than other devices

Because the parts are all separate and because of the large size, desktop computers are not very portable

Usually have a more stable and reliable internet connection since they use a wired system rather than Wi-Fi

Desktops require expensive 'dongles' to access the phone network

All web pages are accessible due to larger screen size than other devices

Use of full-sized keyboard and pointing devices, such as a mouse, make web page navigation much easier

Figure 4.8 Advantages and disadvantages of connecting to the internet with a desktop computer

Exercise 4b

Refer to the notes in Chapter 1 and write an article on the relative advantages and disadvantages of using various devices:

● to access the internet
● to download information from the internet, using these various devices, to allow you to produce a presentation on a topic of your own choice.

Include a conclusion to indicate which device(s) you would choose.

4.2 Network issues and communication

4.2.1 Network security

Many aspects of security (such as hacking, phishing, pharming and viruses) are covered in depth in Chapter 8. This section covers some of the more general aspects of internet security.

When accessing the internet, users have to be very careful of many issues – not all of them obvious. Let us first consider the material found on the internet.

Should the internet be policed?

This question has raged for many years. The internet doesn't presently have any controlling body that ensures that it conforms to certain standards. There are many arguments in favour of having control, and as many arguments against it.

Arguments in favour of some form of control:

- it would help to prevent illegal material being posted on websites (for example, racist/prejudiced and pornographic material, terrorist activities, and so on)
- people find it much easier to discover information that can have serious consequences (for example, how to be a hacker, how to make bombs, and so on); although most of this information can be found in books, it is much easier to find it using a search engine
- it would help to prevent children and other vulnerable groups from being subjected to undesirable websites
- it would help to stop incorrect information being published on websites.

Arguments against some form of control:

- material published on websites is already available from other sources
- it would be very expensive to 'police' all websites and users would have to pick up the bill
- it would be difficult to enforce rules and regulations on a global scale
- it can be argued that policing would go against freedom of information
- laws already exist to deal with those who post illegal material/comments on websites.

One moral issue is the social divide created by computer technology and ICT. This is often referred to as the digital divide: those people who have the necessary IT skills and/or money to purchase and use computer equipment will benefit from the new technology; those who are not able to access this new technology, either through lack of money, skills or simply because they don't live in a country with the necessary infrastructure, are left even further behind, leading to this digital divide.

Inappropriate sites and the accuracy of information

The social and general impacts of using the internet or devices that rely on microprocessors have been discussed in earlier sections. It is now worth spending some time looking at the *quality* of information found on the internet when using a search engine. There are three main aspects to consider:

- reliability of information
- undesirability of certain websites
- security issues.

Reliability of information

- Information on the internet is more likely to be up to date than in books (websites can be updated very quickly).
- It is much easier to get information from websites (search engines quickly link key words together and find information that matches the criteria).
- There is a vast amount of information on the internet that is easier to locate than using the indices in several books.
- Information could also be incorrect, inaccurate or even biased, since it doesn't go through any checking process.
- There is a real risk of information overload, even if the search engines are used properly; it is possible to get millions of **hits**, which may make it difficult to find the relevant information.

Undesirability of certain websites

- There is always a risk of finding undesirable websites.
- There is also a risk of connecting to websites that are not genuine, which could lead to a number of problems (such as undesirable web links, security risks, and so on).
- Security risks (these are a real problem – this topic is covered in Chapter 10 and elsewhere throughout the book).

Security issues

Passwords are used in many instances when accessing the internet, for example when:

- accessing your email account
- carrying out online banking
- accessing social networking sites.

There are many more instances when you might need to type in a password and, in many cases, a user ID. It is important that passwords are protected; some ways of doing this are described below:

- run anti-spyware software to make sure that your passwords aren't being relayed back to whoever put the spyware on your computer
- change passwords on a regular basis in case they have come into the possession of another user illegally or accidentally
- passwords should not be easy to guess or break (for example, don't use your favourite colour, name of a pet or favourite rock group); passwords are defined as either 'strong' (hard to break or guess) or 'weak' (relatively easy to break or guess). Strong passwords should contain:
  - at least one capital letter
  - at least one numerical value
  - at least one other keyboard character (such as @, *, &).

  An example of a strong password would be: Sy12@#TT90kj=0.
  An example of a weak password would be: GREEN.

4.2.2 Authentication

Authentication is used to verify that data comes from a secure and trusted source. It works with encryption to strengthen internet security, for example.

Exercise 4c

Using the information above and information from Chapter 10 (and elsewhere within this book), write an article on the pros and cons of using the internet (rather than other methods, such as consulting books) to search for information when doing some research for a science or geography project.

Remember to draw a conclusion when you have finished giving your advantages and disadvantages.

Exercise 4d

Which of the following are weak passwords and which are strong passwords? Explain your decision in each case.

1 25-May-2000
2 Pas5word
3 ChapTer@15
4 AbC*N55!
5 12345X

User IDs and passwords are authentication techniques. Some forms of authentication include:

- digital certificates (see Section 8.4.4 for more details)
- biometrics (see Section 8.4.4 for more details)
- magnetic stripe cards/id cards/passports.

Magnetic stripe cards were covered in Chapter 2. These cards have a magnetic stripe on one side (made up of tiny magnetic particles on a plastic film). Each particle can act as a north-pole or a south-pole (which corresponds to the two binary values of 0 and 1).

The stripe is read by swiping it through a card reader (see Chapter 2). Data such as name, ID number, sex and date of birth may be contained on a magnetic stripe when used as a security device to allow entry to a building, for example.

Contactless cards can be read from a distance and don't have to be swiped through a card reader. This technology was discussed in Chapter 2. Contactless technology can be used in credit/debit cards, for example, to speed up payments in a shop, but they can also be used as a security device. If the card is in a wallet or a pocket, as the owner of the card walks through a security gate, readers either side of the gate quickly scan the security data stored on the tag/chip embedded in the card. Access will only be allowed if the scanned data matches data in a database.

Some ID cards also use a holographic image (hologram). These are designed to make forgery of the card more difficult. Holographic images change colour or appear to have a moving object when the image is viewed from different angles. As these are difficult to make it stops somebody, for example, simply photocopying a card and using it illegally. The theory behind holograms was discussed in Section 1.5.6.

Another form of security is to have a photographic image of the card user printed on the card surface.

Passports make use of some of the technology described above. Many passports contain an RFID tag/chip, a photograph and a holographic image.

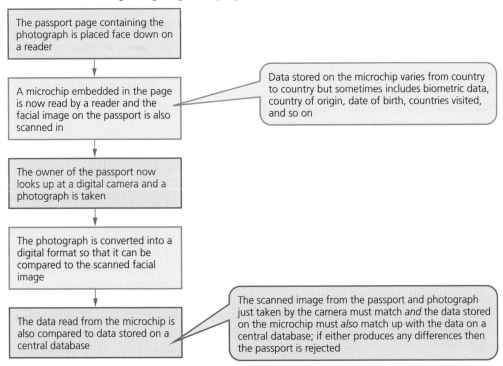

Figure 4.9 What happens when somebody approaches passport control at an airport?

4.2.3 Viruses

The risks of a computer being infected by a virus are discussed in detail in Chapter 8. This section considers how the risk of viruses can be minimised when using the internet or any situation where data is transferred from computer to computer or other electronic devices – it is important to point out that tablets and mobile phones can also be infected by viruses. Any electronic device with a storage capability can be affected by virus attacks.

Ways of preventing or minimising the risk of viruses are outlined below.

Antivirus software

Running antivirus software in the background on a computer will constantly check for virus attacks. Although various types of antivirus software work in different ways, they all have the following common features:

- they check software or files before they are run or loaded on a computer
- antivirus software compares a possible virus against a database of known viruses
- they carry out heuristic checking – this is the checking of software for types of behaviour that could indicate a possible virus; this is useful if software is infected by a virus not yet on the database
- any possible files or programs that are infected are put into quarantine that:
  - allows the virus to be automatically deleted, or
  - allows the user to make the decision about deletion (it is possible that the user knows that the file or program is not infected by a virus – this is known as a false positive and is one of the disadvantages of antivirus software)
- antivirus software needs to be kept up to date since new viruses are constantly being discovered
- full system checks need to be carried out once a week, for example, since some viruses lie dormant and would only be picked up by this full system scan.

Avoiding viruses when accessing the internet

One way to help prevent virus attacks when accessing websites on the internet is to avoid unknown or suspicious-looking websites. If in doubt, don't access the website – look for security indicators such as https or the padlock symbol 🔒.

Also look out for odd behaviour in the URL. When accessing a new website, for example from an advert in an email, copy and paste the URL into the address bar at the top of the page rather than just clicking on the link in the email. This can help to avoid links to bogus/fake websites.

It is also not advisable to open emails (or any attachments) from unknown sources. Essentially, the best form of defence against malicious behaviour when making use of the internet is to apply common sense. Many of these issues will be discussed in more depth in Chapter 8.

Viruses from hardware devices

It is possible to pick up viruses from any device plugged into your computer. Apart from the obvious precaution of scanning the device for viruses, it is still unsafe to plug in a device from an unknown source. Even memory sticks or DVDs from friends or from school could still be infected unless they have also carried out all the necessary precautions.

4.2.4 Data protection acts

Most countries have some form of **data protection act (DPA)**. These are designed to protect individuals and to prevent incorrect or inaccurate data being stored.

Essentially DPAs are set up to protect the rights of the individual about whom data is obtained, stored and processed (i.e., collection, use, disclosure, destruction and holding of data). Any such act applies to both computerised and paper records.

Many data protection acts are based on eight principles, as outlined in Figure 4.10.

In many countries, failure to abide by these simple rules can lead to a heavy fine or even imprisonment to anyone who holds data about individuals.

There are general guidelines about how to stop data being obtained unlawfully:

- don't leave personal information lying around on a desk when not attended
- lock filing cabinets at the end of the day or when the room is unoccupied
- do not leave data on a computer monitor if it is unattended; log off from the computer if away from your desk for any length of time
- use passwords and user ids, which should be kept secure; passwords should be difficult to guess/break and should be changed frequently (see earlier notes on passwords)
- make sure that anything sent in an email or fax (including attachments) is not of a sensitive nature.

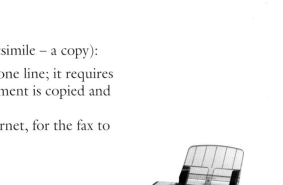

1   Data must be fairly and lawfully processed.

2   Data can only be processed for the stated purpose.

3   Data must be adequate, relevant and not excessive.

4   Data must be accurate.

5   Data must not be kept longer than necessary.

6   Data must be processed in accordance with the data subject's rights.

7   Data must be kept secure.

8   Data must not be transferred to another country unless they also have adequate protection.

Figure 4.10 Main principles of data protection acts

All of the above are in addition to other security safeguards discussed elsewhere in this book.

4.2.5 Network communication

Faxes and emails

There are two basic ways of sending a fax (abbreviation for facsimile – a copy):

- a physical fax (a dedicated machine connected to a telephone line; it requires the number of the recipient to be dialled before the document is copied and then sent electronically)
- electronic faxing (this requires a network, such as the internet, for the fax to be sent).

Physical fax machines

Fax machines have been used for many years to send and receive paper documents.

A standard fax machine allows documents to be sent to another fax machine using a normal telephone line. The user places the document in the fax machine tray, lifts the receiver and dials the fax number of the recipient and then presses <send>. At the receiving end, the document is printed on another fax machine. It can be quite a slow way to send a document if the fax line is busy or if there are several pages to send.

However, a more modern way is **electronic faxing** (or online faxing) which makes use of computer technology and the internet. Electronic faxing has the following advantages over the more traditional method described above:

- costs are reduced as there is no need to buy a fax machine, ink/toner or paper
- transfers using electronic methods are encrypted, improving security
- transmissions are sent to an email account, which is password protected
- there is no issue of a 'busy signal' preventing the fax being sent.

At this point you may be wondering what is the difference between an electronic fax and an email? The simple answer is not a lot. The only real difference is that online faxing is always associated with an email address *and* a fax number. The fax number is similar to the traditional fax number and needs to be known by the sender. Having this number allows a user to send fax messages to the recipient. Once a fax is received, the online fax service provider sends an email with the fax message attached in a tiff or pdf format. The sender of the fax can either use an email account or log into any online account to send the fax.

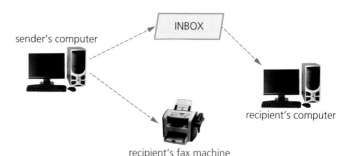

Figure 4.11 Sending an electronic fax

It is important to realise that it is possible to send a fax from your computer to another device connected to the internet *or* to a traditional fax machine, where the document will be printed out in the normal way.

Emails

Electronic mail (email) is discussed in many parts of this book. Emails are particularly useful when sending attachments (for example, documents, videos, music, and so on). Emails can be sent to, or sent from, any device connected to the internet. When sending attachments it is usually important to have a good, stable internet connection – particularly when sending or receiving large files. The basic difference between emails and electronic faxes was described above; all the advantages and disadvantages of emails apply to electronic faxing when it is sent from computer to computer.

Emails require an account with an ISP. When sending an email, it is necessary to include the email address (which **must** be exact), a subject line and any attachments if required.

The recipient simply has to log on to their account and read the emails in their inbox.

It is now worth comparing emails with traditional, physical faxes (as indicated above, there are few differences between electronic faxes and emails so they won't be part of this comparison).

Table 4.2 Comparison of traditional faxes and emails

Traditional faxes	Emails
• They are more likely to be intercepted since the document needs to be printed out and the fax machine is potentially accessible to many people in the office • Signatures on faxes are accepted legally • The quality of the documents printed out can be quite poor at times • If the telephone line is busy (or shared), there can be a considerable delay in sending the fax • It can be a slow process if several documents are to be sent, since each document needs to be scanned before it is transmitted	• More secure than faxes (password protected and usually sent to an individual's computer) • No need to print the document (cost saving and more environmentally friendly) • The document is usually of a much better quality • Unlike paper-based faxes, documents received in emails can be modified or easily copied and pasted into other documents • Documents and files can be sent and received from any device that has internet connectivity • It is much easier to send to multiple recipients at the same time – with a fax you have to dial up the fax number of each recipient before sending • People are more likely to have access to email accounts than a fax machine

Exercise 4e

Carry out an assignment to compare emails, faxes and traditional post as a way to send documents and items to people.

Video conferencing

Video conferencing is a communication method that uses both video and sound. It is a substitute for face-to-face conferences between a number of people, who may be in a different part of the country or live overseas. It is carried out in **real time** and makes use of some form of network. The basic hardware includes:

- webcams
- large monitors/television screens
- microphones
- speakers.

There are a few items to consider when a conference is about to begin:

- it is essential to agree a time and date for the conference to take place
- the delegates in each conference room must log in to the video conference system
- the video conference set-up needs to be checked before the meeting goes live
- webcams need to be placed in the correct position so that all the delegates in the room are within visual contact (the webcams will capture the images and then transmit them to the other delegates – they will see the images on their own large screens)
- microphones need to be placed centrally so that all of the delegates can speak – the sound is picked up by the microphones and transmitted to the other delegates (they hear the voices through speakers in their own conference room)
- it is important for one person to be the main contact in each conference room to make sure that each delegate is able to be heard; this is particularly important if more than two video conference rooms are linked up at the same time.

In addition to the hardware items described above, it is important to realise that software plays an important role in a successful video conference.

Table 4.3 Software used in video conferencing

Software	Description
Webcam and microphone software drivers	It is vital that the correct software is used to ensure that the webcam and microphone transmit their images and sound to the other delegates (these are sometimes referred to as **hardware drivers**)
CODEC	CODEC can stand for **co**der–**dec**oder or **co**mpression–**dec**ompression. The first is used to encode or decode the digital data stream to allow data to be transmitted (encoded) and played back (decoded). The second is used to compress the data before it is transmitted and then decompress it again at the receiving conference room
Echo cancellation software	**Echo cancellation software** allows talking to take place in real time and permits the synchronisation of communication. Microphones can pick up sound from the speakers (i.e. creating an echo); this software copies received signals and checks for parts of the signal that reappear but are delayed slightly. The reappearing parts are removed from the signal (i.e. the echo is removed)

Potential issues with video conferencing

- Potential time lag in responses/delays when talking.
- Jerking images – usually due to poor internet/network performance or a poor bandwidth.
- Can be very expensive to set up in the first place (both the hardware and the software are expensive to purchase and set up correctly).
- There can be problems if the delegates live in different countries where the time zone differences are large.
- Training people to use the system correctly can be both costly and time consuming.
- It can be demotivating for staff if they believe that one of the 'perks' of their job is international travel.
- The whole system relies on a good network connection – if it breaks down or the signal strength is diminished in any way, then the video conference can be almost unusable.

Advantages

- As people are in their own building, it is much easier to access important documents or bring in 'experts' at key parts of the conference – this would be difficult if they were a long way away from their office.
- It is possible to hold conferences at short notice (a conference date can be set up within a few hours as no person needs to travel far).
- Not travelling physically to meetings reduces costs:
  - reduced travelling costs
  - no need to pay for hotel accommodation or venue hire
  - it also reduces the cost of taking people away from their work for two or three days to travel – people are still paid their wage even though they are not in the office, so this is a large 'hidden' cost.
- It may be better to use video conferencing than have delegates travel to potentially unsafe places around the world.

Audio conferencing

Audio conferencing refers to meetings held between people using audio (sound) equipment. The equipment used can be the telephone, a computer (with built-in microphones and speakers) or an internet phone.

Audio conferencing can be done over the telephone network (often referred to as a **phone conference**). The procedure to be carried out when doing a phone conference is detailed below.

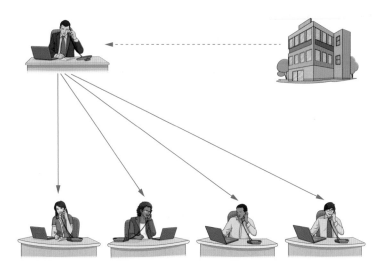

1 The organiser of the phone conference is given two PINs by the phone company. One PIN is the personal PIN (e.g. 2151) given to the organiser and the second PIN is the participants' PIN (e.g. 8422).

2 The organiser contacts all of the participants and informs them of their PIN and the data and time of the phone conference.

3 When the phone conference is about to start, the organiser dials the conference phone number and, once he/she is connected, keys in his/her personal PIN (2151 in this case).

4 The participants then call the same conference number to join in – once they get through they each input the PIN given to them by the organiser (8422 in this case). Without this PIN, it will be impossible to join the phone conference.

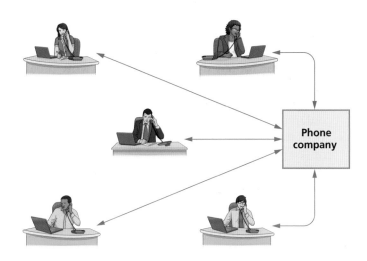

It is possible to hold an audio conference using a computer provided a microphone and speakers are connected. This makes use of **Voice over Internet Protocol (VoIP)**. It is also possible to hook up an internet telephone, which usually plugs into the router or other internet device.

Using VoIP allows an organiser to create a group of people to take part in the conference call. The group is created by dragging and dropping user names and telephone numbers into the group. When the conference is to take place, the organiser clicks on the required group and the conference is initiated. Using VoIP allows communication using voice, instant messaging and video (by using an attached webcam). If some of the users don't have an internet connection or don't have access to a computer, it is possible to add actual telephone numbers (landline or mobile) to the group. The only real drawback is the quality of the sound when using this technique since it is totally reliant on a fast, stable broadband connection – otherwise 'drop out' (loss of voice on occasions), echoing (when the user can hear their own voice being echoed back as they speak) or a very noisy line making it difficult to understand.

Web conferencing

Web conferencing (often referred to as a **webinar**) uses the internet to permit conferencing to take place. Multiple computers are used with this system, all connected over the internet. As with video conferencing, it is carried out in real time and allows the following types of meeting to take place:

- business meetings to discuss new ideas
- presentations
- online education or training.

The only requirement is a computer and a high-speed, stable internet connection. To carry out web conferencing, each user either downloads an application or logs on to a website from a link supplied in an email from the conference organiser.

Delegates can leave or join the conference as they wish. The organiser can decide on who can speak at any time using the control panel on their computer. If a delegate wishes to speak, they raise a flag next to their name. Delegates can post comments using instant messaging for all delegates to see at any time.

Some of the main features include:

- slide presentations using presentation software that can be posted on the conference website in advance of the meeting
- it is possible for any delegate to draw or write on a 'whiteboard' using their own keyboard or mouse
- it is possible to transmit images or videos using the webcam throughout the conference
- documents can be shared by uploading them to the website before the conference begins
- as described earlier, it is possible to chat verbally or by using instant messaging throughout the conference.

As indicated earlier, web conferencing clearly links into video conferencing and audio conferencing through the use of webcams and built-in microphone and speakers. Essentially it is possible to have a conference using any device that allows these functions (for example, tablets and smartphones would both permit this type of group communication).

5 The effects of using ICT

In this chapter you will learn about:

- the effects of ICT on employment
- the effects of ICT on working patterns
- microprocessor-controlled devices in the home.

This chapter considers the effects of ICT on employment as well as our everyday life in the home. The four main areas where ICT has had an effect on employment include:

- **Manufacturing** – robots have replaced human workers in many areas of manufacturing, for example welding car bodies, spraying metal items with paint, assembling items and manufacturing circuit boards.
- **Shop work** – online shopping has reduced the need for high-street shops, leading to a loss of staff.
- **Banking** – the introduction of ATMs and online banking has led to the closure of many high-street branches.
- **Office work** – spreadsheets, word processors and databases have taken over many of the tasks carried out by office staff.

5.1 The effects of ICT on employment

The use of computers and microprocessors has revolutionised many aspects of how we work. From the offices to manufacturing, every task humans do has been affected in some way by electronic devices and their associated software. This has had both positive and negative effects on employment.

5.1.1 Negative effects – job losses

The introduction of ICT systems – whether to improve efficiency, reduce costs or improve safety – has led to redundancies in many areas of industry and commerce. The following sections consider the impact that ICT has had on office work and manufacturing.

Office work

Let us consider a company where the day-to-day tasks are all presently carried out manually by people in the following departments:

- administration
- human resources
- payroll.

By introducing computer systems and new software, the work could be done by fewer staff and in a much shorter time scale. This could lead to many redundancies and the need for the remaining staff to retrain, as they have to learn how to use the new technologies. Skills such as filing and carrying out numerical analysis manually have effectively been replaced by sophisticated software.

Three types of software have had the most impact in offices: word processors, spreadsheets and databases.

Word processors

Word processors make it much easier to modify and update documents. There is no longer a need to file documents in large filing cabinets since all the documents can be stored on hard disks or on solid state storage devices in electronic formats. Documents only need to be printed out when required, which also saves considerable amounts of money and the need for large office space. This clearly leads to huge increases in efficiency and the need for fewer staff to carry out these administrative tasks. It also means that work can be outsourced to countries where the labour costs are lower. This is possible since the documents are stored electronically and can easily be transferred anywhere in the world by email or by newer technologies such as 'cloud storage'.

Spreadsheets

Spreadsheets have revolutionised the way that payroll clerks calculate monthly salaries or wages. There is no longer any need to do the calculations manually or to type out the salary/wage slips. Spreadsheets automatically calculate salary/wages based on hourly rates and the number of hours worked. By linking into databases, it is also possible to carry out all of the deductions, such as tax, insurance and so on. This can be done by using embedded formulas known as macros. This has led to a reduction in staff since a spreadsheet reduces the time taken to calculate salaries/wages – the software effectively replaces several clerks. The software can be set up to do the calculations on a particular day automatically and then print out the salary/wage slips without any manual intervention.

Spreadsheets can be used in many areas where calculations or graphs or charts need to be produced. One good example is a teacher in a college monitoring the progress of their students by entering their marks into a spreadsheet for a number of subjects (see the example spreadsheet above). This type of software has the following advantages in this application:

- graphs and charts can be produced to show how the students compare to each other
- graphs and charts can also be used to show student progress over a given time period; use of 'rolling averages' or trend lines can be used to monitor changes in performance
- it is also possible to use 'conditional formatting' to show which students are performing badly (for example, by highlighting results in red) or well (for example, by highlighting results in green)
- using functions, such as sorting or averages, allows the teacher to quickly see which students are doing particularly well and how they compare against the class average.

These features leave teachers more time to spend on lesson preparations and can be linked into word processors to produce annual student reports to send out to parents. How has the introduction of spreadsheets affected staff at the college? Essentially, the number of administrative staff (who work with the teachers to produce reports, graphs and results sheets) can be reduced, but the teachers need to be fully trained in the use of spreadsheets.

Databases

Other office work, such as human resources, has also been changed by the introduction of computers and software. Tasks such as updating personnel data (e.g. salary, address, phone number, department, etc.) on a regular basis can now be done more effectively using database software. It is possible to cross-check many factors regarding staff working in a company using sophisticated database structures. For example, if new job opportunities were created in a company, the system could automatically cross-check several key factors for its existing staff (such as experience, qualifications, personal qualities and IT skills). A shortlist of potential candidates could then be produced. This would have taken several staff many days if they had to cross-check paper files – the use of databases means the task can be done in minutes. This task would have been further complicated if the company had several sites in different parts of the country. Staff records can now easily be centralised and data can be transferred between sites electronically. This makes it a very quick and easy task to produce a staff shortlist. Obviously, this again has led to a reduction in human resources staff, and the need for intensive training in the use and setting up of effective database structures.

Whilst the use of the above software packages has clearly entailed reducing staff numbers, on the plus side, there has been a huge increase in the need for better trained people, (and good trainers to train them) as well as the creation of new jobs which are IT-related, such as a network manager or IT technicians. The office has also become a more pleasant and safer place to work (no noisy typewriters or the dangers of heavy overfilled filing cabinets).

Manufacturing

Job losses due to ICT have affected industry even more than in the office environment. The introduction of robots, for example, has revolutionised how items such as cars are produced. Car manufacturing makes considerable use of robotics. One robot is capable of doing the same tasks as a number of workers, greatly reducing the need for manual labourers.

Robots are capable of carrying out the following tasks:

- spraying the bodies with paint
- assembling all the body parts
- assembly of the engine and transmission
- fitting the windscreens.

Robots are fitted with different devices, known as end effectors, to allow various tasks to be completed, for example a spray gun (to paint the car body), welding gun (to allow the body parts to be assembled) or vacuum/suction cups (to gently pick up windscreens and attach them to the car). All of these tasks are carried out quickly and accurately, time after time, replacing the need for human labour.

Only the more intricate tasks, such as fitting seats, dashboards and interior trim, are usually carried out by a skilled human workforce.

Factory workers have had to retrain to gain the following new skills:

- maintenance of the robots
- quality control
- design and development
- marketing
- training other workers.

Advantages of robots over humans

- Higher productivity (this can be considerable in mass production factories).
- More consistent results (robots are not necessarily more accurate, but every car is identical, which means a big increase in reliability and easier maintenance for customers).
- They work non-stop without breaks, holidays or time for shift handovers.
- They don't get bored by repetitive tasks.
- They don't go on strike.

Even taking into account expensive maintenance costs, robots still work out cheaper in the long term than paying humans wages.

Disadvantages of robots over humans

- Robots are expensive to purchase and set up in the first place.
- They often need to be reprogrammed for every new task they have to carry out, which can be expensive and time-consuming.
- If an error occurs in the robot's programming, or if it develops a mechanical problem, a number of production errors will occur until the fault has been identified (however, this is becoming less of a problem as self-diagnostics become increasingly sophisticated: robots can detect errors in their own operation and halt production until the fault is rectified).

5.1.2 Positive effects

While the introduction of new software packages and robots has clearly resulted in staff reductions, the positive side is the need for better-trained people, the need for trainers, and the creation of new ICT-related work.

Offices have become more pleasant and safer places to work (no noisy typewriters or the dangers of heavy, overfilled filing cabinets), while the introduction of robots in manufacturing has led to a cleaner, safer, quieter and altogether more pleasant working environment.

There has also been a large increase in job opportunities in some areas, for example:

- network managers and computer technicians
- website designers
- systems analysts
- programmers to write operating systems, applications software (such as spreadsheets and word processors) and computer games
- computer engineers (who build and maintain computer systems)
- computer programmers
- delivery drivers to deliver goods to customers.

5.2 The effects of ICT on working patterns

The introduction of ICT into the workplace has led to a number of changes in working patterns for staff. Essentially, the old concept of the '9 to 5' working day (the normal full-time work pattern) has given way to much more flexible working patterns. The four main additional types of work pattern are shown below.

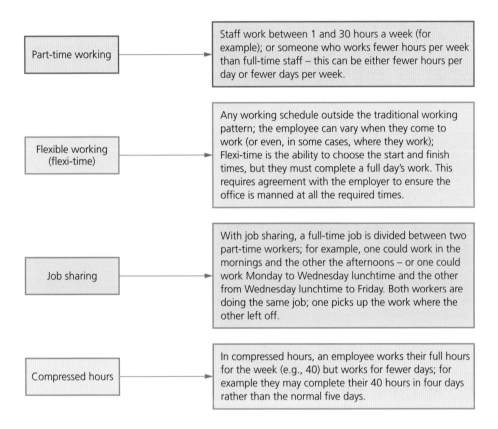

What are the main reasons for having these different work patterns? Essentially this leads to more contented staff, since they can work hours that suit their lifestyle or home circumstances. It can allow them to avoid rush-hour commuting in the morning and evening, and often leads to more highly motivated staff, which is good for staff and company alike.

Obviously employers see advantages in these work patterns as well:

- a contented workforce is more likely to stay in the job, thus reducing the company's recruitment and training costs for new staff
- flexi-time allows them to remain open for longer hours
- job sharing ensures the company has more than one person with a particular skill set
- compressed hours often lead staff to be more focused on their work
- varied work patterns give more flexibility during busy times and during staff sickness.

Table 5.1 summarises the five types of working patterns.

Table 5.1 Different working patterns

Working pattern	Example
Full time	Five days a week, eight hours a day from 9a.m. to 5p.m.
Part time	Five days a week, four hours a day from 10a.m. to 2p.m.
Flexi-time	Five days a week, eight hours a day from 11a.m. to 7p.m.
Job sharing	Five days a week, 20 hours each worker: • Worker 1: 9a.m. to 5p.m. Monday to Tuesday, 9a.m. to 1p.m. Wednesday • Worker 2: 1p.m. to 5p.m. Wednesday, 9a.m. to 5p.m. Thursday to Friday
Compressed hours	Four days a week, ten hours a day from 8a.m. to 6p.m.

The work patterns are illustrated in the following work schedule:

	08:00	09:00	10:00	11:00	12:00	13:00	14:00	15:00	16:00	17:00	18:00	19:00
Mon												
Tue												
Wed						Full	time					
Thu												
Fri												
Mon												
Tue												
Wed					Part	time						
Thu												
Fri												
Mon												
Tue												
Wed								Flexi	time			
Thu												
Fri												
Mon												
Tue				Job	share							
Wed												
Thu								Job	share			
Fri												
Mon												
Tue												
Wed				Compressed		hours						
Thu												
Fri												

5.3 Microprocessor-controlled devices in the home

Many common household devices are now fitted with microprocessors to control a large number of their functions. The devices fall into two main categories:

- labour-saving devices
  - automatic washing machines
  - microwave ovens
  - cookers
  - automatic dishwashers
  - robotic vacuum cleaners

- bread-making machines
- smart fridges and freezers
- other types of device
  - alarm clocks
  - television sets
  - central heating and air conditioning systems
  - home entertainment systems.

Essentially, a microprocessor-controlled labour-saving device allows people to get on with other things while the device carries out their tasks. Microprocessors within the second type of device make them easier to use and give them additional features, such as 'intelligent tuning' in television sets.

Table 5.2 summarises what effects on a person's lifestyle the introduction of microprocessor-controlled devices might have.

Table 5.2 Advantages and disadvantages of microprocessor-controlled labour-saving devices

Advantages	Disadvantages
• People no longer have to do manual tasks at home • There is no longer a need to stay home while food is cooking or clothes are being washed • They give people more time for leisure activities, hobbies, shopping and socialising • It is possible to control ovens and central heating systems, for example, using smartphones – a web-enabled phone allows devices to be switched on or off while the owner is out • Automated burglar alarms give people a sense of security and well-being as they give a very sophisticated level of intruder warning at all times • Smart fridges and freezers can lead to more healthy lifestyles (they can automatically order fresh food from supermarkets using their internet connection) as well as prevent food waste	• Labour-saving devices can lead to unhealthy lifestyles (because of the reliance on ready-made meals) • They tend to make people rather lazy since there is a dependence on the devices • People can become less fit if they just lie around at home while the devices carry out many of the previous manual tasks • Tasks carried out by people in the past are now done by microprocessor-controlled devices, which means there is a potential to lose these household skills

Table 5.3 gives more general advantages and disadvantages of the technology which are not necessarily related to lifestyle changes.

Table 5.3 Advantages and disadvantages of other microprocessor-controlled devices

Advantages	Disadvantages
• Microprocessor-controlled devices save energy since they are far more efficient and can, for example, switch themselves off after inactivity for a certain time period • It is easy to 'program' these devices to do tasks (for example, QR codes on food packaging can simply be scanned and the oven automatically selects the cooking programme, rather than having to turn knobs and press buttons manually)	• The devices lead to a more wasteful society – as it is usually not cost effective to repair circuit boards once they fail, the device is just thrown away • People who are not very confident around electronic devices (technophobes) can find them complex to operate • Leaving devices on stand-by (for example televisions or satellite receivers) is very wasteful of electricity

5.4 Potential health problems related to the prolonged use of ICT equipment

Since health and safety aspects are generally considered together, the potential health issues are covered in considerable depth in Chapter 8, together with ways to minimise or even remove the risks entirely.

6 ICT applications

In this chapter you will learn about:

- communication applications
- data handling applications
- measurement applications
- microprocessors in control applications
- modelling applications
- manufacturing applications
- school management systems
- booking systems
- banking applications
- expert systems
- computers in medicine
- computers in libraries
- computers in the retail industry
- recognition systems
- monitoring and tracking systems
- satellite systems.

This chapter covers a number of applications connected with ICT. Many of the applications bring together notes from earlier and later chapters in the book. Exercises are given at the end of the various sections to help the student develop a better understanding of how these applications make use of various ICT technologies.

6.1 Communication applications

There are several communications systems that make use of ICT technology. For example:

- flyers, posters, brochures and newsletters
- websites
- multimedia presentations
- music scores
- cartoons
- mobile phones
- VoIP (Voice over Internet Protocol)
- business cards and letterheads.

6.1.1 Flyers, posters, brochures and newsletters

Flyers and posters can be produced very easily using one of the many software packages available; most commonly word processing and desktop publishing software. Usually, the flyer or poster will have photos which have been taken specially or have been downloaded from the internet. The following sequence is fairly typical of how such a document could be produced on a computer system:

1 open a word processor, DTP or presentation application
2 create frames, boxes and/or text boxes
3 take photos if necessary using a camera
4 upload the images from the camera or from a CD/ DVD, scan photos, or download photos from the internet
5 save the photos to a file
6 import or copy and paste the photos into the document
7 edit the photos and import from a file or type any text required.

Brochures can also be used to advertise a company. Whilst these can also be produced on a standard computer and then printed out on a laser or inkjet printer, it is usually more professional to go to a specialist company. These companies will have the ability to print on glossy paper and have access to specialist software producing a better final product.

Brochures and flyers can be sent out to every household in a given area; this will ensure that a certain target group receives a company's advertising. A more 'hit and miss' method is to put the documents inside magazines and newspapers. The big disadvantage of both methods is the tendency to throw the documents away (especially those found in magazines and newspapers) unless they actually catch the eye and offer something interesting or useful.

Whilst we have treated brochures and flyers separately, the actual definition of a brochure can include a flyer, a pamphlet or a leaflet.

Brochures can therefore be a single sheet of paper (folded into two, three or more equal parts) or multiple sheets (either stapled or bound in some other way). Generally, single sheet documents are referred to as flyers or leaflets and booklets are referred to as brochures. Posters tend to be much larger sheets of paper which are displayed on buildings, noticeboards or advertising hoardings.

Posters have the big advantage that they are eye-catching and usually very difficult to miss. They are used in many countries on the sides of roads so motorists see the posters on their way to work. By placing the posters in strategic positions, it is of course possible to target certain people rather than the general public (e.g. advertising expensive cars by placing the posters on buildings or advertising hoardings in financial districts in big cities). The disadvantage is the cost of display (the advertising areas can only be rented) and also they are subject to weather conditions, so only have a limited life.

Newsletters are often produced by companies or clubs using many of the methods described above. They contain local information which is read by company employees or club members. The content is pertinent to the organisation and might include:

Figure 6.1 Brochures

Figure 6.2 Flyer/leaflet

Figure 6.3 Poster

- marriages, deaths and births of employees, club members or their families
- fundraising successes by employees or club members
- advertising by outside companies
- news events, such as fundraising, etc.

6.1.2 Websites

Rather than producing flyers and posters by printing them out, it is possible to use websites to do the advertising. This method of advertising requires the company to either develop their own websites or to pay another company to advertise on their website.

Using the first option requires the company to either employ a team of web designers or go to a specialist company with experience in website design. It will also be necessary to buy hardware and software to develop and store the website. This method can therefore be expensive, but the cost doesn't stop there. It will be necessary to use programmers to make sure that the website is safe from hackers and from pharming attacks. The big advantage is that websites offer world-wide advertising capability and there is also no need to buy paper and other consumables or pay people to deliver leaflets or flyers. Companies have to weigh up the advantages and disadvantages of both methods before they decide which is the best advertising method.

Advantages

- Sound/video/animation can be added.
- Links to other websites/hyperlinks can be used.
- Use of hotspots.
- Buttons to navigate/move around the website leading to more information.
- Hit counters to see how many people have visited the website.
- Can be seen by a global audience.
- Can't be defaced or thrown away.
- It is much easier to update a website (and there is no need to do a reprint and then distribute the new version).

Disadvantages

- Websites can be hacked into and modified or viruses introduced.
- Risk of potential pharming.
- It is necessary for the potential customers to have a computer and internet connection.
- It isn't as portable as a paper-based system (although with modern smartphones and phablets this is fast becoming untrue).
- Possible for customers to go to undesirable websites (either by accident or as a result of the pharming attack) – this can lead to distrust from customers.
- There is a need for the company to maintain the website once it is set up – this can be expensive.
- Because it is a global system, it is more difficult to target the correct audience using website advertising.

6.1.3 Multimedia presentations

Presentations that use animation, video and sound or music are generally much more interesting than a standard presentation done on slides or paper.

The presentations are produced using one of the many software packages on the market and then used with a **multimedia projector** so that the whole audience is able to see the presentation.

Advantages

- Use of sound and animation/video effects which are more likely to grab the attention of the audience, and can also make the presentation easier to understand.
- It is possible to have interactive/hyperlinks built into the presentation; this means the presentation could access a company's website or even key files stored on the cloud (such as video footage, images, spreadsheets and so on).
- Use of transition effects allow a presentation to display facts in a key or chronological order.
- The presentations can be interactive.
- They are more flexible; because of the links to websites and other external systems (e.g. the cloud), the presentation can be tailored to suit a particular audience.

Disadvantages

- There is a need to have special equipment which can be expensive.
- Equipment failure can be a disaster when giving multimedia presentations.
- Wherever the presentation is given there may need to be internet access.

- There is a danger when using multimedia in presentations that the focus is on the medium (i.e. the multimedia presentation) rather than the message/facts.
- It is very easy to make a bad presentation with too many animation effects and too much text or images.

Paper-based presentations

It is always possible to produce presentations in a hardcopy format rather than the system described above. This has the following advantages:

- disabled people don't have to go to the venue to see the presentation
- it is possible to print it out in Braille for the benefit of blind people
- the recipient can read the presentation at any time they want
- the recipients have a permanent copy which they can refer to at any time they want.

There are, however, disadvantages:

- the presentation needs to be distributed in some way
- there are no special effects (sound, video, animation)
- there are printing costs (paper, ink, etc.).

6.1.4 Music scores

The generation of music and the production of music scores can now be done by computer systems with the appropriate software. Some of the features of this technology include:

- music samplers and mixers allow the original tracks that were recorded in the studio to be modified in any way that the producer wants
- electronic instruments (like guitars and organs) can play back through electronic effects machines
- synthesisers combine simple wave forms to produce complex music creations
- electronic organs can mimic any other instrument
- the music score can be generated from the music itself using software
- software can automatically correct music notes in a score
- there is no real need to understand music notation to write a music score
- music notes are automatically printed out in the correct format.

6.1.5 Cartoons

Animation can be produced using computer hardware and software. With 3-D animation, objects are designed on a computer and a 3-D skeleton (framework or basic structure) produced. The parts of the skeleton are moved by the animator using key frames (these frames define the start point and end point to give a smooth animation effect). The difference in the appearance of the skeleton in these key frames is automatically calculated by the software and is known as tweening or morphing. The final stage is to make a realistic image by a technique known as rendering.

However, cartoons can simply be freehand drawings and then scanned in or can be computer-generated (possibly with the aid of a graphics pad). The cartoons described in the earlier paragraph are essentially moving images. The example overleaf is a static image but can have the same effect. Essentially, cartoons can add humour to any form of communication and can be a very efficient and effective way to get a message across.

For example:

Mike, I sent you an email. It says can you come downstairs please … your dinner is on the table!!!

As with any form of communication, it is important not to offend anybody and also to make sure the cartoon doesn't become the 'main feature' and the message becomes lost somewhere within the humour.

6.1.6 Mobile phones

Note: refer to Chapter 1 for more information on the use of mobile phones.

Mobile phones communicate by using towers inside many cells networked together to cover large areas. The towers allow the transmission of data throughout the mobile phone network.

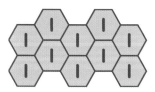

Cell showing tower at the centre. Each cell overlaps giving mobile phone coverage

Figure 6.4 Each cell overlaps giving mobile phone coverage

Each tower transmits within its own cell; if you are driving a car and get to the edge of a cell the mobile phone signal starts to weaken; this is recognised by the network and the mobile phone then picks up the signal in one of the adjacent cells. If a person is making a call or sending a text to somebody in a different country then satellite technology is used to enable the communication to take place.

Mobile phone technology can now be used by computers and tablets. A plug-in device (using one of the available USB ports) or **SIM (Subscriber Identity Module)** card allows the computer to connect to the mobile phone network. This then allows access to the internet.

As a communication device, the mobile phone has many advantages.

As the name suggests, they can be used to make phone calls from any location within the cellular network; this has advantages over the more conventional landline system:

- there is no need to look for an operational public telephone in an emergency
- it is possible to conduct business or personal phone calls on the move
- it is easier to keep in contact with co-workers at the office no matter where you are.

They allow text messaging:

- this is quicker and less expensive than making phone calls
- also text messages can be sent at any time of the day even if the recipient's phone is switched off
- they employ predictive texting where the system completes a word from the first few letters keyed in e.g. key in 'preci' and the phone completes the word as 'precious'; predictive texting also allows the system to remember frequently used words – together they increase typing speed.

Mobile phones allow access to the internet on the move using either the cellular network or a Wi-Fi 'hot spot'.

6.1.7 Internet telephony

One of the most common forms of internet telephony (i.e. having a telephone conversation via the internet) is **Voice over internet Protocol (VoIP)**.

Voice over internet protocol (VoIP) is a method used to talk to people using the internet. VoIP converts sound (picked up by the computer microphone or special VoIP telephone plugged into the USB port of the computer) into discrete digital packets which can be sent to their destination via the internet. One of the big advantages is that it is either free (if the talking is done computer to computer i.e. both computers have VoIP telephones or use their built in/plugged in microphones and speakers) or at a local rate to anywhere in the world (when VoIP is used to communicate with a mobile or land line telephone rather than another computer). Obviously, to work in real time this system requires a broadband ISP. The main problems are usually sound quality (echo and 'weird sounds' are both common faults). Security is also a main concern with VoIP, as it is with other internet technologies.

One of the big advantages of using VoIP is that a webcam can also be used so that it becomes a type of video chat. Whilst this doesn't have the sophistication of a video conference, it is much cheaper (no need for special software and additional hardware items – VoIP uses built-in microphones, speakers and webcams). Usually the video quality is not very good, but this can be improved by using a more expensive webcam connected to one of the computer's USB ports.

6.1.8 Business cards and letterheads

Many IT companies offer to produce business cards and letterheads to any design. The user connects to an appropriate website and they will be given a number of business card templates. The user chooses a template and keys in data such as:

- name of company
- contact details
- image wanted on the business card.

The final version of the business card is then shown. The customer places their order and the business cards are printed and delivered.

Business cards can then be handed out to people as a form of personal advertisement. The use of IT (in this case, a website) has made this a much easier task. Business cards are less likely to be thrown away since they are seen as personal contact. It is also possible to include additional information on the reverse of the card – this could be further advertising of the company's products or it could be advertising another company.

Many of the advantages of having business cards are similar to the advantages of using headed stationery.

The same format used on the business cards can be adopted on a company letterhead (as shown on the right). This helps to project a corporate image. As with the business cards, these pages can be printed on high-quality paper using a laser printer.

Flyers and brochures can be produced (as described earlier) using the same design/logo so it becomes very clear to the customer that the communication all comes from one company.

There are several advantages to a company in using corporate letterheads produced by a printing website:

- professionalism (gives a degree of credibility to the company)
- brand/company awareness (advertises the company by using the same designs on all products)
- legal reasons (it helps if there are any legal actions taken – legitimate documents using the company letterhead is regarded as proof of actual communication)
- advertising (the letterhead can contain many useful pieces of information to advertise the company)
- helps to make the company stand out (will tend to have more impact than a white sheets of paper with a typed company heading)
- can make the company appear larger than it is (this could give a degree of confidence to potential customers).

HODDER CAR SALES
00123 456 7890
AUSTIN MAXI

Exercise 6a

Consider the methods of communication covered in Section 6.1 of this chapter.

1 Write an essay on the relative advantages and disadvantages of using websites, multmedia presentations, flyers and brochures to advertise a company's products.
2 Compare technologies such as VoIP and mobile phones as methods of communication. Consider other information found from within the book when discussing your methods.

6.2 Data handling applications

A number of applications make use of simple data handling techniques, such as:

- surveys
- address lists
- clubs and society records
- school reports
- school libraries.

6.2.1 Surveys

Suppose a small business is interested in finding out information about the buying habits of a number of customers. Questionnaires/surveys will be either handed out to people or will be posted on a website to allow them to be filled in online. Paper questionnaires will be filled in either by ticking/shading in boxes, by connecting two points or by filling in ellipses/circles to select the correct response:

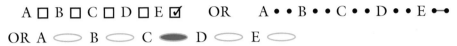

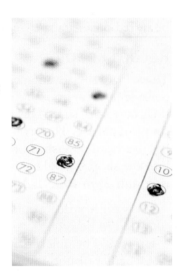

Online questionnaires would tend to use the first option (i.e. using radio buttons) since this is a quick and easy method for gathering data.

However, paper surveys have to be scanned in using OMR or OCR methods and the information is transferred to a database. The advantages of doing this rather than checking each one by hand are:

- faster to get results
- fewer errors
- easier to do a statistical analysis and less expensive (need fewer people).

Online questionnaires have the added advantage that no data preparation is needed at all; the results would be sent directly to a database for analysis.

6.2.2 Address lists

Computers, tablets and mobile phones are all used to store information such as people's home addresses, phone numbers, email addresses or personal data such as date of birth. A typical address book entry may look like the diagram on the right.

The majority of address book applications have features that help the user organise their records into various groupings; such as:

- family
- friends
- work colleagues.

The user can then search by name, grouping, address and so on. Many address book applications also allow synchronisation with tablets and mobile phones. So it is possible to change the data on one system but ensure all devices are kept up to date. As soon as the computer is linked to a tablet or mobile phone then both linked devices will be updated with the latest information.

6.2.3 Clubs and society records

Clubs and societies often keep records of their membership which would typically include: membership number, name, payment details, personal details (phone number, address), their interests etc. A simple database could easily hold all this information making it unnecessary to keep paper records. Consequently, if a particular item of interest (e.g. a talk on F1 motor racing) came up then the computer system could quickly scan all the records on file and find out who would be interested in this topic. They could then automatically contact the member by email or, using mail merge, send out a letter and flyer.

It would also be easy to check on membership subscriptions and send out reminders. This all saves having paper records which are time-consuming to search (and in which details are easy to miss), are easy to lose or misfile, and are more expensive (cost of paper plus filing etc.) and it also saves on space in the office area.

Mail merge is used to find the names and addresses of club members so that reminders can be sent out automatically. The names and addresses would most likely be stored on a database (see further information on mail merge in later chapters).

Record keeping

To evaluate the advantages of using a computer system for record keeping, consider a small bookshop. This shop keeps files on the books in stock and on their customer base. This information could be kept in an electronic form in a simple database. This would make it easy to contact customers if a particular book has just been published or to check on their buying habits. If a customer comes into the shop it would also make it easier to search for a particular book (based on title, author or ISBN). All this leads to several advantages to the shop:

- less office space would be required in the shop since no paper records would need to be kept
- it would be quicker and easier to find details of a particular book or find out whether or not it was in stock
- the system would be less expensive since it wouldn't be necessary to employ somebody to do all the filing and searching
- there would be fewer errors since no manual checking of paper files would need to be done.

There are some disadvantages of the system:

- there would be a need to buy a computer and software to run the system
- time and effort would be required initially to transfer all the existing paper files to the database.

6.2.4 School reports

Computers can be used to keep data on the academic performance of all the students in a school. A database would usually be used to do this. The school could then easily track how well the students were performing over the academic year. The database could be used to produce a printed copy of the student's progress in the form of a report.

This would be considerably easier (and quicker) than writing out a report for each student at the end of the term or year.

A typical database for this application might contain the following fields:

Table 1
StudentID [the student's identification number]
StudName [the name of the student]
TutorGroup [which tutor group the student is in]
Term1Grades [the student's grades for the first term]
Term1Attend [the student's attendance record for the first term]
Term1Notes [this may contain teacher notes about the student's performance]

There may be tables for term 2 and term 3 so that the database contains all the data for the students over the full academic year.

The majority of databases allow the teachers to produce professional-looking reports by carrying out a series of queries. Headed notepaper with the school's name (and possibly logo) will also enhance the appearance of the report.

 FIRE Academy

Semper sursum
Student: 123456 John Doe
Term: end of July 2015

Subject	Grade
Mathematics	A
Science	B
History	D
Languages	E
Art	C
Music	B

Attendance: 97%

Comments: John has continued to work well. He has done particularly well in Maths, Science and Music. His attendance also continues to be excellent.

Mail merge is used to find the names and addresses of parents so that reports can be sent out automatically. The names and addresses would most likely be stored on a database (see further information on mail merge in later chapters).

6.2.5 School libraries

Please refer to Section 6.12 for more details on this topic.

6.3 **Measurement applications**

Measurement applications, using sensors and other electronic hardware (such as a microprocessor), are many and varied.

This type of application involves sensors constantly taking measurement data (such as temperature, rate of rotation or light intensity). Because the data from the sensors are often in an analogue form, they have to be sent to an **Analogue to Digital Converter (ADC)** to turn the data into a digital format. This is needed because microprocessors and computers only understand digital data.

The term 'analogue' means the data is constantly varying and has no discrete values (e.g. the height of mercury in a thermometer to represent temperature). The term 'digital' refers to discrete data which is made up from the binary values 0 and 1. When controlling devices such as pumps, valves, heaters, etc., data/signals (a series of 1s and 0s) from the computer often need to be converted back into an analogue form (e.g. electric signals) using a **Digital to Analogue Converter (DAC)**.

After conversion, the data is sent to a microprocessor where it is processed. However, in measurement applications, the microprocessor simply reviews the data from the sensors (by sometimes comparing it to data stored in memory) and updates its files and sometimes gives a warning signal if the values are outside given parameters. *The microprocessor will take no action to change any of the conditions during the measurement process.*

Examples of measurement applications include:

- weather stations
- scientific experiments (e.g. taking temperature measurements)
- measuring a patient's vital signs on a hospital
- pollution monitoring
- burglar alarm systems.

Advice

Some textbooks will use the term 'signal' instead of data.

6.3.1 Weather stations

Weather stations are set up to automatically gather data from the environment. They are usually unmanned and use a variety of sensors to measure:

- rainfall
- temperature
- wind speed
- wind direction
- (barometric) pressure (air pressure)
- humidity.

The data needs to be gathered 24/7 (i.e. 24 hours a day, every day). This data can then be used by weather forecasters to help predict the weather for the next few days or take a more long-term view by looking at weather patterns.

6.3.2 Measuring a patient's vital signs in a hospital

The following steps show what happens when a computer is used to measure the key vital signs of a patient in a hospital:

- sensors read key vital signs (such as pulse rate, heart rate, temperature, blood pressure, respiration, etc.)
- the data from the sensors is converted into digital using an ADC
- the data is stored in the computer's memory
- the computer compares the data from the sensors with the values stored in its memory (these will be input by the nurse or doctor for a particular patient)
- the results are output on a screen in the form of graphs and/or numerical readouts
- an alarm is activated if any of the data is outside acceptable input values
- the system continues to measure the patient's vital signs until the computer is turned off.

6.3.3 Measuring pollution in a river

The following steps show what happens when a computer is used to measure pollution in a river:

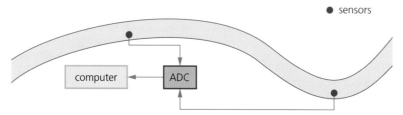

Figure 6.5 Sensors read data from the river (oxygen levels and acidity levels – pH sensor)

- the sensors are placed in at least two different positions so that a pollution comparison can be made
- the data from the sensors is converted into digital using an ADC and sent to a computer
- the computer stores the received data
- the oxygen levels and acidity levels are compared to the historical data stored in memory and they are also compared to *pre-set levels* stored in memory
- the oxygen and acidity levels from the different positions in the river are also compared to see if they are similar – this is used to see if the source of the pollution can be found.

One of two things will now happen: *either* the data is transferred to a CD/DVD or to a memory stick and taken away for further analysis *or* the computer is connected to a mobile phone network and transmits the data back automatically to the monitoring station.

Other sensors, such as light sensors (to see if there are solids or chemicals in the water blocking out light), can also be used.

Advantages

- The computer wouldn't forget to take readings.
- The computer's response time is much faster (very important in the hospital monitoring application).
- Doctors, nurses, scientists, etc. can all get on with other tasks whilst the measurements are taken automatically.

- Computers give 24-hour cover every day.
- The readings will tend to be more accurate.
- Readings can be taken more frequently if done by a computer and sensors.
- It could also be safer since whatever is being measured may have potential hazards (e.g. children falling into the river whilst attempting to take readings or a nurse looking after a patient who has a contagious disease).
- Computers can produce graphs automatically for analysis of results.
- There is a potential cost saving as fewer staff are needed since the measurements are now done by computer (which results in a reduced wages bill).

Disadvantages

- The computer is unable to respond to unusual circumstances.
- Computer equipment and measuring software can be expensive to purchase and set up in the first place.
- A student doing an experiment, for example, will rely on the computer doing the measurement and analysis – it is possible the student will not learn as much using a computer system.
- If the computer malfunctions or if there is a power cut, then the computer cannot be used, and there needs to be good backup procedures in place to cover this eventuality.

Exercise 6b

A student is carrying out an experiment to measure the temperature of a liquid over a 30-minute period. This involves noting down the temperature from a thermometer placed in the liquid; readings are taken every 20 seconds. At the end of the 30 minutes, the student draws a graph of temperature against time:

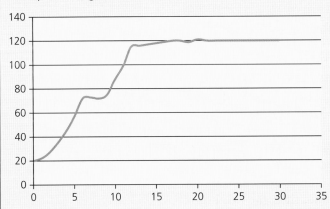

The teacher in charge of the science lesson has decided to do the experiment using sensors and a microprocessor.

1 Describe how the experiment would now be carried out using sensors and microprocessor.
2 Describe the main advantages of doing the experiment using sensors and a microprocessor.

Exercise 6c

A burglar (intruder) alarm system uses various sensors and a microprocessor to detect the presence of intruders. The alarm is set up by keying in a six-digit PIN on a control panel.

1 Name three suitable sensors for this application.
2 Describe how the sensors and microprocessor interact to warn of the presence of an intruder.

6.4 Microprocessors in control applications

In control applications, sensors and a microprocessor or computer are again used. Sensors send data to the microprocessor or computer which then compares the incoming data to stored values or data entered earlier on. As with measuring applications, an ADC may be needed before the microprocessor/computer can process the data.

The microprocessor/computer will check whether the incoming data is outside the given parameters and will take any necessary action. For example, a temperature sensor sends data to a computer which will then check whether the temperature is greater than the preset or stored value. If the temperature is greater than the preset value, the computer will send a signal to switch off a heater. If the temperature is less than the preset value, the computer will send a signal to switch on a heater. There are, of course, many other examples. Unlike measurement applications, the microprocessor/computer will take some action which will ultimately affect the next input value it receives. By doing this, the microprocessor/computer is controlling the application.

Some control applications include:

- automatic washing machines
- automatic ovens/cookers
- central heating systems
- chemical plants
- glasshouse environment control.

> **Exercise 6d**
> Find out how sensors are used in automatic washing machines.

6.4.1 Automatic oven/cooker

An automatic cooker/oven has temperature sensors and a number of controls to set the cooking time (i.e. when to switch the cooker/oven on and off). First of all, the start time and end time (or the actual cooking time) are entered. Finally, the cooking temperature is selected.

The microprocessor checks the set time against the current time and when they are equal, the cooker/oven heating elements are switched on. Once the cooker/oven starts the cooking process, the microprocessor then constantly checks the end time against current time (the end time may be a pre-set value entered by the user or it may be a value calculated by the microprocessor, based on the cooking time entered); when they are equal, the cooking process is stopped.

The microprocessor checks the temperature data sent from a sensor and turns the heating element on if the value less than the preset value chosen by the user. If the temperature is great than or equal to the preset value, then the heating element is switched off by the microprocessor.

Once the cooking process is finished, the microprocessor sends a signal to a beeper to making a beeping sound to indicate that the cooking cycle is completed.

6.4.2 Central heating systems

In the example in Figure 6.6, a gas supply is used to heat water in a boiler. A valve on the gas supply is controlled by a microprocessor and is opened if the heating levels need to be increased. A water pump is used to pump hot water around the central heating system whenever the temperature drops below a preset value.
Note: the water pipes and radiators are not shown in the diagram; only those parts controlled by the microprocessor are shown.

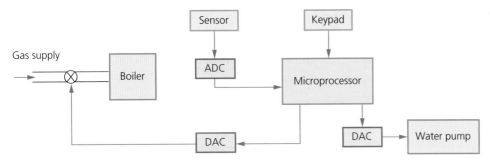

Figure 6.6 A central heating system

So how does this work?

- The required temperature is keyed in and this is stored in the microprocessor memory (this is called the preset value).
- The temperature sensor constantly sends data readings to the microprocessor.
- The sensor data is first sent to an ADC to convert the analogue data into digital data.
- The digital data is sent to the microprocessor.
- The microprocessor compares this data with the preset value.
- If the temperature reading greater than or equal to the preset value then no action is taken.
- If the temperature reading is less than the preset value, then a signal is sent:
  - to an actuator (via a DAC) to open the gas valve to the boiler
  - to an actuator (via a DAC) to turn on the water pump.
- The process continues until the central heating is switched off.

> ### Exercise 6e
>
> Find out how sensors and microprocessors are used to control the following central heating systems:
>
> 1 one which uses an oil burner as the source of heat
> 2 one which uses electric radiators that are switched on and off by the microprocessor.

6.4.3 Chemical process control

A certain chemical process only works if the temperature is above 70°C and the pH (acidity) level is less than 3.5. Sensors are used as part of the control system. A heater is used to heat the reactor and valves are used to add acid when necessary to maintain the acidity. How the sensors and computer are used to control this process is described below:

- temperature and pH sensors read data from the chemical process
- this data is converted to digital using an ADC and is then sent to the computer
- the computer compares the incoming data with preset values stored in memory if the:
  - temperature is less than 70°C, a signal is sent to switch on the heaters
  - temperature is greater than or equal to 70°C, a signal is sent to switch off the heaters
  - pH is greater than 3.5, then a signal is sent to open a valve and acid is added
  - pH is less than or equal to 3.5, then a signal is sent to close this valve
- the computer signals will be changed into analogue signals using a DAC so that it can control the heaters and valves
- this continues as long as the computer system is activated.

6.4.4 Glasshouse environment control

Five different sensors could be used here to control the glasshouse environment; namely, humidity, moisture, temperature, pH and light. To simplify this problem the control mechanisms are shown in Figure 6.7.

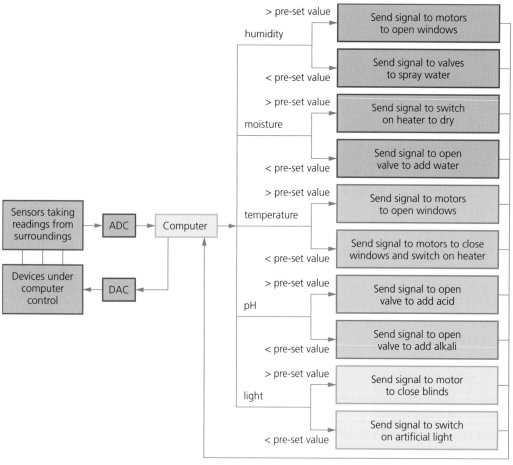

Figure 6.7 Control mechanisms in a glasshouse

Because of the number of sensors, this is clearly quite a complex problem. Let us consider the humidity sensor only. This sends a signal to an ADC which then sends a digital signal to the computer. This compares the input with stored (preset) values and decides what action needs to be taken (follow the orange lines in the diagram above). If humidity is greater than (>) the preset value, the computer sends a signal to a DAC to operate the motors to open windows thus reducing the humidity. If it is less than (<) the preset value, the computer sends a signal to open valves to spray water into the air (follow the green lines in the diagram above). If the reading is the same as the preset value, then no action is taken (this isn't shown in the diagram since it could follow either direction). The control process continues as long as the system is switched on. Similar arguments can be used for all five sensors.

The table on the next page gives a list of possible sensors that might be used in various applications which involve measurement or control.

Sensor type	Possible applications
Temperature	used in the control of central heating systems
	used in the control of/measuring temperatures in a chemical process
Moisture	measuring/used in the control of a glasshouse environment
	measuring moisture levels in any process (e.g. in the production of electronic components)
Oxygen/carbon dioxide	environment monitoring (e.g. measuring the oxygen content in a river to check for pollution)
	measuring carbon dioxide levels in a glasshouse
Light	measuring the light levels in a glasshouse
	measuring for light levels in a dark room (photography)
	used with automatic doors
Infra-red	detecting an intruder by the breaking of an infra-red beam
	allows microprocessor to count items
Pressure	detecting intruders in a burglar alarm system
	counting vehicles as they pass over a bridge
Acoustic	picking up sounds (e.g. footsteps when used in a burglar alarm system)
	detecting liquids or solids moving in pipes/check for blockages in pipes
Motion	detecting movement (as in virtual reality interface devices)
pH	measuring acid/alkaline levels in a river (pollution monitoring)
	used in a glasshouse to measure soil acidity/alkalinity
	used to measure acidity in a chemical process
Proximity/distance	these tend to be another name for the above sensors such as infra-red, motion, etc.)

Exercise 6f

1 i Name the sensors needed in the control of an automatic washing machine.
   ii Describe how sensors and a microprocessor are used to control the wash cycle in an automatic washing machine.
2 Look at Figure 6.7 on page 98. Describe how the pH sensor and light sensor are used to control the soil acidity and light levels in the glasshouse.
3 A street lamp is turned on when it is dark and is switched off when it becomes light again. What sensor is needed to determine whether it is dark or light?
   Describe how the sensors and microprocessor are used to control the switching on and off of the street lamp. Take into account situations such as very heavy cloud cover so that the lamp isn't switching on and off every 30 seconds.

Why use sensors and computer systems to control processes?

A number of advantages were given earlier under the measurement applications section; these advantages are also valid for control applications. There are a couple of additional advantages to consider:

- the response time, if some parameter is out of range, is much faster
- if a process is dangerous it is better to control it from a distance.

The disadvantages are very similar to those given earlier for measurement applications using computers and microprocessors.

6.4.5 Turtle graphics

This is based on the computer language called LOGO and is now usually known as **turtle graphics**. This is essentially the control of the movement of a 'turtle' on a computer screen by a number of key commands which can be typed in.

The most common commands are:

Command	Meaning
FORWARD x	Move xcm forward
BACKWARD x	Move xcm backward
LEFT d	Turn left through d degrees
RIGHT d	Turn right through d degrees
REPEAT n	Repeat next set of instructions n times
ENDREPEAT	Finish the repeat loop
PENUP	Lift the pen up
PENDOWN	Lower the pen

Each square has side length of 20 cm

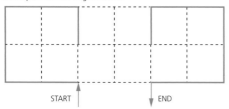

Two different ways to draw this shape are shown below. Option 1 uses a sequence of commands that draw the shape line by line. However, option 2 is a more efficient technique that uses the REPEAT and ENDREPEAT commands. This is used when repeating sequences exist which can be enclosed inside the REPEAT ... ENDREPEAT construct. For example:

```
10   RIGHT 50
20   FORWARD 30
30   RIGHT 50
40   FORWARD 30
50   RIGHT 50
60   FORWARD 30
70   RIGHT 50
80   FORWARD 30
90   RIGHT 50
100  FORWARD 30
110  RIGHT 50
120  FORWARD 30
```

This sequence consists of six repeating commands:

```
RIGHT 50
FORWARD 30
```

and we can therefore write the whole sequence as:

```
10   REPEAT 6
20   RIGHT 50
30   FORWARD 30
40   ENDREPEAT
```

which is considerably more efficient since it only needs four lines rather than 12.

Thus, to draw the shape shown earlier we have the two possible solutions shown in the table on the next page (option 2 makes use of the REPEAT ... ENDREPEAT construct).

Option 1 instructions		Option 2 instructions	
PENDOWN	FORWARD 40	PENDOWN	PENDOWN
LEFT 90	LEFT 90	LEFT 90	FORWARD 20
FORWARD 40	PENDOWN	REPEAT 3	REPEAT 3
RIGHT 90	FORWARD 20	FORWARD 40	RIGHT 90
FORWARD 40	RIGHT 90	RIGHT 90	FORWARD 40
RIGHT 90	FORWARD 40	ENDREPEAT	ENDREPEAT
FORWARD 40	RIGHT 90	FORWARD 20	
RIGHT 90	FORWARD 40	PENUP	
FORWARD 20	RIGHT 90	LEFT 90	
PENUP	FORWARD 40	FORWARD 40	
LEFT 90		LEFT 90	

Exercise 6g

Show how the following sequence could be simplified by using the REPEAT … ENDREPEAT construct wherever possible:

10	PENDOWN	100	LEFT 72
20	LEFT 90	110	PENUP
30	FORWARD 80	120	FORWARD 100
40	RIGHT 72	130	PENDOWN
50	FORWARD 80	140	FORWARD 50
60	RIGHT 72	150	RIGHT 90
70	FORWARD 80	160	FORWARD 50
80	RIGHT 72	170	RIGHT 90
90	FORWARD 80	180	FORWARD 50
		190	PENUP

Exercise 6h

1 Use the REPEAT …. ENDREPEAT commands wherever you can to draw the following shape:

Each side is length 30 mm and the angle shown is 45°.

2 Use turtle graphics to draw the following two-shape drawing. Each side of the regular triangle is 50 mm and each side of the regular pentagon is 30 mm. The angles in the triangle are 60° and the angle shown in the pentagon is 72°. (The distance between the two shapes is 120 mm.)

6.5 Modelling applications

A computer model is the creation of a model of a real system in order to study the behaviour of the system. The model is computer generated and is based on mathematical representations.

The whole idea is to try to find out what mechanisms control how a system behaves. This then makes it possible to predict the behaviour of the system in the future and also see if it is possible to influence this future behaviour.

Computer models have the advantage that they save money, can help find a solution more quickly and can be considerably safer (more of this later). There are many examples of computer models which range from simple spreadsheet representations through to complex flight simulators. The following simple example uses a spreadsheet to do the modelling of a tuck shop in a school:

	A	B	C	D	E	F
1	Item name	Price each ($)	Selling price ($)	Profit per item	Number sold	Total profit per item ($)
2						
3						
4	chew	1.00	1.50	0.50	35	17.50
5	chox	2.00	2.50	0.50	45	22.50
6	gum	3.00	3.50	0.50	30	15.00
7	crisps	1.00	1.50	0.50	45	22.50
8	cake	2.00	2.50	0.50	40	20.00
9						
10					Profit/Loss ($)	-102.50

The formulae behind this spreadsheet are:

	A	B	C	D	E	F
1	Item name	Price each ($)	Selling price ($)	Profit per item	Number sold	Total profit per item ($)
2						
3						
4	chew	1.00	1.50	=(C4-B4)	35	=(D4*E4)
5	chox	2.00	2.50	=(C5-B5)	45	=(D5*E5)
6	gum	3.00	3.50	=(C6-B6)	30	=(D6*E6)
7	crisps	1.00	1.50	=(C7-B7)	45	=(D7*E7)
8	cake	2.00	2.50	=(C8-B8)	40	=(D8*E8)
9						
10			Weekly shop cost	200.00	Profit/Loss ($)	=SUM(F4:F8)-D10

Thus by varying the values in column C or in column E it would be possible to model the shop's profit or loss. This is a very simple model but it shows the principal of using spreadsheets to carry out any type of modelling that can be represented in a mathematical form.

Traffic light simulation

A set of traffic lights are to be modelled at a Y-junction:
   In this computer model it is necessary to consider:

i How and what data needs to be collected.
ii How the computer model is carried out.
iii How the system would work in real life.

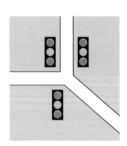

How and what data needs to be collected?
Since the success (or failure) of a computer model depends on how realistic it is, data needs to be collected by watching traffic for a long period of time at the Y-junction. This is best done by using induction loop sensors which count the number of vehicles at each junction. Manual data collection is possible but is prone to errors and is difficult to do over an 18-hour period per day (for example). The sort of data that would need to be collected or considered for collection is as follows:

- a count of the number of vehicles passing the junction in all directions at all different times of the day
- the day of the week (weekends, bank holidays, etc. can alter how the data need be interpreted)
- how long it takes a vehicle to clear the junction

- how long it takes the slowest vehicle to pass through the junction
- whether there are any pedestrian crossings etc. nearby
- whether there are other factors which might affect the junction (e.g. left turns, right turns, filtering, etc.).

How is the computer model carried out?

Data from the above list is entered into the computer and the computer model is run. Once the designers are satisfied that it models the real situation accurately (i.e. by comparing results obtained with actual traffic flow from a number of data sets) then different scenarios can be tried out. For example:

- vary the timing of the lights and see how the traffic flow was affected
- increase the number of vehicles stopped at part of the junction and then change the timing of the lights to see how the traffic flow is affected
- increase or decrease traffic flow in all directions
- consider how emergency vehicles affect traffic flow at different times of the day.

How would the system work in real life?

1 Sensors in the road gather data and count the number of vehicles at the junction.
2 This data is sent to a control box or to a computer (it may need to be converted first into a form understood by the computer).
3 The gathered data is compared to data stored in the system (the stored data is based on model predictions which were used to optimise the traffic flow).
4 The control box or computer 'decides' what action needs to be taken.
5 Signals are sent out to the traffic lights to change their timing if necessary.

Why are computer models done (in general terms)?

- They are less expensive than having to build the real thing (e.g. a bridge!).
- On many occasions it is safer to run a computer model (some real situations are hazardous e.g. chemical processes).
- With computer models it is much easier to try out various scenarios in advance.
- It is nearly impossible to try out some tasks in real life because of the high risk involved or the remoteness (e.g. outer space, under the sea, nuclear reactors, crash testing cars, etc.).
- Time scales are reduced by doing a computer model rather than the real thing (some applications would take years before a result was known e.g. climate change calculations, population growth, etc.).

Other examples of computer models include: population growth, modelling queues at checkouts, training pilots and drivers, running chemical and nuclear plants, crash testing of cars, financial modelling and weather predictions.

Exercise 6i

Create a spreadsheet to do some personal financial modelling. Include the monthly income in one row and then show all the monthly outgoings. For example:

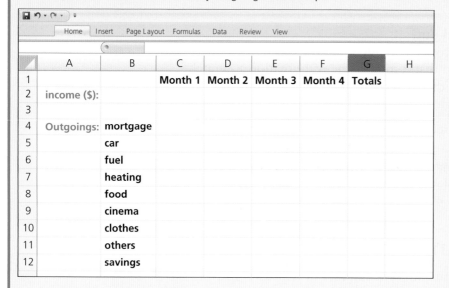

Extend the list as much as you want or change the outgoings to be more realistic if necessary. Insert some values into the spreadsheet and then change a few values to see the effect on your finances. Add extra columns or extra outgoings to extend the spreadsheet. Finally try graphing your income against outgoings for each month and for a year (do a prediction for the year after four months, for example).

Exercise 6j

Here is a list of five computer models and also a list of five reasons why models are carried out. Try to match the five models to the best reason why that model would be done.

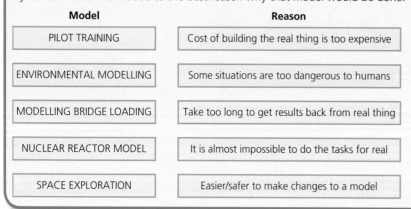

6.6 Manufacturing applications

Manufacturing uses ICT (i.e. automation) in a number of areas to improve productivity, reduce costs, improve consistency and to make factories safer and more environmentally friendly.

One of the most common forms of automation is the use of robots.

Robotics

Robots are used in many areas of manufacturing, from heavy work right through to delicate operations. Examples include: paint spraying of car bodies, welding bodywork on cars, manufacturing of microchips, manufacturing electrical goods and automatic warehouses.

Control of robots is either through embedded (built-in) microprocessors or linked to a computer system. Programming of the robot to do a series of tasks is generally done in two ways:

1 The robot is programmed with a sequence of instructions which allow it to carry out the series of tasks (e.g. spraying a car body with paint).
2 Alternatively, a human operator manually carries out the series of tasks; this can be done in two ways. In our example, we will assume an object is being painted using a robot arm.

   i The robot arm is guided by a worker when spraying the object; each movement of the arm is stored as an instruction in the computer.

OR

   ii The worker straps sensors to his own arm and sprays the object; each movement is stored as a set of instructions in a computer; the sensors send back information such as position relative to the object, arm rotation, and so on – this information forms part of the instructions stored in the computer.

Whichever method is used, once the instructions have been saved, each series of tasks can then be carried out by a robot arm automatically. Each instruction will be carried out identically every time (e.g. assembling parts in a television) giving a consistent product.

Robots are often equipped with sensors so they can gather important information about their surroundings and also preventing them from doing 'stupid things' e.g. stopping a robot spraying a car if no car is present, or stop the spraying operation if the supply of paint has run out, etc.

Robots are very good at repetitive tasks. However, if there are many different tasks (e.g. making specialist glassware for some scientific work) then it is often better to still use human operators.

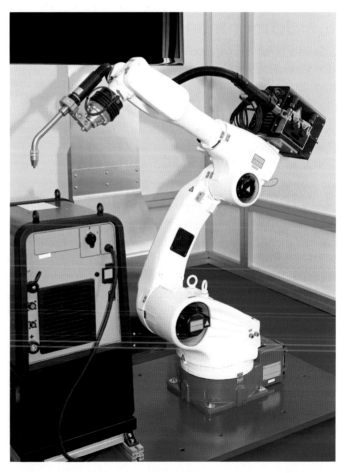

Figure 6.8 Robot arm equipped with a spray gun 'end effector'. Different end effectors allow the robot arm to carry out many different tasks

Advantages

- They can work in environments harmful to human operators.
- They can work non-stop (24/7).
- They are less expensive in the long term (although expensive to buy initially, they don't need wages).
- Higher productivity (don't need holidays, etc.).
- Greater consistency (e.g. every car coming off a production line is identical).
- They can do boring, repetitive tasks leaving humans free to do other more skilled work (e.g. quality control or design work).

Disadvantages

- They find it difficult to do 'unusual' tasks (e.g. one-off glassware for a chemical company).
- They can cause higher unemployment (replacing skilled labour).
- Since robots do many of the tasks once done by humans, there is a real risk of certain skills (such as welding) being lost.
- Because robots are independent of the skills base, factories can be moved anywhere in the world (again causing unemployment).
- The initial set-up and maintenance of robots can be expensive.

> ### Exercise 6k
> Which of these are advantages and disadvantages for the employees and which are for the employers?

6.7 School management systems

Schools have to manage a number of different tasks in the day-to-day running of the school. These include:

- registration and attendance records of the students
- student performance
- organisation of school exams (internal and external)
- creation of timetables
- teacher substitution (when teachers are absent due to illness or training).

6.7.1 School registration systems

The traditional way to record the registration and attendance of a student was to complete daily registers. This was very time consuming since it required a 10-minute session at the beginning and end of each day. It was also prone to error if a student's name was missed at some point during the registration process. There are now a number of possible ways of automating the registration process using hardware and software, some of which are included below.

Method 1

Issue each student with an ID card. This would contain a magnetic stripe (shown in black) on the rear of the card. The student would have to sign the card and also write his unique student ID on the back of the card as well. The magnetic stripe would contain the name of the school, the name of the student, the student's data of birth and their unique ID (registration) number.

Each morning the student would arrive at the school and swipe their ID card through a magnetic card reader. The data read would identify the student and the time and date they entered the school's premises. This data would now be stored on a database. On leaving the school (either at lunchtime or at the end of the day), the ID card would again be swiped. This would now record the leaving time

FIRE-Academy

Paul Smith-012 234 555

and date on the database. This would give a very comprehensive record of when the student attended the school and the number of hours they attended. It would also be a more secure method in the event of, for example, a fire. The school would now be able to account for every student currently showing as being present on the school premises. Using the paper-based system, a student could register then just go home – with this ID card system, the student's attendance would be known at all times.

There are further subtleties that could be used such as (1) use of a PIN to stop another student swiping in with the wrong card (2) use of GPS tracking (see Section 6.16.1) so the exact whereabouts of a student would be known; this would require the addition of a chip in the ID card so that the tracking system could identify them (this is the basis of RFID which was discussed in Chapter 2). At the end of a term (or school year), the database could be interrogated and it would give an accurate attendance record for the student.

Method 2

A second method could make use of biometrics. Each student would have their fingerprints taken. Their personal details (as in method 1) plus fingerprints would be stored on a database. When a student entered the school premises, they would be asked to put their hand on a scanner which would read their fingerprints. Since each student would have unique fingerprints, this system would be very secure. As with method 1, the date and time of entering or leaving the school would be accurately recorded on the database.

Advantages

- Fingerprints are unique, so it would be impossible for a student to sign in pretending to be someone else (with magnetic cards, a student could give his card to a friend and ask them to sign in for him) – this gives more accurate data and improved security.
- ID cards could easily be lost – fingerprints are 'part of you' so can't be lost.
- ID cards could be affected by magnetic fields (e.g. by being placed close to a mobile phone) which would stop them working.
- It is much easier to 'clone' (i.e. make copies of) ID cards than it would be to copy fingerprints (not impossible but very difficult).

Disadvantages

- It would take a long time to collect the initial fingerprints for every student in the school.
- The equipment needed to take and read fingerprints is more expensive than magnetic stripe reading equipment.
- If a student cuts a finger, the fingerprint may not be identified by the system (which would prevent entry to the school).
- There are 'invasion of privacy' issues and some parents may object to having the fingerprints of their children stored on a database.

6.7.2 Student performance

Teachers could make considerable use of spreadsheets to monitor the performance of their students. This was discussed in Section 5.1. Essentially, spreadsheets could record the test results of each student over a term/year. This would allow a teacher easily to see how they were performing against other students in the same subjects. It would also be easy to import data into a report, for example, summarising a student's performance over the academic year.

6.7.3 Exam timetables, subject timetables and teacher substitution

Timetables are often required for the following:

- exams scheduling (both internal and external)
- subject scheduling
- producing cover/substitution plans for teachers who are absent.

For example, at the start of a new academic year, a student may be given their own personal timetable covering their subject allocation:

Timetable for: Paul Smith 012 234 555 Summer term 2016					
	09:00–10:30	10:40–12:10	12:20–13:20	13:30–15:00	15:10–16:40
Monday	Mathematics	History	*lunch*	Science	Science
Tuesday	Geography	Art/Music	*lunch*	ICT	ICT
Wednesday	Sport time	Sport time	*lunch*	Art/Music	Geography
Thursday	Geography	History	*lunch*	Mathematics	Art/Music
Friday	ICT	Mathematics	*lunch*	Science	History

Many factors have to be taken into account when producing timetables for each student:

- availability of teachers
- availability of rooms for each subject
- subject clashes (e.g. a student wishing to do French from a group containing French, History, English and Spanish finds this clashes with their Art/Music lessons and so they have to take History instead of French)
- number of hours for each subject
- making sure double lessons appear for certain practical subjects but ensuring this doesn't happen with others.

Timetables are also produced so that students know when to sit an exam. This allows them to schedule their work correctly.

The main advantages of using software to create timetables is that it is quicker and less error-prone than the older paper-based systems. It is also easier to try 'what if' scenarios to ensure the most efficient use of time is utilised.

Likewise, timetables can be produced to cover classes when teachers are absent. This is often done using the main timetable software since each teacher is allocated a class or non-contact time for each of the teaching periods. In the example above, a teacher would have either a class or a 'free period' for each 1.5 hour session. The main subject speciality of each teacher is also stored so that a subject specialist can be used to cover for absent teachers.

6.8 Booking systems

6.8.1 Theatre and cinema booking systems

Online booking systems rely on the ability to update files immediately thus preventing double-booking etc. which could happen if the system response time was slow. Booking systems are used for transport (flights, trains and buses), cinemas and theatres.

We will consider the theatre booking system to describe how this system works. With this example, we have assumed that the customer has already logged on to the theatre booking website:

- the customer clicks on the performance they wish to see
- a date and time is typed in
- the required number of seats is also entered
- the seating display in the theatre is shown on the screen
- the user selects their seat(s) by highlighting the actual seats on the screen display and then clicks CONFIRM to go to the next part of the process

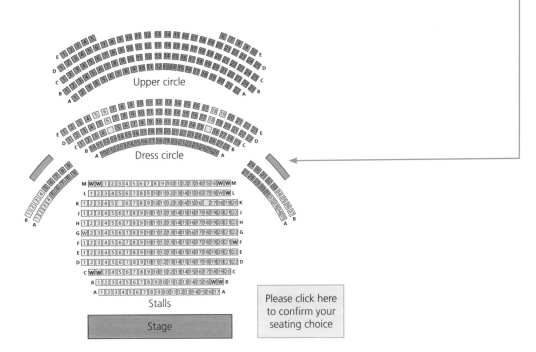

- the database is then searched to check the availability of the selected seats
- if the seats are available, the total price is shown + the seat numbers; this shows on another screen on the web page
- if the customer is happy with this, they select CONFIRM on the screen
- the seats are now temporarily set at NO LONGER AVAILABLE
- the customer then enters their personal details or indicates that they are a returning customer (in which case the website will already have their details)
- the payment method is then selected and payment made
- the theatre seats are then booked in the customer's name
- the final details are again shown on the screen
- an email is sent to the customer which they print out as their proof of purchase (this also acts as their printed ticket when they go to the theatre – an **e-ticket**)
- the database is finally updated with the transaction and the seats become no longer available.

Booking seats at the cinema is obviously a similar series of steps. However, booking flights is slightly more complex since it involves choosing airport, etc.

6.8.2 Flight booking systems

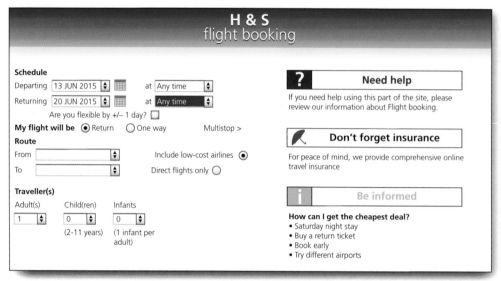

Figure 6.9 An example of an online web page for choosing flights

Exercise 6I

Using the screenshot in Figure 6.9, describe the stages when a person logs on to a flight booking website and makes a booking. Describe how the seats are booked, how double-booking is prevented, how the customer's tickets are produced and how payment is made.

Also investigate the latest ways of creating e-tickets such as Apps on smartphones and so on. Why are these new methods better than printing out a confirmation email to act as the e-ticket?

Advantages of online booking systems

- They prevent double-booking (which could happen in paper-based systems which didn't update the system fast enough).
- The customer gets immediate feedback on the availability of seats and whether or not their booking has been successful.
- The customer can make bookings at any time of the day.
- The customer's email address allows the booking company to attach 'special offers' to them and inform them of such offers automatically.
- It is usually easier to browse the seating plans (particularly on flights) to choose the best seats available at the price.
- It is possible to 'reserve' at seat for a period of time – this allows a customer to 'make up their mind' before finalising the booking of the seat (this was difficult to do with the older paper-based systems).
- Very often there are no printed tickets which saves postal costs and also allows 'impulse' bookings only a few hours in advance.
- Online booking allows the use of modern smartphone and tablet apps technology; the customer is sent a QR code which contains all the booking information necessary (this QR code is stored on the smartphone or tablet and only needs to scanned at the theatre or cinema on arrival). This removes the need to print out tickets (which can get lost) and also removes the possibility of forgeries.

Disadvantages of online booking systems

- The setting up and maintenance of online booking systems is expensive.
- All customers using this service need access to a computer and a reliable internet connection.
- It is often more difficult to cancel the booking and get your money back using online systems.
- If the server is down for maintenance or if the systems breaks down, it becomes impossible to book seats by any method (a temporary paper-based system can't be used because of the risk of double-booking occurring).
- If the websites are not well designed, it can be difficult to make exactly the booking you want or can lead you to make mistakes; this is a particular issue with flight bookings where correcting an error can cost the customer an additional fee.
- Booking online does not allow you to build a personal relationship with the travel agent who might offer free upgrades or special offers which may not be available to online bookings.

6.9 Banking applications

The use of computer technology has revolutionised how we all do our banking transactions. This section will consider:

- the use of automatic teller machines (ATMs)
- internet banking
- telephone banking
- chip and PIN technology
- clearing of cheques
- electronic funds transfer.

6.9.1 Automatic teller machines (ATMs)

Automatic teller machines (ATMs) are places where customers can get cash (or carry out certain other banking activities such as order a statement) using their credit or debit card.

The following sequence shows a typical ATM process:

Sequence for withdrawing cash	What goes on behind the scenes
Customer puts card into ATM	Contact made with bank's computer
PIN is entered using the keypad	PIN is checked to see if it is correct

A number of options are given:
• change PIN
• top up mobile phone
• see account balance
  • on screen
  • printed out
• pay in cheques
• receipt required?
• get a mini statement (e.g. transactions over the last week)
• pay a bill
• make a money transfer
• withdraw cash	

The customer selects the cash option	
A number of cash amounts are shown	Card is checked to see if card expiration date is exceeded or card is reported stolen
The customer accepts one of the options or types in a different amount	Customer's account is accessed to see if they have sufficient funds

⇨ continued…

	Check is made to see if daily limit exceeded
The customer is then asked if they want a receipt	
The card is returned	Transaction is OK
Money is dispensed	Customer's account is updated

There are a few disadvantages with ATMs:

- they are often in places where theft can take place at night
- 'bogus' ATMs can be set up to gather information about the card and retain the card
- some banks charge customers for the use of ATMs.

6.9.2 Internet banking

Using internet banking requires good security. It allows the transfer of sums of money between accounts, payment of bills, ordering of statements, and so on. This is of particular benefit to people who are unable to visit banks during their normal opening hours or if they suffer some disability which makes travelling to the bank difficult. Thus all the advantages of working from home are valid with internet banking. However, it is also true that the disadvantages of using the internet are very valid when applied to internet banking. As the amount of online shopping and banking increases, the impact on society begins to gain in significance.

Online shopping and banking means that more and more people are staying at home to buy goods and services, manage their bank accounts and book holidays etc. This would all be done using a computer connected to the internet and some form of electronic payment (usually a credit or debit card). The following notes give a comprehensive list of the advantages and disadvantages of using the internet to carry out many of these tasks.

Because there is considerable overlap between the advantages and disadvantages of online banking and online shopping, these are both considered together here (see also Section 6.13 for more information on the retail sector).

Advantages of online shopping and banking

- There is no longer a need to travel into the town centre thus reducing costs (money for fuel, bus fares, etc.) and time-wasting; it also helps to reduce town centre congestion and pollution.
- Users now have access to a worldwide market and can thus look for products that are cheaper; this is obviously less expensive and less time consuming than having to shop around by the more conventional methods; they will also have access to a much wider choice of goods.
- Disabled and elderly people can now access any shop or bank without the need to leave home which is of great benefit to them; it helps to keep them part of society since they can now do all the things taken for granted by able-bodied people.
- Because it is online, shopping and banking can be done at any time on any day of the week (i.e. 24/7) – this is particularly helpful to people who work as the shops/banks would normally be closed when they finished work.
- People can spend more time doing other things e.g. going shopping to the supermarket probably took up a lot of time; by doing this online (e.g. setting up repeat items) people are now free to do more leisure activities.
- Many people find it less embarrassing to ask for a bank loan using the internet rather than enduring a face-to-face discussion with bank staff.
- There are often long queues at the banks or checkouts at the shops, so internet banking saves time.

- The shops and banks save money by not having as many staff working for them (reduced wage bill) or hiring of high street premises (reduction in rental costs) – these savings are often passed on to customers in the form of lower interest rates, cheaper goods or higher rates on interest for savers.

Disadvantages of online shopping and banking

- There is the possibility of isolation and lack of socialisation if people stay at home to do all their shopping and banking.
- There are possible health risks associated with online shopping or banking because of a lack of exercise; if people physically go shopping then they are getting some exercise.
- Security issues are a major concern (e.g. hacking, stealing credit card details, etc.) as are viruses and other malware (e.g. phishing, pharming and so on).
- Accidentally using fraudulent bank or shopping websites is always a risk and this is linked to security issues.
- It is necessary to have a computer and to pay for the internet to take part in online shopping and banking.
- Unlike high street shopping, it is only possible to see a picture of the goods, which might not portray the exact colour of a dress for instance (nor can you try something on to see if it suits) before buying them; you also to have wait several days for the goods to arrive; returning goods is also expensive.
- High street shops and banks are closing because of the increase in online shopping or banking and this is leading to 'ghost towns' forming.
- It is easier to make errors with online banking and transfer money incorrectly to different accounts.

Effects on companies due to the spread of online shopping and banking

The earlier discussions all centred around the effects of ICT on people. Companies and other organisations have also been affected by the growth of ICT and online shopping and banking. Some of the effects are listed below:

- companies can save costs here since fewer staff need to be paid and it isn't necessary to have as many shops and banks in high streets to deal with potential customers
- because the internet is global, the potential customer base is increased
- there will be some increased costs, however, because of the need to retrain staff and the need to employ more staff in despatch departments
- there are also costs due to the setting up and maintaining of websites to enable online shopping and banking
- since there is very little or no customer–employee interaction, this could lead to a drop in customer loyalty which could lead to loss of customers (this could also be brought about by the lack of personal service associated with online shopping and banking)
- robberies are less likely due to the decrease in the number of high street banks
- banks also need to employ fewer security staff which has a cost benefit.

6.9.3 Telephone banking

Telephone banking is similar to internet banking. The main difference is that it uses the telephone rather than a computer.

With this system, the customer calls the bank using a telephone. The sequence is as follows:

- the customer keys in their account number
- they are then requested to enter a four-digit PIN or selected numbers from their PIN
- the customer will then hear various options, which might include:
  - press '1' for your balance
  - press '2' to carry out a money transfer
  - press '3' to pay a bill
  - press '4' to talk to one of our representatives
- the customer chooses one of the options (either by pressing the correct key, or some systems ask the customer to speak the number – this relies on voice recognition).

As with internet banking, customers are able to:

- check their balances anywhere in the world
- pay bills or transfer money to another account
- talk with a bank representative.

The advantages of telephone banking are similar to internet banking but with this system there is no need to have a computer and it's possible to talk to an actual human being. Many people still find this a more attractive proposition.

However, compared to internet banking, it can be much slower (there may be a long queue before you can talk to somebody) and the options can be a little more complex to navigate. But it can also be quicker if your computer isn't switched on at the time and you only want a balance enquiry.

Exercise 6m

Using the notes from Sections 6.9.2 and 6.9.3, compare the advantages and disadvantages of using internet banking and telephone banking.

Consider how easy both methods are, the security issues and the need for equipment and communication lines. Also do some research and compare both methods to using banking apps on smartphones.

Put your findings into an article and try to draw some form of conclusion.

6.9.4 Chip and PIN

Many credit cards are equipped with a chip as well as a magnetic stripe – this contains key information such as the PIN.

Chip

This system is designed to enhance security since it is better than relying only on a signature. When paying for items using a chip and PIN card, a form of **electronic funds transfer (EFT)** takes place (see Section 6.9.6). In this example, suppose a customer goes into a restaurant to pay for a meal using a chip and PIN card:

1 The PIN is entered using a keypad.
2 The card is checked to see if it is valid (check on expiry date, whether stolen card, etc.).
3 The PIN is read from the chip on the card and is compared to the one just keyed in.

4 If they are the same, then the transaction can proceed.
   If this is the third attempt at entering the PIN, then the transaction
   is terminated.
5 The restaurant's bank contacts the customer's bank.
6 A check is made on whether they have enough funds.
7 If the card is not valid or there aren't enough funds available, then the
   transaction is terminated.
8 If everything checks out OK, then the transaction is authorised.
9 An authorisation code is sent to the restaurant.
10 The price of the meal is then deducted from the customer's account.
11 The same amount of money is then added to the restaurant's bank account.
12 A receipt is produced as proof of purchase.

6.9.5 Clearing of cheques

This section reviews how banks clear cheques using a centralised clearing centre.

Suppose John uses a bank called Hodder Bank and he pays a cheque for $50 to a company called H&S Ltd who bank with the Smith Bank. How is the H&S bank account credited with $50?

First of all the cheque is sent by the Smith Bank to a centralised clearing centre. The cheque is processed by the clearing centre by first of all passing it through a reader/sorter machine. This machine automatically reads:

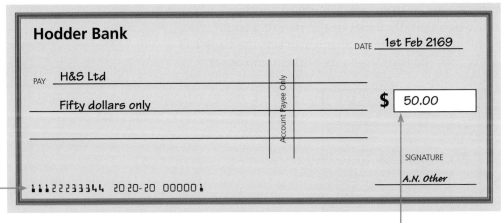

- the amount on the cheque
- the code line (containing account number, sort code and cheque number).

All the cheques are then sorted using their sort codes (unique, six-digit numbers that are used to identify each bank or building society), ready for sending to an exchange centre.

The data from the cheque which has been read is then converted into an encrypted file known as IBDE (Inter-Bank Data Exchange) file. Every IBDE is 'signed' with a digital signature so that the receiving bank can be sure that the data hasn't been tampered with.

Later, Smith Bank delivers the cheque to an exchange centre. The exchange centre then passes the cheque back to the paying bank (Hodder Bank in this case) which then sends it to its own clearing centre.

At the paying bank's clearing centre, the digital signature is first checked and then the cheque is passed through their own reader/sorter machine to make sure the data matches with that on the IBDE file. It also sorts the cheques into branch order (using the sort code).

Later on, Hodder Bank checks to see if John has enough money in his account to cover the cheque, and also that it has been signed, dated and written correctly and is genuine. Based on this information, Hodder Bank decides whether to pay John's cheque to H&S Ltd or return it unpaid to the Smith Bank.

If John's bank decides not to pay the cheque to H&S Ltd, his bank will send the unpaid cheque back to the Smith Bank by special courier.

The decision to return a cheque unpaid must be made on the morning of the day after exchange so the cheque can be returned straightaway to Smith Bank if necessary. A cheque may be returned unpaid for a number of reasons, such as:

- the customer has not got enough money in their account to pay the cheque
- it has not been signed, dated, or written correctly
- it is fraudulent for some reason.

This whole process, known as 'clearing a cheque', takes three working days, so if you pay in a cheque on a Wednesday, Thursday, or Friday, it will actually take five days to clear.

6.9.6 Electronic funds transfer

Electronic funds transfer (EFT) is a system that allows money transfer instructions to be sent directly to a bank's computer system. No actual money is transferred; the whole system relies on electronic transfer of money between accounts. When an EFT instruction is received, the computer system automatically transfers the specified amount from one account to another.

One common use of EFT is the payment of salaries to the staff of a large company. On the day when payment is made, the company instructs the bank to transfer money from their account into the bank accounts of their employees.

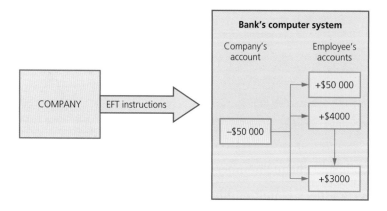

Other examples of EFT include: When a credit/debit card is used to pay for a purchase in a store, the payment is made using a system called **Electronic Fund Transfer at Point-of-Sale (EFTPOS)**. Use of EFTPOS was discussed earlier in Chapter 2.

6.10 Expert systems

Expert systems have been developed to mimic the expertise and knowledge of an expert in a particular field. Examples include:

- diagnosing a person's illness
- diagnostics (finding faults in a car engine, finding faults on a circuit board, etc.)
- prospecting for oil and minerals

- tax and financial calculations
- strategy games (e.g. chess)
- identification of plants, animals and chemical compounds
- road scheduling for delivery vehicles.

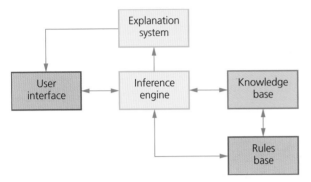

Figure 6.10 A basic expert system is made up of a number of elements

6.10.1 How to set up an expert system

- Experts in the field are interviewed.
- Data is then collected from these experts.
- A knowledge base is first designed and then created (the knowledge from the experts is used to populate the knowledge base).
- The rules base is then designed and created and an inference engine is also designed and created.
- An explanation system is also developed.
- The input screen and output format is also designed and created (this is known as the user interface).
- The expert system is tested against known conditions/scenarios and is also checked to see if it meets the original specification.
- Experts are interviewed about how effective it is before the expert system goes out on general release.

Advantages

- They provide consistent answers and are not affected by emotional reasoning.
- They never 'forget' to answer a question when determining the logic.
- Using expert systems reduces the time to solve a problem.
- They indicate the probability of the given solution being accurate or correct.
- The potential of saving money exists since there is less need for specialists (for example, when carrying out oil exploration).
- Allows areas of the world access to expertise which they couldn't normally afford.

Disadvantages

- They tend to lack common sense in some of the decision-making processes.
- Whilst lack of emotional reasoning is an advantage, it can also be a disadvantage in areas such as medical diagnosis.
- Errors in the knowledge base can lead to incorrect decisions being made.
- They are expensive to set up in the first place.
- Needs considerable training to ensure the system is used correctly by the operators.

6.10.2 Using an expert system

Using oil prospecting as an example, this is the process for using an expert system.

1 An interactive user screen appears (this is often multiple-choice questions or Yes/No responses).
2 The system asks questions about geological profiles.
3 The operator types in the answers to questions/geological profiles.
4 The system then asks questions based on the previous response(s) input by the operator.
5 The inference engine compares answers to questions with the facts stored in the knowledge base using the rules base.
6 The system suggests the probability of finding oil as an output.
7 It also indicates the probable depth of deposits (usually as a percentage probability).
8 The explanation system will also explain how the expert system arrived at its conclusions.
9 It will then make predictions about geological deposits in the soil/rocks.
10 Finally it will produce contour maps showing concentration of minerals, rocks, oil, etc.

Exercise 6n

1 Write a sequence of instructions to show how the following expert systems would be set up:
  • tax calculation system
  • chess
  • engine diagnostics for a racing car.
2 Write a sequence of instructions to show how the following expert systems would be used to diagnose faults or identify things:
  • circuit boards in television sets
  • identify an 'unknown' chemical compound
  • identify a new species of flower
  • produce the best route for a delivery vehicle.

6.11 Computers in medicine

Computers are used in many areas of medicine, such as:

• keeping patient records and pharmacy records
• monitoring of patients in a hospital
• diagnosis of illness using expert systems
• the use of 3-D printers in many areas of surgery.

6.11.1 Patient and pharmacy records

Doctors and hospitals need to keep accurate records of all their patients. This is essential to ensure correct diagnosis and treatment is given. An up-to-date medical history is part of the diagnosis process. Databases are kept by doctors and hospitals so that data can be shared between medical practitioners and pharmacies (e.g. to ensure no drugs are prescribed which interact with each other in an unsafe manner).

Databases also allow a quick and easy search for patient records – this could be very important in an emergency, for example, when accessing the patient's medical history could mean the difference between life and death. It also means that medication can be prescribed without issuing paper prescriptions – an email could be sent to the pharmacy.

The sort of data which would be required on a patient database is as follows:

- a unique identification number
- name and address
- date of birth
- gender (male or female)
- medical history (e.g. recent medicine/treatment)
- blood group
- any known allergies
- doctor
- any current treatment
- any current diagnosis
- important additional information such as X-rays, CT scans, and so on.

6.11.2 Monitoring patients

Note: See also Section 6.3.

By connecting a patient to a computer system, it is possible to carry out 24-hour monitoring of the patient. The computer can monitor:

- heart rate
- respiration (breathing rate)
- brain activity
- blood/body temperature
- blood pressure
- blood sugar levels
- oxygen levels in the blood.

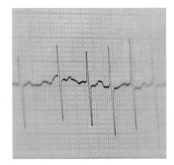

Figure 6.11 Heart beat trace

This is not an exhaustive list, by any means.

The results are shown on a monitor in the form of a digital read-out and/or graphical read-out.

Digital read-outs give the nurse or doctor an immediate value; graphical representations are used to show trends over a period of time. Both methods supply different information. There is often sound output as well in the form of beeps to indicate that the machine is working. It also indicates, for example, the heart rate and gives a warning if the patient's condition suddenly deteriorates. All of these outputs give the nurses and doctors useful information.

As discussed in Section 6.3, the system relies on sensors attached to patients and to a computer system that interprets the sensor data and converts it into a format useful to the nurses and doctors. Using sensors and computers has many advantages over taking readings manually:

- it is more accurate; using a computer system almost removes any chance of error
- they can operate 24/7 and don't require any breaks or get tired
- they never forget to take readings – a nurse could be too busy for example
- readings can be taken more frequently using computer systems
- they are capable of responding much faster to any change in the patient's condition

- they can automatically produce graphs/analyse results
- there is the potential to save money since fewer nurses need to be paid
- computers can monitor several patients at the same time
- they reduce the risk of a nurse being subjected to contagious diseases.

6.11.3 Using expert systems to diagnose patients

Expert systems were discussed in Section 6.10. One of the more common uses of expert systems is to diagnose illnesses in patients.

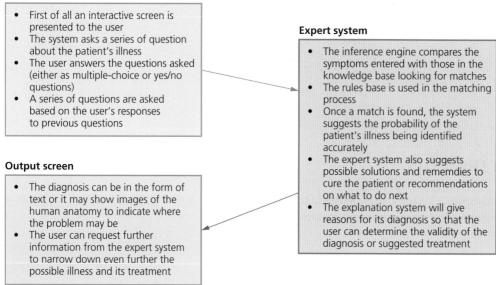

Input screen

- First of all an interactive screen is presented to the user
- The system asks a series of question about the patient's illness
- The user answers the questions asked (either as multiple-choice or yes/no questions)
- A series of questions are asked based on the user's responses to previous questions

Expert system

- The inference engine compares the symptoms entered with those in the knowledge base looking for matches
- The rules base is used in the matching process
- Once a match is found, the system suggests the probability of the patient's illness being identified accurately
- The expert system also suggests possible solutions and rememdies to cure the patient or recommendations on what to do next
- The explanation system will give reasons for its diagnosis so that the user can determine the validity of the diagnosis or suggested treatment

Output screen

- The diagnosis can be in the form of text or it may show images of the human anatomy to indicate where the problem may be
- The user can request further information from the expert system to narrow down even further the possible illness and its treatment

Figure 6.12 A typical patient-diagnosis expert system

6.11.4 Using 3-D printers in medicine

Chapter 2 first introduced 3-D printers. Their use in a number of fields is rapidly progressing. One of the most innovative uses is in the field of medicine. The following is just a small insight into the many developments taking place across the world.

Surgical and diagnostic aids

It is possible to print out anatomical parts using 3-D printers. These are used as an aid towards diagnosis and surgical procedures. The patient is scanned using:

- **CT** (**computed tomography** – which involves producing images of the internal parts of the body in a series of thin slices less than 0.1 mm thick)

OR

- **MRI** (**magnetic resonance imaging** – this uses strong magnetic fields and radio waves to produce a series of images of the internal organs in the body).

A 3-D printer can then reproduce a solid object showing the exact internal organs of the patient. The doctor or surgeon can then show the patient exactly what is wrong and then show them what procedures are required. They also help the surgeons in planning surgical procedures since they can see exactly what is required well in advance of the operation.

3-D printing systems enable blood vessels, major arteries, tumours and so on to be part of the diagnostic, pre-surgical aids. This also allows for patient engagement which would be missing from the more traditional consultation methods.

Some 3-D printers produce hard nylon objects which are used in certain pre-surgical planning. If a patient has suffered a bone break, for example, surgeons can physically test and position screws and plates in the '3-D bone nylon image' prior to the surgery taking place. This reduces the chance of any errors when the actual procedure is carried out.

Prosthetics

3-D printers are now being used to print out prosthetics (false arms, hands and legs). Whilst state-of-the-art myoelectric prosthetics cost tens of thousands of dollars, the price for 3-D printing a prosthetic arm or hand can be as little as $100.

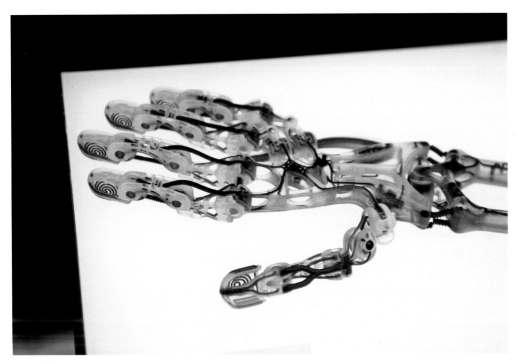

Figure 6.13 This image shows a prosthetic arm produced by a 3-D printer. Whilst the technology may not be cutting-edge, it can be life-changing to an amputee.

There is still much research needed in this field. However, the results to date are very encouraging with many more people from poorer countries now having a chance to replace missing limbs at a fraction of the cost compared to existing methods.

Tissue engineering

Recent advances have allowed the 3-D printing of bio-compatible materials, cells and supporting structures. This has improved the viability of the function of cells within a 3-D printed object. 3-D bio-printing is a very complex process and requires the input from biologists, medical engineers, physicists and other engineers. It has already been used successfully to produce multilayered skin tissue, bone tissue, heart/artery grafts and tracheal splints.

The procedure involves making biological materials by diffusing cells into a bio-compatible scaffold. The bio-printed tissue is then put into an incubator and the cell structure held within the scaffold grows to form actual cellular tissue.

There is still much research to do, but the goal of growing replacement organs, using cells from the actual patient, is getting ever closer thanks to 3-D printing technology.

Design of medical tools and equipment

3-D printers are now being used as part of the product development cycle for medical tools. This allows new medical equipment/tools to be made ready for the market much faster. Traditional methods of producing new equipment/tools are very time consuming and very expensive. 3-D printers create injection-moulding tools which allow several prototypes to be made within a short period of time. Traditional methods require aluminium moulds to be made which is a slow and expensive process. Development time is reduced, on average, by up to 90% and development cost is reduced, on average, by up to 70%. This is important in the field of medicine where it is essential that development time and costs are reduced to a minimum.

6.12 Computers in libraries

Many library systems are now computer-controlled. They usually involve the use of barcodes on the books being borrowed and on the borrower's library card. The following describes a type of computerised library system based on barcodes.

1 Two files will exist containing:
   Book file (this contains a number of records made up of the following fields):

Barcode	Book title	Name of author	Date published	Unique book identifier	Borrower's ID

   Borrower's file (this contains a number of records made up of the following fields):

Borrower's ID	Borrower's name	Borrower's details	Barcode of book borrowed	Unique book identifier	Date due back

2 Thus, when a borrower takes out a book, the barcode is first of all scanned.

- The book details are then found on the book file.
- The system automatically calculates the 'due back' date based on the day the book is taken out.

3 The borrower's library card contains a unique barcode which is then scanned.

- The book file is linked to the borrower's file and both files are updated to indicate which book has been borrowed and when it is due back.
- The date the book is due back is saved in the borrower's file. The system therefore knows when to send out a reminder to the borrower of the book if the return date of the book is exceeded.

4 On a daily basis, the borrower's file is interrogated by the computer to see which books are overdue for return. The sequence of events is summarised below:
- the computer reads a record from the book file
- the corresponding record is read from the borrower's file
- it compares the due date back with the current date
- the borrower details are then found and a letter or email is automatically sent out
- the next record in the book file is then read
- and so on until the whole file has been checked.

Barcodes are not the only way of tracking books borrowed from a library. Some systems use magnetic stripes on the borrower's cards rather than barcodes. The procedure is the same except the card is now passed a magnetic card reader rather than being scanned. The borrower's data and book data are still connected as described above. Some libraries use RFID chips in their books.

6.13 Computers in the retail industry

6.13.1 Automatic stock control system using barcodes

Barcodes now appear on most products sold in shops; they allow quick identification of product details once the barcode has been scanned by a barcode reader. Supermarkets, in particular, use electronic point of sale (EPOS) terminals which incorporate a barcode reader which scans the barcode and retrieves the price of the article and also relays information back to the computer system allowing it to update its files (more of this later).

Figure 6.14 Barcodes are made up of alternating dark and light lines of varying thickness

A number underneath the barcode usually consists of four parts: a country code, manufacturer's code, product code and a check digit. The check digit is a form of validation which is used to make sure no errors occurred during the reading of the barcode.

Barcodes are used in the following applications:

- library book system (see Section 6.12)
- administration systems
- passport/ID cards
- some burglar alarm systems
- equipment checking systems (safety records on maintenance of equipment)
- automatic stock control systems.

The following description is a detailed account of how barcodes are used to automatically control stock levels in a supermarket.

- Barcodes are attached to all items sold by the supermarket.
- Each barcode is associated with a stock file which contains details such as price, stock levels, product description – the barcode will act as the primary key in the file.
- A customer takes their trolley/basket to the EPOS terminal once they have completed their shopping.

- The barcode on each item is scanned at the EPOS.
  - If the barcode can't be read, then the EPOS operator has to key in the number manually.
- The barcode is searched for on the stock file record by record until a match is found.
- Once the barcode has been found, the appropriate record is accessed.
- The price of the item is then found and sent back to the EPOS together with a product description.
- The stock level for the item is found in the record and is reduced by 1 and the new stock level is written back to the file.
  - If the number in stock of the item is less than or equal to the re-order/minimum number in stock, then the computer automatically orders a batch of items from the suppliers (supplier information would be found on another file called the order file or supplier file – the barcode would be the link between the two files).
  - Once goods have been ordered the item is flagged on the file to indicate an order has been placed; this now prevents re-order action being triggered every time this item is scanned until the new stock arrives.
  - When new goods arrive, the barcodes on the cartons will be used to update the stock files; also any flags associated with these goods will be removed so that the stock checks can start to be made again.
- The above procedure is repeated until all the items in the customer's basket/trolley have been scanned.
- When all the items have been scanned, the customer is given an itemised bill showing a list (with prices) of everything they have bought.
- The computer also updates the files containing the daily takings.
- If the customer has a loyalty card, the system will also automatically update their points total.

Some newer supermarkets now allow customers to scan their own items at special checkouts; these basically work the same way as the normal EPOS terminals.

Other retailers use a similar system with only minor differences.

6.13.2 Electronic funds transfer and chip and PIN cards

How electronic funds transfer and chip and PIN cards are used in the retail industry have already been fully described in Section 6.9.

6.13.3 Internet shopping

A discussion on internet shopping, including its advantages and disadvantages, was fully covered in Section 6.9 and won't be repeated here.

Exercise 6o

1 Revisit the earlier sections of this chapter and other parts of the book. Gather together your information and then write an article on the advantages and disadvantages of shopping on the internet compared to shopping on the high street.

Consider aspects such as convenience, costs and security when writing the article.

2 Find out as many areas in the retail industry that use barcodes (including QR codes) and explain why barcodes are used. What other methods exist which could replace barcodes? Why have these other methods not been adopted?

6.14 Recognition systems

6.14.1 MICR, OCR, OMR and RFID

The operation of MICR, OCR, OMR and RFID was discussed in detail in Chapter 2. However, the following additional notes on two uses of OMR are worth studying.

School registers

Newer methods of registering students were mentioned earlier on in this chapter (i.e. use of magnetic stripe cards and biometrics). However, paper-based systems are still used in some schools. These paper-based registers are often scanned in to a computer using OMR. The attendance records are then stored on a central database.

FIRE Academy

Term 1 Week 4 (2016)
Tutor Group: 7AS

Init	Monday am	Monday pm	Tuesday am	Tuesday pm	Wednesday am	Wednesday pm	Thursday am	Thursday pm	Friday am	Friday pm
AA										
RC										
FD										
AE										
BE										
HK										
TL										
SM										
AN										
LN										
AP										
AR										
SW										

The database can be searched or sorted for the data about the attendance of any student.

Multiple-choice question (MCQ) papers

Completed multiple-choice forms are scanned in using OMR. The forms have timing marks down one side – these timing marks pass under the first column sensor of the scanner. These marks indicate the position of each question on the paper. Using OMR software, a template is created to map out the X–Y coordinates of each lozenge (area which is filled in by pencil/ink or left blank) – a value is then assigned to each lozenge. As each MCQ is scanned, a light passes through the scanner which picks up the position of each lozenge which has been filled in by pencil/ink. The position of the filled in lozenges is compared to the corresponding coordinates on the 'answer sheet template'. If the position matches to the X–Y coordinates, then the answer is recorded as being correct. The scanned results are exported to a database or spreadsheet.

If more than one lozenge is filled in for each question, then the OMR software simply discards that result. Marking MCQ sheets using OMR is much quicker and more accurate than doing the task manually. Because the results are automatically exported to a database or spreadsheet, it is much easier to analyse the results.

6.14.2 Automatic Number Plate Recognition (ANPR) System

Automatic number plate recognition (ANPR) systems are used to read the number plates on cars in a number of applications.

In the example that follows, we will describe how ANPR is used in a car park to enable entry and exit to be automatically controlled by a computer system.

Step 1

A sensor detects a vehicle and sends a signal to a microprocessor to instruct a camera to capture an image of the front of the vehicle (often an infrared camera is used to give a clearer image and for use at night).

Step 2

  i An algorithm is used to locate and isolate the number plate from the image taken by the camera. This algorithm also takes into account the size of the number plate and any damage or orientation.   `1 A B C 2 3 4`

  ii The brightness and contrast of the number plate is first adjusted (this ensures that the characters can be clearly read).   `1 A B C 2 3 4`
      Each character on the number plate is then segmented   `1 A B C 2 3 4`

  iii Each character is then recognised using optical character recognition (OCR) software. The characters are converted into a string of editable text by the software.

  iv This text string is then stored on a database.

Step 3

Once all of this has happened, the car park barrier is raised and the motorist is issued with a ticket. The ticket shows the date and time of entering the car park.

Step 4

When the motorist returns to the car park, they insert their ticket into a machine which calculates the car park charges. The payment is registered on the database.

The motorist then drives to the exit barrier and the ANPR system again reads the number plate and checks its database. If the number plate is recognised (and payment has been made), the exit barrier is raised.

> **Exercise 6p**
>
> Do some research to find out other applications of ANPR.
>
> Write down the advantages and disadvantages of ANPR for each application that you find.

6.15 Monitoring and tracking systems

6.15.1 Monitoring/tracking a member of the public

There are a number of reasons why a person may need to be tracked:

- the person may be an offender who is released from prison on the understanding that their whereabouts is known at all times
- an elderly person may need to be tracked to ensure their safety
- it may be necessary to track somebody taking part in a marathon to determine their position and their time to complete the race.

Other applications will exist.

An ankle monitor makes use of RFID technology by inserting a microchip into the device which is strapped to the ankle.

It sends out (at timed intervals) radio frequency signals. These signals contain the person's location and other data. They are tamper-proof devices and automatically alert the authorities if an attempt is made to remove the monitor from the ankle.

Figure 6.15 An ankle monitor

The monitor sends out RF signals which are picked up by a device in the person's home. This unit uses either landline or mobile phone networks to relay the information back to a computer in a control room. If the person isn't at home at an agreed time, an alert is sent to the control room. GPS (see next section) monitoring is also used so that the person can be tracked outside their home. This allows the exact location of the person to be known at all times. The GPS system works by sending signals to a mobile phone which the person must carry with them at all times. CCTV cameras are also used to monitor people in streets and shopping malls in case of crime or any suspect activity.

6.15.2 Cookies

Please refer to Chapter 8 for notes on how cookies are used to keep track of a person's buying habits when using the internet.

6.15.3 Key logging

Key-logging software is covered in Chapter 8. This software is used to monitor each key press on a user's computer. The key presses are sent back to the person who installed the software on the user's computer.

6.15.4 Employee call monitors

Employee call monitoring allows managers to listen in to employees' telephone calls for the following reasons:

- to improve the employees performance (e.g. at a call centre)
- allows the manager/supervisor to join in a call where necessary
- can be used as a training tool
- it allows a company who are concerned about security to monitor all calls
- if the workforce move around, it can be used to make sure they correctly represent the company whilst out of the office.

There are three types of call monitoring:

1 **monitor**: this allows the manager/supervisor to listen in on calls (the line is muted so that neither the employee or the other person being called is aware of their presence)
2 **whisper**: this allows the manager to speak to employees to help them with a call (only the employee can hear the manager/supervisor's voice
3 **barge**: this allows the manager/supervisor to be heard by both the employee and the other person in the call).

6.16 Satellite systems

6.16.1 Global positioning satellite (GPS) systems and satellite navigation

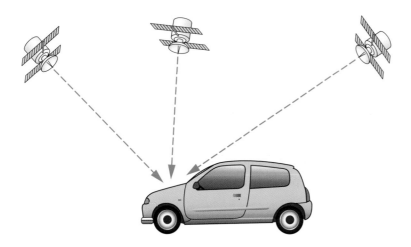

Global positioning satellite (GPS) systems are used to determine the exact location of a number of modes of transport (e.g. airplanes, cars, ships, etc.). Cars usually refer to GPS as **satellite navigation systems** (i.e. satnav).

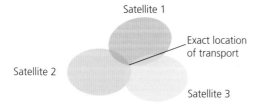

Satellites surrounding the Earth transmit signals to the surface. Computers installed in the mode of transport receive and interpret these signals. Knowing their position on the Earth depends on very accurate timing (atomic clocks are used in the satellites which are accurate to within a fraction of a second per day). Each satellite transmits data indicating its position and time. The computer on board the mode of transport calculates its exact position based on the information from at least three satellites.

In cars, the onboard computer contains stored road maps. With these satnav systems, the car's exact location, based on satellite positioning, can be shown on the map and the driver can also be given verbal instructions such as: 'After 100 metres, take the next left turn onto the A1234'. A screen on the satnav device will also show the car's position in relation to the road network.

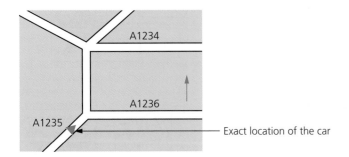
Exact location of the car

Advantages

- The driver doesn't have to consult paper maps, so it is far safer.
- It removes errors (can warn drivers about one way streets, street closures, etc.).
- The system can warn the driver about the location of speed cameras (again aiding safety).
- The system can estimate the time of arrival.
- It is also possible to program in the fastest route, route to avoid towns, etc.
- The system can also give useful information such as location of petrol stations.

Disadvantages

- If the maps are not kept up to date, they can give incorrect instructions.
- Unless the system is sophisticated, road closures, due to accidents or road works, can cause problems.
- Loss of satellite signals can cause problems.
- If an incorrect start point or end point is keyed in the system will give incorrect information.

6.16.2 Geographic information system (GIS)

Geographic information system (GIS) is a computer system that allows us to map, model, query and analyse large amounts of data according to their location.

GIS allows users to create interactive queries, analyse spatial information (this refers to how objects fit together in space) or edit map data. The technology combines maps with computer graphics and databases.

Essentially GIS enables the following:

- amalgamation of information into easily understood maps
- performance of complex analytical calculations and then presentation of the results in the form of maps, tables or graphics (or a combination of all three)
- geographers, scientists and engineers are able to see the data in several different ways in order to see patterns and relationships.

The following example shows how these **layering** techniques are used to produce a visually effective answer to a query made in the GIS system.

Carrying out queries on GIS systems (in a method similar to internet searches) will produce the data which matches the query. The data will be displayed in the form of a diagram, map or set of tables. By zooming into the map, it is possible to find finer details about the layering data used.

Uses

- Emergency services use GIS to send the closest emergency personnel to a location.
- Biologists and environmentalists use GIS to protect animal life and plants in certain vulnerable areas (which meet a certain criteria after carrying out a search on the database).
- Teachers can use GIS in their geography, science or engineering lessons.

6.16.3 Media communication systems

Communication media refers to methods of delivering and receiving data/information using telecommunications.

There are many media used to send and receive information (e.g. fibreoptics, copper cable and Wi-Fi); we will concentrate on the global communication method which makes use of satellites.

Satellites contain antennas, transponders (to allow receiving and sending of data), solar panels (for power from the Sun) and propulsion (to ensure the satellite is in the correct orbit at all times).

Signals are converted to analogue (if necessary) and then beamed to the satellite from a satellite dish on Earth. The signals are delivered by carrier waves which consist of radio waves. Each signal has its own frequency and bandwidth (the larger the bandwidth the more data can be transmitted).

Once the data reaches the satellite it is then resent to Earth. The satellite usually 'boosts' the signal before sending it back to Earth. Often the frequency is changed to prevent the signal received being confused with the signal sent.

The satellite system is used to transmit data from one part of the planet to another. Due to the often great distances, cables would be too costly and there is also the problem of signal deterioration over long distances.

Satellites systems are used to transmit television, telephone and internet data around the world.

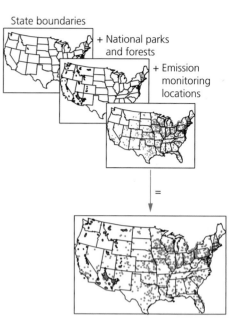

Figure 6.16 Layering state boundaries with national parks and emission monitoring stations produces the final map shown

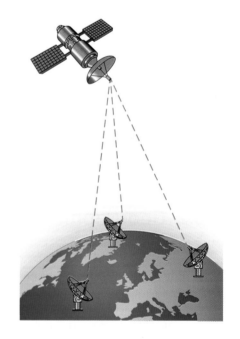

7 Systems life cycle

In this chapter you will learn about:

● systems analysis, including:
  • analysis stage
  • design stage
  • development and testing stage
  • implementation stage
  • documentation
  • evaluation stage.

A systems analysis team is often brought in to review an existing system and suggest a number of improvements. The existing method used may be either a manual, paper-based system, or, more usually, it could already be a computer-based operation that is no longer regarded as adequate for the task.

There are many stages in systems analysis, which are covered in Sections 7.1 to 7.6.

The main stages in the systems life cycle can be summarised as shown in Figure 7.1.

7.1 Analysis

The basic steps in the **analysis** stage can be summarised as shown in Figure 7.2.

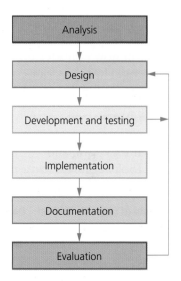

Figure 7.1 The stages in the systems life cycle

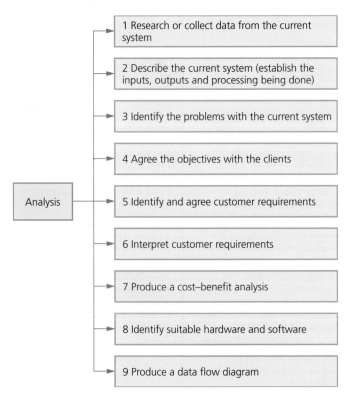

Figure 7.2 Analysis stages

Stages 2 to 8 in Figure 7.3 are sometimes referred to as the **feasibility study** and this can be further broken down as follows:

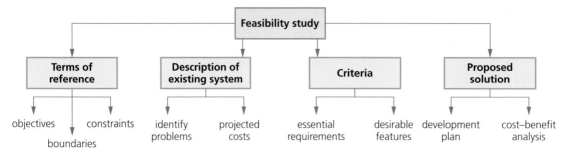

Figure 7.3 Feasibility study stages

We will now consider the first item in the analysis stage – **researching an existing system**. There are four common methods used in fact finding, which have been summarised in Table 7.1 below. The methods are:

- **observation**
- **questionnaires**
- **interviews**, and
- **looking at existing paperwork**.

Table 7.1 Methods of research

Name of research method	Description of research method	Advantages of method	Disadvantages of method
Observation	This method involves watching personnel using the existing system to find out exactly how it works	• the analyst obtains reliable data • it is possible to possible to get an overall view of the system • a relatively inexpensive method	• people are generally uncomfortable being watched and may work in a different way • if workers perform tasks that contravene standard procedures, they may not do this while being watched
Questionnaires	This method involves distributing questionnaires to the workforce, clients or system users to find out their views of the existing system and to find out how some of the key tasks are carried out	• the questions can be answered quite quickly • it is a relatively inexpensive method • individuals can remain anonymous if they want • this method allows quick analysis of the data	• the number of returned questionnaires is often low • the questions are rather inflexible since they have to be generic • there is no immediate way to clarify a vague or incomplete answer to a question
Interviews	This method involves a one-to-one question-and-answer session between the analyst and the employee/customer. It is a good method if the analyst wants to probe deeply into one specific aspect of the existing system	• it gives the opportunity to motivate the interviewee into giving open and honest answers to the analyst's questions • the method allows the analyst to probe for more feedback from the interviewee (it is easier to extend a question) • it is possible to modify questions as the interview proceeds and ask questions specific to the interviewee	• it can be a rather time-consuming exercise • it is relatively expensive (use of analyst's time) • the interviewee can't remain anonymous with this method
Looking at existing paperwork	This method allows the analyst to see how the paper files are kept, look at operating instructions and training manuals, check the accounts, etc. It allows the analyst to get some idea of the scale of the problem, memory size requirements, type of input/output devices needed, etc.	• this method allows information to be obtained which wasn't possible by any of the other methods • analysts can see for themselves how the paper system operates	• it can be a very time-consuming exercise • because of the analyst's time needed, it is a relatively expensive method to use

In Figure 7.2, one of the stages mentioned was the production of a **data flow diagram (DFD)**. DFDs help the analyst by showing the data flows, input and output requirements, processing and the types of data storage needed.

Figure 7.4 shows a type of DFD. The example given covers reserving a seat on a flight – it shows how the data flows from stage to stage, the inputs and outputs, any processing done, and storage (booking system – most likely to be a database stored on a hard disk drive).

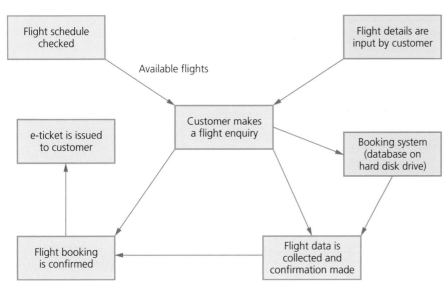

Figure 7.4 Data flow diagram (booking a flight)

Exercise 7a

The data flow diagram shown in Figure 7.4 is one example of the symbols that can be used. Research alternative methods of showing DFDs, and then redo Exercise 6l (page 110) on booking a flight using the alternative DFD symbols you have found.

DFDs in general are used to describe:

- the need to identify inputs, outputs and processing of the current system
- the need to identify problems with the current system
- the need to identify the user and information requirements for the new system
- system specifications:
  - identify and justify suitable hardware for the new system
  - identify and justify new software for the new system.

7.2 Design

Once the analysis has taken place and the systems analyst has some idea of the scale of the problem and what needs to be done, the next stage is to **design** the key parts of the recommended system. A list of tasks is summarised in Figure 7.5, but it is by no means exhaustive.

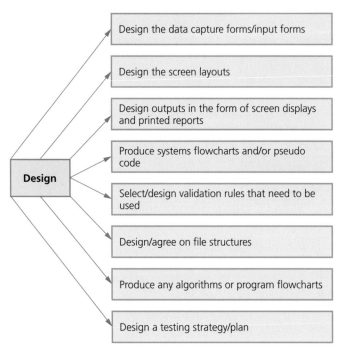

Figure 7.5 Design stage tasks

We will now consider in more depth some of these tasks listed in the design stage.

7.2.1 Data capture forms

These forms allow the data to be input into the system. They will be either paper-based or electronic-based depending on the application.

Paper-based forms need to:

- have a heading to make the purpose of the form clear
- make it clear to the person filling in the form where they must place their answers
- make use of text boxes, which will limit the amount of information collected
- make use of character boxes for data such as surnames, telephone numbers, and so on (each box allows one character only)
- make use of printed text boxes to allow for easy input of items such as date of birth
- make use of tick boxes to make choices easier (such as sex – male or female)
- make sure there is sufficient space to write answers
- use clear fonts and clear text colours to ensure the form is easy to read.

Figure 7.6 shows a typical example, which allows data about a car for sale to be manually completed for later input into a computer database.

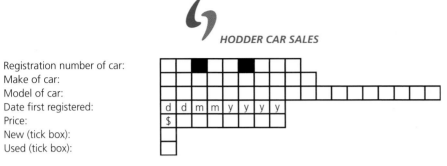

Figure 7.6 Paper-based data capture form

A computer-based data capture form is slightly different. These often have the following features:

- use of text boxes to capture key data clearly
- use of on-screen help when completing the form
- use of drop-down/combo boxes where there are limited choices
- use of radio buttons and tick boxes, requiring a single click of a mouse to select
- automatic validation of data as it is entered
- control buttons (such as next form, clear entry, save, etc.)
- double entry boxes (with verification rules) to check correctness of key data (for example, when keying in an email address).

In the car sales example shown above, the following differences could be used with a computer-based data capture form:

- **registration number**: same as paper-based form
- **make of car**: make use of a drop-down box as there is a limited number of manufacturers
- **model of car**: same as paper-based form
- **date first registered**: use of drop-down boxes for day, month and year
- **price**: use boxes as shown but include a validation check
- **new or used**: use of tick box or radio button to indicate option
- **other features**: a back and forward button (to complete details of all cars), and a save button when form is complete for each car.

> ## Exercise 7b
> Design a computer-based data capture form using the fields given above. Remember that it has to be completed online, so it should include radio buttons, drop-down boxes and so on. It should look a little different to the paper-based form shown in Figure 7.6.

7.2.2 Screen displays and printed reports

The output from any system needs careful consideration since this is part of any user interface and is also the result of some form of processing. Screen outputs should be designed:

- to make sure the size of all the output fields is correct
- so that any instructions/descriptions are clear
- so that the full screen is utilised (avoiding large areas of 'nothing')
- so that colours and fonts (size and type) make the output clear.

Figure 7.7 Screen output example

If the output is on paper then consideration must also be given to the type of output. Items such as headers and footers, fitting the page correctly, whether it should be in colour, and so on, all have to be carefully planned.

Reports (often the output from a database search) should clearly show all the fields that were included in the search criteria – output is usually in the form of a table (the example in Figure 7.8 outputs a list of all sales managers aged over 40).

Employees

Last Name	First Names	Job Title	Business Phone	Address
Pitt	Michael	Sales Manager	001 234 1235	2nd Avenue
Hawkin	Jason	Sales Manager	001 235 1245	4th Avenue
Amin	Manjit	Sales Manager	001 222 3456	9th Avenue
Clark	Katie	Sales Manager	001 234 1119	2nd Avenue
Fawkler	Jemima	Sales Manager	001 299 8745	11th Avenue

Figure 7.8 Report example

7.2.3 System flowcharts

System flowcharts are used to show how data flows through a system and also how decisions are made. They make use of special symbols that represent input/output, processing, decisions and data storage.

Systems analysts use these charts to give an overall view of the proposed system. They don't form the basis of a flowchart from which software can be written but they do show how the processes are carried out and where various hardware devices are used in the system. A sample system flowchart is shown in Figure 7.9 (this is just part of an overall system flowchart showing the flight booking system again).

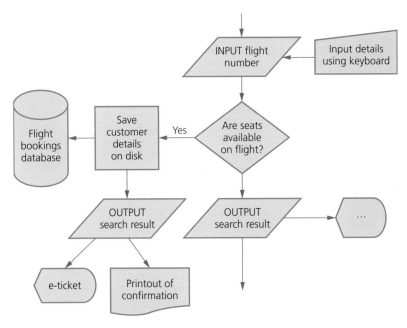

Figure 7.9 Sample system flowchart

7.2.4 Verification

Verification is a way of preventing errors when data is copied from one medium to another (for example, from paper to disk/CD). There are two common ways that verification checks are carried out.

- **Double entry**: in this method, data is entered **twice**, using two people, and is then compared (either after data entry or during the data-entry process).
- **Visual check**: this is the checking for errors by the person who is entering the data; they compare the entered data with the original document (i.e., what is on the screen is compared to the data on the original paper documents – note that this is **not** the same as proofreading).

7.2.5 Validation

Validation is a process where data is checked to see if it satisfies certain criteria when input into a computer; for example, to see if the data falls within accepted boundaries. A number of validation techniques exist; Table 7.2 highlights some of the more common checks used when writing computer software.

Table 7.2 Validation checks

Validation check	Description	Example(s) and comments
Range check	checks whether data is within given/ acceptable values	e.g. to check if a person's age is > 0 but is also < 150
Look-up check	this checks whether the data entered exists and is stored in a table of data	e.g. check is 'senior manager' exists as on option in the query such as: 'PLEASE ENTER YOUR JOB TITLE'
Length check	checks if the input data contains the required number of characters	e.g. if a field needs six digits then inputting a five-digit or seven-digit number, for example, should cause an error message
Character/type check	checks that the input data doesn't contain invalid characters	e.g. a person's name shouldn't contain any numbers, but a person's height should only contain digits

⇨ continued…

Format/picture check	checks that data is in a specific format	e.g. date should be in the form dd/mm/yyyy e.g. xnnnn which shows a person's identification (a single letter followed by five digits)
Presence check	checks if data is actually present and hasn't been missed out	e.g. in an electronic form a person's telephone number may be a required field so, if no data is entered, this should give rise to an error message
Consistency check	checks if fields correspond (tie up) with each other	e.g. if 'Mr' has been typed into a field called 'TITLE' then the 'GENDER' field must contain either 'M' or 'Male'
Check digit	this is an extra digit added to a number which is calculated from the digits (refer to Sections 6.12 and 6.13)	check digits can identify three types of error: • if two digits have been transposed during input e.g., 13597 instead of 13579 • an incorrect digit entered twice, e.g., 13559 in instead of 13579 • a digit missed out altogether, e.g., 1359 instead of 13579

7.2.6 File structures

Designing and agreeing file structures is an important part of the design stage. The fields used in the files need to take the following into account:

- field length
- field name (suitable names should be chosen)
- data type.

A **data dictionary** is used to show suitable field names. An example of a data dictionary is given in Table 7.3.

Table 7.3 Example of a data dictionary

Field name	Field length	Field type	Suitable validation check
product_code	8	alphanumeric	length check
manufacture_year	4	numeric	range check
product_name	20	alphanumeric	none
location_of_stock	4	numeric	character check
colour	2	alphanumeric	look-up check

7.2.7 Design and testing strategy/plan

When producing the software for the new system, it is very important to test it thoroughly in order to:

- make sure it meets the agreed client requirements
- remove any bugs/errors from the system
- make sure it produces the required output for data where the correct output is already known
- check that the software doesn't crash under certain conditions.

To do this, it is necessary to produce a testing strategy or plan to ensure all the possible scenarios have been tested so that the criteria have been met. Refer to Section 7.3.2 for more information on this topic.

7.3 Development and testing

7.3.1 Development

Once the design stage is completed, it is then necessary to create the system and test it fully. This section considers some of the development stages and testing strategies that are often adopted by systems analysts.

- If the system contains files (for example, a database) then the file structure would need to be finalised at this stage (e.g. what type of data is being stored in each field, length of each field, decide on which field will be the key field, how will the data files be linked, etc.). Once the file structure has been determined it is then created and tested fully to make sure it is robust when the system actually goes live.

- Since it is important that the correct data is stored in files (etc.) there are certain techniques that need to be adopted to make sure the data populating the files/database is at least of the right type and that it conforms to certain rules. Validation routines and verification methods are used to ensure this happens. Again, these routines have to be fully tested to ensure they do trap unwanted data but also to make sure that any data transferred from a paper-based system to an electronic system has been done accurately.

- Obviously any system being developed will have some form of user interface. The types of hardware have already been considered; how these are used to actually interface with the final system now needs to be identified. For example, how the screens (and any other input devices) will be used to collect the data and the way the output will be presented. If specialist hardware is needed (for example, for people with disabilities) then it will be necessary to finalise how these devices are used with the system when it is implemented. This will be followed by thorough testing to ensure that the user screens are user-friendly and that the correct output is associated with the inputs to the system.

7.3.2 Testing strategies

Software is often developed in modular form. This method allows the software to be broken down into smaller parts (known as modules). Each part is developed separately by a programmer (or team of programmers) and is then tested to see if it functions correctly. Any problems resulting from the testing require the module to be modified and then tested again.

Once the development of each module is completed, the whole system needs to be tested (i.e., all modules functioning together). Even though each module may work satisfactorily, when they are all put together there may be data clashes or incompatibility, memory issues, etc.

All of this may lead to a need to improve the input and output methods, file/database structures, validation and verification methods, etc., and then test everything fully again. It is a very time-consuming process but it has to be as perfect as possible before the system goes live.

Testing will use many different types of test data, which will fall into one of

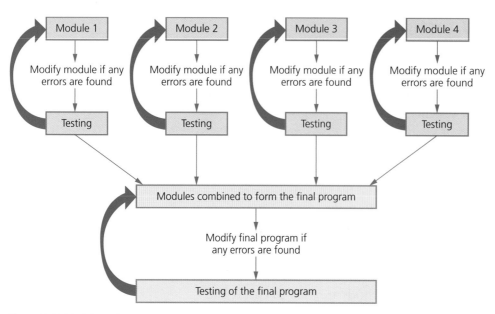

Figure 7.10 Module testing

four categories:

- normal
- abnormal
- extreme
- live.

But we are only going to consider the first three types at this stage.

Let us suppose that one of the fields in a database is the date, which must be in the form dd/mm/yyyy (and also has to be numeric):

- **normal**: this is data that is acceptable/reasonable and has an expected (known) outcome; for example, the month can be *any* whole number in the range 1 to 12
- **extreme**: this is data at the **limits** of acceptability; for example, the extreme values of month can be either 1 **or** 12
- **abnormal**: this is data **outside the limits** of acceptability, or the wrong type of data, and should be rejected or cause an error message; for example, all the following values are not allowed as inputs for the month:
  - negative numbers (e.g., –1, –15, etc.)
  - any value greater than 12 (e.g., 32, 45, etc.)
  - letters or other non-numeric data (e.g., July, etc.)
  - non-integer values (e.g., 3.5, 10.75, etc.).

Once a system has been fully tested, it is then tested with **live data** – this is data

---

Exercise 7c

Use the example of a date in the format dd/mm/yyyy when answering these three questions.

1 Consider the following eight pieces of data and decide whether each data item is normal, extreme or abnormal (tick the appropriate box) for:
  a day (dd)
  b month (mm)
  c year (yyyy).

Data item	Normal	Extreme	Abnormal
15			
12			
7			
1.6			
0			
1			
March			
10			

2 Describe what validation routines could be used to check the date if it was input on the screen as follows:

Day: ☐

Month: ☐

Year: ☐

Describe how it would be possible to avoid errors altogether when inputting the date in the form shown above.

3 Write test data for the following fields in a database (the data should try to cover all possible types of data). The database will store the following information:
- name of resort
- average daily temperature
- number of hours of sunshine per day.

Describe the validation routines that should be written into the database interface to check the above inputs.

with known outcomes. Live data is entered into the new system and the results compared with those produced from the existing system. Further modifications to the software may be needed following this testing procedure.

An example of a results comparison table is shown in Table 7.4.

Table 7.4 Live data comparison table

Live data	Expected result	Actual result	Any actions
January	error message	data was accepted	validation routines on month element need to be altered
0	message output: 'a zero value is not allowed'	computer software crashed	software needs an error trap, such as: IF INPUT = 0 THEN OUTPUT 'no zeros allowed'

7.4 Implementation

Once the system is fully tested, the next stage is to fully implement it. Some of the stages in this process are shown in Figure 7.11.

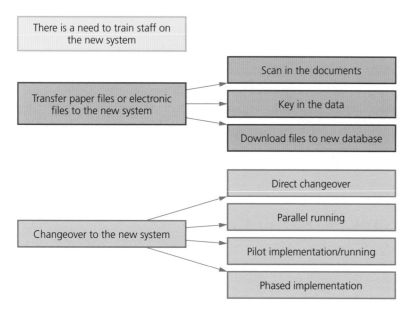

Figure 7.11 The implementation stage

We will now consider **changeover** to the new system in more depth. As indicated above, there are four common methods used for changing over from the old system to the new system. Each one has advantages and disadvantages that need to be weighed up before the most appropriate method is chosen for a particular application.

Table 7.5 Methods of changeover

Implementation method	Design of implementation method	Advantages and disadvantages of the method
Direct	With this method the old system is stopped overnight and the new system introduced immediately	• this method can be disastrous if the new system fails since the old system is no longer available • the benefits are immediate • costs are reduced (since only one system used there is no need to pay for two sets of staff) • less likelihood of a malfunction since the new system will have been fully tested
Parallel	With this method, the old and new systems are run side by side for a time before the new system takes over altogether	• if this new system fails, the old system is still available as a backup • it is possible to gradually train staff • it is more expensive than *direct* since extra staff are needed to run both systems together • it's also more time consuming than *direct* since data needs to be entered into two systems
Pilot	With this method, the new system is introduced into one branch or office of the company and its performance assessed before being introduced elsewhere in the company	• if the new system fails, only one part is affected; the remainder is unaffected • it is possible to train staff in one area only, which is much faster and less costly than *parallel* • the costs are also less than *parallel* since only one part of the system is being used in the pilot warehouse
Phased	With this method, only part of the new system is introduced and, only when it proves to work satisfactorily, is the next part introduced, and so on, until the old system is fully replaced	• if the latest part fails, it is only necessary to go back in the system to the point of failure; hence failure isn't disastrous • more expensive than *direct* since it is necessary to evaluate each phase before moving to the next stage • very time consuming since each part needs to be fully evaluated before making any further changes to the system • it is possible to ensure the system works properly before expanding

Table 7.6 compares the costs, input requirements and risk of failure for all four changeover methods.

Table 7.6 Impact of changeover methods

Changeover method	Relative costs of each method	Input needed by the user	Input needed by systems team	Impact of failure of method
Parallel	High	High	Low	Low
Pilot	Medium	Low	Medium	Low
Phased	Medium	Medium	Medium	Medium
Direct	Low	Medium	Low*	High

*Low if successful, otherwise very high because of amount of input needed.

7.5 Documentation

Once the new system is fully developed, a considerable amount of documentation also needs to be produced for:

1 the end-user
2 people who may need to modify or develop the system further at some later stage.

There is some overlap between the two types of documentation, but the basic requirements are shown below.

7.5.1 User documentation

User documentation is designed to help users to learn how to use the software or system. This can consist of any of the following:

- how to load/install/run the software
- how to save files
- how to do a search
- how to sort data
- how to do print outs
- how to add, delete or amend records
- the purpose of the system/program/software package
- limitations of the system
- screen layouts (input format)
- print layouts (output format)
- hardware requirements
- software requirements
- sample runs (with results and actual test data used)
- error handling/meaning of errors
- troubleshooting guide/help lines/FAQs
- how to log in/log out
- tutorials
- error messages/meaning of error messages
- glossary of terms.

7.5.2 Technical documentation

Technical documentation is designed to help programmers/analysts to make improvements to the system or to repair/maintain the system. This can consist of any of the following:

- program listing/coding
- programming language used
- program flowcharts/algorithms
- systems flowcharts
- purpose of the system/program/software
- limitations of the system
- input formats
- hardware requirements
- software requirements
- minimum memory requirements
- known 'bugs' in the system
- list of variables used (and their meaning/description)
- file structures
- sample runs (with results and actual test data used)
- output formats
- validation rules
- meaning of error messages.

7.6 Evaluation

Once a system is up and running it is necessary to do some **evaluation** and carry out any maintenance if necessary. The following is a list of some of the things considered when evaluating how well the new system has worked; this can ultimately lead to a redesign of part of the system if there is strong evidence to suggest that changes need be made (refer back to Figure 7.1 in the introduction):

- compare the final solution with the original task
- identify any limitations of the system
- identify any necessary improvements that need to be made
- evaluate the user's responses to using the new system
- compare test results from the new system with results from the old system
- compare performance of the new system with performance of the old system
- observe users performing set tasks (compare old with new)
- measure the time taken to complete tasks (compare old with new)
- interview users to gather responses about how well the new system works
- give out questionnaires to gather responses about the ease of use of the new system.

Some results from the evaluation may lead to two things happening:

- update of hardware because:
  - of feedback from end-users
  - new hardware comes on the market, necessitating change
  - changes within the company require new devices to be added or updated
- update of software because:
  - of feedback from end-users
  - changes to the company structure or how the company works that may require modifications to the software
  - changes in legislation that may require modifications to the software.

8 Safety and security

In this chapter you will learn about:

- safety and security when using computers
- data security
- firewalls
- security protocols (SSL and TLS)
- encryption
- authentication.

This chapter covers safety and security issues when using computers in the office or at home. As the use of computers continues to expand, the health risks and security risks continue to increase. Many of these risks are associated with the internet which, by its very nature, poses a great risk to younger people unless they are vigilant at all times. But large businesses are also at risk from hackers, pharming attacks and viruses, for example. Many of the precautions people and business can take are common sense but, equally, it also requires additional knowledge to know how to protect yourself from these external attacks, which can come from anywhere in the world.

8.1 Physical security

The use of computers in the home and business world has increased dramatically over the last few years. This increase brings its own physical dangers, which can cause harm to users unless they take some very sensible precautions.

8.1.1 Health aspects

Health and safety regulations advise that all computer systems have at least tiltable and anti-glare screens, adjustable chairs and foot supports, suitable lighting and uncluttered work stations, and recommend frequent breaks and frequent eye tests.

Table 8.1 lists a number of health risks as well as giving some idea of how each risk can be removed or minimised.

Table 8.1 Health risks

Health risk	Ways of eliminating or minimising risk
Back and neck problems/strain caused by sitting in front of a computer screen for long periods in the same position)	• use fully adjustable chairs to give the correct posture • use foot rests to reduce posture problems • use screens than can be tilted to ensure the neck is at the correct angle
Repetitive strain injury (RSI) – damage to fingers and wrists caused by continuous use of a keyboard or repetitive clicking of mouse buttons, for example	• ensure correct posture is maintained (i.e., correct angle of arms to the keyboard and mouse, for example) • make proper use of a wrist rest when using a mouse or a keyboard • take regular breaks (and do some exercise) • make use of ergonomic keyboards • use voice-activated software if the user is prone to problems when using a mouse and keyboard
Eyestrain caused by staring at a computer screen too long or having incorrect lighting in the room	• ensure that there is no screen flicker as this can lead to eye problems • change to LCD screens where flicker is less of a problem than with CRT screens • take regular breaks (and try focusing on a point that is some distance away) • make use of anti-glare screens if lighting in the room is incorrect; or use window blinds to reduce sunlight reflecting from the screen • users should have their eyes tested on a regular basis (middle vision glasses should be prescribed if the user has a persistent problem such as eye strain, dry eyes, headaches, etc.)

⇨ continued…

Headaches caused by incorrect lighting, screen reflections, flickering screens, etc.	• use an anti-glare screen or use window blinds to cut out reflections (incorrect lighting can cause squinting and lead to headaches) • take regular breaks (and do some exercise) • have your eyes tested regularly and use middle vision glasses if necessary
Ozone irritation caused by laser printers in an office area (dry skin, respiratory problems, etc.)	• proper ventilation should exist to remove the ozone gas as quickly as possible • laser printers should be housed in a designated printer room • change to other types of printer if necessary (e.g., inkjet printers)

8.1.2 Safety aspects

Safety is a different issue to health; health is more generally how to stop people becoming ill or being affected by daily contact with computers. Safety is more concerned with dangers that could lead to serious injury or even loss of life. Some of the more common examples of **safety risks**, together with possible solutions, are listed in Table 8.2.

Table 8.2 Safety risks

Safety risk	Ways of eliminating or minimising risk
Electrocution	• use an RCB (residual current breaker) • check insulation on wires regularly • don't allow drinks near computers • check equipment on a regular basis
Trailing wires (trip hazard)	• use cable ducts to make the wires safe • cover wires and/or have them neatly tucked away (under desks, etc.) • use wireless connections wherever possible, thus eliminating cables altogether
Heavy equipment falling and causing injury	• use strong desks and tables to support heavy hardware • use large desks and tables so that hardware isn't too close to the edge where it can fall off
Fire risk	• have a fully tested CO_2/dry fire extinguisher nearby (not water extinguishers) • don't cover equipment vents (causing equipment to overheat) • make sure that the electrics used in the hardware is fully maintained (i.e. portable appliance testing) • ensure good ventilation in the room (again to stop overheating of hardware) • don't overload sockets with too many items • change to low-voltage hardware wherever possible (e.g., replace CRT monitors with LCD monitors)

In spite of all the above ways of eliminating or reducing the health and safety risks, the individual still has an important role to play. In the home, the user needs to have a good health and safety strategy, and to carry out the following checks on a regular basis:

- check the state of the wires/cables and plugs (check whether any wires/cables are damaged, make sure there are no lose wires in the plugs and make sure the plug isn't broken or cracked)
- make sure that drinks (such as tea or coffee) are well away from the computer
- fix wires along walls and behind desks wherever possible to remove the risk of wires coming into contact with people
- don't cover computers with paper or fabric (e.g., towels or sheets) since these can either block ventilation holes (causing computers to overheat) or these materials could catch fire
- don't plug too many devices into an electric outlet socket – overloading a socket can cause a fire

- make sure you exercise every hour or so to prevent the health risks outlined Table 8.1 from becoming a real issue
- carry out an 'ergonomic assessment' on your work station (there are numerous online questionnaires that will enable you to check whether your work station is set up properly for your own health and safety); it may require you to buy new chairs or computer hardware to minimise the impact of sitting in front of screens or typing for long periods at a time.

8.2 E-safety

First of all, what is the definition of e-safety? It refers to safety when using the internet, i.e. keeping personal data safe and applies to any of the following devices:

- mobile phone
- computer or tablet
- games console
- wireless technology.

Personal data refers to any data concerning a living person who can be identified either from the data itself or from the data in conjunction with other information (for example, 'Peter Smith has blue hair and lives at 40 Green Street' would very clearly identify this individual).

Examples of personal data include:

- name
- address
- date of birth
- medical history
- banking details.

Some personal data is often referred to as sensitive personal data and includes:

- ethnic origin
- political views
- religion
- sexual orientation
- criminal activity.

> ### Exercise 8a
> Do some research and find out why it is important that personal data is kept confidential. Present your notes as an article to discuss with the rest of the class.

E-safety also refers to the benefits, risks and responsibilities when using ICT. The following list is by no means exhaustive but gives some idea of the e-safety issues that can be encountered by users of ICT hardware:

- don't give out **any** personal information to people who are unknown to you; this is especially true online where it isn't possible to physically meet people so that their motives can be fully assessed. Remember that anyone can say anything they want online and it is very difficult to determine whether they are genuine or not
- don't send people photos of yourself – either online or via a mobile phone – unless the person is known to you (it is very easy for somebody to pass

these photos on or even pretend to be you for a number of reasons); this is a particularly large risk on social networking sites

- always maintain your **privacy settings** on whatever device is being used online or during communications. Privacy settings allow the user to control which cookies are stored on their computer or they enable the user to decide who can view certain information about them on, for example, a social networking site

- when accessing the internet make sure the websites being visited can be trusted (two common ways of checking this is to look for http**s** or the padlock sign 🔒); when using search engines, always make sure the device settings are set to 'safe search' and the highest possible level of security is used

- only use websites recommended by teachers and only use a learner-friendly search engine

- only open emails from known sources. It is always a good idea to make sure your internet service provider (ISP) has an effective email filtering feature to ensure unknown emails are placed in the **spam** box

- only email people you know. Think carefully before opening any email and never include the school's name or photos of a student wearing a school uniform in any email

- it is extremely important to be vigilant when using social networking sites, instant messaging or chat rooms:
  - block or report anybody who acts suspiciously or who uses inappropriate language
  - be very careful with the language used in chat rooms
  - always use a nickname and *never* your real name
  - keep private and personal data secret
  - don't enter private chat rooms – stay public (the danger signs in a private chat are: somebody sounds too good to be true, they ask you to go to instant messaging and then to emails, they request your telephone number and then finally suggest that you meet)
  - never arrange to meet anyone for the first time on your own
  - always tell an adult first and meet the person in a public place
  - avoid the misuse of images
  - always use appropriate language
  - always respect people's confidentiality.

It is also important to be careful when using online gaming since this carries its own risks. Many users think that all players are like-minded and, thus, there are no real risks associated with this type of communication. Some of the known risks reported over the years include:

- violence in the game itself, which can lead to violent behaviour in reality
- predators (people who prey on others who they see as vulnerable)
- cyber bullying (the use of electronic communication to bully a person, typically by sending messages of an intimidating or threatening nature)
- use of webcams (the risks here are obvious)
- voice-masking technology (to disguise a voice so you can't tell their sex or age, or even their accent)
- it is often overlooked that online games are also a source of cyber attacks on a user's computer or mobile phone – viruses, phishing or spyware are well-reported examples of problems associated with certain online gaming.

> ## Exercise 8b
> Evaluate your own use of email and social media/networking sites. Which of these e-safety strategies do you use?

The above list is by no means exhaustive but gives some idea of the risks associated with using computers and tablets online. It also indicates that gaming and the use of mobile phones carry equal risks. Basically, any device that allows communication (either through the internet, via phone networks or even via wireless communications) has a number of associated risks. As long as users take simple precautions, the risks are considerably minimised and ICT can be used to its full.

8.3 Security of data

There are a number of security risks associated with any electronic device that connects to a network (internet or mobile phone networks being the most common). This section covers the following risks:

- hacking
- phishing
- smishing
- vishing
- pharming
- spyware
- viruses
- spam
- moderated and unmoderated forums
- cookies.

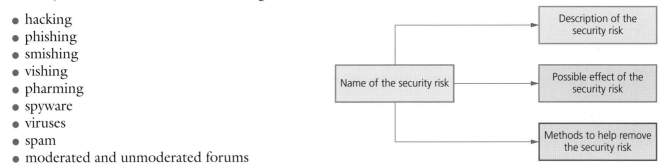

Figure 8.1 Security risks

Each security risk, together with its description, possible effects and how to minimise it, will be set out as shown in Figure 8.1.

8.3.1 Hacking

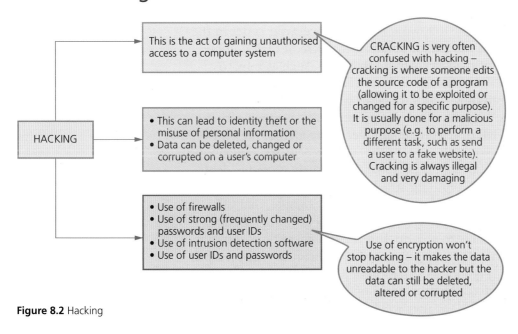

Figure 8.2 Hacking

8.3.2 Phishing

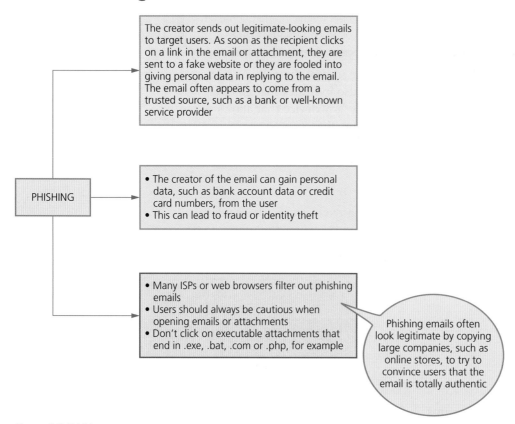

The creator sends out legitimate-looking emails to target users. As soon as the recipient clicks on a link in the email or attachment, they are sent to a fake website or they are fooled into giving personal data in replying to the email. The email often appears to come from a trusted source, such as a bank or well-known service provider

PHISHING

- The creator of the email can gain personal data, such as bank account data or credit card numbers, from the user
- This can lead to fraud or identity theft

- Many ISPs or web browsers filter out phishing emails
- Users should always be cautious when opening emails or attachments
- Don't click on executable attachments that end in .exe, .bat, .com or .php, for example

Phishing emails often look legitimate by copying large companies, such as online stores, to try to convince users that the email is totally authentic

Figure 8.3 Phishing

Malicious use refers to, for example, deletion, fraud, identity theft and selling on personal data. A good example of a phishing attack is when a user is sent an email saying they have ordered an item from an online store. They will be asked to click on a link to see the order details. The link takes the user to a page that shows a product code from a well-known company. A message such as: 'if this order wasn't made by you, please fill out the following form to cancel your order in the next 24 hours' is given. The form will ask for details such as credit card number, user's address and so on. Some of the key clues are that links, such as how to 'contact us', don't work.

Smishing – short for SMS phishing – uses the SMS system of mobile phones to send out fake text messages. It is very similar to phishing as described earlier. These scams often contain a URL or telephone number embedded in the text message. The recipient will be asked to log on to the website or make a telephone call. If they do, they will be asked to supply personal details such as credit/debit card numbers or passwords. As with phishing attacks, the text message will appear to come from a legitimate source and will make a claim, for example, that they have won a prize or that they need to contact their bank urgently. Most people believe that only computers are liable to security threats; mobile phones aren't at risk. This makes smishing a particularly dangerous security threat to many people.

Vishing (voice mail phishing) is another variation of phishing. This uses a voice mail message to trick the user into calling the telephone number contained in the message. As with all phishing attacks, the user will be asked to supply personal data thinking they are talking to a legitimate company.

8.3.3 Pharming

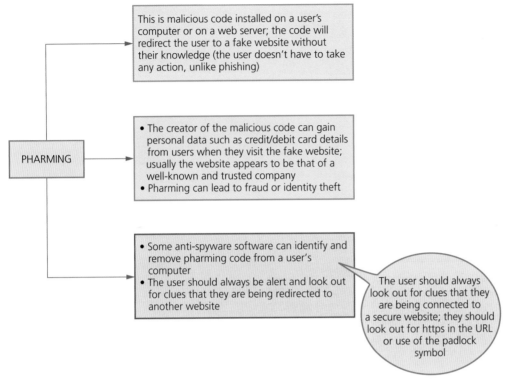

Figure 8.4 Pharming

8.3.4 Spyware and key-logging software

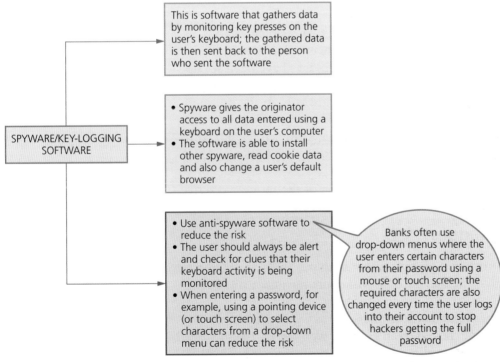

Figure 8.5 Spyware and key-logging software

8.3.5 Viruses

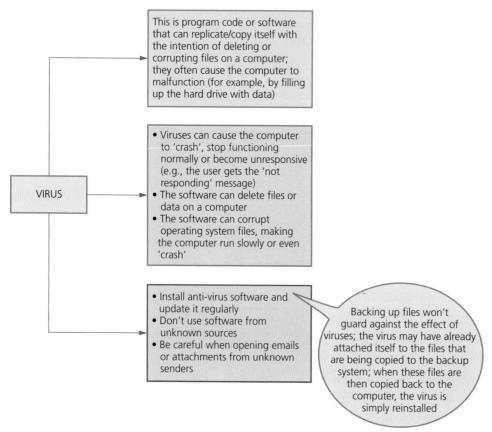

Figure 8.6 Viruses

8.3.6 Spam

Spam, often referred to as junk email, is usually sent out to a recipient who is on a mailing list or mailing group. Spammers obtain these email addresses from chat rooms, websites, newsgroups and even certain viruses that have been set up to harvest a user's contacts list. While spam is rarely a security risk, it can lead to denial of services, for example, by 'clogging up' the bandwidth on the internet. Denial of services is basically an attack on a network that is designed to slow the network down by flooding it with useless traffic. However, spam can be linked to phishing attacks or even the spread of computer viruses, so it should be treated with some caution.

Many ISPs filter out spam or junk mail. However, some of the more overactive ISPs can filter out 'wanted' emails that come from new sources.

Spam prevention techniques

- To obtain the maximum protection possible when using the 'junk email filter' set the protection level to high or to safe lists only. Make sure the junk mail filter is kept up to date.
- Block images in HTML messages that spammers use as web beacons (a web beacon can be a graphic image, linked to an external web server, that is placed in an HTML-formatted message and can be used to verify that your email address is valid when the message is opened and images downloaded).

- Look out for check boxes that are already selected when items are bought online; companies sometimes add a check box (which is already selected) to indicate that you have agreed to sell or give your email address to third party users; make sure that this check box is 'unticked' so that your email address can't be shared.
- Do not sign up to commercial mailing lists.
- Do not reply to an email or unsubscribe from a mailing list that you did not explicitly sign up to in the first place.

8.3.7 Moderated and unmoderated forums

A moderated forum refers to an online discussion forum in which all the posts are checked by an administrator before they are allowed to be posted. Many users prefer this type of forum, compared to an unmoderated one, as the moderator can not only prevent spam, but can also filter out any posts that are inappropriate, rude or offensive, or even those that wander off the main topic.

The internet is essentially an unmoderated forum. No one 'owns' the internet, and it is essentially not policed (this is discussed in more depth in Chapter 9). The only real safeguards are a voluntary cooperation between the users and the network operators. However, most social forums or networking groups on the internet have a set of rules or protocols that members are requested to follow or they will be deleted.

8.3.8 Cookies

Cookies are small files or code that are stored on a user's computer. They are sent by a web server to a user's computer. Each cookie is effectively a small look-up table containing pairs of (key, data) values; for example (surname, Jones) and (music, rock). Once the cookie has been read by the code on the web server or user's computer, the data can be retrieved and used to customise the web page for each individual. These are often referred to as user preferences. For example, when a user buys a book online, the cookies remember the type of book the user chose and the web page will then show a message such as: 'Customers who bought *Cambridge IGCSE ICT* also bought *Cambridge IGCSE Computer Science*'.

The data gathered by cookies forms an anonymous user profile and doesn't contain personal data such as passwords or credit/debit card numbers. Cookies are a very efficient way of carrying data from one website session to another, or even between sessions on related websites. They remove the need to store massive amounts of data on the web server itself. Storing the data on the web server without using cookies would also make it very difficult to retrieve a user's data without requiring the user to login every time they visit the website.

Use of secure servers is always advised. A secure web server is one that supports any of the major security protocols, such as SSL/TLS, that encrypt and decrypt messages to protect them against third party eavesdropping. Making purchases from a secure web server ensures that a user's payment or personal information can be translated into a secret code that's difficult to break.

8.4 Additional security of data online

This section discusses additional ways of keeping data secure when accessing external systems, such as the internet. We will consider:

- firewalls
- security protocols
- encryption
- authentication.

8.4.1 Firewalls

A **firewall** can be either software or hardware. It sits between the user's computer and an external network (for example, the internet) and filters information coming in and out of the user's computer.

Figure 8.7 Firewall

The following list shows a number of the tasks carried out by a firewall:

- to examine the 'traffic' between a user's computer (or internal network) and a public network (for example, the internet)
- checks whether incoming or outgoing data meets a given set of criteria
- if the data fails the criteria, the firewall will block the traffic and give the user (or network manager) a warning that there may be a security issue
- the firewall can be used to log all incoming and outgoing traffic to allow later interrogation by the user (or network manager)
- criteria can be set so that the firewall prevents access to certain undesirable sites; the firewall can keep a list of all undesirable IP addresses
- it is possible for firewalls to help prevent viruses or hackers entering the user's computer network
- it is also possible for firewalls to help prevent hackers gaining access to the user's computer or network. This can be done by blocking IP addresses, but it should be pointed out that hackers can still have access to a computer or network if they are using an **allowed** computer
- the user is warned if some software on their system is trying to access an external data source (for example, an automatic software upgrade); the user is given the option of allowing it to go ahead or request that such access is denied.

The firewall can be a hardware interface that is located somewhere between the computer and the internet connection, in which case it is often referred to as a **gateway**. Alternatively, the firewall can be software installed on a computer; in some cases this is part of the operating system.

However, there are certain circumstances where the firewall can't prevent potential harmful traffic:

- it cannot prevent individuals, on internal networks, using their own modems to bypass the firewall
- employee misconduct or carelessness cannot be controlled by firewalls (for example, control of passwords or user accounts)
- users on stand-alone computers can choose to disable the firewall, leaving their computer open to harmful traffic from the internet.

All of these issues require management control (or personal control on a single computer) to ensure that the firewall is allowed to do its job effectively.

8.4.2 Security protocols

We will now consider two forms of security protocols – sets of rules used by computers to communicate with each other across a network – when using the internet:

- Secure Sockets Layer (SSL)
- Transport Layer Security (TLS).

Secure Sockets Layer (SSL) is a type of protocol that allows data to be sent and received securely over the internet.

When a user logs on to a website, SSL encrypts the data – only the user's computer and the web server are able to make sense of what is being transmitted. A user will know if SSL is being applied when they see https (as part of the website address) or the small padlock in the status bar at the top of the screen. Figure 8.8 shows what happens when a user wants to access a secure website and receive and send data to it.

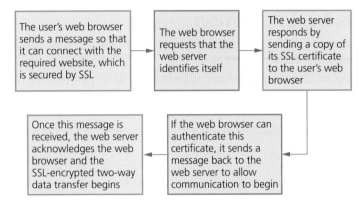

Figure 8.8 Communicating across a network using SSL

Note: SSL certificates are small data files that digitally bind an encryption key to an organisation's details. When installed on a web server, it shows as the green padlock and the https protocol and ensures secure connections from a web server to a web browser.

Transport Layer Security (TLS) is similar to SSL but is a more recent security system. TLS is a form of protocol that ensures the security and privacy of data between devices and users when communicating over the internet. It is essentially designed to provide encryption, authentication and data integrity (data integrity is maintaining the accuracy and the consistency of data) in a more effective way than its predecessor, SSL.

When a website and a user communicate over the internet, TLS is designed to prevent a third party hacking into this communication and causing problems with data security.

TLS is formed of two layers:

- **Record Protocol**: this part of the communication can be used with or without encryption (it contains the data being transferred over the internet).
- **Handshake Protocol**: this permits the website and the user to authenticate each other and to make use of encryption algorithms (a secure session between user and website is established).

Only the most recent web browsers support both SSL and TLS, which is why the older SSL is still used in many cases. But what are the main differences between SSL and TLS, since they both effectively do the same thing?

- it is possible to extend TLS by adding new authentication methods
- TLS can make use of session caching, which improves the overall performance compared to SSL (see the note below to explain this term)
- TLS separates the handshaking process from the record protocol (layer), which holds all the data.

Session caching

When opening a TLS session, it requires a lot of computer time (due mainly to the complex encryption keys being used). The use of session caching can avoid the need to utilise so much computer time for each connection. TLS can either establish a new session or attempt to resume an existing session; using the latter can boost system performance considerably.

Note: a cache is a collection of processed data that is kept on hand and reused in order to avoid costly repeated database queries.

8.4.3 Encryption

Encryption is used primarily to protect data in case it has been hacked or accessed illegally. While encryption won't prevent hacking, it makes the data meaningless unless the recipient has the necessary decryption tools described below.

Encryption uses a secret key that has the capability of altering the characters in a message. If this key is applied to a message, its content is changed, which then makes it unreadable unless the recipient also has the same secret key. When this secret key is applied to the encrypted message, it can be read.

The key used to encrypt (or encode) the message is known as the **encryption key**; the key used to decrypt (or decipher) the message is known as the **decryption key**. When a message undergoes encryption it becomes **cypher script**; the original message is known as **plain text**. Figure 8.9 shows how these are linked together.

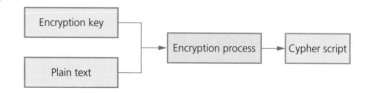

Figure 8.9 Encryption

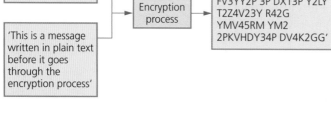

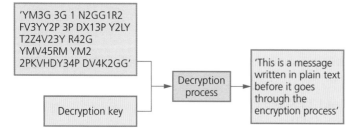

Figure 8.10 Example of the encryption and decryption process

8.4.4 Authentication

Authentication is used to verify that data comes from a secure and trusted source. It works with **encryption** to strengthen internet security. In this section we will consider digital certificates, passwords and biometrics in their authentication roles.

Digital certificates

A **digital certificate** is a pair of files stored on a user's computer – these are used in the security of data sent over the internet. Each pair of files is divided into:

- a public key (which is known by anyone)
- a private key (known to the computer user only).

For example, when sending an email, the message is made more secure by attaching a digital certificate. When the message is received, the recipient can verify that it comes from a known or trusted source by viewing the public key information (this is usually part of the email attachment). This is an added level of security to protect the recipient from harmful emails. The digital certificate is made up of six parts:

Figure 8.11 Digital IDs

- the sender's email address
- the name of the digital certificate owner
- a serial number
- expiry date (the date range during which the certificate is valid)
- public key (used for encrypting messages and for digital signatures)
- digital signature of certificate authority (CA) – an example of this is VeriSign.

Operating systems and web browsers maintain lists of trusted CAs (see Figure 8.11 for an example).

Passwords

When logging on to a system (for example, a bank website), a user will be asked to type in their **password** – this should be a combination of letters and numbers that would be difficult for somebody else to guess. Strong passwords should contain upper case and lower case characters, as well as numbers and other keyboard symbols, for example: Rn5K;2mL/8.

When the password is typed in, it often shows on the screen as ******** so nobody overlooking can see what the user has typed in. If the user's password doesn't match up with the user ID then access will be denied. Many systems ask for the password to be typed in twice as a verification check (check on input errors). To help protect the system, users are only allowed to type in their password a certain number of times – usually three times is the maximum number of tries allowed – before the system locks the user out. After that, the user will be unable to log on until the system administrator has reset their password.

For example, if a user forgets their password when using the internet, they can request that the password is sent to their email address. The password is never shown on the computer screen for reasons of security.

Passwords should be changed on a regular basis in case they become known to another user or even a hacker. In particular, it is important to prevent other people gaining access to your password by way of spyware or viruses – many methods to guard against this have been discussed earlier in this chapter.

It is often necessary to use a user ID or log in ID as well as a password. This gives an additional security level since the user ID and password must match up to allow a user to gain access to, for example, a bank website.

Biometrics

Biometrics relies on certain unique characteristics of human beings; examples include:

- fingerprint scans
- signature recognition
- retina scans
- iris recognition
- face recognition
- voice recognition.

157

Biometrics is used in a number of applications as a security device. For example, some of the latest mobile phones use fingerprint matching before they can be operated; some pharmaceutical companies use face recognition or retina scans to allow entry to secure areas. We will now consider two of these biometric techniques in a little more detail.

Fingerprint scans

Images of fingerprints are compared against previously scanned fingerprints stored in a database; if they match then access is allowed. The system compares patterns of 'ridges' and 'valleys', which are fairly unique (accuracy is about one in 500).

An example of its use would be as a security method for entering a building. Fingerprint scanning techniques have the following advantages in this application:

- everybody's fingerprints are unique, therefore this technique would improve security since it would be difficult to replicate a person's fingerprints
- other security devices (such as magnetic cards) can be lost or even stolen, which makes them less effective
- it would be impossible to 'sign in' for somebody else since the fingerprints would match up to one person only on the database
- fingerprints can't be misplaced; a person always has them!

What are the disadvantages in this application?

- relatively expensive to install and set up
- if a person's fingers are damaged through an injury, this can have an effect on the scanning accuracy
- some people may regard it as an infringement of civil liberties.

Retina scans

Retina scans use infrared light to scan the unique pattern of blood vessels in the retina (at the back of the eye). It is a rather unpleasant technique, requiring a person to sit totally still for 10 to 15 seconds while the scan takes place. It is very secure as nobody has yet found a way to duplicate blood vessels patterns (the accuracy is about one in ten million).

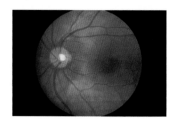

Table 8.3 Comparison of the six common biometric techniques

Biometric technique	Comparative accuracy	Comparative cost	Devices needed	Social acceptability	What can interfere with the procedure
Fingerprint scans	high accuracy	medium	scanner	medium	damaged fingers (e.g., cuts)
Signature recognition	low accuracy	medium	an optical pen	high	signatures can change with time
Retina scans	high accuracy	high	digital camera	low	irritation of the eye
Iris recognition	high accuracy	high	digital camera	low	wearing of glasses
Face recognition	medium–low accuracy	medium	digital camera	high	facial hair or glasses
Voice recognition	medium accuracy	medium	microphone	high	background noise or person has a cold

Table 8.4 Comparison of the advantages and disadvantages of the six common biometric techniques

Biometric technique	Advantages	Disadvantages
Fingerprint scans	• one of the most developed biometric techniques • very high accuracy • very easy to use • relatively small storage requirements for the biometric data created	• for some people it is very intrusive, since it is still related to criminal identification • it can make mistakes if the skin is damaged (e.g., cuts)
Signature recognition	• non-intrusive • requires very little time to verify (about five seconds) • relatively low-cost technology	• if individuals do not sign their names in a consistent manner there may be problems with signature verification • high error rate (one in 50)
Retina scans	• very high accuracy • there is no known way to replicate a person's retina	• it is very intrusive • it can be relatively slow to verify retina scan with stored scans • very expensive to install and set up
Iris recognition	• very high accuracy • verification time is generally less than five seconds	• very intrusive • uses a lot of memory for the data to be stored • very expensive to install and set up
Face recognition	• non-intrusive method • relatively inexpensive technology	• it is affected by changes in lighting, the person's hair, their age, and if the person is wearing glasses
Voice recognition	• non-intrusive method • verification takes less than five seconds • relatively inexpensive technology	• a person's voice can be recorded easily and used for unauthorised access • low accuracy • an illness, such as a cold, can change a person's voice, making absolute identification difficult or impossible

Exercise 8d

Find out which applications use each of the biometric techniques described in this section. Consider all the advantages and disadvantages of each method and make conclusions about its suitability for the applications you found.

Online credit fraud

In spite of all the security systems described above, online credit card fraud is still too common. It basically happens for the following reasons:

- hackers gaining access to a user's computer through the use of spyware, phishing or pharming; any of these methods can trick a user who is not particularly IT literate; the user can be tricked into giving personal and financial details that enable the hacker to gain full access to a user's account; this can lead to unauthorised purchases or even removal of money from an account if it remains undetected for a few days
- the breaking of passwords through a number of techniques is an all-too-familiar risk; if passwords are weak or no encryption is used then it is a relatively easy task to break these passwords and allow illegal access to bank and credit card accounts
- it is always a good idea to type in a web address or URL rather than 'copy and paste it' from an email or other website. Sometimes the web address/URL is altered very slightly in the email and the user ends up visiting a fake website. Once they visit the fake website it is possible that they will give personal and financial details to a fraudster without the user's knowledge – by physically typing in the web address the user will ensure they get it right and avoid such risks
- if the user is using wireless technology, it is very important for internet access to be password controlled since it is relatively easy to tap in to wireless networks without password protection

- if a user logs in to an account or website in a public place (such as an airport using the available Wi-Fi 'hotspots') it is necessary to be very vigilant; there is always a risk that somebody is monitoring internet usage in the area and will try to tap in to the data that is going to and from any computer using this wireless link
- even large organisations can be subject to cybercrime; in recent years, the cloud and some large retail companies have been the targets for hackers, which leaves customers very vulnerable.

There are a number of simple precautions users can take:

- always use varied and complex passwords for all your accounts (see earlier notes)
- check the accuracy of bank accounts continually and resolve any discrepancies immediately
- only provide personal information on sites that have 'https' in the web address or have the padlock icon in the web browser
- don't provide personal information to any unsolicited requests for information; this is often a sign of phishing
- don't open emails or attachments from unknown senders
- delete any messages from your spam folder on a regular basis
- report any suspicious phishing activity to the company that is used by the perpetrator
- only download software from sites that can be trusted.

Cloud security

Several computer (especially tablets and laptops) and mobile phone manufacturers encourage customers to store or backup their files on a medium known as the **cloud**. Users purchase cloud storage and can then access all their files (for example, photos, videos, music or e-books) from any device anywhere in the world. This has obvious advantages:

- you don't need to carry memory sticks around with you if you want to access your files away from home
- you don't have to pay for large storage capacity on your computer/tablet or mobile phone
- because the cloud is controlled by external companies, they will ensure that your files are backed up and therefore reduce the possibility of losing irreplaceable data
- the ability to synchronise (sync) files ensures they are automatically updated across all devices; this means that the latest version of a file saved on a desktop PC, for example, is also available on other devices, such as a smartphone
- cloud storage is also ideal for collaboration purposes; it allows several users to edit and collaborate on a single file or document – there is no need to worry about tracking the latest version or which user made the changes.

In spite of all these obvious advantages, there are still security worries about using cloud storage. The main fears are data security and data loss.

Data security

Companies that transfer vast amounts of confidential data from their own systems to a cloud service provider are effectively relinquishing control of their own data security. This raises a number of questions:

- What physical security exists regarding the building where the data is housed?
- How good is the cloud service provider's resistance to natural disasters or power cuts?
- What safeguards exist regarding personnel who work for the cloud service company? Can they use their authorisation codes to access confidential data for monetary purposes?

Data loss

There is a risk that important and irreplaceable data could be lost from cloud storage facilities. Actions from hackers (gaining access to accounts or pharming attacks, for example) could lead to loss or corruption of data. Users need to be certain sufficient safeguards exist to overcome these potentially very harmful risks.

In late September 2014, three breaches of security involving two of the largest cloud service providers showed why many of the above fears make people a little nervous of using this facility to store their important files:

- the XEN security threat, which forced several cloud operators to reboot all their cloud servers; this was caused by a problem in the XEN hypervisor (a hypervisor is a piece of computer software, firmware or hardware that creates and runs virtual machines)
- a recent case where a large cloud service provider permanently lost data during a routine backup procedure
- the celebrity photos cloud hacking scandal, where over 100 'interesting' photos of celebrities were leaked; hackers had gained access to a number of cloud accounts, which enabled them to publish the photos on social networks and to sell them to publishing companies.

All of the reasons above have made individuals and companies nervous about using cloud service providers. A 'game' between hackers and owners of online service companies continues to simmer. Considerable amounts of advice have been given in this chapter. Provided users are vigilant in their use of any device connected to the internet then the possibility of being a victim of cybercrime is considerably reduced.

⑨ Audiences

In this chapter you will learn about:

- how to tailor ICT solutions according to the audience
- copyright legislation
- legal, moral, ethical and cultural implications of ICT solutions
- policing of the internet.

This chapter will consider the importance of researching your audience before an ICT solution is implemented – this ranges from presentations through to actual ICT systems which run companies. No matter how large or small the task, consideration of the people involved with the presentation or full solution must be taken into account.

The legal, moral, ethical and cultural aspects of ICT solutions will also be considered together with the age-old question 'Should the internet be policed?'

At the end of the chapter, you should have some idea about the importance of the above topics, particularly in the multicultural and litigation-driven society we now live in.

9.1 Audience appreciation

When planning and creating ICT solutions, it is important to consider the audience who will either use or take part in the solution. The following list shows a number of factors that should be considered – not all of them are relevant to every proposed solution, of course.

- The age of the target group (young children will have a different appreciation and response compared to a more mature group of adults, for example).
- The experiences of the audience (a board of company directors would expect a different approach compared to an audience composed of teenage school children).
- The expectation of the audience (for example, if you are advertising or giving a presentation on a new restaurant, an older audience would expect to see fine wines and good waiter service; whereas a group of students would be more interested in pizzas and fast counter service).
- Knowledge of the audience (for example, graduates in maths would expect to see a different approach to a solution than a group of history students).

When starting to look at the ICT solution, some or all of these factors need to be taken into account. Some research needs to be done first to find out about the target audience. This could be done by:

- interviewing a cross section of the target group to find out how to engage the audience (if this involves a major ICT solution, then this may have to involve many of the techniques that were described in Chapter 7)
- giving out questionnaires to people in the target group to find out their background, interests, and so on, so that the final solution can be tailored to meet the full expectation of the audience
- carrying out market research – this could involve the two techniques described above, but would certainly involve a more sophisticated and in-depth analysis of the data received (it would all depend on how large the 'affected' audience is likely to be).

9.1.1 Giving a sample presentation to an audience

Let us now consider a phone company who market a number of different mobile phones. The company has decided to do two presentations regarding the sales and features of the four different mobile phones they market and sell:

- one presentation is to be given to the sales team who will receive different bonus payments depending on the phone sold
- a second presentation is to be given to a potential group of customers.

How would these two presentations differ? The first group (the sales team), will have technical knowledge and will be interested in the profitability of each sale. The second group (end-users), will only be interested in the price and the features found on each phone.

The language used, the need for multimedia, the length of the presentation, the need for audience participation (an interactive approach) and the examples used to illustrate certain points are all key factors when writing the presentations. Let us look at each of these in turn:

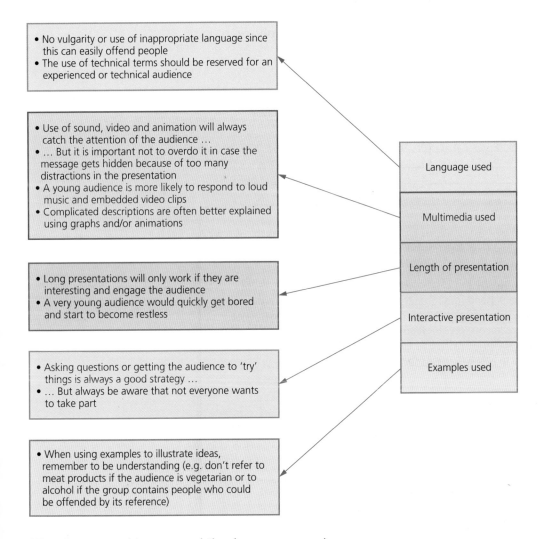

Now let us consider our mobile phone presentation.

The data to be used in the two presentations is based on the following:

- sales of each phone over three years
- selling (retail) price of each phone
- percentage profit made on each phone
- how the prices and profit margin changed over the three-year period

Table 9.1

	2014		2015		2016	
	Retail price	% profit	Retail price	% profit	Retail price	% profit
Neophone	$400	35%	$440	37%	$450	40%
Rappia	$525	29%	$560	31%	$590	30%
Wintry	$350	40%	$380	40%	$400	41%
Samstalk	$650	25%	$700	27%	$750	30%

- features of each phone (do they have a camera, memory size, do they have a touch screen and do they have an MP3 player).

It is worth remembering here that customers would be more receptive to colours, supporting images and special effects (e.g. slide transitions). Whereas the sales team (who already know about selling the phones) simply want to know the facts. Customers, on the other hand, really want to be 'entertained' by the phone presentation.

Table 9.2

	Mobile phone features			
	Camera	Memory	Touchscreen	MP3 player
Neophone	√	16 GB	√	√
Rappia	√	32 GB	X	√
Wintry	√	16 GB	X	X
Samstalk	√	64 GB	√	√

Exercise 9a

Produce the two presentations for the scenario given in Section 9.1.1:

- for the marketing and sales team
- for a group of customers.

Using your knowledge from Section 9.1 and from Chapter 19 (Presentations), consider how to present the information in Table 9.1 and Table 9.2 to the two groups. Also consider what information you might want to have in each presentation and any additional information you might need.

For the mobile phone features, you may like to use icons such as:

- built-in camera

- memory

- touchscreen

- MP3 player.

Additional example

This second example (which is the introduction to Exercise 9b) considers producing a presentation on the 'increase in world population over the next ten years'. The presentation is to be given to two different audiences:

- adults
- children of primary school age (5 to 11 years old).

We have already covered aspects of an adult audience. What needs to be considered when presenting to young children?

- careful consideration needs to be given to font type used; a large font size is more likely to make young children interested
- bright colours will keep their attention
- use of the correct language (for example, to say 'the world population is 7.1 billion for which China accounts for 1.4 billion' is acceptable to adults; young children won't understand the figures or the statistics so the presentation would need to say 'the world's population is very big; for example, 60 million people live in the UK. But some countries, such as China, are much bigger than this', and so on)
- use of lots of images to make it amusing (and have sound effects as well)
- use of slide transitions and animation to keep their attention.

Exercise 9b

Produce two slide presentations on 'changes to the world population'. One presentation is aimed at an adult audience and the other is aimed at a very young audience (5 to 11 years). Write down your reasons for the features of each presentation you produce.

It is important to remember that the example given in Section 9.1.1 was a presentation to two very different groups of people. However, the audience may be the actual users of the ICT solution. To meet the audience requirements in this case also requires a number of key considerations, for example:

- how skilled is the workforce (the interface might need to be icon-driven if the staff are either computer-illiterate or not very skilled)
- how old is the workforce (is the interface appropriate for all the age ranges who will use the system)
- are any of the staff disabled (different disabilities require different methods to allow them to interface with a computer system)?

Exercise 9c

A small company employs a workforce where 35% of the staff are disabled, have learning difficulties or come from an ethnic minority. The company markets various food products.

- 10% of the staff have little or no hand or arm movement.
- 10% of the staff have learning difficulties.
- 15% of the staff come from ethnic minorities.

Write an article on the features needed in a computer interface to cope with the range of different staff that work within the company.

9.2 Legal, moral, ethical and cultural appreciation

9.2.1 Software copyright and privacy

Software is protected by copyright laws in much the same way as music CDs, videos and articles from magazines and books are protected.

When software is supplied on CD or DVD there are certain rules that must be obeyed. It is illegal to:

- make a software copy and then sell it or give it away to a friend or colleague
- use software on a network or in multiple computers unless a licence has been acquired to allow this to happen
- use coding from the copyright software in your own software and then pass this software on or sell it as your own without the permission of the copyright holders
- rent out a software package without permission to do so from the publishers
- use the name of copyrighted software on other software without agreement to do so.

Software **piracy** (illegal copies of software) is a big issue amongst software companies. They take many steps to stop the illegal copying of software and to stop illegal copies being used once they have been sold. There are a number of ways software is protected either by making the installer agree to certain conditions or by methods which require the original software to be present for it to work:

- when software is being installed, the user will be asked to key in a unique reference number or **product key** (a string of letters and numbers) which was supplied with the original copy of the software (for example: 4a3c 0efa 65ab a81e)
- the user will be asked to click 'OK'/'I AGREE' or put a cross in a box to agree to the licence agreement before the software continues to install
- the original software packaging often comes with a sticker informing the purchaser that it is illegal to make copies of the software; the label is often in the form of a **hologram** indicating that this is a genuine copy
- some software will only run if the CD-ROM, DVD-ROM or memory stick is actually in the drive; this stops illegal multiple use and network use of the software
- some software will only run if a **dongle** is plugged into one of the USB ports.

Note: A dongle is a small device, usually plugged into one of the computer's USB ports. It is used to allow wireless communications with devices, such as a keyboard, and for the use of protected software (e.g. it may contain important files and the software will only run if the dongle is plugged into the computer).

The Federation Against Software Theft (FAST) was set up in the UK many years ago to protect the software industry against piracy. FAST prosecutes organisations and individuals who are involved in any copyright infringements. There are legal penalties for anyone found guilty of such infringement.

Similar organisations exist in many countries to globally protect software from piracy. The following extract is a typical example of how strict the anti-piracy laws are in many countries:

> **TRADERS FINED $100,000**
>
> Two eBay traders (from the US) agreed this week to pay a total of $100,000 in damages after they were caught selling illegal copies of Norton security software. The SIIA settled the case against the two traders who also agreed to stop selling illegal software and provided SIIA with records identifying their customers and suppliers.

Reproduced with the kind permission of out-law.com.

9.2.2 Legal, moral, ethical and cultural implications

Note: it is also worth looking at Chapters 5, 8 and 10 for further information on the legal implications of ICT.
Definitions:

- **Legal** covers the law; whether an action is punishable by law.
- **Morality** governs the private and personal interactions between people and is usually determined by the person concerned.
- **Ethics** governs professional interactions, for example, codes of behaviour practised by a society or group of people sometimes going against an individual's own sense of morality.
- **Culture** refers to the attitudes, values and practices shared by a society or group of people.

Essentially, anything which breaks the law is termed *illegal*. Examples from ICT would include copying software and then selling it without the permission of the copyright holders. This was covered in Section 9.2.1.

Morality covers the human desire to distinguish between right and wrong. The only problem here is that culture can get in the way. What may be immoral in some cultures is regarded as acceptable practice in other cultures. Because something is immoral, it isn't necessarily illegal (and vice versa). Altering websites or creating fake websites is not in itself illegal; provided the person who carries out the act doesn't try to gain from their actions – it is simply an immoral act since it can cause distress to others who aren't aware that it was simply a harmless prank. As soon as they try to obtain personal and financial data then it becomes an illegal act. Some people regard hacking as simply immoral – this again ceases to be true if the act of hacking leads to breaking national security, or financial gain or leads to revealing personal information which leads to distress. It can be a very thin dividing line between an immoral act and an illegal act.

Unethical behaviour is essentially breaking a code of conduct. For example, if somebody works for a software company and passes on some of the ideas to a rival company, this would be regarded as unethical behaviour. Unless the software passed on is part of national security, then it isn't actually illegal to do this.

The importance of culture is less clear-cut. Writing software games that make fun of religion could be seen by certain people as unacceptable behaviour – but some cultures would find it funny and wouldn't understand why it was seen as offensive. When writing computer games, for example, programmers need to be careful that they don't include items which some cultures would find offensive or obscene. Again, this may not be seen as unethical and certainly not illegal, but nonetheless can cause distress.

Exercise 9d

Suppose John works for a company during the day that develops and markets software for use by car manufacturers. In the evening, he works with a small team who write software for computer games. Consider which of the following can be termed unethical, immoral or illegal (it is possible some things may be regarded as all three):

1 John uses some of the software routines from his day job when writing computer games.
2 John claims that the software routines he uses from his day job were all written by himself.
3 John has some of his software written overseas, but only pays them a very low wage to do the work.
4 John writes some of his computer games using the computer systems in his day job.
5 To help advertise his computer games, John hires a 'hacker' who breaks into websites so that 'pop ups' appear which advertise the games free of charge.
6 Some of the games software written by John's company makes fun of people who have certain disabilities.
7 Some of the games that John writes collect information from the user's computer and send the data back to John's computer.

Once you have decided the answers to the above seven statements, write down other activities which fall into the illegal, unethical or immoral category. For each activity, give reasons why they fall into one or more of these categories.

At the end of Exercise 9d you should have come to the following conclusions: statements 1, 2 and 4 are unethical; statements 2, 3 and 6 are immoral; statements 5 and 7 are illegal. But this can vary in some countries; for example, statement 1 may be illegal in certain parts of the world.

9.2.3 Should the internet be policed?

This is a question which continues to cause much discussion. Recent events in hacking (e.g. the hacking of Sony Films in USA) and in terrorism (e.g. the 2015 terrorist attacks in France) have brought increasing pressure from many people to start policing the internet. Those that support freedom of speech argue that the internet only works because it isn't policed. Many security departments and governments believe that the hacking and terrorism attacks could have been stopped by having tighter laws (allowing them to 'eavesdrop' on any data transmission on the internet). There are many points that support both sides of the argument.

Arguments in favour of some form of internet control

- It would prevent illegal material being posted on websites (e.g. racist comments, pornography, terrorist activities, and so on).
- People find it much easier to discover information which can have serious consequences (e.g. how to be a hacker, how to make a bomb, and so on); although this can be found in books, it is much easier for a novice to find the required information using a search engine.
- Some form of control would prevent children and other vulnerable groups from being subjected to undesirable websites.
- Some form of control would stop incorrect information being published on websites.

Arguments against some form of internet control

- Material published on websites is already available from other sources.
- It would be very expensive to police all websites and users would have to pay for this somehow.
- It would be difficult to enforce rules and regulations on a global scale.
- It can be argued that policing would go against freedom of information/speech.
- Many topics and comments posted on websites are already illegal and laws already exist to deal with the offenders.
- Who is to decide what is illegal or offensive – many things are only offensive to certain people (e.g. religious comments) but not to the majority.

Having read the arguments for and against policing, you may wish to enter into your own debate as to whether freedom of speech is so important that the risks of more internet legislation would be too damaging. However, you might argue that losing some of your freedom of speech is a small price to pay for your own physical safety.

⑩ Communication

In this chapter you will learn about:

- communication constraints when using emails
- email groups
- cloud storage
- spam
- the internet
- intranets
- the world wide web (www)
- blogs, wikis and social networking sites
- searching the internet for information.

This chapter covers certain aspects of using the internet. We will consider rules and regulations when sending emails and also look at several features of the internet. In particular, we will define and explain many of the internet terms used and how to search for information on the internet. The chapter also considers the differences between the internet, the world wide web and intranets.

10.1 Communication with other ICT users using email

10.1.1 Constraints

Emails are now one of the most common ways of communicating between people. However, there are many rules we need to follow to ensure the security of the messages sent and also to prevent people from writing things that are regarded as unacceptable. The first part of this chapter considers these constraints.

Laws

Many countries have laws to protect people against the misuse of emails. The following diagram is a guideline to the rules that most countries require companies and individuals to abide by when sending out emails.

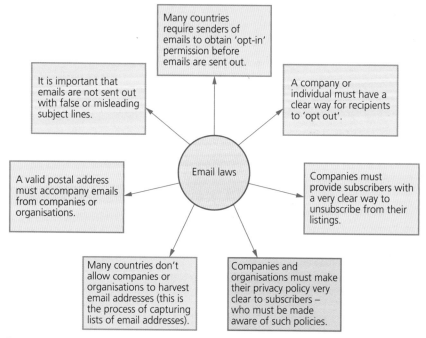

Figure 10.1 Email laws

Acceptable language

The language used by people when writing emails must lie within an acceptable code of practice. The following is a list of unacceptable content to be used in emails, text messages and online forums:

- obscene images
- language that is regarded as abusive, profane, inflammatory, coercive, defamatory or blasphemous
- racist, exploitative, violent messages
- use of illegal materials in messages.

This list doesn't cover everything but gives some idea of what is not acceptable when posting messages or items on the internet. In many countries there are very stiff penalties for going outside the above boundaries, and it is not regarded as adequate that recipients can simply delete images or messages.

It is essential that anyone writing emails or posting messages on, for example, bulletin boards, is aware of the above constraints.

Copyright

It is very important to realise that emails are subject to copyright laws. Just because it is relatively easy to forward an email does not mean it is always legal to do so. This is also true of any attachments sent with an email.

As with web pages, the copyright in an email is determined by its content.

Printing, copying or forwarding emails is generally not considered a breach of copyright unless the sender has indicated clearly that the message is confidential or the subject of copyright law. It is important that the recipient checks this out before forwarding it on to somebody else. Most companies or organisations will clearly set out their policies on sending emails and the material that they contain. This will be particularly true if the sender's email address is part of the company's name, for example A.N.User@company_name.com. Emails and attachments from companies and organisations will usually contain a copyright statement, such as:

> Any dissemination or copying of this email or attachment is strictly prohibited unless you are the intended recipient or are responsible for delivering the message to the intended recipient. If you have received this email in error, please let us know and then delete the original email and any attachments.

It is common for the message to then make some statement that the views and opinions in the email may not represent those of the company, and that the contents may be subject to disclosure under the Freedom of Information Act. Companies are clearly very concerned about any potential risk of copyright infringement.

Security and password protection

It is very important to consider the security of emails. Many security aspects have been covered elsewhere in this book but some of the factors to consider are repeated here for completeness.

Some methods of increasing the security of emails include:

- using strong passwords when logging on to your email (for example, the name of your pet dog is a weak password; strong passwords contain a combination of letters, numbers and other symbols: Sy12@#TT90kj=0 would be regarded as a strong password)
- changing passwords on a regular basis

- using spam filters to remove suspicious emails to a 'junk folder' or even to block the email entirely
- running anti-virus and anti-spam software at all times on your computer to protect against emails from unknown or malicious sources.

Emails are said to be vulnerable to both **passive** and **active** attacks. Passive attacks include the release of email material to other users without your consent. Active attacks involve the modification of your messages or even denial of service (i.e., overloading your system by sending thousands of emails, which basically 'clogs up' your computer and makes internet access almost impossible). Active attacks can also involve viruses or phishing attacks (these are covered elsewhere in the book).

Netiquette

Netiquette is a shortened form of the phrase inter**net** eti**quette**, which refers to the need to respect other users' views and display common courtesy when posting views in online discussion groups or when sending out emails. It is very important to consider what you write always since the reader can't see your facial expressions or body language. What may have been intended to be humorous could offend somebody if they misunderstand your message and make the wrong conclusions. Always be aware of this when posting messages or sending emails.

There are a number of rules governing netiquette – one such source is *The Core Rules of Netiquette* by Virginia Shea (published in 1994); but the following diagram gives the reader some idea of what constitutes netiquette.

1. Don't be abusive – don't threaten people or use personal violence.
2. Don't send spam – don't repeatedly send somebody the same information.
3. Be clear and succinct with your message – don't waffle.
4. Remember that posts are public in most cases and can be read by anyone.
5. Always check your spelling and grammar – give a good impression.
6. Respect people's privacy and don't discuss or publish information that might embarrass somebody.
7. Forgive people's mistakes – don't be compelled to respond to an error.
8. Don't use CAPITAL LETTERS to highlight comments – this is seen as 'shouting' in emails, text messages and online forums.
9. Don't plagiarise – always acknowledge quotes used in any messages you write.
10. Don't use too many emoticons as they might annoy your readers.

Figure 10.2 Rules of netiquette

10.1.2 Spam

Any unsolicited email sent over the internet is regarded as **spam**. It is often sent to multiple recipients and can range from being simply annoying to dangerous – spam can contain viruses or be part of a phishing scam (see earlier chapters). The origin of the word is open to debate: it ranges from the name of an old war-time foodstuff called spam to a word used in an old BBC Monty Python television comedy sketch ('spam, spam, spam, spam, spam, spam…' – a word repeated many times!).

Spam can affect many online operations (for example, YouTube) where links (called 'spambots') are posted within videos that send users to another website.

While some regard spam as a cheap way of advertising to many people at the same time, most people consider it to be a big nuisance. The main disadvantages are:

- it uses up people's time
- it generally annoys people
- it uses up valuable bandwidth on the internet, slowing it down
- it can have viruses attached or even be part of a phishing scam
- it can clog up users' inboxes.

Spam is not just a problem for computer users – it can also affect mobile phones. In this case it is usually text messages being send to multiple phones. They are sometimes referred to as 'spasms' (spam SMS) – at the basic level they just annoy people, but in some countries or with some mobile phone providers, users are charged for each message they receive. It then becomes more than just an annoyance! (Look back at Chapter 8 for ways to prevent spam.)

10.1.3 Email groups

Email groups are used for a number of purposes:

- it is easier for a user to send out multiple emails if the addresses are all grouped together under a single name; the user only needs to use that single name in the 'to' box
- companies and organisations can group people together for marketing purposes, for example according to age, ethnicity, hobbies, favourite music and so on – this means that each email can target specific groups
- 'spammers' can create email groups by buying addresses of people from certain companies or from software that 'raids' address books on computers or email companies – this means that several thousand people can be sent spam by simply pressing the <enter> key
- companies use email groups to set up meetings (for example, for a video conference) to ensure that everybody is always invited to attend – it would be easy to forget a person if the email addresses were all typed in individually; this way you can be sure all the correct people are sent messages.

10.2 Effective use of the internet

10.2.1 The internet

The **internet** is a worldwide collection of networks that allows users to:

- send and receive emails
- chat online (using text, voice and/or video)

- transfer files from computer to computer (using file transfer protocols)
- browse the world wide web.

In 2015 it was estimated that over three billion people use the internet across the world. The internet isn't actually owned by any single person or organisation. It is a concept rather than something tangible (that is, something that can be touched) and relies on a physical infrastructure that allows networks to connect to other networks.

The **world wide web** (the web, or www) is only *part* of the internet, which users can access by way of a **web browser**. It consists of a massive collection of web pages and has been based on the **hypertext transfer protocol (http)** since 1989. The world wide web is a way of accessing information over the medium known as the internet; the two terms 'www' and 'internet' are clearly not the same thing and should not be confused.

10.2.2 Intranets

Many companies use an **intranet** as well as the internet. An intranet is defined as 'a computer network based on internet technology but designed to meet the internal needs for sharing information within a single organisation or company'. *Access* to an intranet is usually confined to a company or organisation and, unlike the internet, is not available to the general public.

Intranets reside behind a **firewall** and are only accessible:

- internally to members of the company, or
- to people given various levels of access who are external to the company (see later).

There are a number of reasons for adopting intranets rather than using the internet:

- intranets are safer since there is less chance of external hacking or viruses
- it is possible to prevent external links to, for example, certain websites
- companies can ensure that the information available is specific to their needs
- it is easier to send out sensitive messages in the knowledge that they will remain within the company
- intranets offer better bandwidth than the internet, thus there are fewer connection limits than with the internet (that is, the number of bits per second that can be transmitted are usually higher within an intranet)
- it is possible to create **extranets** that allow intranets to be extended outside the organisation but with the same advantages as an intranet; this allows, for example, trading partners to have controlled access to some of the information (commercially-sensitive information is password protected).

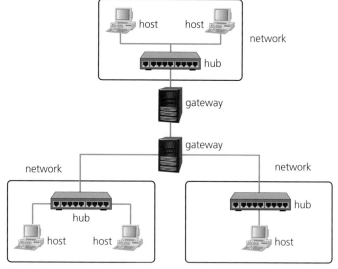

Figure 10.3

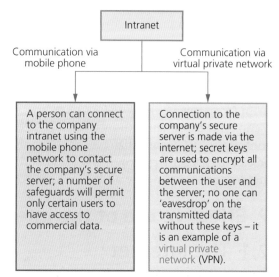

Figure 10.4 Connecting to an intranet though a mobile phone network or virtual private network

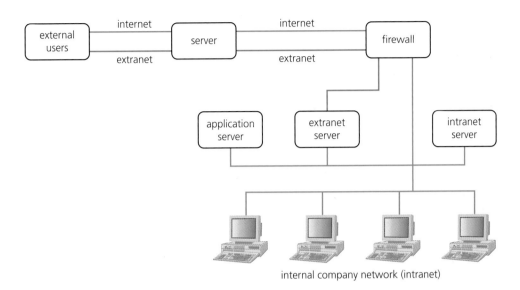

Figure 10.5 How intranets, extranets and the internet can be connected together

What are the differences between the internet and an intranet?

- The term 'internet' comes from the phrase: **inter**national **net**work.
- The term 'intranet' comes from the phrase: **int**ernal **r**estricted **access net**work.
- An intranet is used to give local information relevant to the company or organisation whereas the internet covers topics of global or general interest.
- It is possible to block certain websites using the intranet; while this is also possible with the internet, it is more difficult.
- An intranet requires password and user ID entry and can only be accessed from agreed points/computers; the internet can be accessed from anywhere in the world provided the user has an ISP account.
- An intranet is behind a firewall, which gives *some* protection against hackers, viruses, and so on; this is more difficult to do with internet access since it is open on an international scale.
- The internet can be public access, whereas intranets tend to be private access.

10.2.3 Cloud storage

Cloud storage is a method of data storage where data is stored on offsite servers – the physical storage covers hundreds of servers in many locations. The same data is stored on more than one server in case of maintenance or repair, allowing clients to access data at any time. This is known as **data redundancy**. The physical environment is owned and managed by a hosting company.

Security aspects of **cloud storage** were discussed in Chapter 8.

There are three common systems:

- **Public cloud**: this is a storage environment where the customer/client and cloud storage provider are different companies.
- **Private cloud**: this is storage provided by a dedicated environment behind a company firewall; customer/client and cloud storage provider are integrated and operate as a single entity.

- **Hybrid cloud**: this is a combination of the two previous environments; some data resides in the private cloud while less-sensitive/less-commercial data can be accessed from a public cloud storage provider.

Instead of saving data on a local hard disk or other storage device, a user can save their data 'in the cloud'. The advantages and disadvantages of doing this will now be discussed.

Advantages

- Customer/client files stored in the cloud can be accessed at any time, from any device, anywhere in the world, provided internet access is available.
- There is no need for a customer/client to carry an external storage device with them, or even to use the same computer, to store and retrieve information.
- The cloud provides the user with remote backup of data with obvious advantages to alleviate data loss/disaster recovery.
- If a customer/client has a failure of their hard disk or backup device, cloud storage will allow recovery of their data.
- The cloud system offers almost unlimited storage capacity.

Disadvantages

- Security aspects of cloud storage were discussed in Chapter 8.
- If the customer/client has a slow or unstable internet connection, they could have problems accessing or downloading their data/files.
- Costs can be high if a large storage capacity is required; it can also be expensive to pay for high download/upload data transfer limits with the customer/client internet service provider (ISP).
- The potential failure of the cloud storage company is always possible – this poses a risk of loss of all backup data.

10.2.4 General internet terms

A number of terms have been introduced in this chapter – this section considers the definition of these terms.

Hypertext transfer protocol (http and https)

Hypertext transfer protocol (http) is a set of rules that must be obeyed when transferring data across the internet. Protocols are sets of rules agreed by the 'sender' and 'recipient' when data is being transferred between devices. When a web page is being accessed, entering 'http://' at the front of an address tells the web browser that http rules for communication are to be obeyed.

If http is omitted from the address, most web browsers now default to http.

When some form of security (for example, SSL or TLS) certification or encryption is used (refer to Chapter 8) then the protocol is changed to https (this is often seen as the padlock symbol 🔒. The letter 's' after http refers to 'secure'.

Because of encryption, it is slower to use https than http, so it is usually only adopted when sensitive or private data is being transferred across the internet.

Web browsers and URLs

A **web browser** is software that allows a user to display a web page on their computer screen. They interpret or translate the HTML (hypertext markup language – see later chapters) from websites and show the result of the translation. This can often be in the form of videos, images or sound. Most web browsers share the following features:

- they have a 'home' page
- they have the ability to store a user's favourite websites/pages
- they keep a history of the websites visited by the user
- they give the ability to go backward and forward through websites opened
- they have **hyperlinks** that allow users to navigate between web pages; these hyperlinks are shown as <u>blue underlined text</u> or use a small picture, such as a pointed finger , under a phrase or image. By clicking on these hyperlinks the user is sent to another website or web page.

Web browsers use **uniform resource locators (URLs)** to access websites, retrieve files and so on. They are represented by a set of four numbers, for example 109.108.158.1 (i.e., <u>http://109.108.158.1</u>).

However, this is not very user friendly, and an alphanumeric format is usually used instead:

> **protocol://website address/path/filename**

where:

- **protocol** is usually http or https
- **website address**:
  - domain host (www)
  - domain name (name of website)
  - domain type (.com, .org, .co, .net, .gov)
  - sometimes a country code is given (.uk, .us, .de, .cy)
- **path**, which is a web page (if omitted then root directory of website)
- **filename** is the item on the web page

For example, **http://www.hoddereducation.co.uk/igcse_ICT**

An error will occur if any part of the URL is incorrect. Most frequently, error page 'HTTP 404' will display on the computer screen.

The web browser translates the web server name into an IP address (for example, 109.108.158.1). The HTML is returned and is shown as a correctly formatted page on the screen.

File transfer protocol (ftp)

File transfer protocol (ftp) is a network protocol used when transferring files from one computer to another computer over the internet. It is similar to http (used for the transfer of web pages and data) and smtp (simple mail transfer protocol – used when transferring emails); ftp is an application protocol for the transfer of files across the internet.

Web browsers can be used to connect to an ftp address in much the same way as you would connect to an http address, for example <u>ftp://username@ftp.example.gov/</u> .

Internet service provider (ISP)

An **internet service provider (ISP)** is a company that provides users with access to the internet. It is normal to pay a monthly fee for this service. When a user registers with an ISP, an account is set up and they are given login details that include a user ID and password.

An ISP has the equipment and telecommunications line access required to have internet access – usually broadband connections, which use copper cables, or, more recently, fibre-optic cables.

So what is the difference between an ISP and a web browser?

- ISPs provide the user with access to the internet for a monthly fee
- web browsers allow a user to view web pages.

10.2.5 Blogs, wikis and social networking sites

Blogs

Blogs (we**b logs**) are personal internet journals where the writer (blogger) will type in their observations on some topic (for example, a review about the latest movie release) and perhaps provide links to some relevant websites.

Blogs tend to range from minor projects (such as the performance of a rock star) through to important social issues. However, the comments made on blogs are **not** immune from the law: bloggers can still be prosecuted for writing offensive material.

Features of blogs:

- updated on a regular basis by the author
- usually organised in reverse chronological order (most recent to least recent entry)
- normally public – anyone can read them
- entries normally come from a single author
- other internet users can't change blogs – they can only read them.

Microblogs are similar to blogs but are most often used on social networking sites to make short, frequent posts. The posts can be done using instant messaging, emails or other social networking vehicles (such as tweets). Social networking sites use microblogs to allow members to update their personal profiles, for example.

Another version is a **b-blog** – short for business blog – which is used by businesses to promote themselves on the internet.

Wikis

Wikis are web applications or websites that allow users to create and edit web pages using any web browser. A wiki will support hyperlinks and uses a very simple syntax (known as wiki markup) to create pages. They are often described as 'web pages with an <edit> button'.

Features of wikis:

- anyone can edit, delete or modify the content
- many authors can be involved in a wiki
- it is possible to organise a page any way that the author(s) wish(es)
- shows/keeps track of all entries – i.e. it stores a document history
- can be easily edited using a web browser
- allows large documents to be seen by many people – it is easier than emailing several people.

Social networking sites

Social networking sites focus on building online communities of users who share the same interests and activities. They enable people to share photos, videos and music, hobbies, favourite eating places, and so on. The members do this by creating public profiles and thus form 'relationships' with other users. The dangers of such sites were covered earlier in Chapter 8.

Features of social networking sites:

- each member is provided with free web space
- each member can build their own private and public profiles
- it is possible to upload content such as text messages, photos and videos
- it is possible to 'write on each other's wall'
- members are given free instant messaging and video chatting
- it is possible to email other members within the community
- members can create pages where they can post photos, articles, and so on
- it is possible to invite people to become friends
- members have control over who can access their private or personal data.

10.2.6 Searching the internet for information

One of the most useful and powerful aspects of the internet is the ability to easily search for vast amounts of information on almost any given topic. There are basically two ways to locate information:

- The first is to type in the URL if you know the name of the website you wish to access.
- If you don't know where to find the information you are looking for, the second method is to use a **search engine**.

Opening a website from a URL

As discussed earlier in the chapter, the URL contains the protocol, site address and file name. If you type http://www.cie.org.uk in to a web browser as shown here, you will go to the home page for the website.

If you know the URL for a page within the website, you can type the full entry into the web browser to get a particular page. For example, if you want the IGCSE subjects page within the website, you could type in the full URL: http://www.cie.org.uk/programmes-and-qualifications/cambridge-secondary-2/cambridge-igcse/subjects/ to get this page.

If you want to use this page frequently, you can add it to your 'favourites', which saves you having to type in the URL every time.

It is also possible to search through the website using the navigation tools until you find the web page you are looking for.

Search engines

Search engines are useful if you don't know the URL of the website or if you want to find some information but don't know where to look. Many search engines exist, and they search for websites using a variety of methods, but they all have one common underlying feature: they use the words entered in the search box and look up in their database of web pages to find out which of them match your search string.

Obviously, the more detailed or specific your search string, the more accurate the results (known as 'hits') will be. For example, if we type **ICT textbooks** into a typical search engine, the following options will appear:

As you can see about 1.5 million 'hits' or web pages have been found. This is a lot of information. We could narrow down the search by now typing in **ICT textbooks+Hodder+IGCSE** – we now get a much reduced selection:

We now have reduced the number of web pages to 217 000, which is a vast reduction. However, the search can be further refined using the advanced search option.

> Add this text if known and it will search for both words together, not just for either word.

The result is now only about 2000 hits.

Once the information is found it can then be saved or used as follows:

- saved as a favourite (as described earlier) and accessed when required
- by adding hyperlinks in a document, so that this web page can be accessed when required
- by using 'Print Screen' (or the equivalent – it varies from computer to computer) and then pasting the saved information into a word processor page
- copy and pasting the information into another document.

It is important to acknowledge your sources of information when doing this, both to avoid plagiarism and because the information may be subject to copyright.

As we have already said, the internet is a vast and very useful source of information, but it is important to be aware of its disadvantages as well its advantages.

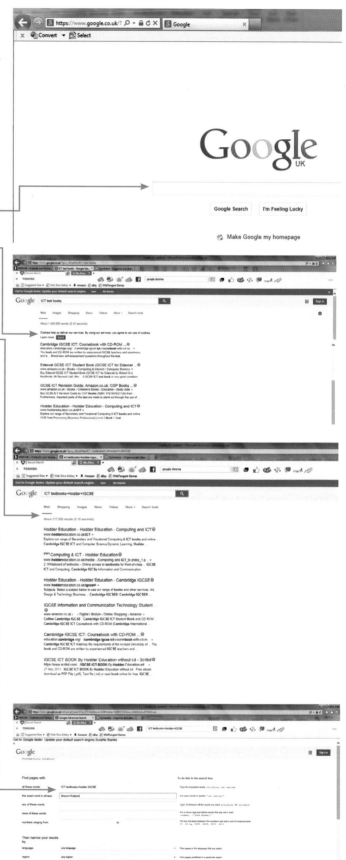

Advantages

- Information on the internet tends to be up-to-date since it is quicker and easier to amend web pages than, for example, to reprint books.
- The internet has vast, almost limitless, amounts of information.
- Searching for information using a search engine is fast and easy.
- People can look for information in the comfort of their own home – there is no need to travel to a library to find the required book or books.
- Unless the required book can be found in a library, there is a need to buy it – information on the internet is usually free of charge.
- Pages on the internet can have multimedia elements (for example videos, animations, cartoons and music/voiceovers) that make learning more interesting and often make it easier to understand the topics – unless textbooks have accompanying CD-ROMs, this option is not available in books.

Disadvantages

- The internet is not regulated – anything can be posted on a web page and, consequently, information may be biased or totally incorrect (books, on the other hand, usually undergo some form of review before being published).
- There is always the risk of accessing inappropriate websites when using search engines; these can take many forms and can be very distressing to certain people.
- It is too easy to be distracted when searching on the internet – users can find computer games or enter social networking sites instead of doing their work.
- There is always the risk of 'information overload' if the user lacks the necessary experience or expertise when using search engines.
- Because it is very easy to copy material from the internet, there is a huge risk of plagiarism; this is more likely to occur than when using books since this requires considerably more effort than a simple copy and paste.
- Some research skills are lost when using the internet as search engines do all the work for you.

Why are internet searches to find relevant information not always fast?

When using search engines, there is always the danger of information overload. It is possible for millions of sites to be found matching the given criteria. Unless the user narrows down their search criteria, it can take a long time to find out exactly what they are looking for. Also, if the user is uncertain of what needs to be asked, it can also take a long time to obtain only relevant information.

While search engine companies deny it, certain websites are also placed at the top of their lists. When a user keys in certain words, these websites in the list always show up first in the search results and may not contain exactly what the user is looking for. Search engines also rank the time it takes to load up pages from websites – the fastest are given priority when the results appear on the screen. All of this means that the user may not find exactly what they are looking for when using the search engine.

The actual operation of search engines is very complex and is beyond the scope of this book.

Why isn't it always easy to find reliable information on the internet?

When using a search engine to find information on the internet, there is no guarantee that the material returned is accurate or unbiased. Essentially, anybody is able to set up a website and write whatever they like without it having to be first verified (the only stipulation is that the material posted doesn't break any laws – if it does, then the author is liable to criminal prosecution). However, the material can be inaccurate or unverified and it can also be biased towards one way of thinking only. Unlike books, the material posted on websites doesn't have to be checked by other people to ensure it is factually correct. It is also possible for search engines to suggest websites that are completely out of date so that the information displayed on the web pages is no longer correct or relevant. It is arguable whether or not policing of the internet would improve this situation – this was covered in some detail in Chapter 9.

How can you evaluate the reliability of information found on the internet?

- Anybody can set up a website (claiming to be factually accurate), so information is not necessarily reliable or accurate.
- Some commercial websites will be biased (to advertise their products, for example).
- If a website has excessive advertising it could be unreliable (due to pressures from those advertising on their website).
- If the advertising on a website is related only to its own products it could be unreliable (again due to arguments claiming that their products are the best to carry out a specific task).
- It is possible to use the final part of a URL to identify a website's reliability – for example, websites ending with: .ac and .gov are more likely to be reliable.
- If a comparison of information from reliable sites or reliable/authenticated student books is made, this will often help to show if the information is reliable.
- It is always a good idea to see if responsible bodies have endorsed the website.
- Check if the website has links to other reliable websites or to unreliable websites.
- If a website has testimonials, this can indicate reliability.
- If the date of the last update was a long time ago it is likely to be unreliable or out of date.

If the author of the website has good credentials, then it is more likely for the content to be reliable

Exercise 10a

Research a number of search engines and write down ways to narrow down searches using different symbols and key words (such as '+' and 'OR'). Take screenshots of your results to see how using these symbols and keywords narrows down the number of results shown.

Section 2

Practical

⑪ File management

In this chapter you will learn how to:

- identify different file types and their uses
- describe the need for a hierarchical file/folder structure
- use a hierarchical file/folder structure to save work
- save files using appropriate file names
- save and print files in a variety of formats
- describe why generic file formats are needed
- export data into package-specific file formats and generic file formats
- describe the need to reduce file sizes for storage or transmission
- identify when it is necessary to reduce file sizes for storage or transmission
- reduce file sizes using file compression.

For this chapter you will need this source file from the CD:

- remora.jpg.

11.1 What is a generic file type?

Generic file formats allow you to save files so that they can be opened on any platform. The files may not contain all of the formatting that can be saved in a package-specific format. Using generic formats allows files created on a PC to be read/imported on an Apple Mac and vice versa.

Some file types, such as those used by *Microsoft Office* – for example *Excel* spreadsheets (.xlsx), *Word* documents (.docx) and *Access* databases (.accdb) – are not generic. It is not always possible to open files from these packages on other platforms.

Common generic text files include:

- **comma separated values**: these files have a **.csv** file extension. This file type takes data in the form of tables (that could be used with a spreadsheet or database) and saves it in text format, separating data items with commas.
- **text**: these files have a **.txt** file extension. A text file is not formatted and can be opened in any word processor.
- **rich text format**: these files have a **.rtf** file extension. This is a text file type that saves some of the formatting within the text.

Common generic image files include:

- **graphics interchange format**: these files have a **.gif** file extension. This format stores still or moving images and is an efficient method of storing images using a smaller file size, particularly where there are large areas of solid colour. It is widely used in web pages.
- **joint photographic expert group**: these files have a **.jpg** (or sometimes a .jpeg) file extension. This format stores still images only, not moving images. It is an efficient method of storing images using a smaller file size and is widely used in web pages.
- **portable document format**: these files have a **.pdf** file extension. This is a document that has been converted into an image format. It allows documents to be seen as an image so that they can be read on most computers. The pages look just as they would when printed but can contain clickable links and buttons, form fields, video and audio. You can protect a document in pdf format to stop others from editing it. Text can be copied and pasted into a word processor or sometimes edited using PDF writing software.

- **portable network graphics**: these files have a **.png** file extension. It is a file format that compresses graphics (image) files without any loss of image quality. It was created to replace graphics interchange format and is now the most-used **lossless compression** format used for images on the internet.
- **moving picture experts group layer 4**: these files have a **.mp4** file extension. It is not a single file format; it is a multimedia **container** that is used for storing video files, still images, audio files, subtitles and so on. This container is often used to transfer video files on the internet.

Common generic audio files include:

- **moving picture experts group layer 3**: these files have a **.mp3** file extension. It is a compressed file format used for storing audio files. This format cannot store still or moving images. The file sizes are relatively small but have near CD quality, which makes them suitable for use on the internet.

Common generic files used for website authoring include:

- **cascading stylesheet**: these files have a **.css** file extension. This is a stylesheet that is saved in cascading stylesheet format and attached to one or more web pages (often written in HTML) to define the pages' colour scheme, fonts and so on.
- **hyper text markup language**: these files have a **.htm** (or sometimes a .html) file extension. This text-based language is used to create markup that a web browser will be able to display information as a web page.

Common generic compressed files include:

- **Roshal archive**: these files have a **.rar** file extension. This is a container that can hold almost any file types in a compressed format. It is used to reduce the number of bytes needed to save a file, either to save storage space or to reduce transmission time when sent from one device to another. It was developed for Windows by Russian software engineer Eugene Roshal (and takes its acronym from 'roshal **ar**chive').
- **zip**: these files have a **.zip** file extension. This is a container that can hold almost any file types in a compressed format. It is used to reduce the number of bytes needed to save a file, either to save storage space or to reduce transmission time when sent from one device to another.

11.2 Manage files effectively

11.2.1 Locate and open stored files

Make sure that you are familiar with the file structure of your local system. If you are using a stand-alone computer, files are likely to be stored on local hard disks or SSD drives. If you are using a networked system, files are likely to be stored on a network drive, usually in a secure area where only you have access. Each system is different and you must use the 'This PC' icon from the *Windows 8 Start Screen* to access these drives.

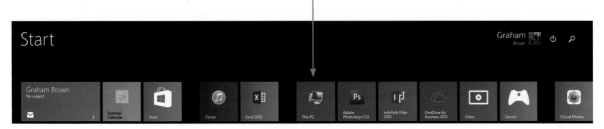

The path to your current location is shown at the top of the window.

The left pane is used to locate the drive that you wish to use.

The right side of the window shows the files and subfolders in this folder. It also gives you other useful information such as the date the file was saved and the file type. Some of this information will be used later in this book.

You can use these elements and the scroll bars to locate your stored files.

On most computers, double clicking on the file icon will open the file in the most suitable application. There are times when you may wish to use other programs to open a file; for example, in the website authoring section you may wish to open a file in both a browser and in *Notepad*. In this case you can either:

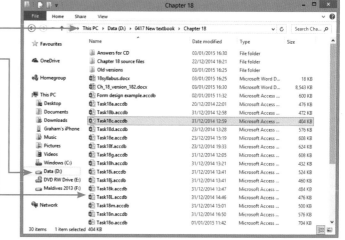

- open the application and load the file from there
- drag the file into an open application, or
- right mouse click on the filename and use Open with....

11.2.2 Save your work

Work should always be saved using a planned folder structure. Here is an example of part of a folder from the development of Chapter 18 of this book.

Advice

In some schools, network managers may have disabled some of these methods of opening files. This is to help increase the network security and keep your work safe. If this is the case, use one of the other methods to open files.

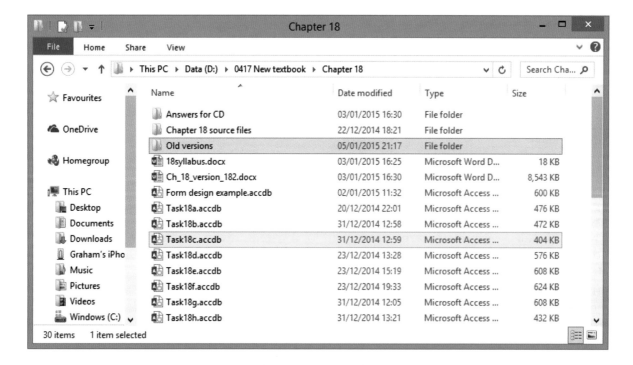

You can see that separate folders are used to hold each different area of the development. The answers for the teacher's CD are stored in a subfolder, as are the source files. There's also a folder for old versions of the files created during the chapter's development; this has been used so that the working folder does not get filled with lots of copies of the same file – the old versions of the files are dragged into the 'Old versions' folder at the end of each work period.

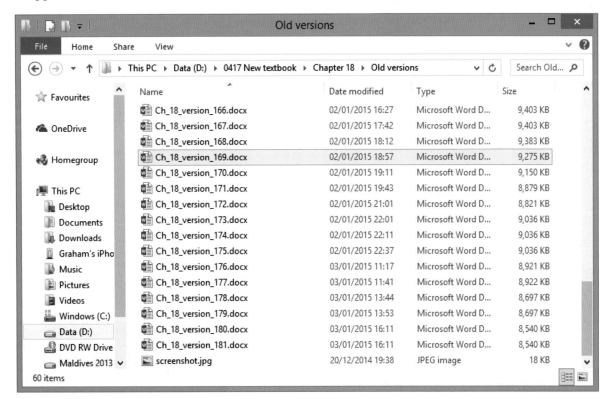

This is a small part of the 'Old versions' folder. You can see that different versions of the same file have been saved as it was worked on. In some cases, where major additions or deletions were made, there are even two files with different names saved less than a minute apart. You can see that each file has been saved with a meaningful filename that includes a version number. This is really useful if you need to go back and look at your previous work. When the folders get very full, I keep the last 20 versions of a file, plus every fifth file from the early versions (versions 5 and 10, and so on). I then archive the other files before deleting them from the hard disk drive. Choose meaningful file names which give clues as to the contents of the file. This makes it easier for you to find the work in your user area when you look back at a later date.

Task 11a

Create a new folder to store your work for this chapter in. Call this folder Task11b.

Open the **File Explorer** window by pressing the <Windows> and <E> keys together. Click the left mouse button to select the drive that you will use as your work area.

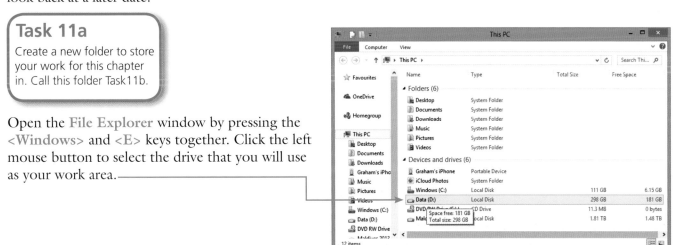

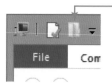

Then click on the New folder icon and name this folder Chapter 11. The location of this will depend on the structure of the system you are using. Go into this folder and create new subfolders for the other task in this chapter. Call this folder Task11b.

Make sure you are in the folder Task11b. This is where you will save your work later in the chapter.

11.2.3 Save, export and print in different formats

Most of the details for this section of the syllabus are covered in the following chapters. Although there are similarities in the methods of saving, exporting and printing, these have been covered in detail for each application package used.

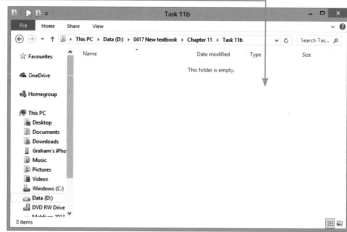

Where evidence of how you answered a question is required, you can always take a screen shot and submit that as evidence. The Snipping Tool is very useful. Select the search bar with the keyboard by pressing the <Windows> and <F> keys together. Select the Everywhere search.

Enter the text Snip into the search box. The result should look similar to this.

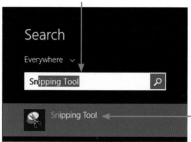

Click on the Snipping Tool icon, which opens a small window on the screen. Click on New.

The screen will change colour. Drag the cursor over the area to be snipped. The snipped image can now be copied and pasted as evidence of your method.

If you use screen shots, make sure that each screen shot shows all the information. Your name, Centre number and candidate number must be on all work and, if items such as a 'browser view' are required, you must show that your web page is displayed in a browser and not in an editing package.

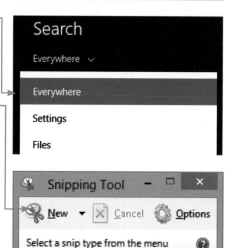

From the File tab in most *Microsoft Office Suite* packages, you have option to:

- Save – to save the current file with the same filename
- Save As – to save the current file with a new name, and/or new file type, and/or in a new location
- Print – to print the current file
- Export – to export, save a copy in .pdf format, or to change the file type in some packages.

11.3 Reduce file sizes for storage or transmission

11.3.1 Why reduce file sizes?

All computer systems have a limited storage capacity so the most efficient use of that storage space is important. The speed at which files are transmitted (sent) between one device and another also depends on the size of the data being transmitted. This does not just affect transmission speeds on the internet, but also between computers and devices such as printers and network servers, and so on. This is important when sending files as email attachments. The larger the file size, the more time it takes to transmit.

11.3.2 Reduce file sizes

The largest files stored and transmitted are often image files. Still images can vary in size: images with lower-resolution graphics, which are often used for web pages to speed up the loading time of the page, can be very small but, the higher the image resolution, the larger the file. Video files (because they contain thousands of still images) tend to be the largest files stored and transmitted. There are exceptions to this rule however. Large database management systems, such as that used by the Driver and Vehicle Licensing Agency (DVLA) in the United Kingdom, require immense amounts of storage. These systems continue to grow, especially as organisations start to hold digital images (such as drivers' photographs) within their systems. File sizes must be kept as small as possible, but not to the point where images become so pixelated that they are not clear.

This will mean resizing and/or resampling image files so that they require less storage space and take less time to load. Resizing changes the physical dimensions (width and height) of an image, while resampling changes the quality of an image.

Resize an image

This method is used to physically resize an image in a graphics package and then to save the new image (usually with a new filename). This method has the advantage of reducing the file size of an image so that a web page will be displayed more quickly. It has the disadvantage of using lower-resolution images, which can appear pixelated, particularly if you wish to enlarge them.

Task 11b

Open the file **remora.jpg**. Save a copy of this file in your Task11b folder. Resize this file to 80 pixels wide. Save it as **remora1.jpg**. Reduce the resolution of the image further by downsampling and save the new image as **remora2.jpg**.

Open your Task11b folder in the File Explorer window. In a File Explorer window open the source CD and click on the file you need; hold down the left mouse button and drag it from the folder on the source CD into the Task11b folder.

Open the image **remora.jpg** in your graphics manipulation package. In *Adobe Photoshop* images are resized using the Image menu, followed by the Image Size... option.

This opens the Image Size window. To set the image width to 80 pixels, change the value in the Width: box.

The image will maintain its aspect ratio as long as there is a tick in the Constrain Proportions box. To intentionally distort an image you would remove this tick and enter a height as well as a width for the image. Click on [OK].This will alter the size of the image within the package, like this.

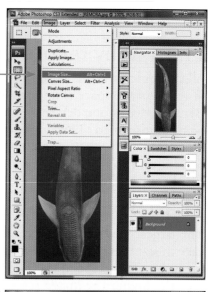

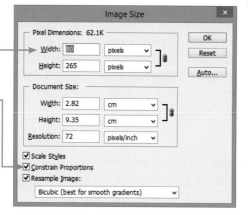

To save the new image, select File, then Save As... and enter the new filename **remora1.jpg** before clicking on [Save]. As this image will be saved in JPEG format, you are given options on the image quality that you require. These can be selected by typing a number between 1 and 12, using the slide bar, or selecting from the drop-down menu: 1 is the smallest file size that you can have and gives the poorest quality images; 12 is the highest quality but results in large file sizes, which are much slower to download over the internet.

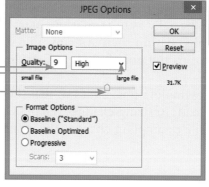

Resample an image

The process of changing the quality of an image is called resampling. Images can be downsampled, meaning fewer pixels are used for the image, as you have just done by reducing the image quality. Images can also be upsampled by adding more pixels. Downsampling reduces the file size and therefore makes the web page load more quickly. Save the same image again, downsampling it by lowering the resolution when saving. If you look at your Task11b folder you should see that the file sizes have decreased at each stage.

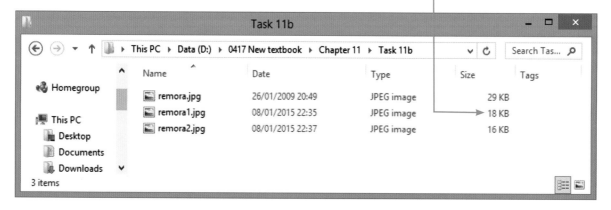

Use file compression

If a document contains lots of formatting or lots of images, its file size tends to be quite large. To reduce the file size for transmission (if the file is not to be edited), you can turn the file into portable document format using the FILE tab, followed by Export. Select the Create PDF/XPS button. ─────────────────────────────────→

Enter the new filename and click on Publish to create a pdf which, because it is an image, should have a smaller file size, like this. ──

If you need to send multiple files, the most efficient way is to compress the files together as a single zip file. To do this you must open File Explorer by pressing the <Windows> and <E> keys. Hold down <Ctrl> and select the files to be zipped. With these files selected, click the right mouse button to get the menu. Move the cursor down to the Send to option and a second menu appears. Click the left mouse button on Compressed (zipped) folder. ──────

Edit the name of the folder if appropriate.

Export

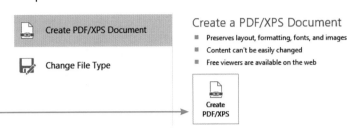

Create a PDF/XPS Document

- Preserves layout, formatting, fonts, and images
- Content can't be easily changed
- Free viewers are available on the web

Ch11_version_8.docx	09/01/2015 09:24	Microsoft Word Document	1,448 KB
Ch11_version_8.pdf	09/01/2015 09:45	Adobe Acrobat Document	738 KB

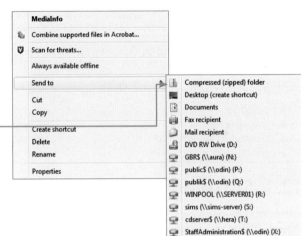

12 Images

In this chapter you will learn how to:

- place images into documents and presentations
- resize an image
- wrap text around an image
- place an image with precision
- place a border around an image
- rotate an image
- crop an image
- reflect an image
- adjust the colour depth of an image
- adjust the brightness and contrast of an image
- maintain the aspect ratio of an image
- adjust the aspect ratio of an image to distort an image where appropriate.

Other syllabus sections on images covered in this chapter include:

- understanding the need to reduce image resolution to increase transmission speed
- reducing the resolution of an image to reduce its file size.

For this chapter you will need the following source files from the CD:

- dog.png
- snow.rtf
- snowangel.png
- snowball.jpg
- snowman.jpg
- trees.jpg
- winter.pptx.

12.1 Software tools

You will need to know how to place image files into different application packages. Where this is required in a web page please refer to Section 21.2.7. Images are unlikely to be included in the spreadsheets and databases elements of the course. However, images will be placed in both word-processed documents and presentations. First you must select images appropriate for the document's audience.

Task 12a

A short news article is to be given to young adults aged 15–25.

Open the document **snow.rtf**. Insert a suitable image from clip art and the images **snowball.jpg** and **trees.jpg** at the end of the document.

Open the Search window by pressing the <Windows> and <F> keys together. Use the drop-down arrow to select Everywhere. ————

This task requires a document rather than a presentation, although the methods shown are identical in both packages. Type Word into the search box and select Word 2013. ————

This opens *Microsoft Word*. Open the file **snow.rtf** and replace the text <Your Name> with your name, Centre number and candidate number. Create a new folder called Task12a. Save your document in this folder with the filename Task12a as a *Word* document (*.docx).

12.1.1 Use images in a document or presentation

Read the contents of the document **snow.rtf** to see what it is about. Task 12a asks for a 'suitable image from clip art'; only when you have read the contents and considered the audience will you know which images will be suitable and which will not.

12.1.2 Import an online image

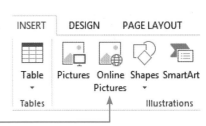

Many packages, like *Microsoft Word* and *Microsoft PowerPoint* used to include a number of free clip art images with the software but now images are imported from the internet. Move the cursor and click where you wish to place the image. Select the INSERT tab, then in the Illustrations section click on the Online Pictures icon.

Select where you wish to look for the image and in the search box enter the type of image you want. After reading **snow.rtf**, I think an image of a snowman might be the most appropriate for this task.

Press the <Enter> key. The search results are displayed.

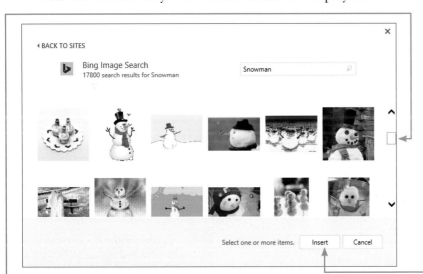

Use the scroll bar to view the images. In this case there are more than 17 000 to choose from. When you have selected the first one appropriate for the task (lots of these images are appropriate for this age group), click on the image to highlight it, then click Insert.

This places the image in your document.

Advice

Please note that you **must** ask for, and be given permission to use an image in any publication. Copyright law in many countries will not allow you to use an image belonging to another person without their written consent.

Many copyright holders are happy for students to use their images for educational purposes without charging them, but you must obtain their permission to do so.

12.1.3 Import an image provided for the task

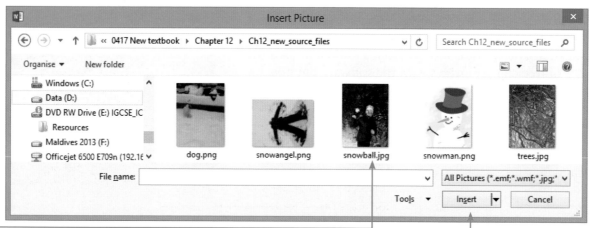

Select the INSERT tab, followed by Picture. This opens the Insert Picture window. Browse through the folders and files until you locate the file **snowball.jpg**.

Click the left mouse button on this file followed by Insert.

This will insert the image into the document. Save the document as task12a.

You will notice that the images have just been placed at the end of the document. These will now need manipulating so that they become a part of the document, rather than just appended to the end.

12.2 Edit an image

It is important that an image included in any document, presentation or publication should, as mentioned earlier in the chapter, be appropriate to the subject matter. If a document was about the snow, you may expect to see an image like this.

Read the question and text carefully to try to understand which image would be the best and why. Does this image need editing? Is the image the correct shape to fit the position you wish to place it? If the image needed to be in landscape orientation you would need to crop the image. Where do you crop it? If you crop the top off the image the watering can on the wall will be lost which gives the viewer an idea of the depth of the snow, but so do the bricks in the wall. Do you crop the bottom from the image and remove lots of the white snow? The choices are yours depending upon what message you want the image to give. Is it the depth of the snow? Is it the dog playing in the snow?

If this image needs to be in landscape orientation and no alternative image is available, then you must crop the image rather than compressing or distorting it. Images should retain the correct proportions between width and height; this is called the 'aspect ratio'.

12.2.1 Resize an image

Task 12b

Open the file task12a.

Resize the image **snowball.jpg** to 8 cm high and maintain its aspect ratio. Place this at the top right of the first paragraph.

Resize the image of the snowman to 2.8 cm high and 2 cm wide. Place this image at the top left of the second paragraph. Ensure that the text wraps around both of these images.

Find the image **snowball.jpg** in your document. To obtain a drop-down menu, right click with the mouse on this image. From this menu select the Size and Position... option. ──────────────

Advice

If the Size and Position... option does not appear, select Format Picture... followed by the Size tab.

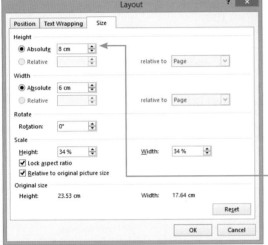

This opens the Layout window which should be in the Size tab. If not, select it.

The task instructs you to resize the image, maintaining its aspect ratio. This means to keep the height and width in the same proportions as the original image, usually to ensure that you do not distort it. To do this, ensure that the two tick boxes related to the aspect ratio are both selected.

Change the Height: of the image to 8 cm and click on ⟨ OK ⟩.

Use a similar method to resize the image of a snowman to 2.8 cm high by 2 cm wide. Select the snowman image and open the Size window for that image. In this case different lengths and widths have been specified, but you have not been instructed to crop the image. This means that you will probably distort the image from its original proportions. To do this, ensure that both of the aspect ratio tick boxes have their ticks removed. ──────────────

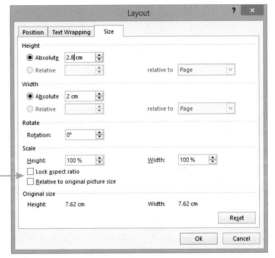

Use the Height: box to change this setting to 2.8 cm and the Width: box to 2 cm.

This will change the proportions (aspect ratio) of the image from this,　　　to this.

Notice how the second image is slightly thinner but the same height. This task is continued in the next section.

Advice

If evidence of an image size or the aspect ratio is required, you can use screen shot evidence of this window.

12.2.2 Wrap text around an image

Task 12b asks you to place the resized **snowball.jpg** image at the top right of the first paragraph. You are expected to align the image to the margins and to the top of the paragraph and there is a further instruction to wrap the text around the image. It is often wise to set the text wrapping first, then place the image. Click the left mouse button on the image to select it (which opens Picture Tools), then the FORMAT tab followed by the drop-down arrow next to the Wrap Text icon. ──────────────→

Wrap
Text ▾

You get a drop-down menu with layout options. Useful ones include:

- **In Line with Text:** This places the image as an in-line graphic and is treated as a text character within a line of text. It will move with the text surrounding it if new text is inserted or deleted.
- **Square:** This places the image on the page and the text wraps (flows) around it. Use **More Layout Options…** to specify the type of wrapping that you require.
- **Tight:** This places the image on the page and the text wraps (flows) around it, like **Square**, but you cannot control the distance of the text from the image for the top and bottom settings, although you can to the left and right, using **More Layout Options….**
- **Through:** This places the image on the page and the text wraps around the image with preset values.
- **Top and Bottom:** This places the image with the text above and below the image, but not wrapped to the side.
- **Behind Text:** This places the image behind the text. It can be used to set a background image in a document.
- **In Front of Text:** This places an image over the top of the text.
- **More Layout Optons:** This can be used to give more options to the selected layout types above. For example: if a **Square** layout is selected you can specify where you wish to flow the text around the image and the distance of the text from the image on each side. This option also allows you to control the positioning of the image on the page.

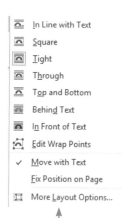

For this task, set the **Text Wrapping** of the image to **Tight** using the drop-down menu.

Advice

This menu can also be found by right clicking the mouse on an image and selecting **Wrap Text**.

Advice

Packages like *Microsoft PowerPoint* will not give text wrap options. Sometimes you have to layer objects on the slide or on the page in a document. To do this click the right mouse button on the image and use the options like **Bring to Front** and **Send to Back**. This is also useful for placing overlapping images in a presentation or document.

12.2.3 Place an image with precision

You will be expected to place images precisely. To move and place this snowball image, click and hold the left mouse button on the image and drag it to the top right corner of the first paragraph. There are two methods of placing the image: the first is to drag it until the green guidelines appear at the top and right side of the image like this:

The second method is to roughly place the image. Right click on the image again. Select the **Size and Position…** option to open the **Layout** window. Select the **Position** tab.

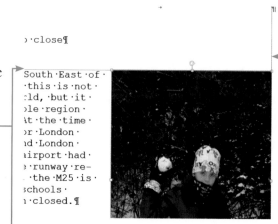

Set the Horizontal alignment to Right aligned to the Margin.
Set the Vertical alignment to Top aligned to the top of the line of text.

Click the ⬚ OK ⬚ button to place the image. Check that this has worked correctly. If not, this is usually due to the image being placed with too little precision when it was dragged and dropped. Try dragging and dropping the image again and repeat the process.

Repeat this process, placing the resized image of the snowman at the top left of the second paragraph like this.

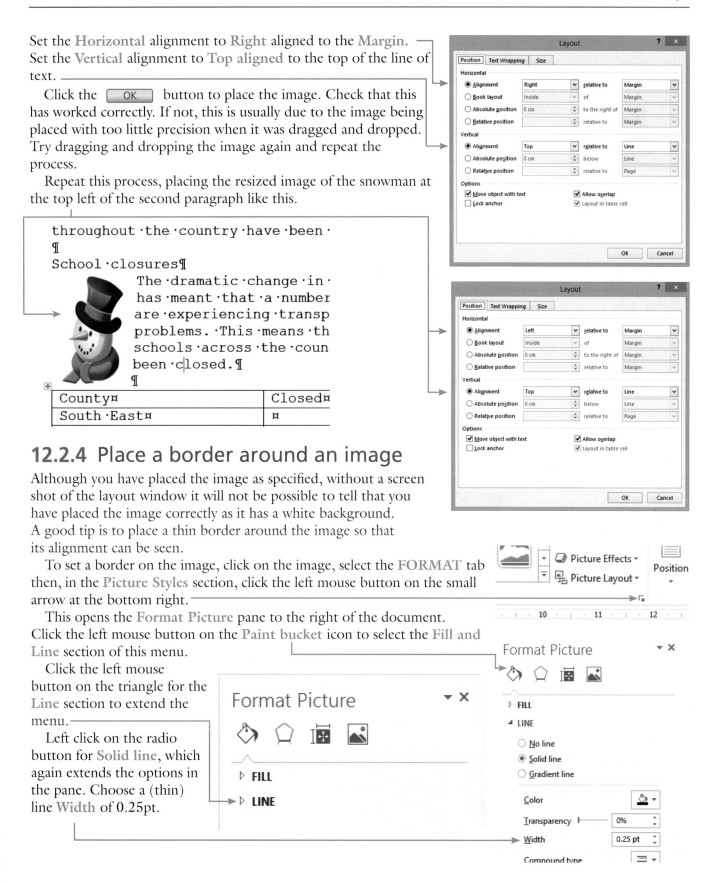

12.2.4 Place a border around an image

Although you have placed the image as specified, without a screen shot of the layout window it will not be possible to tell that you have placed the image correctly as it has a white background. A good tip is to place a thin border around the image so that its alignment can be seen.

To set a border on the image, click on the image, select the FORMAT tab then, in the Picture Styles section, click the left mouse button on the small arrow at the bottom right.

This opens the Format Picture pane to the right of the document. Click the left mouse button on the Paint bucket icon to select the Fill and Line section of this menu.

Click the left mouse button on the triangle for the Line section to extend the menu.

Left click on the radio button for Solid line, which again extends the options in the pane. Choose a (thin) line Width of 0.25pt.

The border now shows the precision placing of the image.

```
throughout ·the ·country ·have ·been ·c
¶
School ·closures¶
```

```
The ·dramatic ·change ·in ·
has ·meant ·that ·a ·number
are ·experiencing ·transp
problems. ·This ·means ·th
schools ·across ·the ·coun
been ·closed.¶
¶
```

County¤		Closed¤
South ·East¤		¤

Save your document as task12b.

Task 12c

Open the file task12b.

The image **trees.jpg** has been taken on a digital camera. Place this image to the right of the table, aligned to the right margin. Resize this image if needed.

Place the image **trees.jpg** at the end of the document, as shown earlier in the chapter. Click on the drag handle and drag the vertical borders in the table to narrow the column widths so that all text shows without wrapping, but no extra white space is shown.

The table should change from this to this.

Using the ruler at the top, you can tell that the image will need to fit into a space from about 7 cm into the page to 16 cm in. This means the image width should be about 9 cm wide (16 − 7 = 9). Use the methods learnt earlier in this chapter, to resize the image to 9 cm wide whilst maintaining its aspect ratio. Set the text wrap so as to allow the image to sit to the right of the table. Drag the image into the correct position to the right of the table.

12.2.5 Rotate an image

Because the image has been taken using a digital camera and saved, the original image is upside down. The image could be saved and adjusted in an external graphics package, or can be adjusted in the Format Picture pane within *Microsoft Word*. Click the left mouse button on the Pentagon icon to select the Effects section of this menu.

Click on the triangle to open the 3-D Rotation options.

To turn the image upside down, we must rotate the image through 180 degrees. Select the Z Rotation section and use the small arrows until the image has been fully rotated.

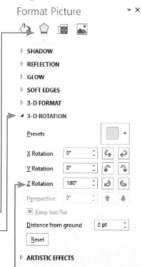

Save your document as task12c.

Task 12d

Open the file task12c.

Crop the image **trees.jpg** to remove the bottom 25% of it.

12.2.6 Crop an image

To **crop** an image is to cut off part of the image. This changes its aspect ratio but does not distort the image. Right mouse click on the image **trees.jpg** to get two menus and left click on **Crop**.

The drag handles for the image will change to crop handles. Drag the centre crop handle at the top of the image down so that about 25% (1/4) of the image is selected (so that it becomes grey) like this.

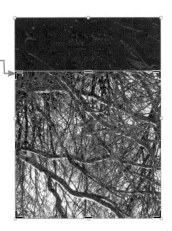

Look carefully at this image and you will see that with the crop tool selected, the image is upside down. This is because this image has already been rotated through 180 degrees in Section 12.2.5 but cropping takes place on the original image. You will notice that you have dragged from the top of the image rather than the bottom of the image. Click the left mouse button on the text and the image will be cropped and appear the right way up, with the snow on the top of the branches, like this.

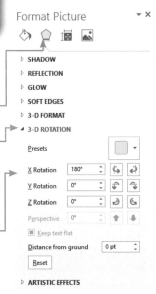

This image will need moving so that it aligns with the top of the table and right margin.

Save your document as task12d.

Task 12e

Open the file task12d.

Reflect the image **snowman.jpg** so that the snowman faces the other two images.

12.2.7 Reflect an image

To reflect an image, left mouse click on the image and select the Format Picture pane, then click on the Pentagon icon to select the Effects section of this menu. **Do not** select Reflection, but click on the triangle to open the 3-D Rotation options. With the 3-D Rotation features, a reflection (flip) from left to right is an X rotation of 180 degrees and a (flip) reflection from top to bottom is a Y rotation of 180 degrees. Sometimes it is easier to perform these functions in a graphics package before placing the image.

For this task, set the X rotation of 180 degrees, like this.

Save your document as task12e. The finished document should look like this.

Winter weather forces schools to close
By <Your Name>

On Monday February 2nd 2009 the South East of England was hit by snow. I know this is not unusual in many parts of the world, but it was interesting to watch the whole region grind to a virtual standstill. At the time of writing this article the major London airports of Heathrow, Gatwick and London City were all closed. Stansted airport had been closed but has just had one runway re-opened. Travel chaos has ensued, the M25 is closed in many places and many schools throughout the country have been closed.

School closures

The dramatic change in the weather has meant that a number of areas are experiencing transport problems. This means that many schools across the country have been closed.

County	Closed
South East	
Essex	250+
Hertfordshire	100+
Middlesex	80+
Sussex	50+
North	
Greater Manchester	100
Lancashire	70
Cumbria	34
Durham	70
Northumberland	33
Yorkshire	1

This table shows the number of schools reported closed. It is interesting to note that although the snow is no heavier in the South East of England, one of the eastern Counties has reported more than 250 of its schools are closed.

This gave the children lots time to play in the snow, snowballing, making snowmen and snow angels. The snow gave an added dimension, producing some very picturesque scenes, many captured on camera.

Task 12f

Open the file **trees.jpg**. Save the image as a .png file.

Adjust the colour depth of this image to 16 bits per channel and save the new image as **trees2.png**.

12.2.8 Adjust the colour depth of an image

These functions will be performed in *Adobe Photoshop*. Open the package and open the file **trees.jpg**. Save the image using the FILE tab, then Save As. Keep the filename as **trees** and change the Format to **PNG**.

All colour JPEG images have a colour depth of 24 bits which is 8 bits per colour channel (greyscale JPEG images have less). If you need to do lots of editing to an image it is better to change the colour depth before starting, so as to reduce the image degradation (sometimes seen as blurring) when making the changes. Changing the colour depth of an image also changes the file size. A file with a 48 bit colour depth (16 bits per channel) needs twice the storage space of a file with a 24 bit (8 bits per channel) colour depth.

Select the Image tab, followed by Mode, then change the colour depth from 8 Bits/Channel to 16 Bits/Channel.

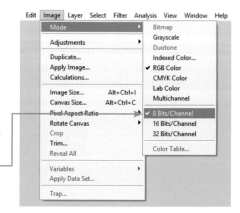

Save the image again but change the filename to **trees2** and keep the Format as **PNG** as JPEG does not support 48 bit images. The difference in the file sizes can be seen here.

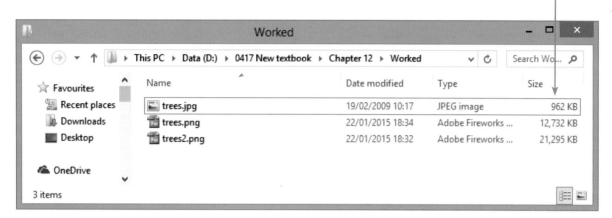

Task 12g

Rotate the file **trees2.png** through 180 degrees and save the new image as **trees3.png**.

Open the file **trees.png** in *Adobe Photoshop*. Select the Image tab, followed by Rotate Canvas. From the sub-menu select **180°**.

Save the new image as **trees3.png**.

Task 12h

Increase the brightness of the image **trees3.png** and decrease the contrast, so the image can be used as a background. Save the new image as **trees4.png**.

12.2.9 Adjust the brightness and contrast of an image

Open the file **trees3.png** in *Adobe Photoshop*. Select the Image tab, followed by Adjustments. From the sub-menu select Brightness/Contrast... which opens the Brightness/Contrast window.

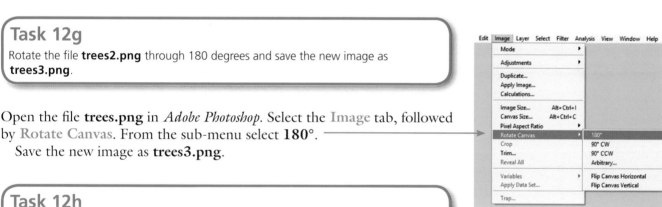

Use the two sliders to edit both the Brightness and the Contrast until the image looks appropriate for the task.

Save the new image as **trees4.png**.

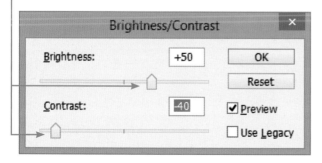

Advice

The brightness and contrast of an image can also be edited with the packages in *Microsoft Office* in a similar way using the right-hand icon from the Format Picture pane, then selecting PICTURE CORRECTIONS and the sliders for Brightness and Contrast.

Activity 12a

Open the image **snowangel.png** in a suitable package. Reduce the colour depth to 8 bits per channel. Rotate the image 90 degrees clockwise. Save the image as **snowangel1.png**. Save the image again as **snowangel1.jpg**. Show evidence of the finished image, the filenames and file sizes.

Activity 12b

Open the presentation **winter.pptx** in a suitable package. Crop the bottom 30 % from the image **dog.png**, reduce its contrast and increase its brightness. Place it to fill the slide so that it becomes a background image.

Find an appropriate image of a snowman. Resize it to 2 cm high. Place it 1 cm from the top of the slide and 1 cm from the left of the slide with no border.

Activity 12c

Open the file you saved in Activity 12b. Reflect (flip horizontally) the image of the snowman. Place a 1pt red border around this image.

(13) Layout

In this chapter you will learn how to:

- use software tools to prepare a basic document to match the purpose and target audience
- create a new document
- open an existing document
- place objects into the document
- enter and edit data including text and numbers
- create a table
- format a table and its contents
- wrap text around a table
- explain why headers and footers are needed
- create headers and footers
- use a header and footer
- align the contents of the header and footer consistently within a document
- place automated objects in headers and footers.

For this chapter you will need these source files from the CD:

- text1.rtf
- table1.csv
- text2.rtf
- table2.csv
- activity13c.rtf.

13.1 Basic documents

This chapter will help you develop your document layout skills. The word 'document' does not just relate to a word-processed document, but can be a piece of written or printed material, or an electronic file that provides information or evidence or that serves as an official record. These can even include images such as photographs. Such documents will therefore include word-processed documents from *Microsoft Word*, reports from a database using *Microsoft Access*, spreadsheets, graphs and charts using *Microsoft Excel*, a presentation using *Microsoft PowerPoint* or a web page. Even though each of these packages requires different practical skills, they have many common elements which work in similar ways.

New documents need to be created with regard to the target audience, which will often be a major factor in setting the styles that will be used within the document (more details can be found in Chapter 14). One other very important element will be the accuracy of your data entry. Always check your documents for typing errors. More help will be given on proofing in Chapter 15.

Plan it

Plan your document before starting it by making sure that you know:

- What is the purpose of the document?
- Who is the target audience?
- How will I make it suitable for this audience?
- What is the appropriate medium?
- What is the appropriate package?

13.1.1 Create a new document

The method used to create a new document in most of these applications will depend on whether the package is already open in the computer.

Create a new document if the package is already open

To create a new document in most of these applications (databases, graphs, charts and web pages are different), open the application package and click on the FILE tab followed by New. It is worth saving your new document as soon as you have started it, and saving your work often using the methods shown in Chapter 11.

Create a new document if the package is not open

This method does not apply to web pages. Open the application package. It may open a new document when the package is opened. In this case go to Section 13.2. If it does not automatically open a new document, then the Start screen for the package will open. If you are using a home computer, down the left side is a list of recently used files that could be selected. It is unlikely that this will appear in many school systems due to the security settings placed by your network administrator. In the bottom left corner of the window will be an option to Open other.... The rest of this depends upon the package, if it is *Microsoft Word* you will see 🖿 Open Other Documents, if it is *Microsoft Access* you will see 🖿 Open Other Files, if it is *Microsoft Excel* you will see 🖿 Open Other Workbooks, etc. Double click on this text and double click to select New from the left menu. Open a new blank document/workbook/database, etc by selecting the top left icon in the window. It is worth saving your new document as soon as you have started it, and saving your work frequently using the methods shown in Chapter 11.

13.1.2 Open an existing document

The method used to open an existing document in most of these applications will depend upon whether the package is already open in the computer.

Open a document if the software is already running

If the software is already running, in most applications (except databases, graphs, charts and web pages), click on the FILE tab followed by Open. It is worth saving your new document as soon as you have opened it, with a different version number using the methods shown in Chapter 11. This will make sure that the original file that you have opened is kept without changes.

Open a document if the software is not running

This method does not apply to web pages. Open the software package and the Start screen for the software will open. If you are using a home computer, down the left side is a list of recently used files that could be selected. It is unlikely that this will appear in many school systems due to the security settings placed by your network administrator. In the bottom left corner of the window will be an option to Open other.... The rest of this depends upon the package, if it is *Microsoft Word* you will see 🖿 Open Other Documents, if it is *Microsoft Access* you will see 🖿 Open Other Files, if it is *Microsoft Excel* you will see 🖿 Open Other Workbooks, etc. Double click on this text and locate your file within your storage area from the Computer icon. It is worth saving your new document as soon as you have opened it, with a different version number using the methods shown in Chapter 11. This will make sure that the original file that you have opened is kept without changes.

13.2 Place objects into a document

> ## Task 13a
>
> Create a new document. Open the file **text1.rtf** and insert the file **table1.csv** as a table within the document. Change the document heading to 'Winter weather forces schools to close'. Save the document as task13a.

13.2.1 Place text

Before starting this task, examine the files **text1.rtf** and **table1.csv**. As Task 13a makes no mention of the purpose of the task or its audience we cannot answer the first three questions from the 'Plan it' section above. After examining the two files:

- the most appropriate medium would appear to be printed on paper (or if used electronically as a downloadable document)
- the most appropriate package would appear to be a word processor (although this may be converted into portable document format if used as a downloadable document).

Open the document **text1.rtf** in *Microsoft Word*. As you do this, when you get to the **Open** window, you may need to change the file type to **All Files**.

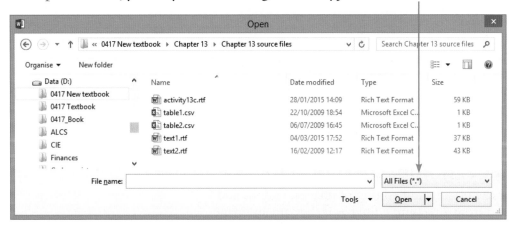

If you do not you may not be able to see all the files that are needed for this task in the **Open** window. Left mouse click on **text1.rtf** and select [Open ▾].

Use the **FILE** tab and **Save As** to save this document with the filename task13a as a *Word* document, rather than in rich text format.

13.2.2 Place a table from a .csv file

Open *Microsoft Word*. Open the file **table1.csv** as a new *Word* document. An alternative to copying and pasting the table into the document would be to place the .csv file in the document as an **embedded object**. This is really useful if you wanted to update the table within another package like a spreadsheet, but is not as useful when you have little time to keep updating objects embedded into a document.

The file **table1.csv** looks like this when it has been opened in *Word*.

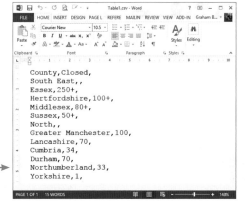

Advice

If you have to combine more than one file (sometimes with different file types), open each file as a new document, then copy and paste from one document to another. This method can reduce any problems that could occur with embedded objects.

Now you need to edit it, to turn the comma separated values into a table and copy it into the file that you recently saved. Highlight all the text (hold the <CTRL> key and tap the <A> key) and then select the INSERT tab followed by the Table icon.

Click the left mouse button on Convert Text to Table....

Because the text is highlighted it will be placed within the cells of a table.

This opens the Convert Text to Table window. Click on [OK] to create the table. If *Word* has not offered you the correct values for rows and columns because the .csv file contains both commas and carriage returns, then the table may need editing by either removing blank rows and/or columns. In this example, it has created an extra column to the right.

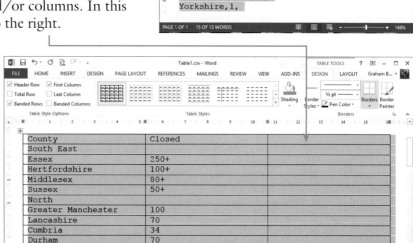

To remove this column, first click the left mouse button in a cell in the right-hand column. This removes the highlighting from the table. In the same cell, right mouse click to obtain a drop-down menu. From this menu select the Delete Cells... option.

Choose the radio button for Delete entire column followed by [OK].

Copy this table and paste it in place of the text <*Place table here*> in the document that you saved as task13a. This task is continued in Section 13.2.4.

13.2.3 Place an image, graph, chart or database extract

Please refer to Chapter 12 for the placing and editing of images. Graphs and charts can be copied and pasted from *Excel* and edited as if they are an image within a document. If a database extract is to be included in another form of document, export this (as shown in Chapter 18) before copying and pasting this into the document.

Place a screen shot in a document

To take a screen shot of the current screen use the <Print Screen> or <Prt Scr> key on your keyboard. This captures an image of the screen contents (the same as Copy) and places it in the clipboard. Paste this image into a document. To take a screen shot of a single window use <Alt> and <Prt Scr>. To take a screen shot of part of a window use the Snip tool (as shown in Chapter 11). Please note that if you want to show a drop-down menu that you are using in the screen shot, you must capture the whole screen and crop unused areas from the image. See the section on cropping images in Chapter 12.

13.2.4 Enter and edit data

Data can include text and numbers. For the purposes of a document, both can be entered and edited in the same way through the keyboard.

Advice

For screen shots in an evidence document, make sure that it is easy to read the contents of the screen shot but **do not** crop off the information that may be needed, for example: your name, Centre number and candidate number, the filename or the evidence that you are using a web browser rather than an editing package.

Enter text or numbers in a document

Open the file task13a. To change the document heading, highlight the existing heading and overtype this with the new heading from the task. Although this seems one of the easiest tasks, it is one where a significant number of students fail to check their data entry. You will need to be 100 per cent accurate with all data entry, including the use of capital and lower case letters. The document should now look like this.

Save the changes to this document.

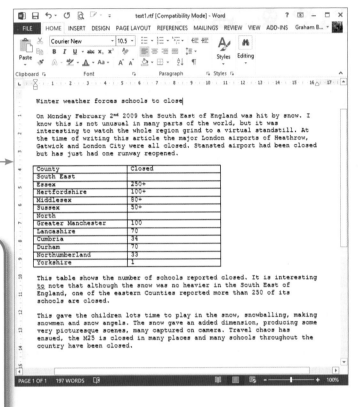

Edit text or numbers in a document

Task 13b

Open the file task13a.

Move the last sentence in the document so that it becomes the last sentence in the first paragraph.

Add a new subtitle 'School closures' just above the table, and add this new paragraph between the subtitle and the table:

'The dramatic change in the weather has meant that a number of areas are experiencing transport problems. This means that many schools across the country have been closed.'

In the third paragraph change the word 'was' to 'is', and add the word 'has' between 'counties' and 'reported'.

Save the document as task13b.

There are a number of techniques that could be used to move the last sentence to the end of the first paragraph. These include cut and paste, copy and paste then delete the original and drag and drop. It is recommended that you learn and practise all of these methods.

All three methods require you to highlight the correct section of text. A useful tip (especially if you are right-handed) is to highlight from the end of the text back to the beginning rather than the other way around. Highlight the text like this.

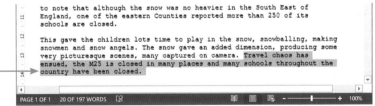

Editing methods

You can now choose your method from the following.

Cut and paste
Right mouse click within the highlighted area to get the drop-down menu, then select **Cut**. This removes the sentence and places it in the windows clipboard. Move the **cursor** to the end of the first paragraph and right mouse click to obtain the drop-down menu again. This time select **Paste**.

Copy, paste and delete
Right mouse click within the highlighted area to get the drop-down menu, then select **Copy**. This copies the sentence to the clipboard but does not remove it.

Move the cursor to the end of the first paragraph and right mouse click to obtain the drop-down menu and select **Paste**. Move back to the original sentence, highlight it and press the <Delete> key on the keyboard. Although this method takes longer than method 1, it does not remove the original sentence until the end of the process, so if you accidentally lose the sentence from the clipboard the original is still present.

Drag and drop

Click the left mouse button in the highlighted area and hold this down, moving the cursor to the end of the first paragraph. Release the left mouse button at that point and you will drop all of the highlighted text there.

Whichever method you have used, make sure that the character spacing between the sentences and the line spacing between paragraphs matches the rest of the document. Check carefully for any inconsistencies.

To add the subtitle, move the cursor to the end of the first paragraph and press the <Enter> key twice. (This will keep the same paragraph spacing as the rest of the document.) Now type the text 'School closures' followed by the <Enter> key. Type the new paragraph given in Task 13b. Go back and check for data entry errors and the consistency of spacing. Correct any errors.

To change the word 'was' to 'is', locate the word and highlight it. Type in the word 'is' and it will replace the original. To insert the word 'has', place the cursor between the words 'counties' and 'reported'. Make sure that there is a single space on each side of the cursor before you type the word 'has'.

Save your document as task13b. The finished document should look like this.

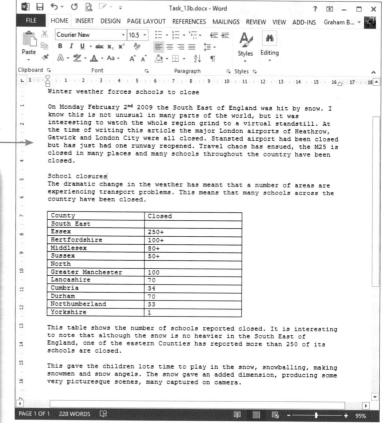

Advice

Use <Ctrl><X> to cut, <Ctrl><C> to copy and <Ctrl><V> to paste.

Advice

Drag and drop is easy when both positions are on the screen at the same time, but harder when you need to scroll through the document before dropping.

Activity 13a

Open the file **text2.rtf** from the CD and insert the file **table2.csv** as a table within the document after the paragraph that ends 'This table shows the number of schools closed in some of the local authorities:'.

Change the document heading to 'Snow brings disruption to Britain'.

Move the last paragraph in the document so that it becomes the first paragraph.

Add the following text as a new paragraph immediately before the paragraph that starts 'Flights were suspended ...':

'Heavy snowfalls were reported to the north of London. London was also affected but not to the same extent as the disruption that had been caused the week before.'

In the last paragraph change the word 'weird' to 'unusual' and add the word 'national' between 'many' and 'newspapers'.

Save and print this document.

13.2.5 Create a table

Tables of data may need inserting into your word-processed documents or presentations. You have already inserted a table from a .csv file in Task 13a.

Task 13c

Open the file task13b.

Add to the end of the document the following text as a new paragraph:

'Temperatures recorded at one weather station in Ross-on-Wye during the week read:'

Below this add this table:

	Maximum	Minimum
2nd Feb	3	−1
3rd Feb	5	−3
4th Feb	5	−3
5th Feb	2	−1
6th Feb	2	−1
7th Feb	5	−3
8th Feb	4	−2

Save the document as task13c.

Open the file task13b and add the text given above as a new paragraph to the end of the document.

To create a new table you must first work out how many rows and columns the table contains. By counting them, you can work out that this table contains three columns and eight rows. Move the cursor to the correct place in the document, then select the INSERT tab, the Tables section and click on the Table icon.

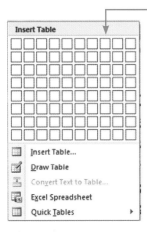

This will open the Insert Table drop-down menu. Move the cursor over the grid until it highlights the three columns and eight rows that you need, like this. ——▶

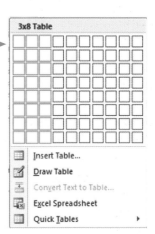

Click the left mouse button in the last highlighted cell of the grid and this will insert a three by eight table into your document. Add the text from the task into this table. You can move the cursor into the next cell by pressing the <Tab> key. If you need more rows than the eight available, move the cursor into the last cell of the table and press the <Tab> key to create a new row. If you need lots of new rows, hold down the <Tab> key. Save the document as task13c.

209

Activity 13b

Create a new document with the title 'Skills to practise using tables'. Create this table, below the title.

Function	How	Feature		
Insert	Insert tab	Table		
	Right click	Rows		
	Right click	Columns		
Delete		Rows		
Format		Cells	Alignment	Left, right, centre, fully justified
				Top, centre, bottom
			Colour, shading	
		Rows	Breaks across page	
		Gridlines	Show	
			Hide	
Text wrapping		Cells		

Save this document.

13.2.6 Format a table

Tables can be formatted so that they can be aligned left, right or centrally between the margins. Text can be wrapped around the table or not as required. These features are found in the table properties: click the right mouse button in any cell of the table, then select Table Properties... and the Table tab within the Table Properties window. The table alignment can be selected in the Alignment section and text wrapping around the table can be switched on or off in the Text wrapping section.

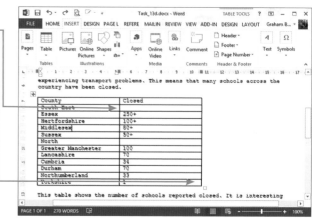

Task 13d

Open the file that you saved in Task 13c.

Narrow the columns in the top table so that there is a minimum of white space but no text wraps within a cell.

Set the text wrapping options for this table so that the body text of the document flows around the table.

Save the document as task13d.

Open the file that you saved in Task 13c. Move the cursor into the top table and grab the vertical gridline.

Drag this to the left while holding down the left mouse button so that it almost reaches the right edge of the longest data item. Repeat this with the right-hand gridline.

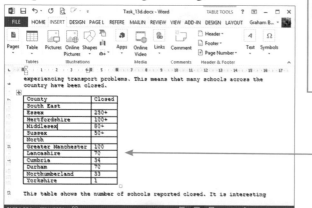

The table will look like this.

Click the right mouse button in any cell of the table, then select Table Properties... and the Table tab within the Table Properties window. Move the cursor into the Text wrapping section and select Around to wrap the body text around the table. Click on OK to complete this. The table should look like this.

Save the document as task13d.

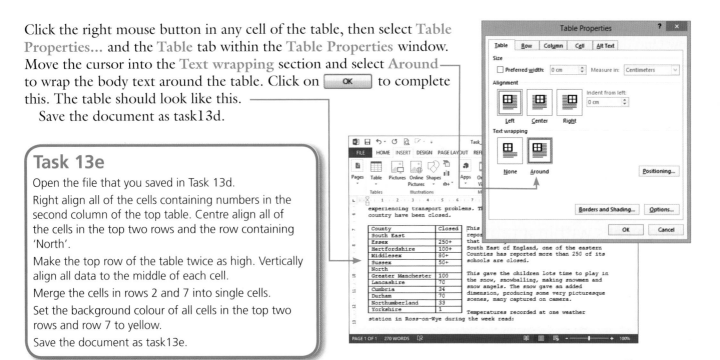

Task 13e

Open the file that you saved in Task 13d.

Right align all of the cells containing numbers in the second column of the top table. Centre align all of the cells in the top two rows and the row containing 'North'.

Make the top row of the table twice as high. Vertically align all data to the middle of each cell.

Merge the cells in rows 2 and 7 into single cells.

Set the background colour of all cells in the top two rows and row 7 to yellow.

Save the document as task13e.

Align cell contents within a table

Move the cursor into the top table. To highlight all the cells containing numbers, left mouse click in the top cell containing numbers and drag the mouse down. Select the HOME tab. In the Paragraph section find the four icons for text alignment. Click on the third icon to right align the contents of these cells.

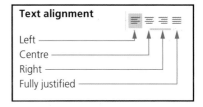

Text alignment

Left
Centre
Right
Fully justified

Highlight all cells in the top two rows of the table as described above, hold down the <CTRL> key and drag over the contents of the cell containing 'North' so that all five cells are highlighted like this.

Select the HOME tab. In the Paragraph section find and click on the second icon for text alignment.

Vertically align cell contents within a table

To make the top row of the table twice as high, grab the gridline below the top row and drag down so that it changes from this to this.

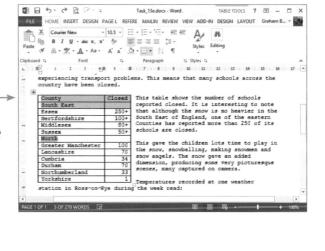

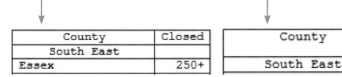

County	Closed
South East	
Essex	250+

County	Closed
South East	

You can see that the cell contents are aligned to the top of the cells in this row (and the rest of the table). You must vertically align all data to the middle of each cell. Highlight all the cells in the table and click the right mouse button in one of these cells. Select Table Properties... and the Cell tab. Click in Center then [OK] so that it changes from this to this.

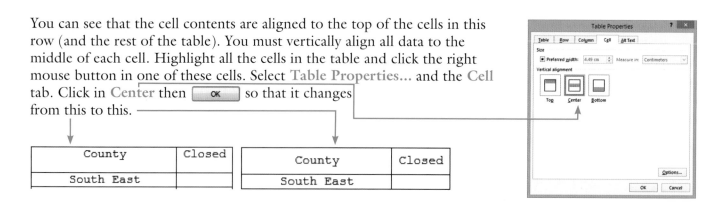

County	Closed
South East	

County	Closed
South East	

Merge cells within a table

Highlight both cells in row 2 of the table and click the right mouse button in one of these cells. Select Merge Cells from the drop-down menu. Repeat this for row 7. The table now looks like this.

Set the background colour to cells within a table

Highlight all cells in rows 1, 2 and 7 together. Select the HOME tab. In the Paragraph section click on the small triangle to the right of the Shading icon to get a drop-down menu/palette.

The palette gives you a range of greyscale shadings, the theme colours that are available, plus some of the standard colours. If the colour that you require is not present use the More Colors... option.

For this question we need yellow so click on the yellow block in the palette.

Save the document as task13e.

County	Closed
South East	
Essex	250+
Hertfordshire	100+
Middlesex	80+
Sussex	50+
North	
Greater Manchester	100
Lancashire	70
Cumbria	34
Durham	70
Northumberland	33
Yorkshire	1

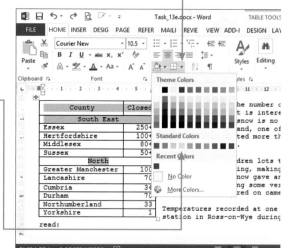

Advice

The Shading icon can also be found by clicking the right mouse button when the text has been highlighted in a small menu like this.

Task 13f

Open the file that you saved in Task 13e.

Remove all gridlines from the lower table except those cells containing the maximum and minimum temperatures during this week.

Save the document as task13f.

Add and remove gridlines from a table

To work on the second table, click the right mouse button in the table. Select Table Properties... and the Table tab. Select the option for Borders and Shading....

This opens the Borders and Shading window with the focus of the borders applied to this table.

To remove all borders (the four lines around the outside) and gridlines (the lines within a table) click on None, followed by OK twice. The borders and gridlines within the table will usually show as faint dashed lines that are visible on the screen but not when printed. Highlight the cells containing the maximum and minimum temperatures for the week, like this.

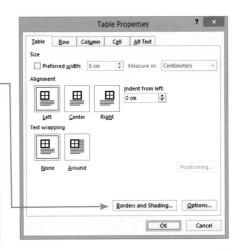

	Maximum	Minimum
2nd Feb	3	-1
3rd Feb	5	-3
4th Feb	5	-3
5th Feb	2	-1
6th Feb	2	-1
7th Feb	5	-3
8th Feb	4	-2

Click the right mouse button on one of these cells, select Table Properties..., the Table tab, then Borders and Shading....

As the Borders and Shading window opens, click on Grid to set the gridlines back.

Note that the focus of the borders applied to only these cells after selecting <OK> twice. Save the document as task13f.

The completed table will now look like this.

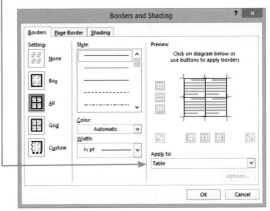

	Maximum	Minimum
2nd Feb	3	-1
3rd Feb	5	-3
4th Feb	5	-3
5th Feb	2	-1
6th Feb	2	-1
7th Feb	5	-3
8th Feb	4	-2

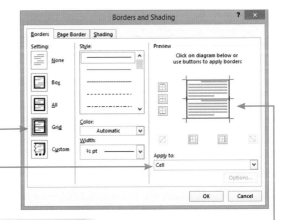

Activity 13c

Open the file **activity13c.rtf** in a suitable software package.

Merge all cells in the top row into a single cell. Centre align the text both horizontally and vertically. Shade this cell with a mid-grey background colour.

Merge cells 1 and 2, and merge cells 3 and 4 in row 2 of the table. Centre align all text in row 2 horizontally. Shade all three cells in this row with a light grey background colour.

Merge cell 1 in both rows 5 and 6. Merge cell 2 in both rows 4 and 5. Format each cell in rows 3 to 5 as it specifies in the table.

Replace the text <Your name> with your name.

Save the document.

Advice

A quick method of editing the borders is to click on this diagram.

Change the line widths, colours and turn lines on and off. Create a new table and play with the different options to see what they do.

13.3 Headers and footers

13.3.1 What is a header and footer?

A header is the area of a document between the top of the page and the top margin. A footer is the area of a document between the bottom of the page and the bottom margin. You can insert text or graphics into headers and footers. This might include the author's name, the document's filename, page numbering, or even a company logo. Headers and footers can be found in many printed documents, including those that have been word processed or desktop published, and in presentations, reports from spreadsheets and databases and in web pages.

13.3.2 Why are headers and footers needed?

Headers and footers are needed to make sure that each page (or pair of facing pages) has elements like the page number, book/document/chapter, logo, titles, filename etc. placed consistently within them. If these are placed in the header or footer, they only have to be placed once but will repeat on every (or every other) page. This saves the author a great deal of time and effort, not having to duplicate their work on every page.

13.3.3 Create headers and footers

In all the packages within *Microsoft Office* the headers and footers have already been created and these can be opened, edited, resized etc. rather than created. Most of these application packages use the INSERT tab to access the header and footer. *Microsoft Access* uses the design view of a report and has not only page headers and footers but also report headers and footers (see Chapter 18 for further details). Headers and footers are not used in website authoring at this level. Each package has a different method of entry.

Open headers and footers in *Microsoft Word*

Open *Microsoft Word*, then from the INSERT tab, find the Header & Footer section and select either the Header or Footer icon. ⎯⎯⎯⎯⎯⎯⎯⎯⎯⎯

Some standard themed settings are available for you to choose from if you wish, but I recommend the option to Edit Header/Footer is used.

Open headers and footers in *Microsoft Excel*

Open *Microsoft Excel*, then from the INSERT tab, find the Text section and select the Header & Footer icon. ⎯⎯⎯⎯⎯⎯⎯⎯⎯⎯

Open headers and footers in *Microsoft PowerPoint*

Open *Microsoft PowerPoint*, then from the INSERT tab, find the Text section and select the Header & Footer icon. ⎯⎯⎯⎯⎯⎯⎯⎯⎯⎯

To make the footer visible tick the check box next to footer. If slide numbers are required click on the check box next to slide numbers and then click on Apply to All (see Chapter 19 for more details).

13.3.4 Align headers and footers

Task 13g

Open the file that you saved in Task 13f.

Add your name on the left in the header, the text 'Historical Study' in the centre of the header and the text 'England 2009' on the right in the header.

Save the document as task13g.

Use the ruler

Open the file task13f in *Microsoft Word*. Make sure that the ruler is visible at the top of the document. If it is not visible select the **VIEW** tab and in the **Show** section tick the checkbox next to **Ruler**. Open the header from the **INSERT** tab, with **Header**, then **Blank** header. Click the left mouse button on the text [Type here] in the header so that it looks like this.

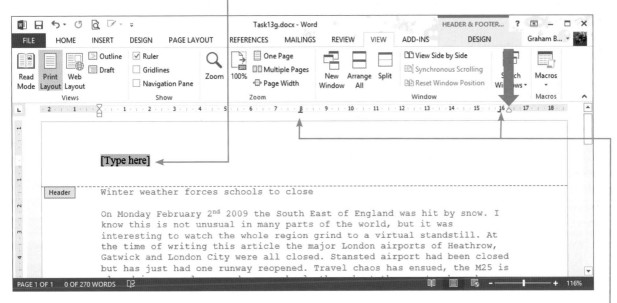

Check the alignment of the tab stops on the ruler before entering any text or object. In this case there are two tab stops placed on the ruler.

The left one of these is a centre aligned tab and show the centre of the page (although it is not precise in this example) and the right-hand tab stop shows the right-hand edge of the page, although we can clearly see that this does not match the full width (shown with the red arrow). These two **must** be placed together for the header to align to the edge of the body text. Grab the right-hand tab stop and drag this so that it sits over the right margin stop. Be careful not to drag the tab stop off the ruler or it will be removed. If this is difficult, hold down the <Alt> key whilst dragging it to stop it snapping to *Word*'s hidden gridlines.

Advice

<Ctrl> <Z> undoes the previous action and is a good tip if a tab stop has been accidentally removed. This will undo your last action.

The right tab stop should look like this.

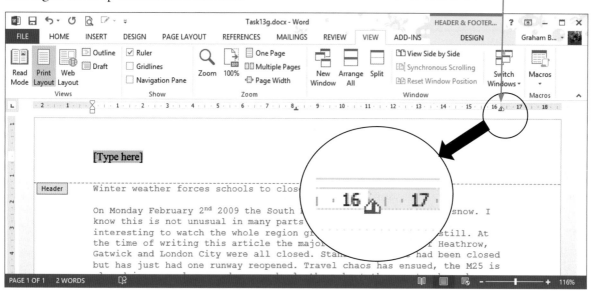

The right margin and tab stop have been placed at 16.3 centimetres from the left edge. The centre tab stop needs to be placed at 8.15 centimetres (half of this width). Use the left mouse button to drag the centre tab stop to this position.

Advice

You can always use the scale at the bottom right corner of the window to zoom in, if positioning the tab stop is difficult.

Click again on the text [Type here] and enter your name. Press the <Tab> key and enter the text 'Historical Study'. As you type this text you will see that it always stays exactly in the centre of the page. Press the <Tab> key again and enter the text 'England 2009'. As you enter it you should notice it always stays right aligned to the tab stops. The finished header looks like this.

Advice

Practise getting absolutely precise measurements for your tab stops.

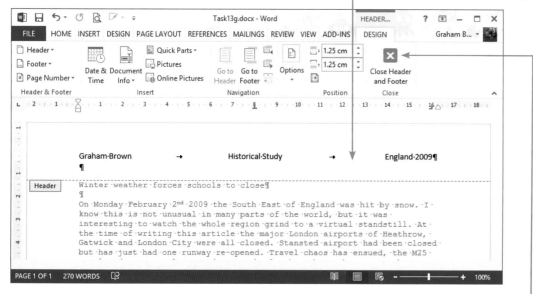

Double click the cursor in the body text to view the page showing the header and footer or double click on Close Header and Footer to return to Draft

View which will not show you the changes you have just made.
Save your document as task13g.

More on tab stops

There are four types of tab stop that you may need to use. These are:

Type of tab stop	Looks like	What does it do
Left tab	All text and numbers	Aligns tabbed text, so that the left edge of the text is in a fixed position.
Centre tab	All text and numbers	Aligns tabbed text, so that the centre point of the text is in a fixed position.
Right tab	All text and numbers	Aligns tabbed text, so that the right edge of the text is in a fixed position.
Decimal tab	400000.53 4.3 2134	Aligns tabbed text, so that numeric data aligns with the decimal point in a fixed position.

Example:

Left	Centre	Right	Decimal
Left tabbed	Centre tabbed	Right tabbed	$0.13
Left again	more centre tabbed	right	$1234.45
Left	Lots of centre aligned text	small right	$23.45

Tab stop positions can be added, edited or cleared from the Tabs window. To open this select the **HOME** tab, In the **Paragraph** section, double click to select the **Paragraph** group's dialog launcher in the bottom right corner.

Then from the paragraph window select the Tabs button.

This can be used to create new tabs, these are the tab stops for the example above.

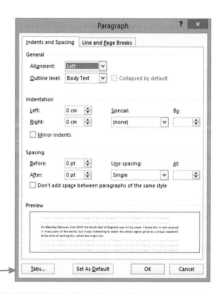

Task 13h

Open the file that you saved in Task 13g.

Place in the footer the text 'Saved on' followed by the date, then the text 'at' and the time on the left, with the page number page in the centre, and the automated filename and file path on the right.

Save the document as task13h.

13.3.5 Place automated objects in headers and footers

Open the file task13g in *Microsoft Word*. Make sure that the ruler is visible at the top of the document. Open the footer from the INSERT tab, with Footer, then the Blank (Three Columns) footer. Change the position of the right-aligned tab stop so that it precisely matches the page margin. Change the centre tab so that it is placed precisely half-way between the margins, like this (see Section 13.3.4).

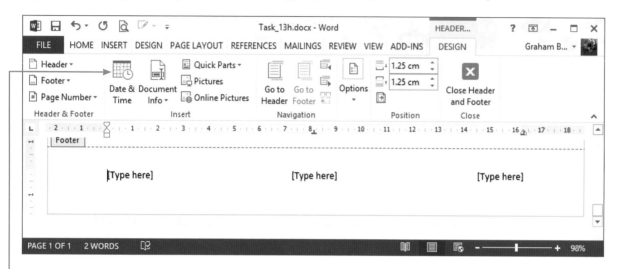

Automated date and time

Move the cursor over the left [Type here] and click the left mouse button to highlight it. Enter the text Saved on followed by a space, then click on the icon for Date & Time.

This will open the Date and Time window. Choose an appropriate date format, as the question does not tell you which one to use. This is a portrait page so a shorter version would be better. I have chosen the top option from the menu followed by OK.

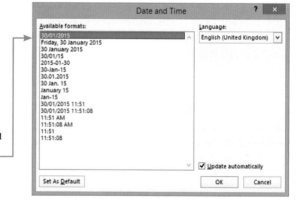

Type another space, the word 'at' followed by another space. Click on the icon for Date and Time and choose an appropriate time format followed by OK.

Automated page numbers

Move the cursor over the centre [Type here] and click the left mouse button to highlight it. Select the icon for Page Number to get the drop-down menu.

As we have moved to the correct position on the page already, click the left mouse button on Current Position. This opens another sub-menu from which you can choose the type of page numbering you require. Again, this is a portrait page so a shorter version would be better. I have chosen the top option Plain Number.

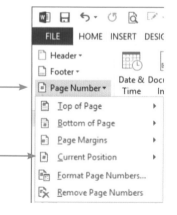

Automated filename and file path

Move the cursor over the text [Type here] and click the left mouse button to highlight it. Select the icon for Document Info to get the drop-down menu.

To add the file name and file path to the footer click the left mouse button on File Path.

Sometimes if you have used long file and folder names, or there is a long file path, the header or footer may look crowded. Do not change the tabs as these will have been set to match the question, even if sometimes it looks unusual like this.

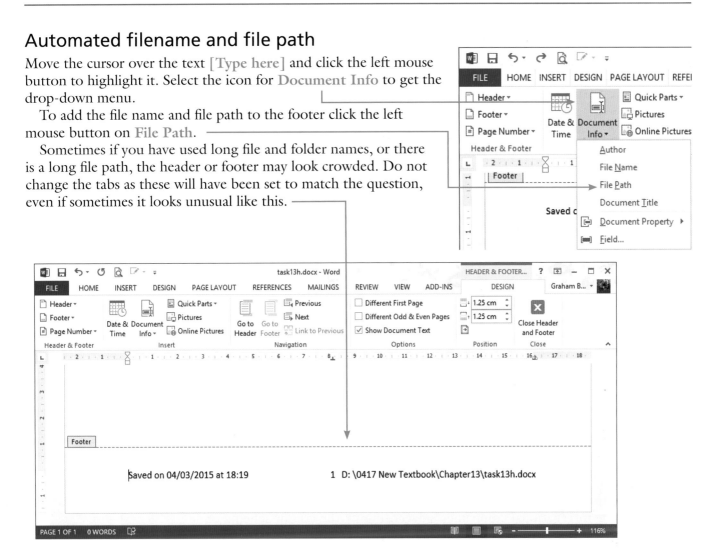

Save your document as task13h.

Activity 13d

Open the document that you saved in Activity 13c. Save it with the filename activity13d.

Place in the header: the text 'Created by' and your name, and an automated filename on the right. Place in the footer: the text 'Page number' followed by an automated page number in the centre, and the text 'Last updated:' followed by the date and time on the right.

Save the document.

(14) Styles

In this chapter you will learn how to:

- explain what a corporate house style is
- make sure that all work produced matches specified house styles and has consistency of presentation
- produce documents which conform to a corporate house style
- take into account the audience when creating or selecting a style
- create and edit styles for page layout including: text alignment, spacing between lines, spacing between paragraphs, spacing before and after headings
- create and edit styles including: font type (serif, sans-serif), font face, point size, font colour, text enhancement, bulleted lists, numbered lists
- create and apply paragraph style(s) with a new style name
- produce evidence of the styles you have created.

For this chapter you will need these source files from the CD:

- activity14a.rtf
- activity14b.rtf
- advice.rtf
- lists.rtf.

14.1 Corporate house styles

14.1.1 What is a corporate house style?

Most companies and organisations have a corporate house style. This is sometimes called 'corporate branding'. This can be seen on a company's products, printed stationery (like letterheads and business cards), advertising, websites and often on company vehicles. House style can range from company logos to recognised colour schemes, fonts, point sizes etc. You will probably recognise many international companies' advertising by the colour scheme or other stylistic features that they use, long before you can read the company name on the material. In ICT terms, you should always adopt a specific style for the work that you produce. Anything produced for a company will usually have a logo, colour scheme, font style, paragraph style, page layout (particularly if using headed notepaper), page formatting and defined styles for bullets and numbering.

When you produce work, it is important that you apply these styles to every element that you produce, whether it relates to a document, presentation or any other form of communication, especially when it is for customers or clients. The most important part of applying styles, is to make sure that you have consistency of presentation.

14.1.2 What is the purpose of a house style?

A house style is used to make sure that all documents and other materials from an organisation have consistency. It is used to save time in planning, setting up, creating and formatting documents and other materials. It is also designed to support brand recognition and reduces the risk of mistakes in documents, like typing errors in an address or telephone number, or missing an important element like a logo.

14.1.3 Match the specified house style

You must always make sure that all work produced matches the house styles given to you which may look like these examples.

Example 1 House style for a website

Create and apply the following styles to all web pages:

Style	Definition
h1	Font – Arial Bold, if this is not available Arial, if neither of these fonts are available, the browser's default sans-serif font. 24 point font. Black. Italic.
p	Font – Times, if this is not available Times New Roman, if neither of these fonts are available, the browser's default serif font. 11 point font. Black.
table	Gridlines visible and 2 points thick. Light grey background colour. Foreground colour #100080.

Example 2 House style for a presentation

The master slide must have:

- a yellow background
- a 4 point thick dark blue horizontal line 4 cm from the top of the slide
- the logo logo.jpg placed in the bottom left corner of the screen
- the text **Corporate House Styles** in a navy blue, underlined, 36 point serif font, above the line, with no text wrap, aligned to the right of the slide
- automatic slide numbers in the bottom right corner
- 1st level bullets formatted in a 24 point blue (#0000FF) italic sans-serif font with a hollow disc bullet style.

Example 3 House style for a word-processed document

Create, store and use the following paragraph styles:

	Font style	Font size	Alignment	Enhancement	Line spacing	Spacing before	Spacing after
Heading	sans-serif	24 point	right	bold, italic	Single	0	6 point
Subhead	sans-serif	16 point	centre	underlined	Single	0	6 point
Body text	serif	11 point	left		Single	0	11 point
Bulleted list	serif	10 point	left with 2 cm indent		Single	0	0 point
Header	serif	10 point	to page margins	bold			
Footer	serif	10 point	to page margins	bold			

Different techniques are required to apply these styles, each technique being package specific. However, the results would be that each document, web page or presentation slide would have the same formatting, colour scheme and layout. In the case of the website, the styles would be applied in a cascading stylesheet (see Chapter 21), for the presentation the master slide would be created and a theme applied (see Chapter 19) and for a document styles are defined and applied to the text and layout of a the page.

14.1.4 Font styles and sizes

Serif and sans-serif

Text can be changed to have different font faces, colours and sizes and can have a number of enhancements added. These are useful for making text stand out. Font faces are grouped into two main categories: serif fonts and sans-serif fonts. These are not the name of the font face, but are the generic categories that describe the properties of the font.

A serif font looks like this: **This is a serif font** and a sans-serif font looks like this: **This is a sans-serif font.**

Strokes   No strokes

The word 'serif' describes the short strokes at the end of individual letters. Sans-serif fonts do not have these short strokes. If you are asked to set text in a sans-serif font, you must find any font in your word processor that does not have these serif strokes.

Serif fonts are often used in newspapers and books as they are usually easier to read than sans-serif fonts. It would be appropriate to use sans-serif fonts for emphasis or for titles or subtitles. It is not sensible to use more than two different font faces on any page. You can use other enhancements to make text stand out such as bold, italics, underline and highlighting. Other elements like coloured text and backgrounds can also be used to emphasise text.

Font size

Font sizes are measured in points. There are 72 points to an inch (which is just over 2.5 cm). If you are asked to produce text of an appropriate size, for most adults 10 point is appropriate as body text, but older readers may prefer 12 point. Anything above 14 point is generally unsuitable as body text for adults, but may be ideal for children. In stories for children learning to read (ages four to six) it may be appropriate to use a 20 or 24 point font size to make it easier to make out the letter shapes. Larger font sizes would also be appropriate as body text for the partially sighted. Much depends upon the target audience.

Font face

The font face is the design of the typeface. Different fonts like Arial, Arial Narrow and **Arial Black** all have the same design for each letter but have different widths. Some fonts can be the same size but appear to be different heights. For example, all of these fonts are 11 points high:

ALGERIAN, *Brush Script Std*, *Edwardian Script ITC* and Arial.

The height of the font is measured using the measurement from the top of the letter with the tallest ascender (often the letter 'h'), to the bottom of the one with the longest descender (i.e. the bit that descends below the line, often the letter 'f').

14.2 Create styles in a document

For this chapter we will focus on the application of styles within a word-processed document. The document contains layout and font styles. In *Microsoft Word*, the layout styles are stored in a document template which is usually hidden from you. As you create a new document, a set of default styles are applied to it. They include the page orientation, margin settings, settings for the header and footer as well as different font styles which *Microsoft* have called 'Themes'.

Open the file task13h in *Microsoft Word*. Save this as task14a. We will start in the header. Open the header of the document and highlight all the text in the header, like this.

Task 14a

	Font style	Font size	Alignment	Enhancement	Spacing
Header	serif	10 point	to page margins	bold	
Footer	serif	10 point	to page margins	bold	

Open the document you saved as task13h. Create, store and use the following styles in this document.

Save the document as task14a.

Graham Brown   Historical Study   England 2009

Header   Winter weather forces schools to close

Select the HOME tab. In the Font section find the drop-down menu for the font face.

Set the font face to Times New Roman which is a serif font. Set the Font Size to 10 point using the drop-down menu next to the font size.

The text in the header does align to the page margins (you took great care getting that right in Chapter 13) so the last part of this style is to embolden (add the bold enhancement) to this text. With all the header text highlighted select the HOME tab and in the font section click on the icon for bold.

The header will now look like this.

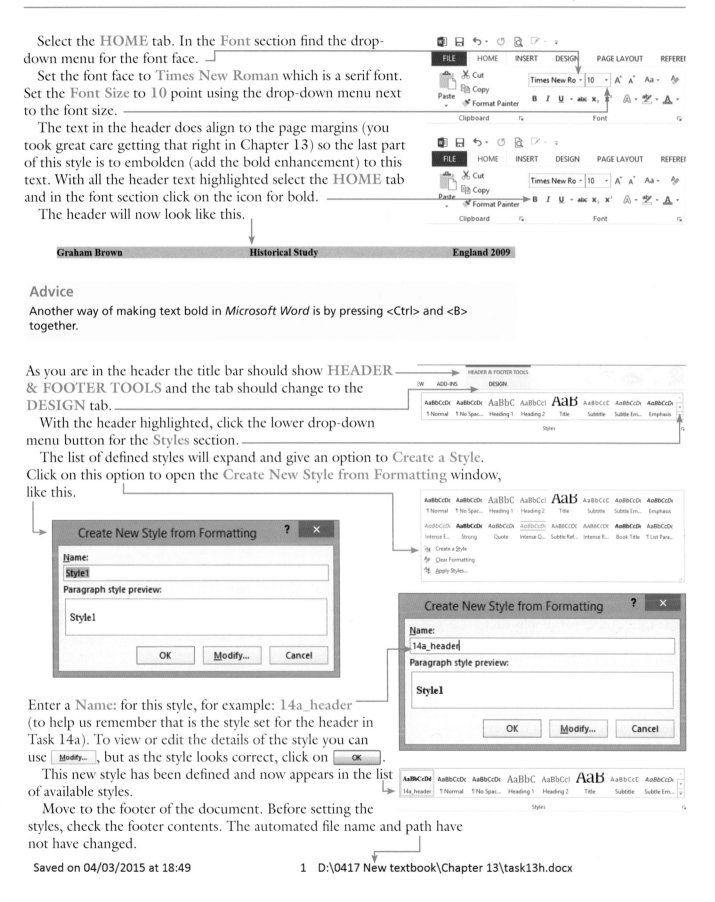

| Graham Brown | Historical Study | England 2009 |

Advice

Another way of making text bold in *Microsoft Word* is by pressing <Ctrl> and <B> together.

As you are in the header the title bar should show HEADER & FOOTER TOOLS and the tab should change to the DESIGN tab.

With the header highlighted, click the lower drop-down menu button for the Styles section.

The list of defined styles will expand and give an option to Create a Style. Click on this option to open the Create New Style from Formatting window, like this.

Enter a Name: for this style, for example: 14a_header (to help us remember that is the style set for the header in Task 14a). To view or edit the details of the style you can use Modify... , but as the style looks correct, click on OK .

This new style has been defined and now appears in the list of available styles.

Move to the footer of the document. Before setting the styles, check the footer contents. The automated file name and path have not have changed.

Your file path will not be the same as the one shown here. To update this, click the right mouse button on the filename/path to get the drop-down menu. Click on Update field. The filename will have changed to look similar to this.

Saved on 04/03/2015 at 18:48   1   D:\0417 New textbook\Chapter 14\task14a.docx

Highlight all of the footer, select the HOME tab then click the left mouse button on the style you called 14a_header.

Saved on 04/03/2015 at 18:48   1   D:\0417 New textbook\Chapter 14\task14a.docx

The footer should change from this to this.

Saved on 04/03/2015 at 18:55   1   D:\0417 New textbook\Chapter 14\task14a.docx

Save the document.

Task 14b

Open the document you saved as task14a. Add the text 'Winter wonderland or woe?' as a new main heading at the start of the document. Create, store and use the following styles in this document.

	Font face	Font size	Alignment	Enhancement	Line spacing	Spacing before	Spacing after
Heading	sans-serif	24 point	right	bold, italic	Single	0	6 point
Subheading	sans-serif	16 point	centre	underlined	Single	0	6 point
Body text	serif	11 point	left		Single	0	11 point

Save the document as task14b.

Advice

Use the ¶ Show/Hide icon from the home tab to show all hidden characters like returns and tabs.

Open the document that you saved in Task 14a. Move to the top of the document and add the text 'Winter wonderland or woe?' as a main heading before the subheading 'Winter weather forces schools to close'. Remove all blank lines from the document using the cursor and <Delete> key.

When defining the font styles, always start with the body text. Many people start by highlighting all the text using <Ctrl> and <A>, but for this task, just highlight the first paragraph. This will let you practise applying this style to the other paragraphs later.

Select the HOME tab. In the Font section, set the font face to Times New Roman. Set the Font Size to 11 point using the drop-down menu. In the Paragraph section, select the text alignment to left using this icon.

In the Paragraph section select the Paragraph Settings arrow to open up the Paragraph window. Move to the Spacing section.

Select Single for the Line spacing: and type the value (sometimes you can use the up and down arrows) in the After: box.

Click on ☐ OK ☐ to format this paragraph. From the HOME tab click the lower drop-down menu button for the Styles section.

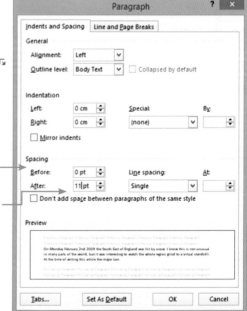

Click on Create a Style to open the Create New Style from Formatting window. Enter a Name: for this style, for example: 14b_body (to help us remember that is the style set for the body text in Task 14b). To view or edit the details of the style you can use Modify... , but as the style looks correct, click on OK .

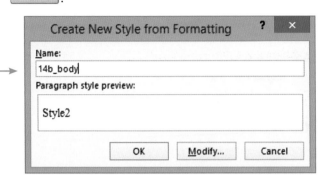

Click the cursor into each paragraph in turn, then then click the left mouse button on the style you called 14b_body.

Highlight the text for the main heading. In the Font section, set the font face to Arial which is a sans-serif font (i.e. it does not have serifs). Set the Font Size to 24 point. In the Paragraph section, select the text alignment to the right using this icon.

Open up the Paragraph window (as described on the previous page). In the Spacing section, leave the line spacing as single (as no spacing has been specified), but change the After: to 6 point. Click on OK to close this window. With the heading still highlighted, go to the Font section and click the left mouse button on the icon to embolden the text (i.e. to make it bold).

Click the left mouse button on the icon to italicise the text (i.e. to make it italic). From the Styles section, use Create a Style to open the Create New Style from Formatting window. Enter a Name: for this style, for example: 14b_heading, then click on OK .

Use the same method to set the font style to the same sans-serif font (Arial) as the heading style. It is good practice to use as few fonts as possible within a document, two or three are acceptable. Set the size to 16 point and spacing as for the heading style. To centre align the text, move to the Paragraph section and use this icon.

In the Font section select the underline icon.

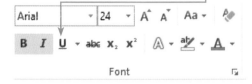

Use Create a Style and call this style 14b_sub-head. Click on each subheading in turn and click on this style. Save the document which should look similar to the one shown on the next page.

Advice

If you are asked to enhance text (e.g. … make this text bold …), do not use other enhancements as well (e.g. underline or italic).

Graham Brown   Historical Study   England 2009

Winter wonderland or woe?

Winter weather forces schools to close

On Monday February 2nd 2009 the South East of England was hit by snow. I know this is not unusual in many parts of the world, but it was interesting to watch the whole region grind to a virtual standstill. At the time of writing this article the major London airports of Heathrow, Gatwick and London City were all closed. Stansted airport had been closed but has just had one runway reopened. Travel chaos has ensued, the M25 is closed in many places and many schools throughout the country have been closed.

School closures

The dramatic change in the weather has meant that a number of areas are experiencing transport problems. This means that many schools across the country have been closed.

County	Closed
South East	
Essex	250+
Hertfordshire	100+
Middlesex	80+
Sussex	50+
North	
Greater Manchester	100
Lancashire	70
Cumbria	34
Durham	70
Northumberland	33
Yorkshire	1

This table shows the number of schools reported closed. It is interesting to note that although the snow is no heavier in the South East of England, one of the eastern Counties has reported more than 250 of its schools are closed.

This gave the children lots time to play in the snow, snowballing, making snowmen and snow angels. The snow gave an added dimension, producing some very picturesque scenes, many captured on camera.

Temperatures recorded at one weather station in Ross-on-Wye during the week read:

	Maximum	Minimum
2nd Feb	3	−1
3rd Feb	5	−3
4th Feb	5	−3
5th Feb	2	−1
6th Feb	2	−1
7th Feb	5	−3
8th Feb	4	−2

Activity 14a

Open the file **activity14a.rtf**. This document has four headings, a table, a bulleted list and body text. Add your name to the left in the header. Add an automated date and time on the right in the footer. Create, store and use the following styles in this document.

	Font style	Font size	Alignment	Enhancement	Line spacing	Spacing before	Spacing after
Heading	sans-serif	20 point	centre	bold, underlined	single	12 point	6 point
Body text	serif	12 point	fully justified		1.5	0	6 point
Header	sans-serif	12 point	to page margins	italic			
Footer	sans-serif	12 point	to page margins	italic			

Do not format the table or bulleted list. Save and print this document.

14.2.1 Editing styles in a document

Task 14c

Open the document you saved as task14b.

Change all the subheading styles to have a dark blue font with a yellow highlighted background.

Save the document as task14c.

Open the document that you saved in Task 14b. Highlight the top subheading. Select the HOME tab and in the Font section click the left mouse button on the small triangle to the right of the Font Colour icon.

This opens a colour palette, which looks like like this.

Select a dark blue font colour from the pallete, if the exact colour you are looking for is not present you can use the more colours option to see more. For this task the dark blue in the standard colours section looks ideal so select that one.

With the subheading still highlighted, left click the mouse button on the small triangle to the right of the Text Highlight Colour tool.

This opens the text highlighter palette. Select the yellow highlighter colour which will highlight the selected text. To change the style we created for the subheading, move the cursor to the Styles section and right mouse click on the style 14b_sub-head to open a drop-down menu. Use the left mouse button to select the option for Update 14b_sub-head to Match Selection.

You will notice that the colour of the font has changed in the style, you have modified that part of the style but the highlighting has not appeared.

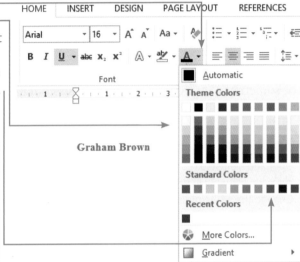

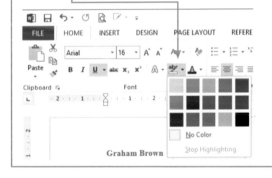

That is because not every feature of the word processor can be set into a document's saved styles. The new style has been applied to every subheading in the document, without the need for you to change the colour by hand.

As the highlighting does not save with the styles, which will need to be completed for each subheading, in this case just the one, but in a large document that could be time consuming. Highlight the subheading School closures in yellow. Save the document as task14c.

14.2.2 Use format painter

If you need to copy the formatting from one part of a document and apply it to another, for example if you have just set some text red and emboldened and want to copy that formatting onto another area of text you can use the **format painter**. Place the cursor within (or highlight) the text you wish to copy the formatting from and click the left mouse button. Select the **HOME** tab. In the **Clipboard** section, click on the **Format Painter** icon. Move the cursor to the text that you wish to format. If it is a single word then click the left mouse button anywhere within that word. If the area is more than one word, highlight the new text and the formatting from the original text will be applied to this text.

Format painter is very useful for copying styles in spreadsheets and presentations as well as in word processing.

Advice

Use the **Format Painter** with care, it copies paragraph formatting as well as font formatting. For example, if the area copied from is part of a bulleted list, when the format is applied, the new text also becomes a bulleted list in the same style.

14.2.3 Use lists

There are two types of list that you need to know about: bulleted lists and numbered (or sometimes lettered) lists. Bulleted lists contain a bullet point (character) at the start of each line to show that it is a new item in a list of other similar items.

Task 14d

Open the file **lists.rtf** and place your name on the right in the header in a 14 point serif font. Place the filename in the centre of the footer.

Change the 11 items listed into a bulleted list. Use a bullet of your choice. Make sure that this bulleted list is indented by at least 3 cm.

Set items 2 to 6 inclusive as a sub-list with a different bullet of your choice, indented by at least 4 cm.

Save the file as task14d.

Open the file and create the header and footer as described earlier. To add bullet points to a list, highlight all of the text to be added, in this case all 11 items. Select the **HOME** tab, the **Paragraph** section and click on the **Bullets** icon. ———

This will place bullet points next to each of the list items. To choose the type of bullets used, select the drop-down handle instead of the icon. ———

Select the type of bullet point that you require from **Bullet Library**. In this case, you can choose any symbol like the ☑. The bulleted list will look like this.

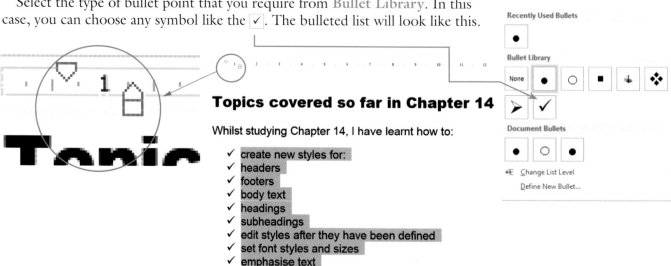

Notice how the bulleted list has been indented automatically in from the left margin, although not by at least 3 cm. To indent it further, you need to change the paragraph setting on the ruler.

Highlight all the bulleted list. On the ruler, click the left mouse button on the rectangle (not the triangle) and hold it down whilst dragging the handle to the right. Make sure that both handles are more than 3 cm to the right of the margin. The finished ruler should look like this.

The bulleted list will now be indented like this.

To create the sub-list, highlight only items 2 to 6 (headers to subheadings). Click the left mouse button on the **Increase Indent** icon.

Topics covered so far in Chapter 14

Whilst studying Chapter 14, I have learnt how to:

- ✓ create new styles for:
- ✓ headers
- ✓ footers
- ✓ body text
- ✓ headings
- ✓ subheadings
- ✓ edit styles after they have been defined
- ✓ set font styles and sizes
- ✓ emphasise text
- ✓ use format painter
- ✓ use lists

You may need to click this a few times to move the indented sub-list far enough to the right.

Select the type of bullet point that you require from **Bullet Library** for this sub-list. Save the document.

Topics covered so far in Chapter 14

Whilst studying Chapter 14, I have learnt how to:

- ✓ create new styles for:
  - • headers
  - • footers
  - • body text
  - • headings
  - • subheadings
- ✓ edit styles after they have been defined
- ✓ set font styles and sizes
- ✓ emphasise text
- ✓ use format painter
- ✓ use lists

Task 14e

Open the file saved in Task 14d.

Change the first level bulleted list into a numbered list using arabic numerals, and the second level list into a lettered list starting with a).

Save the file as task14e.

Open the file and highlight the entire bulleted list. Select the **HOME** tab, the Paragraph section and click on the Numbering icon.

Paragraph

This will place numbers next to each of the list items. To choose the type of numbering used, select the drop-down handle instead of the icon.

Select the type of numbering that you require from Numbering Library. In this case you can choose the arabic numerals as that was specified in the task. The extra indentation for the first level bullet points has been lost, so this will require you to reset the tab stop positions for these items.

Highlight the second level bullets and move the tab stop to the correct position. Again use the Numbering Library from the drop-down list to choose the correct formatting for these items. It should look like this.

Make sure that, if the bulleted list contains short items that would make up the end of a sentence, it has a colon before the list, each list item starts with a lower case character and only the last item in the list has a full stop. Add the full stops to the appropriate places before you save the file.

Word will often try to place capitals on each list item, but this is not correct as each one is not a new sentence. You must adjust these to get a list looking like this.

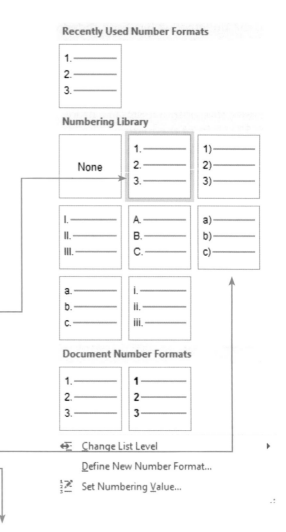

Topics covered so far in chapter 14

Whilst studying chapter 14, I have learnt how to:

1. create new styles for:
   a) headers
   b) footers
   c) body text
   d) headings
   e) subheadings.
2. edit styles after they have been defined
3. set font styles and sizes
4. emphasise text
5. use format painter
6. use lists.

Activity 14b

Open the file **activity14b.rtf** and place your name on the left, today's date in the centre and the filename on the right in the header. Make the blue text into a bulleted list, using a bullet of your choice. Make sure that this bulleted list is indented by at least 2 cm. Make the green text into a numbered list, using numbers followed by a bracket. Make the red text into a bulleted sub-list, indented from the numbered list using different bullet points. Change the colour of all the text to black.

Save the file with a new name.

14.2.4 Define styles for lists

Open the file task14c and **advice.rtf** in your word processor. Copy and paste the contents of **advice.rtf** into the document before the paragraph that starts 'Temperatures …'. Click inside the paragraph that starts 'The United States government …' and set the style to 14b_body that you defined earlier.

Start by setting up the first level bullet style on the single line that starts 'Before winter approaches …'. When you set this text to an 11 point serif font, you must use the same font as the body text, so it is easier to use format painter 🖌 from the body text, then to change the list type to a numbered list select the numbered list icon.

Change the indent to exactly 1 cm using the ruler. Change the line spacing to single line with no spacing before and after. From the Styles section, use Create a Style. In the Create New Style from Formatting window, enter a Name: for this style, for example: List-L1, then click on [OK]. To set up a style for the second level list, apply the new style List-L1 to the single line that starts 'Rock salt or more …'. Click the left mouse button on the Increase Indent icon.

Then click on the select the drop-down handle next to the Bullets icon. Select the type of bullet point that you require from Bullet Library. In this case choose an arrow to match the question.

From the Styles section, use Create a Style. In the Create New Style from Formatting window, enter a Name: for this style, for example: List-L2, then click on [OK].

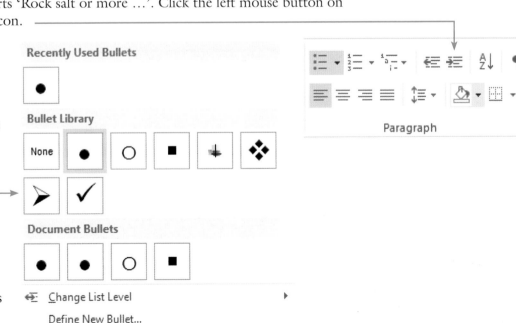

Highlight all the other level 2 bullets in the document and click on the List-L2 style.

Highlight the other two level 1 lists in the document and click on the List-L1 style.

Save the document as task14f. The completed list should look like this.

AaBbCcDd | AaBbCcDd | **AaБ** | AaBbC | 1. AaBbC | ➤ AaE
14a_header | 14b_body | 14b_headi... | 14b_sub-h... | List-L1 | List-L2

website. The United Kingdom government did not offer similar advice to its citizens. The advice from the United States is to prepare for a winter storm by doing the following:

1. Before winter approaches, add the following supplies to your emergency kit:
    ➤ Rock salt or more environmentally safe products to melt ice on walkways.
    ➤ Sand to improve traction.
    ➤ Snow shovels and other snow removal equipment.
    ➤ Sufficient heating fuel. You may become isolated in your home and regular fuel sources may be cut off. Store a good supply of dry, seasoned wood for your fireplace or wood-burning stove.
    ➤ Adequate clothing and blankets to keep you warm.
2. Make a Family Communications Plan. Minimize travel. If travel is necessary, keep a disaster supplies kit in your vehicle.
3. Bring pets/companion animals inside during winter weather. Move other animals or livestock to sheltered areas with non-frozen drinking water.

Temperatures recorded at one weather station in Ross-on-Wye during the week read:

Activity 14c

Open the file you saved in Activity 14a. Save this file as activity14c. Edit and update the contents of the footer.

Create, store and use the following styles in this document.

	Font face	Font size	Alignment	List type	Line spacing	Spacing before	Spacing after
List level 1	serif	12 point	Left – indent 1.5 cm	Bulleted list with arrow	Single	0	0
List level 2	serif	12 point	Left – indent 3 cm	Bulleted list with square bullet	Single	0	0

Save the file with a new name.

14.2.5 Evidence of your styles

If you are required to produce evidence of the styles you have created or amended, select the HOME tab. In the Styles section, click the right mouse button on the style that you have defined and want to evidence.

Select Modify from the drop-down list to open the Modify Style window. Hold down the <Alt> key and press <Prt Scr> to copy a screen shot of this window into the clipboard. This can then be pasted as evidence of your method.

Advice

Do not create a screen shot with the mouse hovering over a style in the Styles window. Whilst this shows much of the style definition it does not show the font face that you have selected.

(15) Proofing

15.1 Software tools

You will need to spell check all word-processed documents before submitting them for assessment. Select the REVIEW tab and in the Proofing section click on the Spelling & Grammar icon. The spelling and grammar check starts automatically. Any words or phrases found in a document that are not in the dictionary will be flagged as an error. Do not worry about the differences in spelling that can occur with dictionaries from different regions, for example 'centre' and 'center'. Be careful not to change the spelling of names, especially of companies, people or places. Each time an error is flagged, read it carefully and decide whether to change or ignore the spelling, using the buttons in the pane.

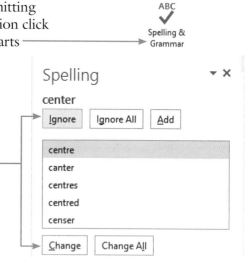

15.1.1 Spell check

You need to make sure that your work is spelt correctly and contains no data entry errors or 'typos' (these are mistakes that you make when typing in the data). Errors may already exist in the documents you have to work on. Sometimes these are spelling errors which look like this: ⟶ **speeling**. Errors like this need correcting.

What is spell check?

Spell check is a test carried out by the word processor on the text. As you work, it checks each word and compares it to those held in its dictionary. If the words match then the word processor moves on and checks the next word. If the word does not match one in the dictionary, then it uses a red wavy underline to highlight the word to suggest it may be an error.

Does the spell check always work?

If the word processor shows the red wavy underline, it may not be a spelling error. The red underline tells you that *Word* has compared this word to its dictionary and not found a match. Sometimes, as in the case above, it is a spelling

error; at other times words like 'Tawara' are flagged as a spelling error
because the dictionary does not have the name of this (made-up) place
within it. When a person's name is entered into a word processor, some
names will be shown as an error and other names will not.

Suggested spellings

When *Word* shows you an error, right mouse click on it and a drop-down
menu of suggested words will appear, like this.

For the word 'Tawara' no change needs to be made, but in the case of
a genuine error like this, a list of suggested words is shown. Choose the
word which is the most appropriate, in this case it would be 'spelling'.

Other errors

Sometimes other errors may be flagged as spelling errors, like this.

This example shows a repeated word 'not' which needs removing. Delete the
extra word to correct this error.

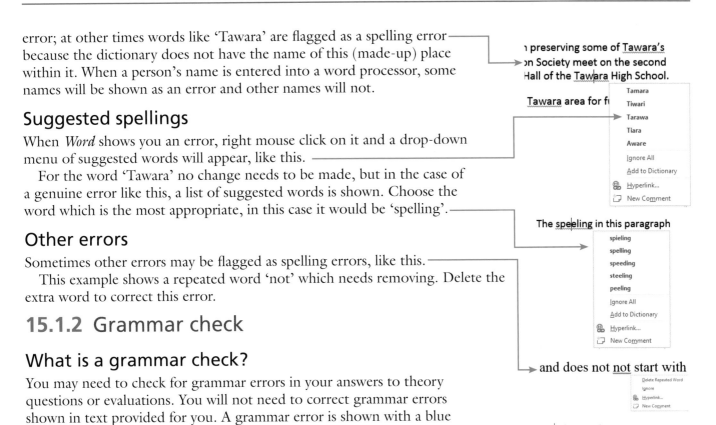

15.1.2 Grammar check

What is a grammar check?

You may need to check for grammar errors in your answers to theory
questions or evaluations. You will not need to correct grammar errors
shown in text provided for you. A grammar error is shown with a blue
wavy underline like this.

In this case it is not a proper sentence and does not start with a capital letter.
Edit the text (by deleting the extra word) to correct this type of error.

> **Activity 15a**
>
> Open the file **activity15a.rtf**. Remove all errors, save and print the document.

15.1.3 Validation routines

What is validation?

Validation is checking that data entered is reasonable. It is often a process where
data is checked to see if it satisfies certain criteria when input into a computer,
for example, to see if data falls within accepted boundaries. For further details of
validation, including the types of validation, see Section 7.2.

Appropriate type of validation

In practical examinations you may be required to apply appropriate validation rules
in the data handling or data analysis sections. It is important that for each question
you review all the different validation types, and decide which would be most
appropriate, for example you would not use a type check on a book title as book/
movie titles can contain any type of character (in fact you would be unlikely to find
a validation check of any kind to check this type of data). A length check would
not pick up transposed digits in an ISBN but could be used as well as a check
digit for double checking. Another example is that a range check is unlikely to be
appropriate on a bar code.

Task 15a

The data file **gym.csv** will be used both to create a database and in a spreadsheet. Select the most appropriate validation type for the month field in this data.

Examine the data in the file **gym.csv**. Using the list of validation types in Section 7.2 compare each type of check to see if it could be applied to the data in the month field. Use a table similar to the one below to help you.

Validation check	Appropriate?	Selected?
Range check	Yes, Select integer, >0 AND <13	Yes
Length check	Yes, Restrict to 2 characters, but would not stop 13, 14 etc.	
Character/type check	No, database would restrict to numbers if numeric data selected. Yes in spreadsheet, need to check numeric not text, but would not restrict to correct values.	
Format/picture check	No.	
Limit check	No, would only restrict one end of the range.	
Presence check	Yes, would be appropriate but would only check something had been entered.	
Consistency check	No, this is a single field with no other related field/s.	
Check digit	No.	

After working through each type of validation check, it is most appropriate to use a range check.

Task 15b

Create a database with the file **gym.csv**. Validate the month field.

Validation in *Access*

Using the methods shown in Chapter 18, examine the file **gym.csv** and use it to create a new database. Open the table in Design View and select the Month field. In the General tab, move the cursor into the Validation Rule box.

We decided above that the most appropriate validation rule to apply to this field was a range check with >0 AND <13. The field has already been set to a numeric field with Integer sub-type. Type the validation rule into this box.

In the Validation Text box add suitable text that tells the user that they have made a data entry error and gives them information as to what is acceptable data for this field. It may look like this.

Save the database.

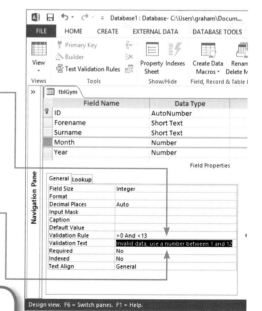

Task 15c

Add to the database saved in Task 15b, a new field called <Title>. Validate this field to make sure only Mr, Mrs, Miss, or Dr are allowed.

Open the database saved in Task 15b and using the methods shown in Chapter 18, add a new field called Title to the Gym table with the data type Text. Set the Field Size to 4 characters, as 'Miss' is the longest entry and this has four letters. Set the Validation Rule for this field to restrict the data entry to only 'Mr', 'Mrs', 'Miss' or 'Dr'. Add an appropriate message as Validation Text. The finished field should look similar to this.

Open the table and add a new record to the database. Try entering this date: 14/14/1992, and this title: 'Ms'. What happens and why?

Save the database.

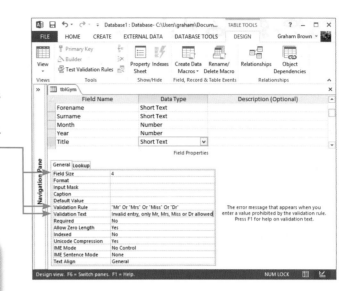

Task 15d

Create a spreadsheet with the file **gym.csv**. Validate the cells in rows 2–30 of the month column.

Validation in *Excel*

Using the methods shown in Chapter 20, examine the file **gym.csv** and use it to create a new spreadsheet. We decided above that the most appropriate validation rule to apply to this field was a range check with >0 AND <13. Highlight cells C2 to C26. Select the DATA tab, then in the Data Tools section, select the Data Validation icon.

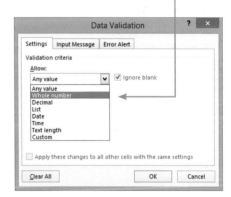

This opens the Data Validation window. Click to select the Settings tab (if it is not already selected), and move the cursor into the Allow: section. Select the drop-down list, then choose Whole number to make sure that only integers can be entered into these cells. When this value has been selected more options appear within this window.

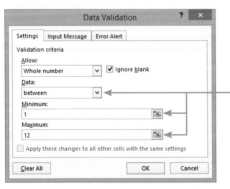

From the drop-down list in the Data: box, select between (if it is not already selected). Using 'between' in *Excel*, means that you have to give the smallest and largest acceptable values. In the Minimum: box enter 1, (which is extreme data as it is the smallest acceptable value) and in the Maximum: box enter 12.

Select the Error Alert tab.

Select an appropriate title for this error message and enter it in the Title: box. In the Error message: box enter a similar message to the one entered in Task 15b. It may look like this.

Click on OK. Test your validation routine with normal, abnormal and extreme data. Save the spreadsheet.

Task 15e

Add to the spreadsheet saved in Task 15d, a new column 1 with the label Title. Validate the cells in rows 2–30 of this column to make sure only Mr, Mrs, Miss, or Dr are allowed.

Open the spreadsheet saved in Task 15d and using the methods shown in Chapter 20, insert a new column before column 1. In cell A1 add the label Title. Highlight cells A2 to A26. Select the DATA tab, then in the Data Tools section, select the Data Validation icon to open the Data Validation window. Select the Settings tab (if it is not already selected), and move the cursor into the Allow: section. Select the drop-down list, then choose List. In the Source: box enter the text Mr, Mrs, Miss, Dr as the list of possible acceptable entries, like this.

Select the Error Alert tab. Select an appropriate title for this error message and enter it in the Title: box. In the Error message: box enter a similar message to the one entered in Task 15c. Click on OK . Test your validation routine with all four pieces of normal data and with abnormal data. Try things like 'dR', 'dr', 'mr' or 'mR' as part of your abnormal data. There will be no extreme data as this is not a range of possible answers with a highest and lowest value. Save the spreadsheet.

15.2 Proofing techniques

Proofing techniques are not the validation checks that you have studied in Section 15.1 but other ways of reducing the number of errors in your work. The term 'proofing' in printing means to make sure that the work is accurate. It should include checking not only spelling, punctuation and grammar, but also page layout, including:

- the correct application of styles
- the correct margin settings
- images placed as specified
- text wraps as specified
- images not distorted
- objects fitting within the boundaries of a page/column/slide
- objects not overlapping (unless specified in a question)
- no lists (bulleted or numbered) split over two columns/pages/slides
- no tables (bulleted or numbered) split over two columns/pages/slides
- no blank columns, pages or slides
- no widows or orphans.

Part of the proofreading and error correction will be to check for widows and orphans. A widow is the last line of a paragraph that appears alone at the top of a new page or column. An orphan is the first line of a paragraph (or heading) that appears alone at the bottom of a page or column. Even though you may have applied automatic widow and orphan control, it is always good practice to check that these have been removed. It is possible that you did not apply it to every paragraph. Make sure that other objects, like bulleted or numbered lists, tables, graphs and database or spreadsheet extracts are not split over two columns or pages. Again, inserting appropriate breaks should avoid these problems.

15.2.1 Accuracy of data entry

It is important that you read through all of the work and make sure that the text or data that you have typed is 100 per cent accurate. Check that your documents have consistency in all areas, not only fonts and styles, but also in line spacing and paragraph spacing. It is very easy to follow the instructions, for example to remove a page break, only to find that you have accidentally inserted an extra carriage return. If you have inserted section breaks or page breaks, make sure that there are no blank pages.

The importance of accurate data entry

It is critically important that data entered into computer systems is accurate. For example: if your school stores your doctor's telephone number on its system and this number contains an error, in an emergency they may not be able to contact the doctor. Another example is if a bank took $10 000 from a bank account, rather than $10, then this would have serious consequences financially. Errors in numeric data will cause problems if any calculations are performed. Imagine the costs of a data entry error if a rocket was being sent into outer space and one of its navigation systems was given some data with an error in it, or the consequences of a data entry error in the control of a nuclear reactor.

Common data entry errors

The most common data entry errors include: spelling errors, errors in the use of capital letters (like Capital letters Placed in tHe middle of A sentence, or not used where instructed) and transposed numbers (like 21 instead of 12). All of these errors can be removed by carefully checking every item of data entered when you have completed each step. Visually verify every character that you enter.

Other common errors are found in the spacing of characters in text entry, (like: sometimes words have   too many spaces between them.There are even times when spaces are missed). There are sometimes factual errors, even if someone else has proofread and corrected your work, although you would hope this was not the case. It is possible that you may get source files in different forms that contain errors for you to correct.

At the end of every piece of work, check it carefully for data entry errors and consistency of your presentation.

15.2.2 Verification

What is verification?

Verification is a way of preventing errors when data is copied from one medium to another (e.g. from paper to disk/CD). Verification does not stop all errors, but helps to reduce the errors made when data is entered into the computer, by checking the accuracy of data entry. There are two common ways that verification checks are carried out. These are called 'visual verification' and 'double data entry'.

> **Advice**
>
> If the word 'verification' is used in a question, call this method 'visual checking'. If the word is not used in the question call it 'visual verification'.

Visual verification

Visual verification can also be called a visual check.

Visual verification is checking for data entry errors by comparing the original paper documents with the data entered into the computer. This does not make sure the data is correct. For example: if the original document contained an error (e.g. the telephone number 842211 was recorded as 841122) then this error would be copied onto the computer. This is not the same as proofreading.

Double data entry

Data is entered into a system twice (often by two different people). The two sets of data are then compared by the computer and any differences in the data is flagged as an error and can be corrected by the user. A simple example of this is when you are asked on a website to create a new password, you must enter the password twice. The computer checks the two passwords are the same before allowing you to continue. This does not check that the passwords are correct, for example if you make the same spelling error in both passwords the data will verify, but would still contain an error. In the case of these passwords the computer will check they are the same as the second password is entered. In the case of documents, two people would enter the data and the computer would verify they are the same after all the data has been entered.

Why are validation and verification needed?

Validation and verification, when used together, will help to reduce the number of errors in data entry. Even together they do not stop all data errors occurring. For example, if a school has a telephone number of 842211, but this is recorded in the original documents as 841122. This error would not be found or corrected through visual verification or double data entry. If the most appropriate validation is applied (to either a database or spreadsheet) for example: to make sure that all telephone numbers are six digits long and start with a 5, 8 or 9. Again 841122 would pass the validation tests but if someone then tried to telephone the school it would not work.

A company supplying electricity sends bills to its customers that are between $100 and $500. You need both validation and verification because:

- data might be sensible but has not been transcribed/transferred accurately, for example an electricity bill for $329 may have been copied as $320 – it is still sensible but has not been copied accurately
- data might have been transcribed/transferred accurately but may not be sensible, for example an electricity bill of $3000.

Using validation in addition to verification would trap both errors, verification for the first example and validation for the second.

15.2.3 Proofreading

Although detailed knowledge of proofreading is not part of the Cambridge IGCSE syllabus, it is a term often used (incorrectly) by students. Proofreading is part of the proofing process. Proofreading is not a form of verification. It is the careful reading and re-reading of a document (before it is finally printed) to detect any errors in spelling, grammar, punctuation or layout, whether or not they were in the original document. This process is more than just verification; verification simply checks the transcription of data from one medium to another. If the original data contains errors then the verified data will contain the same errors. Proofreading should help to remove many of these errors by checking that the data is correct, not just accurately transcribed.

(16) Graphs and charts

In this chapter you will learn how to:

- select the most appropriate graph or chart for a given task
- create a graph or chart
- label a graph or chart
- extract segments from a pie chart
- change chart colours to print in black and white
- add a secondary axis
- set axis scales.

For this chapter you will need these source files from the CD:

- employees.csv
- project.csv
- rainfall.csv
- webhits.csv.

Important: please study Chapter 20 before starting this chapter.

16.1 Chart types

You may be asked to select an appropriate chart for a purpose. Which chart is the most appropriate is often very difficult to work out. The choice will be between a pie chart, a bar chart and a line graph.

16.1.1 Pie charts

If you are asked to compare percentage values, a pie chart is often the most appropriate type because pie charts **compare parts of a whole** or fractions of a whole. An example would be comparing the percentage of children who preferred ice cream, jelly or trifle.

16.1.2 Bar charts

Bar charts show the difference between different things. A bar chart is traditionally a graph with vertical bars, but it is called a column graph in *Excel*. This is a little confusing but to create a vertical bar chart you would need to use the 'column chart' and for a horizontal bar chart (with the bars going across the page) you would need to use the 'bar chart'. An example would be showing the number of items sold by five people in the same month.

Advice

Do not use stacked column charts or stacked bar charts.

16.1.3 Line graphs

Line graphs are used to plot **trends** between two variables. An example would be plotting the temperature of water as it was heated against time. You could then find any point in time on the graph and be able to read the corresponding temperature, even if the temperature had not been taken at that time.

16.2 Create a chart

To create a chart, you have to highlight the data that you wish to use. This is highlighted in the same way as other data in the spreadsheet. Sometimes you need to create a graph or chart using contiguous data (the data you use for this is in columns which are next to each other, e.g. columns B and C). Other times you need to create a graph or chart using non-contiguous data (the data you use for this is in columns which are not next to each other, e.g. columns B and F). To select non-contiguous data, hold down the <Ctrl> key while making your selections.

Task 16a

Open the file **employees.csv**. This shows the job types, the number of employees with that job type and the percentage of employees with that job type.

Create an appropriate graph or chart to show the number of employees with that job type.

Open the file and highlight only cells A1 to B8 (which is an example of contiguous data). The highlighted data should look like this. ──────→

	A	B	C
1	JobTitle	Number of staff	Percentage
2	Director	3	0.048387097
3	Engineer	12	0.193548387
4	Analyst	4	0.064516129
5	Sales	16	0.258064516
6	Programmer	9	0.14516129
7	Tester	5	0.080645161
8	Clerical	13	0.209677419
9		62	

This highlighted area will be the cells used to produce the graph. Notice that the cells containing the column headings (A1 and B1) have been included in this selection as they will be used as the labels in the chart (they can be changed later if the question asks for different labels).

Decide what type of chart you will need for this task. Look at the data and decide if it compares parts of a whole, shows trends between two variables or shows the difference. In this task the data shows the different numbers of employees in each job type, so a bar chart is the most appropriate chart type, and in this case you can use a vertical bar chart.

Select the INSERT tab and find the Charts section. ──────→

Select a vertical bar chart (labelled Column in *Excel*); this can be selected using the small icon of a bar chart or, in this case, it could also be found using *Excel*'s 'Recommended Charts' (please note that this feature does not always select the most appropriate type chart for a given task). Click on the bar chart icon and the Insert Chart window appears, with the vertical bar chart (called a column chart in *Excel*) selected. If you select the wrong chart type you can always click on the chart types on the left of this window to change it. Selecting each chart type from the left, and each sub type from the icons along the top of this window, you can see the different graphs and charts to choose from. Select the chart shown and click OK. ──────

The chart will look similar to this. ──────
Save this as task16a.

Advice

Keep your charts simple – do not use 3-D charts or add features that are not a necessary part of a task.
A simple chart is often more effective.

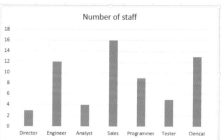

Task 16b

Open the file **employees.csv**.

Create an appropriate graph or chart to show the percentage of employees with that job type.

Open the file and, using the <Ctrl> key and the mouse, highlight cells A1 to A8 and C1 to C8 (which is an example of non-contiguous data). Do not highlight any other cells. The highlighted spreadsheet should look like this. ──────

	A	B	C
1	JobTitle	Number of staff	Percentage
2	Director	3	0.048387097
3	Engineer	12	0.193548387
4	Analyst	4	0.064516129
5	Sales	16	0.258064516
6	Programmer	9	0.14516129
7	Tester	5	0.080645161
8	Clerical	13	0.209677419
9		62	

Decide what type of chart you will need for this task. Again, look at the data and decide if it compares parts of a whole, shows trends between two variables or shows the difference. In this task the data compares parts of the whole, so a pie chart is the most appropriate chart type. Select the INSERT tab and find the Charts section. Then select a Pie chart and the 2-D Pie.

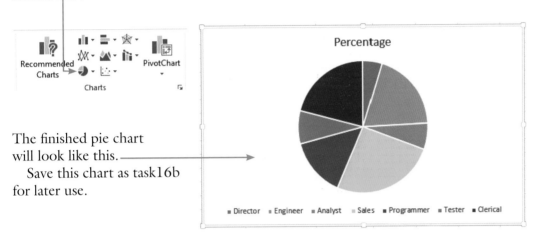

The finished pie chart will look like this.

Save this chart as task16b for later use.

Task 16c

Open the file **rainfall.csv**.

Create an appropriate graph or chart to show a comparison of the monthly data for towns A and B.

Open the file and highlight cells A1 to C15. Decide what type of chart you will need for this task. Again, look at the data and decide if it compares parts of a whole, shows trends between two variables or shows the difference. This task mentions periods of time, which suggests a trend. In this task, it is seeing how the total amount of rainfall changes/varies over a period of 12 months. Because specific dates are used and the rainfall is cumulative, a line graph is the most appropriate chart type. As there are two towns shown in the data, you will make a comparative line graph using both data sets. Select the INSERT tab and, in the Charts section, select a Line graph and the 2-D Line (the top left icon).

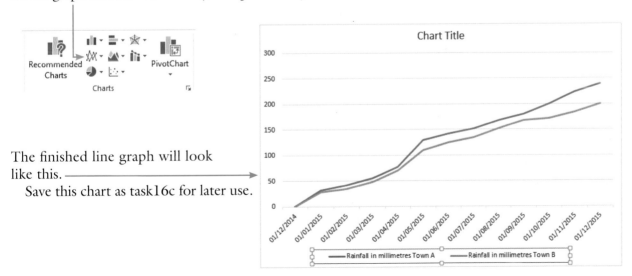

The finished line graph will look like this.

Save this chart as task16c for later use.

16.3 Label a chart

> **Task 16d**
>
> Open the chart saved in Task 16a and add appropriate chart labels.

Open the chart saved in Task 16a. Although *Excel* attempts to complete the chart – it has added a chart title and axis labels – it is still incomplete. All charts need fully labelling. Use the **Chart Elements** icon to add other elements, in this case value and category axis labels. Move the cursor into each label box and type each label.

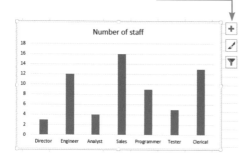
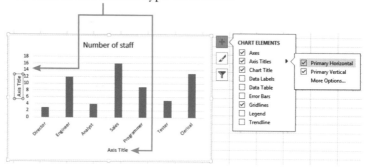

If you are given the chart title, enter it very carefully and exactly as shown in the question paper; if not, change the text in the question into a chart title so that it gives as much information as possible to the reader. Include your name, Centre number and candidate number in the chart labelling. As there is only one set of values (data series) in this chart, a legend (or key) is not needed. Save this chart for later use. The finished chart may look like this.

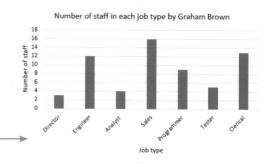

> **Activity 16a**
>
> Open the file that you saved in Activity 20a. Use this data to produce a vertical bar chart comparing the number of days worked for each person, except Aminat and Sukrit. Add an appropriate title and labels to the chart. Do not include a legend.

> **Activity 16b**
>
> Open the file **webhits.csv**. This contains data about the number of members of an online book club and the average number of website hits each week over a nine-year period.
>
> Create and label an appropriate graph or chart to show a comparison of these two sets of data.

> **Task 16e**
>
> Open the chart saved in Task 16b.
>
> Display all segment labels and percentage values on the chart. Do not display a legend. Extract the segment for engineers. Make this segment red.

Advice

The category axis in a vertical bar chart is the *x* axis and displays the names of the different categories; the value axis is the *y* axis and displays the number values.

Open the chart saved in Task 16b. Click on the chart with the left mouse button and use the **Style icon** to display a list of styles to choose from. You can scroll through the list and choose the style you want.

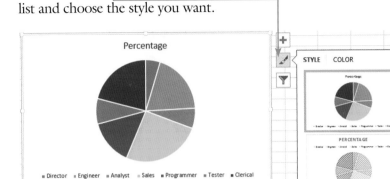

Careful selection here can save you a lot of work. Sometimes the best choice can also contain a legend but this is easy to remove. Select the **Chart Elements** icon and remove the tick from the legend box.

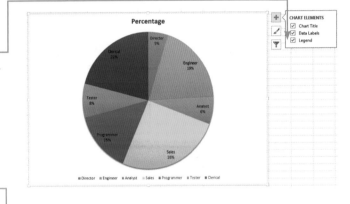

To extract the segment for Engineer, click the left mouse button on the segment (but not on the labels), hold the mouse button down and slowly drag the segment out in the direction shown by the red arrow.

The chart changes from this to this.

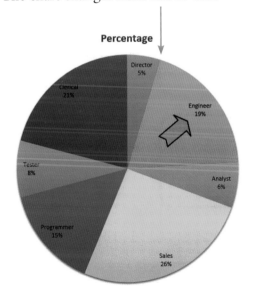

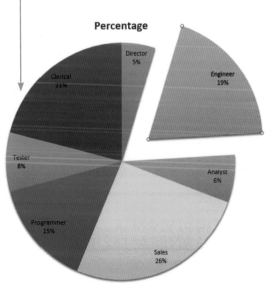

To make this segment red, right mouse click on the segment for engineers and select the **Fill** tool.

The drop-down palette of theme colours appears. For this task, select the red colour for the segment and the task is almost complete.

Use the same method so that the text is easy to read, like this.

The **Fill** tool is very useful in many types of chart, including bar charts, for changing the colours of different segments or bars. If a chart (or a document including a chart) has to be printed in black and white, it would be very difficult to tell which segment or bar is which. So that charts displayed or printed in black and white are easy to read, use the range of texture, pattern and gradient fills to make each bar or segment look different.

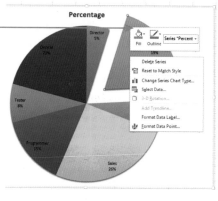

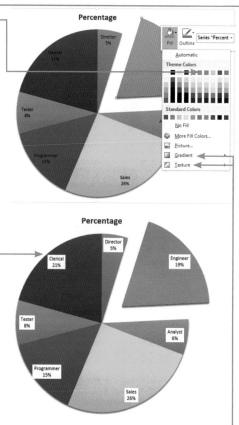

Advice

It is worth spending time browsing through each of these chart layouts to see what is available.

Activity 16c

Open the file that you saved in Activity 20m.

- Create a pie chart showing the name of each house (the colours) and the percentage of the class in that house.
- Add the title 'Percentage of students in each house'.
- Change the colour of each segment to match the name of the house.
- Extract the segment for the Yellow house.

Activity 16d

Open the **project.csv**.

Create a pie chart to compare the number of hours worked by the people with each type of job. Make sure that each type of job can be clearly identified when printed in black and white.

16.4 Use secondary axes

Task 16f

Open the file **rainfall.csv**.

Create an appropriate graph or chart to show a comparison of the rainfall and average temperatures for each month in only town A. Add a second value axis to the chart for the temperature series and label and scale these axes appropriately.

Open the file **rainfall.csv** and highlight the dates and data for town A; this is in cells A1 to B15 and D1 to D15. Select the INSERT tab then, in the Charts section, select the Insert Combo Chart icon.

Use the bottom option to Create Custom Combo Chart, which allows you to compare two values using bar charts and/or line graphs and opens the Insert Chart window set to Combination charts.

Both of the data series chosen show trends between two variables (rainfall will be plotted against the date, and average temperature will be plotted against the date) so using line graphs for both series would be the most appropriate chart types. To make this happen choose the Chart Type as Line for both series, like this.

It is difficult to read the values for the temperature, so adding and scaling a second value axis will make it easier to read the graph.

Click the left mouse button in the tick box for Secondary Axis for the temperature data series (the one shown in orange).

Your graph will now look similar to this. Click the OK button to create the chart.

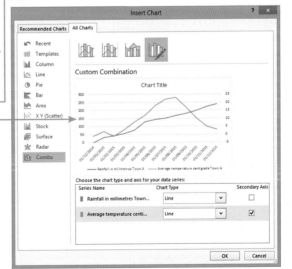

Excel has attempted to scale these axes but you are now going to adjust them further. You will change the primary axis so that it is set between 0 and 250 and the secondary axis so that it is set between –2 and 24. These values have been extracted from the original data: the total cumulative rainfall is 240 mm (so we will choose 250, so that the scale can go up in steps of 50); the temperature changes between –1 and 23 degrees (so we will use –2 and 24 so the scale can go up in steps of 2). For this axis it would be acceptable to use the values –5 to 25 suggested by *Excel*.

To change the primary axis values, double click on the axis labels like this.

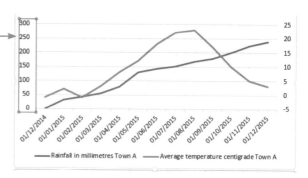

This opens the Format Axis pane at the right side of the window. In the Axis Options sections the Axis Bounds are set to 0 and 300. We want the bounds set to 0 and 250, so edit the Maximum boundary to 250. Press the <Enter> key or click the left mouse button to refresh the chart.

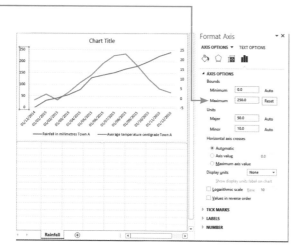

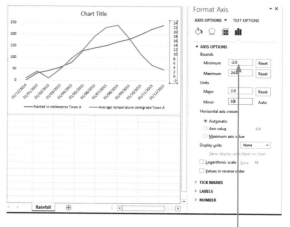

Follow a similar procedure for the secondary axis. Double click the left mouse button on the axis then change the axis settings with a Minimum value of −2, a Maximum value of 24 and, in the Units section, set the Major Unit to 2. The Minor Unit will change automatically.

It is important to label these axes appropriately. Label the primary axis (the left one) 'Cumulative rainfall in millimetres' and the secondary axis 'Average temperature'. Label the category axis 'Date'. Label the chart with a meaningful title, such as 'Comparison of rainfall and temperature in town A by <your name>'. These changes should leave the chart looking like this.

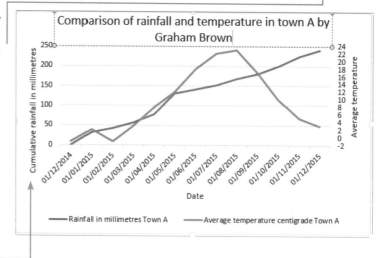

Save the file.

Activity 16e

Open the file that you saved in Activity 16b.

Add a second value axis to the chart for the number of members and set the maximum value for this axis to 3200 and keep the minimum value at 0.

17 Document production

17.1 Format text and organise page layout

17.1.1 Format pages

You may be presented with documents with different page layouts and given instructions to reformat them. Do not assume that a document is already set as specified. If it is in text (.txt) format, it will use the default settings of your word processor. If it is opened in rich text format (.rtf) or was saved as a *Word* document, it will keep the settings used to save the file.

Task 17a

Open the file saved in Task 14f.

Change the page size to A5 and the orientation to landscape. Set the top and bottom margins to 3 cm and the left and right margins to 3.5 cm. The document is going to be bound along the top edge. Add a 2 cm gutter to the document.

Save the file with a new name and print the document.

Open the file saved in Task 14f and save the document as task17a. Move into the footer and right mouse click on the date and time to get the drop-down menu. Select Update. Repeat this for the filename. Double click on the body text to leave the footer.

Set the page size

Select the PAGE LAYOUT tab and in the Page Setup section click the left mouse button on the icon at the bottom right corner of the box, to open the Page Setup window. This window can be used to change the page size, orientation (to make the page tall or wide) and the page margins. To change the paper size, select the Paper tab. The Paper size: can be selected from the drop-down list. For this task, select A5 from this list.

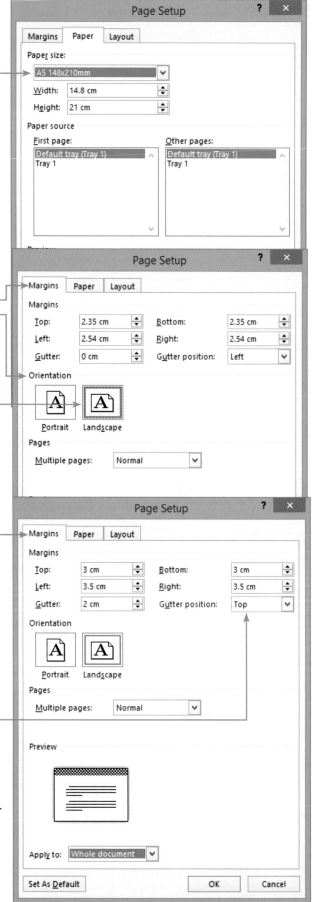

Set the page orientation

To change the page orientation, remain in the Page Setup window and select the Margins tab.
Find the Orientation section of the window.
Click the left mouse button on the landscape icon to change from portrait to landscape.

Set the page margins

Remain in the Page Setup window and in the Margins tab. To set the top and bottom margins to 3 cm, select the Margins section.
Either highlight the text within the Top: and Bottom: boxes and type in the new values, or use the scroll handles to change the values in each of the boxes.
Change the left and right margins to 3.5 cm using a similar method in the Left: and Right: boxes. Click on OK .

Set the gutter

If the document is to be part of a bound book or booklet, a gutter will be needed. This is an area outside the margins that is used to bind the book together. The gutter is set in the same way, in the Margins section of the window. The gutter can be placed to the left or top of the page, depending upon the type of binding to be used. In this case change the Gutter: size to 2 cm and the Gutter Position: to Top.

Edit headers and footers

You worked with headers and footers in Section 13.3. Use the methods learnt there to change the tab stops in the header and footer so that all text aligns to the page margins.

After doing this you can see a problem with the header and one with the footer.

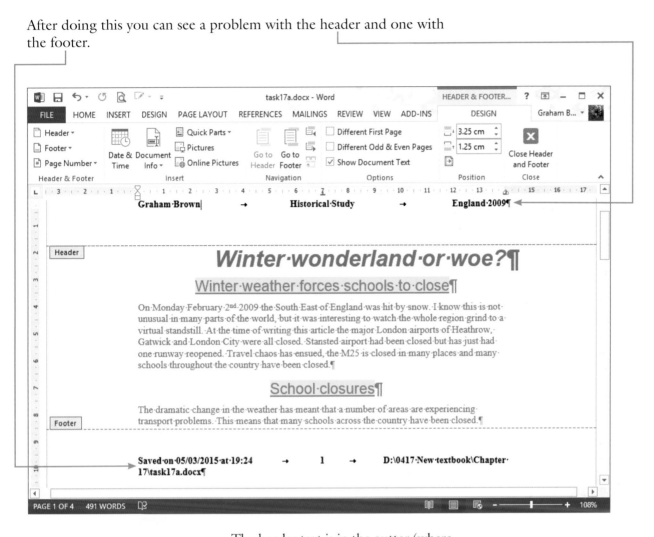

The header text is in the gutter (where the pages would be glued or bound). To change the vertical alignment of this header text, select the PAGE LAYOUT tab. In the Page Setup section click the left mouse button on the icon at the bottom right corner of the box, to open the Page Setup window. Select the Layout tab within this window. In the From edge: section, *Word* has set the distance from the Header text to the top of the page at 1.25 cm. This is the default value on my computer but the value shown on yours may differ. Take this value and add the 2 cm depth of the gutter to it, so on my computer it will become 1.25 + 2 = 3.25. Enter the new value, either by typing it or using the small arrows at the side. The window will change from this to this.

Click on OK. You will see the text move out of the gutter area.

The text on the right in the footer is too long to fit into the space provided by the word processor so it has wrapped onto the next line. This is because a file name and file path is required and now that the page is A5 (which is half the size of A4) it does not fit.

There are two ways to solve this problem.

Change the font style

You can choose a narrower font face like Arial Narrow rather than Arial for sans-serif, or **Bodini MT Poster Compressed** rather than Times New Roman for serif. Make this change to all the serif or sans-serif style definitions so that it happens automatically. Although this may help, it may also make the text very difficult to read, especially in a serif font.

Change the file name or path

Word has already attempted to split this onto a second line. It will only split filenames and paths that contain spaces. Remove all the spaces from the filename and path to change it from this to this.

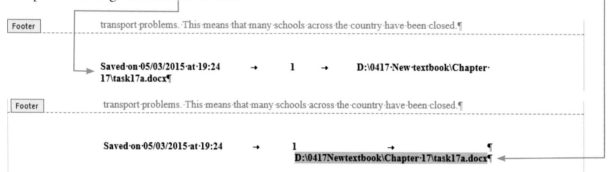

Changing the file name or path to make them shorter (but still meaningful) is the best solution. Use the methods you learnt in Chapter 11 to do this. Save the document. The finished footer may look like this.

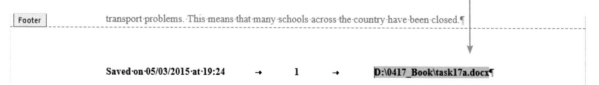

17.1.2 Widows and orphans

If you start a paragraph of text on one page or column but there is not enough room on the page to get the last line typed in, the single line of text which appears at the top of the next page or column is called a widow. Similarly, sometimes you start a paragraph at the bottom of a page or column but you can only type in one line before the rest of the text goes onto the next page. The first line of the paragraph at the bottom of the page or column is called an orphan. These should be avoided when producing a document. They can be manually avoided by inserting a Page Break or Column Break. For more information on breaks, refer to Section 17.1.3.

You can set up *Word* to avoid widows and orphans automatically. To do this, select the PAGE LAYOUT tab, then in the Paragraph section, click the left mouse button on the icon at the bottom right corner of the box, to open the

Paragraph window. Now select the Line and Page Breaks tab so that the window looks like this.

To get *Word* to avoid widows and orphans, select the Widow/Orphan control tick box and click on OK.

17.1.3 Use page, section and column breaks

Breaks can be used within a document to force text onto a new page or into the next column (if columns are being used), or to define areas with different layouts, for example where part of a document is formatted in landscape orientation and part is in portrait.

Page break

This forces the text onto the start of a new page, leaving white space at the end of the previous page. It is particularly useful for removing widows and orphans from your document, although *Word* can be set up to do this for you.

Column break

A column break is used to force the text into the top of the next available column, which may be on the same page or may be on the next page. This is also useful for removing widows and orphans.

Section break

A section break is used to split areas of a document with different layouts. There are two types of section break: one forces a page break as well as the change in layout and the other is a continuous break, which allows different layouts on the same page.

> ## Task 17b
> Open the file saved in Task 17a.
>
> Keep only the two titles on the first page of the document. Set the orientation of the first page to portrait and the rest of the document to landscape. Set all of the body text except the table into two columns, with a 3 mm spacing and vertical line between the columns.
>
> Save the file with a new name.

Open the file saved in Task 17a. Move the cursor to the place where the first break needs to be inserted. This will be just before the text 'On Monday ...'. Because this break will be the separator between two different types of layout (page 1 being portrait and page 2 onwards being landscape), a section break for a new page needs inserting rather than just a page break. To do this, select the PAGE LAYOUT tab and click on the Breaks icon.

This drop-down list will appear. In Section Breaks, click the left mouse button on Next Page.

Advice

If you select the Home tab on the Toolbar and click on the Show/Hide ¶ icon, the section break will be visible like this:

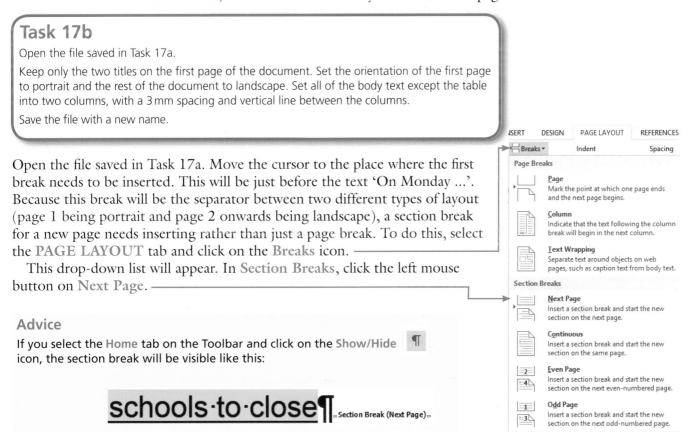

As the document is currently in landscape orientation, move the cursor to page 1, the section that needs to be changed to portrait orientation. Then select the PAGE LAYOUT tab again, followed by the Orientation icon and click on Portrait. You will notice that the word processor has only changed the orientation of this page (because you inserted the section break).

The header and footer settings have not been automatically amended for the new layout of this page, so we need to edit them. Double click the left mouse button into the header on **page 2**. Look in DESIGN tab of the HEADER & FOOTER TOOLS. You can see that this shows that the header in section 2 is linked to the header in section 1.

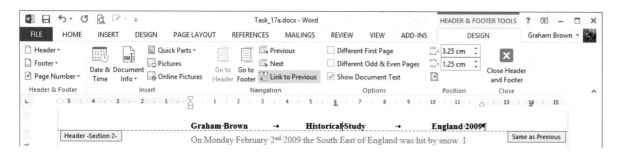

Click on the icon for Link to Previous so that the highlighting on this icon and the Same as Previous box are not seen. Now move the cursor into the header for page 1 and edit the tab stops for this section only, like this.

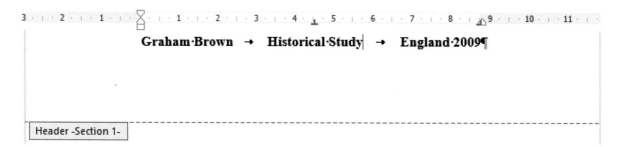

Repeat this for the footer. The text does not fit across the page so press the <Return> key after each item to move the next onto a new line like this.

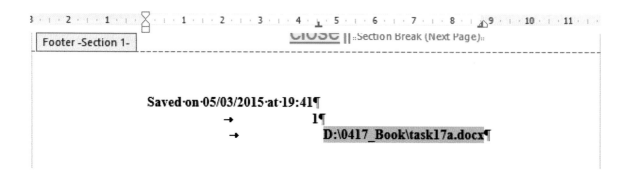

This task is continued in the next section.

17.1.4 Use columns

Columns can be used to give a layout similar to that found in a newspaper. You may be required to format a document, or part of a document into a number of columns. If you are going to have different column settings for different parts of the document, you must decide where you are going to split the document into the different sections. However, this information is often given to you in the question.

For Task 17b you need to add three more section breaks to the document, so that the body text and the tables can have different layouts. These section breaks need to be at the start and end of the first table and at the start of the second table. Where the text and table do not need to be on different pages, you will set these as continuous section breaks. It may look like this. ——————————————

Where the table is split over two pages, you will use a section break for next page.

Move the cursor to the place where you want each break inserted (i.e. before the first table), then in the PAGE LAYOUT tab click on the Breaks icon, followed by the Section Breaks option for Next Page. This is needed so that the table is not split over two pages. Move to the end of the first table and place a Continuous section break. Move to the start of the second table and place a Continuous section break.

Click the left mouse button to place the cursor within the text of the first paragraph. From the PAGE LAYOUT tab click on the Columns icon. ——————————————

Do not select the option for two columns; although this would give you the correct columns it will give you default values for the column spacing and would not give you the vertical line. Instead select the More Columns option at the bottom of the drop-down list. ——————————————

This opens the Columns window. Change the Presets from One column to Two. ——————————————

Place a tick in the Line between box to place the vertical line. Change the Spacing: from its default value to 0.3 cm (3 mm).

Make sure that the Apply to: box contains a reference to This section before clicking on ⬛OK⬛. Move the cursor into the paragraphs after the table and repeat this process for the final section of the document.

Advice

If you have just formatted the first section like this, moving the cursor into the final paragraph and pressing <Ctrl> and <Y> will repeat your last action. This is much quicker than repeating this process.

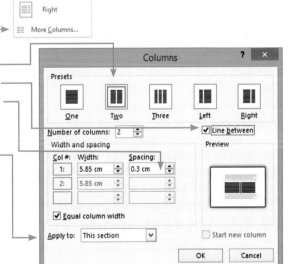

School·closures¶

The·dramatic·change·in·the·weather·has·meant·that·a·number·of·areas·are· experiencing·transport·problems.·This·means·that·many·schools·across·the· country·have·been·closed...................Section·Break·(Next·Page)...................

Saved·on·05/05/2015·at·22:39 → 2 → D:\0417_Book\Task_17a.docx¶

Graham·Brown → Historical·Study → England·2009¶

County¤	Closed¤
South·East¤	
Essex¤	250+¤
Hertfordshire¤	100+¤
Middlesex¤	80+¤
Sussex¤	50+¤
North¤	
Greater·Manchester¤	100¤
Lancashire¤	70¤
Cumbria¤	34¤
Durham¤	70¤
Northumberland¤	33¤
Yorkshire¤	1¤

Continuous)...................
This·table·shows·the·number·of· schools·reported·closed.·It·is· interesting·to·note·that·although·the· snow·is·no·heavier·in·the·South·East· of·England,·one·of·the·eastern· Counties·has·reported·more·than· 250·of·its·schools·are·closed.¶

This·gave·the·children·lots·time·to· play·in·the·snow,·snowballing,· making·snowmen·and·snow·angels.· The·snow·gave·an·added·dimension,· producing·some·very·picturesque·

scenes,·many·captured·on·camera.·¶

The·United·States·government·offered·lots·of·advice·about·preparing·for·lots·of· snow.·This·advice·and·more·details·can·be·found·in·community·centres·or·on·

Sometimes when you have followed all the necessary steps, a page does not look as it should. In this case, page 2 has a heading which has become an orphan. To solve this problem, insert a column break just before the heading. Save the document.

Task 17c

Open the file saved in Task 17b.

Set the first level bullets to be indented by 3 mm and the second level bullets to be indented by 6 mm from the margin.

Save the file with a new name.

Open the document saved in Task 17b. Select the HOME tab and modify the styles List-L1 and List-L2 so that List-L1 has a 0.3 cm indent and List-L2 has a 0.6 cm indent.

Graham·Brown → Historical·Study → England·2009¶

On·Monday·February·2nd·2009·the· South·East·of·England·was·hit·by· snow.·I·know·this·is·not·unusual·in· many·parts·of·the·world,·but·it·was· interesting·to·watch·the·whole·region· grind·to·a·virtual·standstill.·At·the·time· of·writing·this·article·the·major· London·airports·of·Heathrow,·Gatwick· and·London·City·were·all·closed.· Stansted·airport·had·been·closed·but· has·just·had·one·runway·reopened.· Travel·chaos·has·ensued,·the·M25·is· closed·in·many·places·and·many· schools·throughout·the·country·have· been·closed.¶

The·dramatic·change·in·the·weather· has·meant·that·a·number·of·areas·are· experiencing·transport·problems.·This· means·that·many·schools·across·the· country·have·been·closed.¶

School·closures¶

Saved·on·05/03/2015·at·20:02 → 2 → D:\0417_Book\task17b.docx¶

Activity 17a

Open the file **activity17a.rtf**.

Change the page size to A4 and the orientation to portrait. Set all the margins to 4 cm and remove the gutter.

Place the date on the left, the filename in the centre and the time on the right in the header. Place your name on the left and an automated page number on the right in the footer. Ensure that the header and footer are 2 cm from the top and bottom of the page respectively.

Print the document.

Save the file with a new filename.

Activity 17b

Open the file you saved in Activity 17a.

Change the body text of only the first page so that it is set in two columns with a 1 cm spacing and a vertical line between the columns.

Save the file with a new filename.

Activity 17c

Open the file saved in Activity 17b.

Change the page margins to 2 cm and the alignment of the header and footer to fit the margins. Ensure that the header and footer are 1 cm from the top and bottom of each page.

Add a new title 'Arctic blast grips the United Kingdom' at the start of the document. Place the two titles on a single portrait page with a single column. All other text should be on landscape pages, in three columns with 1.5 cm column spacing.

Save the file with a new filename.

17.1.5 Set text alignment

Text can be aligned in four basic ways. It can be aligned:

- to the left margin with a ragged right margin which is called 'left aligned'
- to the centre of the page, which is called 'centre aligned'
- to the right margin, which is called 'right aligned'
- to both margins which is called 'fully justified'.

As you saw in Section 14.1, the text is aligned by selecting the text and then using the using the alignment icons. These icons are found in in the **Paragraph** section under the **HOME** tab.

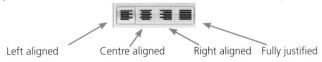

Left aligned   Centre aligned   Right aligned   Fully justified

---

Activity 17d

Open the file **activity17d.rtf** and place your name in the centre of the header.

Make only the title a 36 point sans serif font that is centre aligned and fits in a single, full width column.

Move the third paragraph so that it becomes the last paragraph. Fully justify the body text.

Centre align the second paragraph. Left align the third paragraph. Right align the fourth paragraph.

Make the first word 'grew' in the story 16 point, the second 'grew' 20 point and the third 'grew' 24 point.

Save the file with a new name.

17.1.6 Set line spacing

Line spacing is usually set as part of a defined style. More details of setting the line spacing as part of a style can be found in Section 14.1. Different line spacing can be used to present different page layouts. The most commonly used layouts are single line spacing, 1.5 line spacing and double line spacing. To change the line spacing in a paragraph, select the **HOME** tab, and look in the **Paragraph** section to find the **Line spacing** icon. Select this icon to open this drop-down menu.

Although you can change the line spacing of a paragraph from here, select **Line Spacing Options...** to open the **Paragraph** window, which gives you more options.

To change the line spacing, select the **Line spacing:** drop-down menu. This will allow you to define an exact number of lines, which is very useful for title pages, where lines may be spaced out, perhaps needing to be five or six lines apart.

Ensuring that line spacing on a page is consistent is just as important as setting the line spacing. It is often wise to select all text and adjust the line spacing together. If you move, copy, insert or delete text from your document, always check that the line spacing is correct after you have made any change. Each paragraph and heading can have the spacing before and after it set using the same **Paragraph** window. This is set in the **Spacing** section, where the space before and after any paragraph (a title is counted as a paragraph) can be edited.

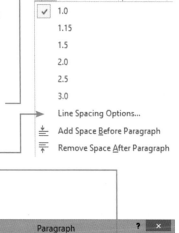

Activity 17e

Open the file that you saved in Activity 17d.

Make the first paragraph single line spacing, the second paragraph 1.5 line spacing and the third paragraph double line spacing. Do not change the line spacing in the rest of the document.

Set the heading spacing to 12 spaces before and 24 spaces after the paragraph.

Save the file with a new name.

17.1.7 Set tabulation settings

Paragraphs can be formatted with different settings for the first line of a paragraph and the other lines in a paragraph. These settings are all changed on the ruler, which looks like this.

On the left side of the ruler are two settings for the left margin. The top pentagon adjusts the first line of the paragraph, the bottom pentagon aligns the rest of the paragraph, and the rectangle below moves the whole paragraph.

Task 17d

Open the file **tabulation.rtf** and place your name on the left in the header.

Set the first line of the first paragraph as indented text, indented by 2.5 cm. Indent the whole of the second paragraph by 2.5 cm. Set the fourth and fifth paragraphs as hanging paragraphs with a 2.5 cm tab. In the fifth paragraph make the text 'Good Use' a subheading.

Save the file with a new filename.

Open the file and place your name in the header.

Click the left mouse button in the first paragraph. Drag the top triangle to the right by 2.5 cm, like this.

To indent the whole of the second paragraph, click in that paragraph and then drag the small rectangle across to the right by 2.5 cm like this.

Highlight both the fourth and fifth paragraphs and drag the bottom triangle to the right by 2.5 cm like this.

To make the text 'Good Use' a subheading, remove the full stop and space at the end of it and replace it with the <Tab> key. The finished document looks like this.

Activity 17f

Open the file that you saved in Activity 17c.

Add the text 'History item 1' as a new line to the start of the document. Format this text in the same style as the rest of the page. Change the title 'Weather update' to 'February 2009'.

Set all of the text on the first page to be spaced five lines apart and all other text in the document to be single line spacing with no spacing before each paragraph and 24 point spacing after each paragraph. Indent all the text on the second page by 5 mm.

Save the file with a new name.

This·paragraph·contains· indented·text.·This·means·that·the·left·margin· on·the·first·line·is·indented·from·the·rest·of· the·paragraph.·The·top·margin·setting·on·the· ruler·is·indented·to·the·right·of·the·lower· margin·setting.¶

The·whole·of·this·paragraph· has·been·indented·from·the· left·margin·and·is·called·an· indented·paragraph.·This·is· sometimes·used·to·show·sub- text·within·a·document,·or·for· showing·a·quotation·from· another·author.¶

This·paragraph·is·a·normal·paragraph·with·no· indents·and·no·hanging·first·line.·The·margin· settings·on·the·ruler·are·directly·above·each· other.¶

This·paragraph·is·called·a·hanging·paragraph.· This·means·that·the·first·line· of·the·paragraph·is·aligned·to· the·margin·and·all·other·lines· are·left·hanging.·The·bottom· margin·setting·on·the·ruler·is· indented·to·the·right·of·the· top·margin·setting.¶

Good·use → One·really·good·use·of·a· hanging·paragraph·is·for·short· titles·like·this·one·to·be· followed·by·the·relevant·text.· By·setting·a·tab·stop·on·the· first·line,·the·short·title·can·be· used·as·a·heading.·This·layout· can·give·each·heading·a· powerful·effect·on·the·page,· without·any·other·text· enhancement·like·enlarging·or· emboldening·the·text.·¶

17.1.8 Format bulleted or numbered lists

Although individual styles can be set for small portions of text, it is better to set these as defined styles and apply the styles to parts of the document, in this case lists. These elements have already been covered in Section 14.2.3.

17.2 Edit a table

It is recommended that you study Sections 13.2.5 and 13.2.6 before starting Section 17.2.

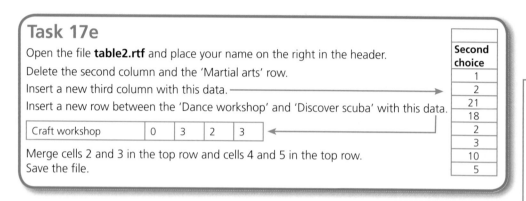

Task 17e

Open the file **table2.rtf** and place your name on the right in the header.

Delete the second column and the 'Martial arts' row.

Insert a new third column with this data. ────────────────────

Insert a new row between the 'Dance workshop' and 'Discover scuba' with this data.

| Craft workshop | 0 | 3 | 2 | 3 |

Merge cells 2 and 3 in the top row and cells 4 and 5 in the top row.
Save the file.

Second choice
1
2
21
18
2
3
10
5

Open the file **table2.rtf** and place your name on the right in the header.

Delete a column

To delete the second column, move the cursor to any cell in this column, and click the right mouse button, to get the drop-down menu like this. ──────

Select Delete Cells..., which will open the Delete Cells window. Select the radio button for Delete entire column. ──────

Click on OK .

Delete a row

Repeat this method to delete the 'Martial arts' row. Right mouse click in any cell in this row and select Delete Cells.... This time select the radio button for Delete entire row before clicking on OK .

Insert a column

To insert a new third column, right click the mouse in any cell in the second column to obtain the drop-down menu. Select Insert, then Insert Columns to the Right. This will insert the column. Enter the text shown in the task into the cells.

Insert a row

Use a similar method to insert the new row. Click the right mouse button in any cell in the 'Dance workshop' row. Select Insert, then Insert Rows Below. This will insert the new row. Enter the text shown in the task into the cells.

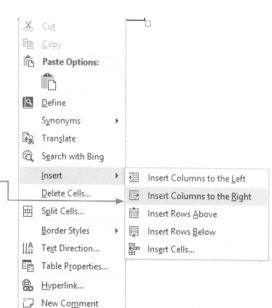

Merge cells

To merge cells 2 and 3 in the top row, highlight both these cells and then click the right mouse button on one of the highlighted cells to get the drop-down menu. Select Merge Cells.

Repeat this for the two cells placed to the right of the cells that you have just merged. Save the file. The completed table should look like this:

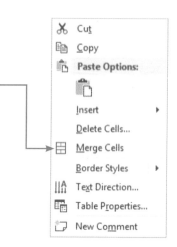

Activity	X population		Y population	
	First choice	Second choice	First choice	Second choice
Jewellery making	0	1	1	2
Paintballing	39	2	37	19
Boulogne trip	52	21	56	18
Rock workshop	3	18	2	3
Dance workshop	0	2	2	10
Craft workshop	0	3	2	3
Discover scuba	4	3	8	8
Beauty	4	10	1	9
Ceramic painting	0	5	1	2

Activity 17g

Open the file that you saved in Activity 13b.

Delete the top row and second column of the table.

Insert a new row above the row containing the word 'Format'. Insert the text 'Columns' in cell 2 of this new row. Insert a new fourth column with this data. →

Horizontal
Vertical
.

In column 1 merge the cell containing 'Insert' with the blank cells below it. Repeat this for the cell containing 'Delete' and the one containing 'Format'. In column 2 do the same for the cell containing 'Cells' and the one containing 'Gridlines', and the same for the cell 'Alignment' in column 3.

Save the file with a new name.

Format a table

All of the required knowledge and skills for this section have already been covered in Section 13.2.6. These include:

- setting horizontal text alignment to left, centre, right and fully justified
- setting vertical cell alignment to top, centre or bottom
- formatting cells and their contents, such as: showing and hiding gridlines, wrapping text within a cell and shading or colouring cells.

Activity 17h

Open the file that you saved in Activity 17g.

Right align all the cells in the first column. Left align all other cells in the table.

Set the background colour of all cells in the first column to light grey. Ensure that there is no text wrapped within the cells of the table. Vertically align all data to the middle of each cell. Remove the gridlines from any unused cells.

Save the file with a new name.

17.3 Mail merge

17.3.1 What is a mail merged document?

A mail merged document is created to save the repeated typing of similar documents that are designed to be sent to different people. It uses a master document and a source file containing data. Data, like the names and addresses of people to send the letter to, is taken from the source file and placed into a copy of the original document. This is done automatically.

17.3.2 Why are mail merged documents used?

Mail merge is used to save retyping or editing lots of documents. It saves time (and therefore money) and helps to reduce the number of errors that may occur in editing or retyping the document. The most common use of mail merged documents is to produce personalised letters for a number of people. The contents of the letter have parts that are the same for all people and parts that are personal to the reader. When using the mail merge, the parts that are the same for all people only need to be typed once, even if hundreds of letters are to be created. The personal part of this letter is added using a placeholder, which will hold the individual information taken from the data source. The placeholders can hold information from a data source and/ or instructions called merge codes (sometimes called field codes). The information from the data source is often a person's name and address, but may also include information about products that they have bought from a company.

You will be given a copy of a document that will become your master document. This contains the parts for all people. You will also be given a source file, which may be a database, spreadsheet or text file. You will need to merge the files into a number of personalised documents.

17.3.3 Create a mail merged document

Create a master document

A master document will usually be supplied to you as a source file. However, if a document to be used as a master document is only small you may be asked to create this document. The source document may be provided in a format suitable for use with any word processor. For example, it might be in a .rtf (rich text format) or a .txt (text format) file. This may need importing or opening in your word processor program and you will need to save it as a word-processor (.docx) file. You will need to import or create the document, carefully spell check and proofread the document and check that it has a consistent layout. You must then save two copies of this document as word-processed (.docx) files, making sure that you have a backup copy before you start to add the placeholders. You may need to go back to this backup copy if you experience any problems.

Task 17f

Use the file **mailmerge.rtf** as the master letter for a mail merge and the file **mmstudents.csv** as the data source file. In the master letter:

- insert relevant merge fields from the data source file to replace the text shown in chevrons, e.g. <field>
- replace the text <Date> with today's date in DD MMMM YYYY format
- replace the Headteacher's name with your name.

Save the file.

Open the file **mailmerge.rtf**. Save this as a *Microsoft Word* document because rich text format will not keep mail merge fields. Spell check and proofread the document. Correct any errors found (there are two).

You will notice that this document contains some text in chevrons <like this>. The text within the chevrons (and the chevrons) will each need to be replaced by a merge code.

Insert a special field into a mail merged document

Special fields that are automatically updated can be added to any word-processed document. In Section 13.3 we added date fields into the header and footer areas of documents. Move the cursor over the first of these and highlight the text <Date> which you will replace with the automated date. To do this select the INSERT tab, then in the Text section select the Quick Parts icon. ──────

This will open a drop-down menu. Select the option for Field....────────────────────────

This will open the Field window which looks similar to this.──

Using the drop-down menu from the Categories: section, select Date and Time. ──────

Select the date from the Field names: drop-down list. This can be the date that the mail merge was created, the date it was saved, the current date or the date the document was printed. For this example, you can select the Date field name. ──────

As you select it, the Date formats: list appears. The question asked for the format DD MMMM YYYY, scroll down through each of the formats until the date is displayed as required. ──────

Click on [OK] to insert the placeholder for the date. This part of the letter should look similar to this.──────

Save the document again.

There are many different types of automated fields that can be placed into a document, for example the filename, number of words, number of chapters, name of author, file size, etc.

Attach the source file to the master document

For all mail merge functions use the MAILINGS tab. As the letter has already been created, move the cursor into the Start Mail Merge section and select the icon to Select Recipients. ──────

You can see that many of the other icons are 'greyed out' as the document has no source file attached to it, but these will become active icons later on. As you select the icon a drop-down list appears. Select Use an Existing List.... ──────

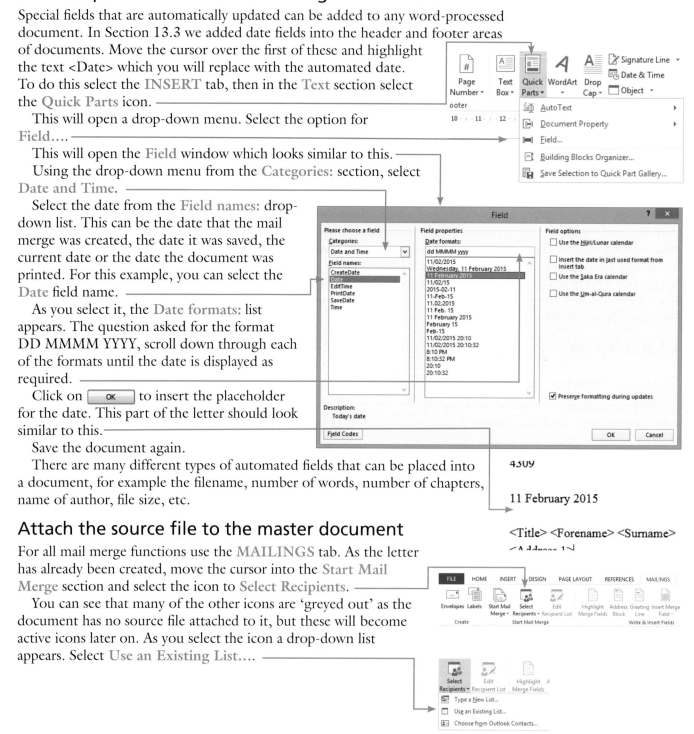

Use the left part of the Select Data Source window to move from the default 'My Data Sources' folder into the folder that holds the file **mmstudents.csv**.

Select this file and then click on [Open]. At this point you will see many of the previously greyed out icons appear ready for you to use. Save the document so that the path to the attached data source is also saved with the document.

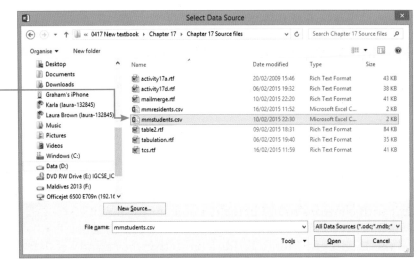

Advice

Once you have attached the data source **do not** save the document or data sources into different folders, or move them into different folders, or the links to the source document will not work.

Check that the data source is attached

From the MAILINGS tab, in the Start Mail Merge section click the left mouse button on the Edit Recipient List icon.

This will open the Mail Merge Recipients window. Check that the data in here matches that source file.

If you need to select only certain people to send this mail merged letter to, you would untick the check box for those people who did not need a letter. This task does not tell us who to prepare the letters for, so make no changes at this point. Click on [OK] to return to the document.

Insert merge fields into a mail merged document

Move the cursor over the first place where the merge field is to be placed and highlight the text <Title>. Do not highlight the spaces around this text. You are going to replace this text with the merge field for the person's title (e.g. Mr, Mrs, Miss, etc). Click the left mouse button on the Insert Merge Field icon to get a list of the available merge fields from the source data.

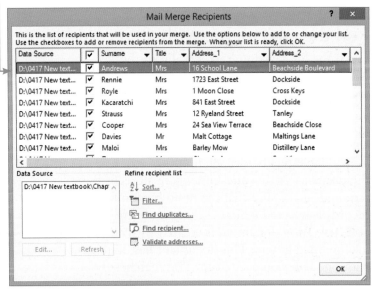

These are shown in the Insert Merge Field window. Click in the Fields section on Title.

Click the left mouse button on [Insert]. This part of the document will change from this to this. ——————

¶	¶
<Title><Forename>·<Surname>¶	«Title»·<Forename>·<Surname>¶
<Address·1>¶	<Address·1>¶
<Address·2>¶	<Address·2>¶

You can see that *Microsoft Word* has placed double chevrons around the fieldname, to show that it is a field rather than text. Repeat this process for all of the other text with chevrons round in the document. To show which fields you have set as merge fields you can click on the **Highlight Merge Fields** icon so that they stand out. Replace the Headteacher's name with your name. The document should now look like this. ——————

Save the file as task17f.

17.3.4 Run the mail merge

> ### Task 17g
>
> Run the mail merge saved in Task 17f so that individual letters are produced for all students.
>
> Save the letters.

Run the mail merge with all records

Open the file saved in Task 17f. From the **MAILINGS** tab, select from the **Finish** section the **Finish & Merge** icon. ———

Select from the drop-down menu the option to **Edit Individual Documents…** so that you can check the contents of the individual letters before sending them to the printer. For this question where all records are required, make sure that the radio button for all the records is selected before clicking on [OK]. ———

A new *Word* document is created with all of the mail merged letters. This document has 25 pages, with one letter on each page. This matches the 25 records in the source data file. Save the merged letters as task17g.

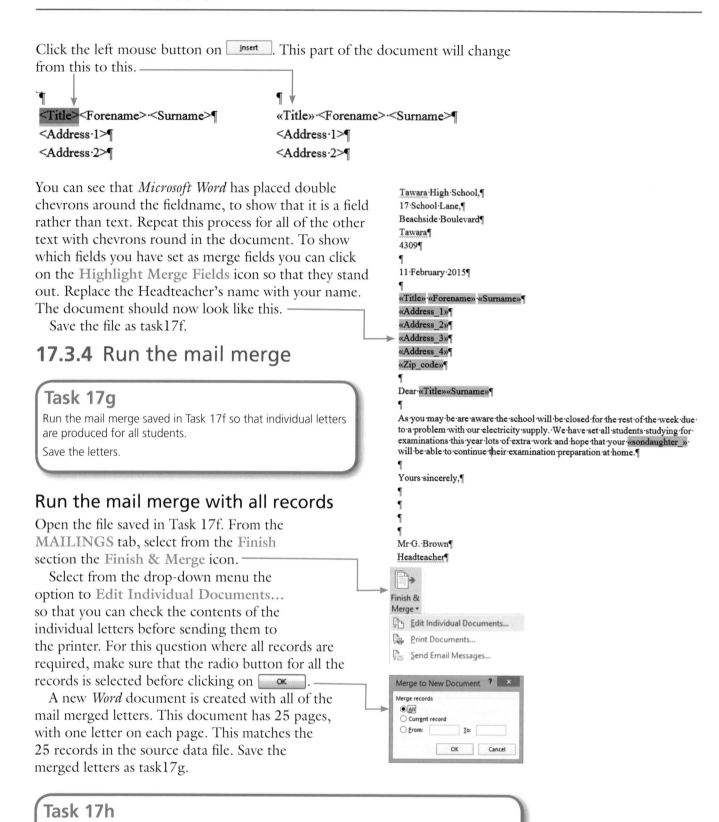

Tawara·High·School,¶
17·School·Lane,¶
Beachside·Boulevard¶
Tawara¶
4309¶
¶
11·February·2015¶
¶
«Title»·«Forename»·«Surname»¶
«Address_1»¶
«Address_2»¶
«Address_3»¶
«Address_4»¶
«Zip_code»¶
¶
Dear·«Title»·«Surname»¶
¶
As·you·may·be·are·aware·the·school·will·be·closed·for·the·rest·of·the·week·due·to·a·problem·with·our·electricity·supply.·We·have·set·all·students·studying·for·examinations·this·year·lots·of·extra·work·and·hope·that·your·«sondaughter_»·will·be·able·to·continue·their·examination·preparation·at·home.¶
¶
Yours·sincerely,¶
¶
¶
¶
¶
Mr·G.·Brown¶
Headteacher¶

Finish & Merge ▾
- Edit Individual Documents…
- Print Documents…
- Send Email Messages…

Merge to New Document
Merge records
● All
○ Current record
○ From: ___ To: ___
[OK] [Cancel]

> ### Task 17h
>
> Run the mail merge saved in Task 17f so that individual letters are produced for only the students from Port Peppard.
>
> Save the letters.

Run the mail merge with selected records

Edit
Recipient List

Open the file saved in Task 17f. To select the data for the letters, select from the MAILINGS tab, in the Start Mail Merge section, the Edit Recipient List icon.

This will open the Mail Merge Recipients window which will look like this.

Use the horizontal scroll bar to examine the data.

Find the field containing Port Peppard. In this data source this is the Address 3 field.

Remember or write down the name of this field.

You could go through each record and remove the tick against every record that does not have Address_3 as Port Peppard. This would not be a very efficient way of doing this and may take a lot of time. You may also make mistakes, for example, removing one accidentally. To select the correct records click the left mouse button on the text to Filter....

This opens the Query Options window. Make sure that the Filter Records tab has been selected. In the top row of the table, under the heading Field:, use the drop-down menu to select the Address_3 field. As you select this a drop-down menu appears in the next box below the text Comparison:. Select the option for Equal to if it is not already visible. In the box below the text Compare to: type the data to be compared with, in this case Port Peppard.

Take care that you do not make any typing errors. When you have completed this, click on OK .

From the MAILINGS tab, select from the Finish section the Finish & Merge icon. Select from the drop-down menu the option to Edit Individual Documents.... Even though we have filtered the number of letters so that they are only sent to people living in Port Peppard, make sure that the radio button for all the records is selected before clicking on OK . The new merged document has six pages with the six letters addressed to only those living in Port Peppard. Save the merged letters as task17h.

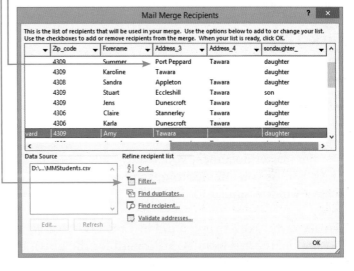

Task 17i

Run the mail merge saved in Task 17f so that individual letters are produced for only the girls from Port Peppard.
Save the letters.

Other filters can be used in the Query Options window. Look at the data again and find out which field you would use to find the girls. You cannot use the title field as this is the title of the parent, not the gender of the student. Open the file saved in Task 17f and in the **Query Options** window set up the Filter to find only those students with the **Address_3** field **Equal to** (as the **Comparison:**) **Port Peppard** (as you did for Task 17h). Move the cursor down into the second row of the query. As the students live in Port Peppard **and** are girls, select **And** from the drop-down list on row 2.

In the **Field** box for this row, select the **son/daughter** field (note how this has changed to sondaughter_ because *Word* could not handle the use of the / in the original source data, this will not change the outcome of the merge). In the **Comparison:** box select **Equal to**, and type in the **Compare to:** box the word **daughter**. When you have completed this, click on OK .

Finish & Merge to get only three letters. Save the merged letters as task17i.

17.3.5 Print mail merge documents

Save your work regularly using the methods shown in Section 11.2. Mail merge documents will need to be printed so that they show the master document and the finished documents (often letters) after the merge has been run.

> ### Task 17j
> Print the master document created in Task 17f showing the merge and field codes.

Print the master document

You will always do this to show the merge codes within the document. Open the master document you saved in Task 17f. As you attempt to open the file a window similar to this will appear.

To allow the work that you did in Task 17f, (that is choosing the records from Port Peppard for the girls), to be included you must click the left mouse button on Yes . The document opens and looks like this.

The merge codes are visible inside the chevrons. This will show the name of the field and the fact that it is a merge field. You may notice that the field used for the Date is not shown.

You can see more detail for each field by clicking the right mouse button on a field and from the drop-down menu, selecting **Toggle Field Codes.**

Tawara High School,
17 School Lane,
Beachside Boulevard
Tawara
4309

16 February 2015

«Title» «Forename» «Surname»
«Address_1»
«Address_2»
«Address_3»
«Address_4»
«Zip_code»

Dear «Title» «Surname»

As you may be are aware the school will be closed for the rest of the week due to a problem with our electricity supply. We have set all students studying for examinations this year lots of extra work and hope that your «sondaughter_» will be able to continue their examination preparation at home.

Yours sincerely,

Mr G. Brown
Headteacher

This will display the full details of the field and change from this to this.

«Title» «Forename» ·   { MERGEFIELD "Title" } «Forename»

«Address_1»   «Address_1»

If you wish to display the field codes in this format, take screen shot evidence and use that because the field codes in this format cannot be sent to the printer.

To show evidence of the date field and its formatting, right click the field (this one is not a merge field) and select Toggle Field Codes. This will display the full details of the field and change from this to this.

16 February 2015   { DATE \@ "dd MMMM yyyy" * MERGEFORMAT }

«Title» «Forename» «Surname»   «Title» «Forename» «Surname»

You can see that the format of the field is also displayed (the question asked for 'with today's date in DD MMMM YYYY format') showing the correct formatting. Again, this will not print, so screen shot evidence will need to be provided.

Task 17k
Print the merged letters saved in Task 17i for the girls from Port Peppard.

Print the merged documents

Open the merged letters saved in Task 17i. Check that each letter is addressed to the girls and that the address contains Port Peppard. Print these letters as a normal *Word* document using the FILE tab then Print.

Activity 17i
Use the file **tcs.rtf** as the master document for a mail merge and the file **mmresidents.csv** as the data source file.

In the master document:

- insert relevant merge fields from the data source file to replace the text shown in chevrons, e.g. <field>
- replace the text <Date> with today's date in DDDD, DD MMMM YYYY format
- replace the text <Your Name> with your name
- run the mail merge so that individual letters are produced for all residents.

Save the file.

Print only the first and last letter. Print the master document showing the merge and field codes.

Activity 17j
Print the merged letters saved in Activity 17i for the residents who live in Eccleshill.

Activity 17k
Print the merged letters saved in Activity 17i for the residents who live in Dunescroft or Stannerley.

(18) Data manipulation

In this chapter you will learn how to:

- describe flat-file and relational database structures
- create a flat-file database from an existing data file
- create a relational database from existing data files
- define database structures
- describe the key features of data entry form design
- create and edit a data entry form
- enter different forms of data into a database
- add a field to an existing table
- search for subsets of data
- extract summary data
- produce a report
- export data and reports for use within another package
- use formulae within a database
- sort data within a database.

For this chapter you will need these source files from the CD:

- cars.csv
- customers.csv
- orders.csv
- stationery.csv
- students.csv
- teachers.csv.

18.1 Create a database structure

18.1.1 What is a database?

A database is an organised collection of data. A database program is software which stores and retrieves data in a structured way. This includes the data that is stored and the links between the data items. All databases store data using a system of files, records and fields:

- A **field** is a single item of data, such as a forename or date of birth. Each field has a field name that is used to identify it within the database. Each field contains one type of data, for example numbers, text or a date.
- A **record** is a collection of fields, for example all the information about one person or one item. These may contain different data types.
- A **file** (in database terms) is an organised collection of records, usually where all the records are organised so that they can be stored together. A file can have one or more tables within it.

Although all databases have these three elements in common, there are two types: **flat-file databases** and **relational databases**.

18.1.2 Flat-file databases

A flat-file database stores its data in one **table**, which is organised by rows and columns. For example, in the following database about teachers, each record (row) in the table contains data about one person. Each column in the table contains a field, which has been given a field name, and each cell in that column has the same, predefined data type.

Teacher_ID	Forename	Surname	Subject	Room
AVA	Anthony	Varela	Maths	51
GBA	Graham	Barney	Science	14
JKW	Jennie	Kwong	English	42
PTY	Paul	Tyrell	Science	8
SJR	Sarah	Jordan	English	39

18.1.3 Relational databases

A relational database stores data in more than one linked table, stored in a file. Relational databases are designed so that the same data is not stored many times. Each table within a relational database will have a key field. Most tables will have a **primary key** field that holds unique data (no two records are the same in this field) and is the field used to identify that record. Some tables will have one or more **foreign key** fields. A foreign key in one table will point to a primary key in another table.

Using the earlier example, if we wanted to add to the table the names of each student taught by each teacher using a flat-file database, the table would look like this:

Teacher_ID	Forename	Surname	Subject	Room	Student_ID	Student_FName	Student_SName
AVA	Anthony	Varela	Maths	51	G12345	Jasmine	Hall
AVA	Anthony	Varela	Maths	51	G12346	James	Ling
AVA	Anthony	Varela	Maths	51	G12348	Addy	Paredes
AVA	Anthony	Varela	Maths	51	G12349	Hayley	Lemon
AVA	Anthony	Varela	Maths	51	G12351	Jennie	Campbell
GBA	Graham	Barney	Science	14	G12345	Jasmine	Hall
GBA	Graham	Barney	Science	14	G12348	Addy	Paredes
GBA	Graham	Barney	Science	14	G12349	Hayley	Lemon
JKW	Jennie	Kwong	English	42	G12345	Jasmine	Hall
JKW	Jennie	Kwong	English	42	G12349	Hayley	Lemon
JKW	Jennie	Kwong	English	42	G12351	Jennie	Campbell
PTY	Paul	Tyrell	Science	8	G12346	James	Ling
PTY	Paul	Tyrell	Science	8	G12351	Jennie	Campbell
SJR	Sarah	Jordan	English	39	G12346	James	Ling
SJR	Sarah	Jordan	English	39	G12348	Addy	Paredes

If the data is split into two tables – one for the teachers and one for the students – that are linked together, it can be stored and retrieved more efficiently, like this:

Teachers' table

Teacher_ID	Forename	Surname	Subject	Room
AVA	Anthony	Varela	Maths	51
GBA	Graham	Barney	Science	14
JKW	Jennie	Kwong	English	42
PTY	Paul	Tyrell	Science	8
SJR	Sarah	Jordan	English	39

Students' table

Student_ID	Student_FName	Student_SName	English	Maths	Science
G12345	Jasmine	Hall	JKW	AVA	GBA
G12346	James	Ling	SJR	AVA	PTY
G12348	Addy	Paredes	SJR	AVA	GBA
G12349	Hayley	Lemon	JKW	AVA	GBA
G12351	Jennie	Campbell	JKW	AVA	PTY

These two tables are linked with a 'one-to-many' relationship, because one teacher's record is linked to many students' records. The primary key fields (which **must** contain unique data) are the Student_ID and Teacher_ID.

18.1.4 Why use a relational database?

From the example above you can see how much internal memory and external storage space is saved by not storing data more than once. Imagine the space saved for a school with over a hundred teachers and over a thousand students, or in a national database with data on every driver and every vehicle registered in a country.

There are three common types of changes which can be made to the data contained in a database. Records/data can be added, edited or deleted. Because data is not repeated in a relational database, each change to an item of data or to a record has to be made only once. It is also much easier for users to produce reports from a relational database, where data is held in two or more tables, than from two or more flat-file databases.

Although people often think that it is quicker to search using relational rather than flat-file databases (in some cases, where indexed values are used, it can be true), it is not always the case. It depends on the structure of both databases and the quantity of the data being searched.

You will need to create both flat-file and relational databases, but the data for these will be provided. You will be using *Microsoft Access*, which is part of the *Microsoft Office* suite. When used with a single table *Access* is a flat-file database, but it can also be a relational database when used with more than one linked tables.

18.1.5 Data types

When you create a new database you will set a data type for each field. The data type tells *Access* how to store and manipulate the data for each field. You will usually decide what data type should be used for each field. There are a number of data types that you can use and different packages may have different names for them. The list below shows the generic names for these data types but, depending on the package used, you may have different names. For example, in *Access* an **alphanumeric** field is called a text field. The three main types of field are **alphanumeric**, **numeric** and **Boolean**.

- **Alphanumeric** data can store alpha characters (text) or numeric data (numbers) that will not be used for calculations. In *Access* this is called a text field.
- A **numeric** data type (as the name suggests) is used to store numeric values that may be used for calculations. This does not include numeric data such as telephone numbers, which should be stored in an alphanumeric data type. In *Access* this is called a number field. There are different types of numeric field including:
  - **integer** sub-type, which store whole numbers. In *Access* you can select an integer field or a long integer field. It is wise to use a long integer field if it is going to contain three or more digits

- decimal sub-type, which will allow a large number of decimal places, or a specified restricted number, if this is set in the field properties when the database is created
- currency sub-type, which allow currency formatting to be added to the display. This includes currency symbols and regional symbols. The database does not store these symbols as this would use up valuable storage space
- date and time sub-type, which store a date and/or time as a number.
- A Boolean (or logical) data type stores data in a Yes/No (or True/False, 0/−1) format.

There are other data types, such as autonumber (which generates unique numbers) but as they are not available in all packages you do not need to worry about them. Some packages, such as *Access*, have long and short versions of their data types (for example, long text and short text) but these are still versions of alphanumeric data types.

Other data types that are not studied in depth here can often be found in commercial databases, for example placeholders for media such as images, sound bites and video clips. These are often used in web applications where a back-end database holds the media to be displayed in another application, such as a webpage.

As stated above, you will be using *Access. Microsoft Excel* is **not** suitable for database tasks as you cannot define data types.

Task 18a

You work for a small garage called 'Dodgy Dave's Motors'. This garage sells used cars. Using a suitable database package, import the file **cars.csv**. Assign the following data types to the fields.

Field name	Data type
Who manufactured the car?	Text
Model	Text
Colour	Text
Price that we bought the car for	Numeric/Currency/2 decimal places
Price that we will sell the car for	Numeric/Currency/2 decimal places
Year	Numeric/Integer
Extras	Text
Does the car need cleaning?	Boolean/Logical

Some field names are inappropriate. Create appropriate and meaningful field names for those fields. You may add another field as a primary key field if your software requires this.

Save the database.

It is important to make sure that you use the field names exactly as given in the question paper, unless you are asked to provide appropriate and meaningful field names. In this task you are asked for appropriate and meaningful field names, so start by looking at the detailed descriptions given instead of the field names, or even examine the data to work out what information the fields contains.

For this task, the descriptions help you to work out meaningful field names. These should always be short enough to allow printouts to fit easily on to as few pages as possible. The first example is Who manufactured the car?; this could be shortened to Manufacturer or even Make. Make is short, meaningful and appropriate, so use that. Price that we bought the car for could be changed to Purchase Price, Purchase, P Price, P_Price or just PPrice. Although *Access* will allow any of these, do **not** use field names with spaces in as they may cause problems if you try to do more complex operations with the database. You could use any of the other three options, as all would be acceptable. For this task, use PPrice. Similarly, the next field can be called SPrice. Consider the final field, Does the car need cleaning?. Simply using the fieldname Clean could give the wrong idea, as it could mean 'Does the car need cleaning?' or 'Is the car clean?'. It is sensible to plan this and make the changes in the .csv file before importing the data into *Access*.

Open the **cars.csv** file in *Excel*. Move into the relevant cells and type in the new field names. Check the spelling carefully before resaving the data file. Save it with the filename **cars1.csv** so that you do not lose the original data file. Task 18a is continued in the next section.

18.1.6 Create a flat-file database from an existing file

Advice

Check that the data files are in the correct format for your regional settings before attempting this section (see Introduction, page viii).

Open *Access* and select the Blank desktop database icon.

Set the filename to task18a and select Create.
This should open a new database similar to this.

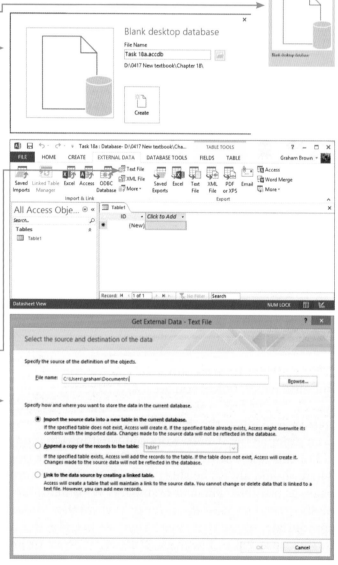

To import the file **cars1.csv** (remember, we saved it with a new filename in an earlier section) for the task, select the EXTERNAL DATA tab.

In the Import & Link section, double click on the Text File icon, as files saved in .csv format are text files with each data item separated from the next by a comma. This icon opens the Get External Data – Text File window, like this.

Use the Browse... button to find the file **cars1.csv** and ensure that the top radio button is selected. This will make sure that the data is saved in a new data table. Click on OPEN, then click on OK.

Advice

A large number of students perform poorly on these questions in examinations because they select the bottom option to link the database to data held in a spreadsheet.

The Import Text Wizard window will open. As comma separated value (.csv) files are delimited files (the comma is the delimiter), select the Delimited radio button and click on [Next >].

For the next part of the wizard, make sure that Comma is selected using the radio buttons (unless you have changed the .csv file so that it uses semicolons as delimiters). Examine the first row of the data and decide whether this row contains the field names that you need or if it contains the first row of data. If the first row contains the field names click on the First Row Contains Field Names tick box. As you tick this box, the first row changes from this to this.

Click on [Advanced...] to open the Import Specification window.

Check that all the field names and data types match those specified in the task. In this case the PPrice, SPrice and Valet fields do not have correct data types. The PPrice and SPrice fields need changing to numeric (currency) fields and the Valet field needs changing to a Boolean (Yes/No) field.

Advice

.txt and .rtf files may have different characters to separate each data item. If either of these file types is to be used, open the file in Notepad and examine the data. Work out which character is the separator and select this instead of a comma or semicolon.

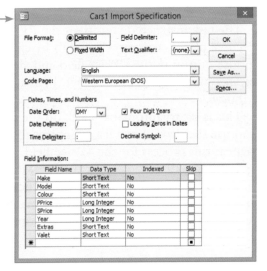

To change the PPrice field into a numeric field with a currency subtype, click on the Data Type cell for this field and use the drop-down list to select the Currency data type. Repeat this process for the SPrice field.

For the Valet field, use the drop-down list to change the Text data type into a Yes/No data type. When all of these changes have been made, click on OK. Select Next > twice. In the next screen, ensure that the radio button for Let Access add primary key is selected – this adds a new field called ID to the table; *Access* will use this as the primary key field. Click on Next > and in the Import to Table: box, enter tblCars. This is a meaningful table name as 'tbl' shows you that it is a table and 'Cars' gives relevance to the data. Click on Finish to import the data and on Close to close the wizard. Double click on tblCars to display the table like this.

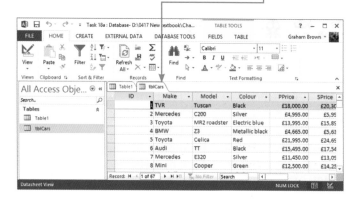

Changes to the data types or other properties can be made from the HOME tab. In the Views section click on the Design View icon.

The task instructed you to set the PPrice field to two decimal places. You can check this by clicking the left mouse button in the PPrice field and viewing the number of Decimal Places in the General tab at the bottom of the window.

This is set to automatic. Click on the cell containing Auto and use the drop-down list to set this to two decimal places. Repeat this process for the SPrice field.

To change the Boolean field so that it displays Yes or No (it does not store the data like this), click in the Valet field and, in the General tab, select the Format cell. Use the drop-down list to select the Yes/No option.

Save the database as task18a.

Advice

If you need percentage values, set an integer or long integer data type and select Percentage from the Format drop-down menu for this field.

Advice

The icon in the Views section of the HOME tab will let you change between Datasheet and Design View.

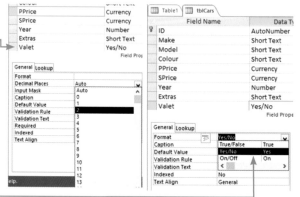

Activity 18a

You work for a shop selling office supplies called 'Easy as ABC'. Using a suitable database package, import the file **stationery.csv**. Use these data types for each field.

Field name	Data type
Code	Numeric/Integer
Type of product to be sold	Text
Description of the product to be sold	Text
Quantity of items in each pack	Numeric/Integer
Colour	Text
Sales price	Numeric/Currency/2 decimal places
Purchase price	Numeric/Currency/2 decimal places
Discount	Boolean/Logical

Some field names are inappropriate. Create appropriate and meaningful field names for those fields. Use the Code field as your primary key. Save the database.

18.1.7 Enter data using a table

Task 18b

Open the database that you saved in Task 18a. Add this new car to the database.

Make	Model	Colour	PPrice	SPrice	Year	Extras	Valet
Ford	Focus	Silver	1350	2285	2008	Alarm Central Locking Alloy Wheels	Yes

Data is normally entered into a database using a form but, if a form is not asked for, it may be quicker to use the table to enter new data.

Open the database saved in Task 18a. First click on the Enable Content button.

Double click the left mouse button on the table name to open the table in Datasheet View.

To make sure that all the columns are fully visible, click the left mouse button on the grey square to the left of the ID field name to highlight the entire datasheet. Move the cursor between two field names until it looks like this and then double click.

This will adjust the display widths of the columns. Scroll down the list of cars until you reach the entry with a star next to it, which will allow you to add a New car at the bottom.

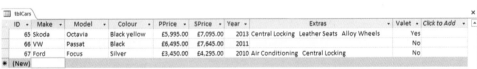

Click the cursor in the Make cell for the new car and add 'Ford'. The new ID number will automatically appear in the ID field, as you set this field as an AutoNumber type. Move the cursor and enter the Model, Colour, Year and Extras data from the task in the same way. You can always use copy and paste for some data. For example, if you need to make sure the spelling of 'Focus' is correct, copy and paste it from record 67 above. For the PPrice and SPrice fields, enter only the numbers (and decimal point if this is required). Do not attempt to enter any other characters, such as the currency symbol. As you press the <Enter> key after adding the prices *Access* will set the data into currency format. Each time you press the <Enter> key, *Access* automatically saves the changes you made to the data. The Valet field will automatically default to 'No'. Move into this field and enter 'Yes' in this cell. *Access* will automatically save each item of data as you enter it.

Check your data entry carefully using visual verification. This is when you compare the original data on paper (in this case, in the Task 18b brief) with the data that you have entered into the computer. Data entry errors in a database may cause problems when you try to use the database to search or sort. Save the database as task18b.

18.1.8 Add a field to an existing table

> ### Task 18c
>
> Open the file that you saved at the end of Task 18b.
>
> Add a new field to the database called PDate. Add the purchase date of 20 December 2014 for the last car added to the database.

Open the database and open the table tblCars in Design View. Move to the empty row below the Valet field and enter the Field name PDate. ——————

In the Data Type box use the drop-down list to select the Date/Time type. ——————

Choose the most appropriate Format for the question. In this case, the task asks for a Long Date format.

Save the database as task18c and select the Datasheet View. Move the cursor into the PDate field for the new record (the Silver Ford Focus) and use the Calendar icon to select the correct date. ——————

You may need to double click to the right of the PDate column to widen the column. Save the database as task18c.

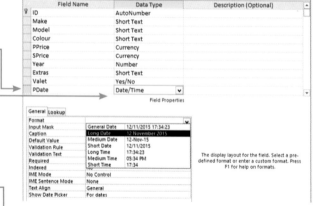

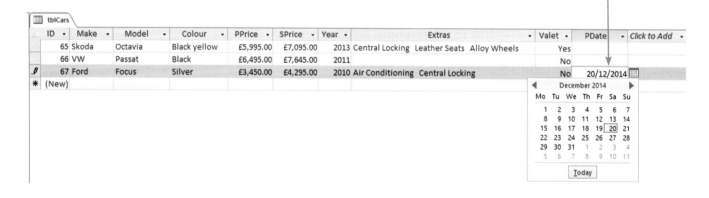

Activity 18b

Open the file saved in Activity 18a.

Add these three items of stationery to the database.

Code	Type	Description	Quantity	Colour	SPrice	PPrice	Discount
44282	Lever Arch File	Laminated Lever Arch Files	1	Red	57.22	28.96	No
44283	Lever Arch File	Laminated Lever Arch Files	1	Yellow	57.22	28.96	No
47478	Spine Label	Eastlight Spine Lables	100		30	13.86	Yes

18.1.9 Create a relational database from existing files

Task 18d

You work for Tawara High School. You will edit some data about the Mathematics Faculty. Using a suitable database package import the file **teachers.csv**.

Use these field names and data types:

Field name	Data type
SCode	Text
FName	Text
SName	Text
Subject	Text
Room	Numeric/Integer

Set the SCode field as a key field.

Import the file **students.csv** as a new table in your database.

Set the Student_ID field as a key field.

Create a one-to-many relationship as a link between the SCode field in the Teachers' table and the Maths field in the Students' table.

Use the techniques you practised in Task 18a to import the two tables into the database so that each table looks like this.

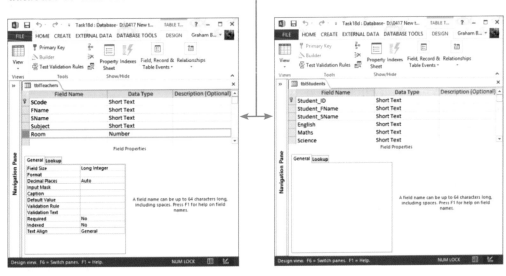

Select the DATABASE TOOLS tab and double click on the Relationships icon to open the Show Table window.

Double click on each of the table names to place the table in the Relationships tab.

After both tables have been added, click on [Close] to see the Relationships tab like this.

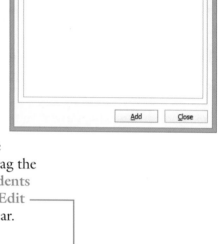

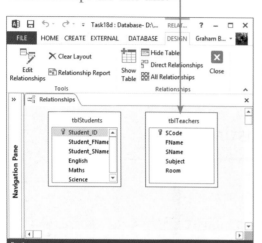

Move the cursor to sit over the bottom right corner of the Students table so that it changes to a drag arrow; expand it slightly so that all the field names are fully visible.

To create the one-to-many relationship between the SCode field in the Teachers' table and the Maths field in the Students' table; click the left mouse button down in the tblTeachers table on the SCode field. Hold down this button, drag the cursor and drop it in the tblStudents table over the Maths field. The Edit Relationships window will appear.

This window shows the link between the fields in both of the tables. The bottom of the window displays the type of relationship that you have created. You cannot change it here: if the relationship is not the correct type, you have probably missed setting one of the key fields. To correct this, click [Cancel], add the key

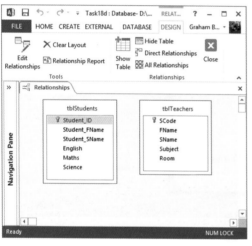

field and redo this task. You will be expected to show how you created the relationship. A screen shot of this window taken with the <Alt> and <Prt Scr> keys will copy this into the clipboard. Paste this into the document that you will present as evidence of your method. When you click [Create] the window will disappear and the Relationships tab will look like this.

In this relationship SCode is the primary key field in tblTeachers and Maths is the foreign key field in tblStudents. If you wish to view or edit the relationship again, you can double click the mouse on the relationship line that joins the two tables.

Save the database.

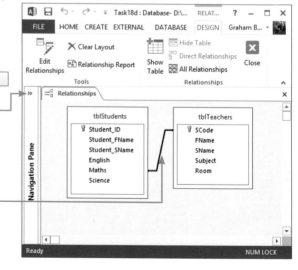

Activity 18c

Open the file saved in Activity 18b.

Import the file **orders.csv**. Use these field names and data types:

Field name	Data type
Order_No	Numeric/Integer
Customer_No	Text
Product_Code	Numeric/Integer
Units_Sold	Numeric/Integer

Assign a new field as a key field. Import the file **customers.csv**. Use these field names and data types:

Field name	Data type
Customer_ID	Text
Name	Text
Address_1	Text
Address_2	Text
Address_3	Text
Zip_Code	Text
Discount_%	Numeric/2 decimal places

Set the Customer_ID field as a key field. Create a one-to-many relationship between the Code field in the Stationery table and the Product_Code field in the Orders table. Create a one-to-many relationship between the Customer_ID field in the Customers table and the Customer_No field in the Orders table.

Take screen shot evidence showing the:

- field names and data types used in these two tables
- relationships between the three tables.

18.1.10 Create a data entry form

Task 18e

Open the file saved in Task 18d. Add new data entry forms to collect data for all fields in both of the tables.

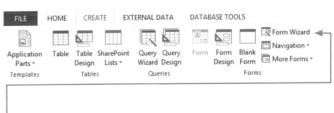

Open the file saved in Task 18d. The best way to create a data entry form is to select the CREATE tab, then click on the Form Wizard.

The Form Wizard window opens. Select the table that holds the fields that you will include in the form. If the form needs fields from more than one table then select a query (you will use these later in the chapter). We will create the first form by selecting tblStudents, so leave that selected in the top selection box.

You can move each field across into the form using the
`>` key but, as we want all the data from this table on the form, use the double arrow key.

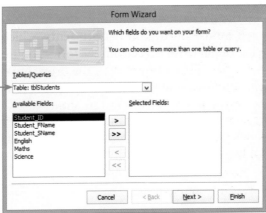

All of the fields move into the selected fields box. Click on Next > . Choose that layout of the screen that you require (I chose Columnar for this task) before clicking on Next > again. Change the title of the form to frmStudents so that you can easily tell that it is a form. Click on Finish to open the form.

The bottom of the form has a navigation bar which can be used to move from record to record like this.

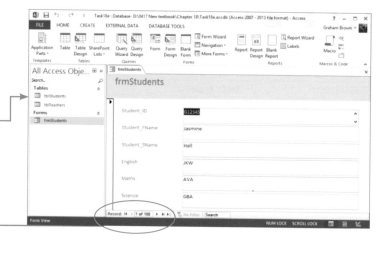

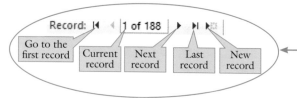

Repeat this process for tblTeachers to create the second data entry form, which should look like this.

The data entry form may need editing to make it easier for a different target audience to use. Using short and meaningful field names to store the data may not be easy for other users to understand, particularly if they do not work with databases regularly. For example, if children were to add their data, simple questions would be better than encoded field names, along with instructions on how to complete the form.

Save the database as task18e.

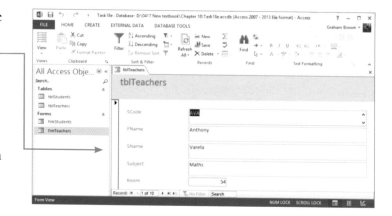

18.1.11 Edit a data entry form

Task 18f

Open the file saved in Task 18e. Edit the data entry form for student data to make it easier for students to enter their own data.

Open the database saved in Task 18e. Double click the left mouse button on frmStudents, which is in the list of database objects under forms, on the left.

Select the HOME tab, then the drop-down arrow in the View section to pull down the different ways of viewing the form. Select Design View.

Click on the minimise button to hide the list of database objects, giving you more room to work.

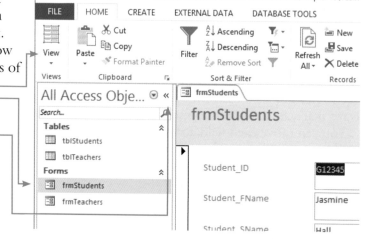

From the Tools section of the Toolbar, select the Property Sheet icon. This will open the Property Sheet for the current object. Move the cursor into the Form Header and click on the outline so that it changes to orange.

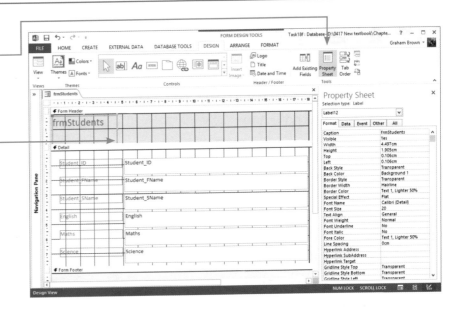

Highlight the text in this label box and change it to a more suitable heading. If the text does not fit in the label box, grab the drag handles and make it larger. You may not be able to see the lower drag handles; if you need to use them, drag the Detail bar down slightly, but remember to move it back up again later. If you wish to change the font, colours or formatting of the text (or any other form element) this can be done in the Property Sheet. In this example I have changed the Text Align to Center, Fore Color and Back Color by clicking on them, then on the . . . icon, then by choosing colours from the palette.

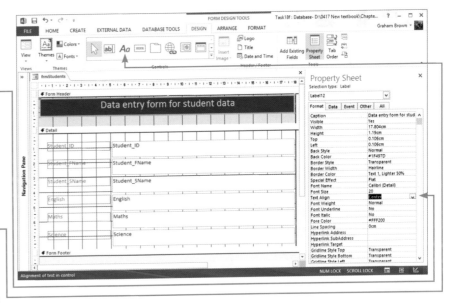

As students would be expected to enter their own data, it is important to tell them what to do. From the Controls section of the toolbar, select the Label icon.

Drag a new label box into the header and enter some instructions to help the students to understand what to enter, like this.

In the Detail row each field has two boxes: the left one is the label box and this is what is displayed to the user; the right box is a text box and this is joined to the data table. This box is where, when the form is displayed in Form View, the user will enter the data. Select each label in turn and edit the text. You may need to resize some of the label boxes so that all the text fits. Each box has a large drag handle in the top left corner that will allow you to drag the box around the form to rearrange the form without resizing the box. This is useful if you are creating your form to a particular design. From the View section of the

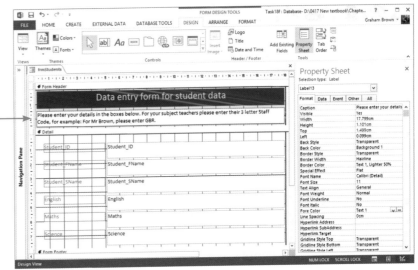

toolbar, use the drop-down arrow under the View
icon to select Form View like this. ———————

Save the database as task18f.

18.1.12 Enter a new field on to an existing form

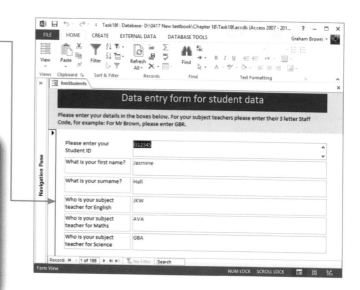

Task 18g

Open the database that you saved in Task 18f.

Two new fields are to be added to the students' data. Use these field names, data types and field descriptions:

Field name	Data type	Description
Year_Group	Numeric/ Integer	The school year between 7 and 11 inclusive
Tutor	Text	The name of the student's tutor

Open the database. Remember you hid the Navigation Pane. Restore it using the arrow ▶.

Open tblStudents in Design View. Enter the Field Name, Year_Group (you cannot shorten it to Year as this is a reserved word in *Access*, try it and see…). The data type always starts in Short Text format; click on that cell and use the drop-down menu to select Number. ———————

Type the field description into the Description box. This helps to document the database. Add the new Field Name, Tutor on the next row. To help improve the form and to save lots of storage space, we know that the tutors' initials are three characters in length. In the General tab at the bottom, set the Field Size to 3. Save the changes to the table, close it and open frmStudents in Design View. Pick up the top of the Form Footer and drag it down to give enough room to add the two new fields.

The Year_Group field could appear on the form as a text box but, as this data can only hold five possible values (because Tawara High School only has years 7, 8, 9, 10 and 11) it would be a suitable field for radio buttons (*Access* calls these Option Buttons) within an option group. From the Design tab select the Option Group icon.

Drag the frame for the Option Group into the Detail section of the form, clicking the left mouse button once; this action will open the Option Group Wizard window. Enter six label names, one item on each row – in this case Year 7, Year 8, Year 9, Year 10, Year 11 and an additional option for 'No year group selected' – before clicking on [Next >]. ———————

In the next window choose the top option for Yes, the default choice is: and select the option you typed in for No year group selected. Click [Next >]. Each label has a value assigned to it. *Access* has tried to assign values for you but we need to change all of the settings in this example. For Year 7 set the value to 7, Year 8 set to 8, and so on. For No year group selected set the value to 0. When you have changed all of the values click [Next >]. ———————

XYZ

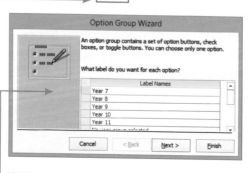

In the next window, change the radio button from the top option to Store the value in the field:. Using the drop-down menu to the right, select the Year_Group field. This will make sure that, when a radio button is selected, the value for that radio button is stored in the correct field within the table. Click [Next >] to choose the style of options selected (radio buttons, tick boxes or toggle buttons) and to choose how the Option box will appear on the form. Click [Next >] again when you have made your choices. Give the frame a meaningful caption such as Which year group are you in? before selecting [Finish].

The option block will look similar to this in Design View.

To add the Tutor field to the form, select the Text Box icon from the toolbar.

Drag the text box for the Tutor field on to the form; you do not need much space as this field only needs to hold three characters.

Resize the label box on the left and add the text 'Tutor' as the label. The text box looks like this.

Click the cursor on the Unbound text box and, within the Property Sheet for this control, select the Data tab. In the Control Source box, use the drop-down menu to select the Tutor field.

The text box changes from unbound to show the Tutor field.

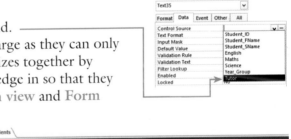

The text boxes for English, Maths and Science are also too large as they can only contain three-lettered staff codes, so reduce these three field sizes together by selecting all three text boxes together and dragging the right edge in so that they match the Tutor field. Save the database. The finished Design view and Form view look like this.

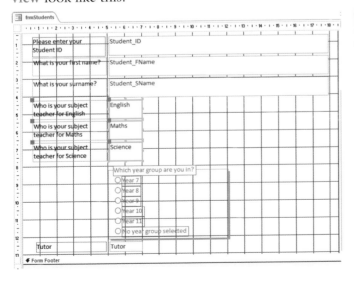

18.1.13 Key features of a well-designed form

The most important feature of form design is to keep the form simple, with clear questions, using closed questions where possible. This will limit the different answers to be stored in the database and will make it easier to search the database. A well-designed form has similar fields grouped, but not crowded, together with white space between each data entry box.

This form has many features of a well-designed data entry form. The form has a title that states what data is being collected. There are instructions on filling in the form. The questions are not just the field names but written questions. Each field has appropriate space for the data that will be added, and there is space between each field. The form has been appropriately filled by the text boxes but there is enough white space to keep it from being overcrowded. Radio buttons (or drop-down menus) are used where possible. There are navigation buttons on the form (already added by *Access*) to allow a user to add new records and move between records. In this form all of the data is important; in some forms key fields can be highlighted to show that this data must be completed before the record can be saved.

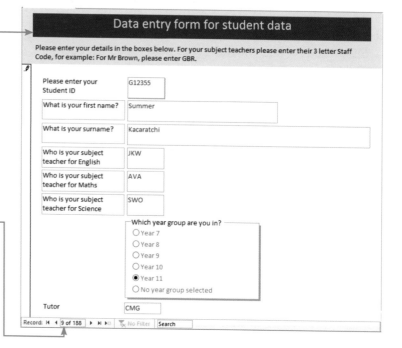

18.2 Manipulate data

18.2.1 Perform searches

You can search for data in *Access* using a query. This allows you to select a subset of the data stored in your table. Each query is created and saved, and can be used again later. If new data is added to the table, when you open a query again it will select the subset from all the data, including the new data.

> **Task 18h**
>
> Open the file that you saved at the end of Task 18c.
>
> A customer would like a car made by Ford. Find the customer a list of all the cars in the garage made by Ford.

Open the database that you saved at the end of Task 18c. You do not need to open the table that you created earlier. Select the **CREATE** tab and find the Queries section. Click on the **Query Wizard** icon.

This is the easiest way of performing a search and opens the New Query window. Select the Simple Query Wizard and click on OK.

In the Simple Query Wizard window, make sure that the correct table name has been selected in the Tables/Queries box. As this is your first query this is the only option in this box, but each time you create a new query it will be shown here. If you select a previous query rather than the table, you are likely to get incorrect results.

For this task it would be appropriate to show the customer all the fields except the ID field, the price that the garage bought the car for (the PPrice field) and the date the garage purchased the car (the PDate field). Move all of the fields into the query using the double arrow key.

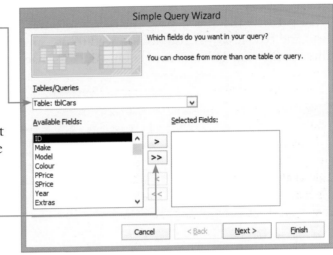

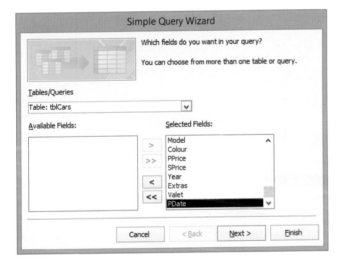

Select the ID field, the PPrice field and the PDate field in turn and click on the single arrow to remove them from the selection. When you have got only the required fields, click Next >. Select Next > again.

Enter a name for the query. This query may be turned into a report at some point and the name you give the query may become the title for the report. You may therefore wish to add your name to the query name, like this.

Select the radio button for Modify the query design before clicking on Finish.

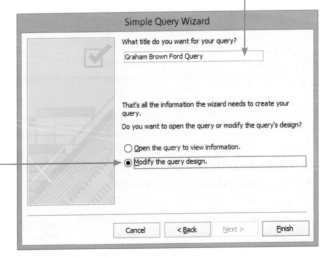

This opens the query in Design View. Datasheet View can be seen by selecting the drop-down list under the View icon. However, at the moment the query will still contain all of the records as we have not yet performed the search, so make sure you are in Design View.

To perform the query, move the cursor into the Criteria: row of the Make field and type in Ford. You do not need to use speech marks as *Access* will put these in for you. This will extract only the cars made by Ford.

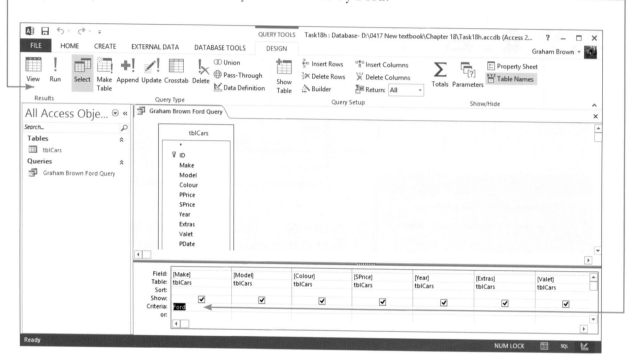

Now select the Datasheet View to see the results of the query. The number of records can be seen at the bottom of the window in this view. There should be 25 Ford cars in the query. Save the database as task18h.

Task 18i

Open the file that you saved at the end of Task 18h.

The manager would like to see all the details of all the Fords that need valeting.

Create a query in a similar way to the one for Task 18h. Make sure you have tblCars selected and not your Ford query. Select all the fields and, when in Design View, enter Ford in the Criteria: row of the Make column and Yes in the same Criteria: row for the Valet column. The selection will look like this and only two cars will be found using this search.

Advice

This is called an AND Query, because the Make has to be Ford AND the Valet field has to be Yes.

Field:	Make	Model	Colour	SPrice	Year	Extras	Valet	
Table:	tblCars	tblCars	tblCars	tblCars	tblCars	tblCars	tblCars	
Sort:								
Show:	☑	☑	☑	☑	☑	☑	☑	
Criteria:	"Ford"						Yes	
or:								

Task 18j

Open the file that you saved at the end of Task 18i.

The manager would like to see all the details of all the cars made by Ford or Vauxhall.

Create a query in a similar way to the one for Task 18i. In the Simple Query Wizard window, make sure that the correct table name has been selected in the Tables/Queries box. If you select one of the previous queries rather than the table, you are likely to get incorrect results.

Select all the fields and, when in Design View, enter Ford or Vauxhall in the Criteria: row of the Make column. The selection will look like this and 37 cars will be found using this search.

Save this as task18j.

Field:	Make	Model
Table:	tblCars	tblCars
Sort:		
Show:	✔	✔
Criteria:	"Ford" Or "Vauxhall"	
or:		

Advice

Another way of doing this is to type Ford in the Criteria: row and Vauxhall in the or: row.

Task 18k

Open the file that you saved at the end of Task 18j.

The sales manager would like to see details of all the cars in stock **not** made by Ford.

Create a query in a similar way to the one for Task 18j. Select all the fields and, when in Design View, enter Not Ford in the Criteria: row of the Make column. The selection will look like this and 43 cars will be found using this search.

Save this as task18k.

Field:	Make	Model
Table:	tblCars	tblCars
Sort:		
Show:	✔	✔
Criteria:	Not "Ford"	
or:		

Task 18l

Open the file that you saved at the end of Task 18k.

The manager would like to see all the details of all the cars that have alloy wheels.

By examining the data in the database you can see that the text 'Alloy Wheels' could appear in the Extras field. It may not be the only extra that a car has – there could be other extras listed before it or after it within the field.

To find all the cars with this extra you must create a query in a similar way as for Task18k. Select all the fields and, when in Design View, enter *Alloy Wheels* in the Criteria: row of the Extras column. The stars tell *Access* that you are performing a **wildcard search**. This is a search which looks for the words 'Alloy Wheels' (including the space) anywhere in the Extras fields' contents. The selection will look like this and 35 cars will be found using this search.

Save this as task18l.

Field:	[Year]	[Extras]	[Valet]
Table:	tblCars	tblCars	tblCars
Sort:			
Show:	✔	✔	✔
Criteria:		*Alloy Wheels*	
or:			

Advice

To search for something that is at the start of the data, use Text*; for example, Bl* in the Colour field will find all the cars with the first colour Blue or Black, but would not find colours such as Light Blue. Placing the star at the start of a search string will only find those things ending with the search string.

Task 18m

Open the file that you saved at the end of Task 18l.

The sales manager would like to see details of all the cars in stock for sale for less than or equal to £4125.

Create a query in a similar way as for Task 18l. Be careful not to use symbols such as < or £ in the query name. Select all the fields and, when in Design View, enter <=4125 in the Criteria: row of the SPrice column. The selection will look like this and 19 cars will be found using this search.

Field:	SPrice	Year
Table:	tblCars	tblCars
Sort:		
Show:	☑	☑
Criteria:	<=4125	
or:		

Similar mathematical formulae can be used, with < for less than, > for greater than, >= for greater than or equal to, and = for equals. These mathematical formulae cannot be used for queries involving text fields but can be used for any numeric, date or time fields.

Task 18n

Open the file that you saved at the end of Task 18g.

Find Mr Varela a list of all the students that he teaches for Maths; include in this extract his full name and teaching room.

Open the database that you saved at the end of Task 18g. Create a new query using the Query Wizard. This is the easiest way of performing a search and opens the New Query window. Select the Simple Query Wizard then, in the Tables/Queries box, select the table tblTeachers. Move across to the right the FName, SName and Room fields. Move back into the Tables/Queries box and select the table tblStudents. Select (by moving them from Available fields: to Selected fields:) the Student_Fname, Student_SName and Maths fields, like this.

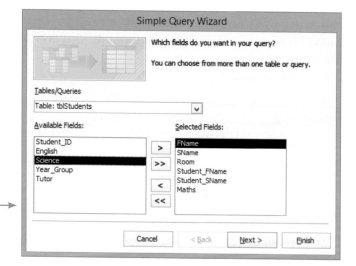

Click on [Next >]. Continue through the wizard until you get to the query in
Design View. Move the cursor into the Criteria: row of the Maths field and type
in AVA.

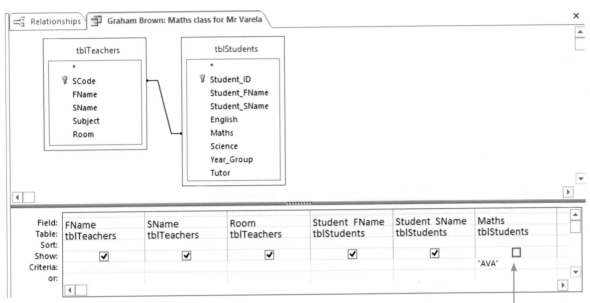

Open the query in Datasheet View to check that you have done the query as
specified. The Maths field does not need to be shown; to hide it (do not delete it
or the selection of the data will also be lost) move back into Design View. Move
the cursor into the Show: row of the Maths field and remove the tick from the
check box. This field is present in the query but will not be shown. This query
should return 31 records. Save the database as task18n.

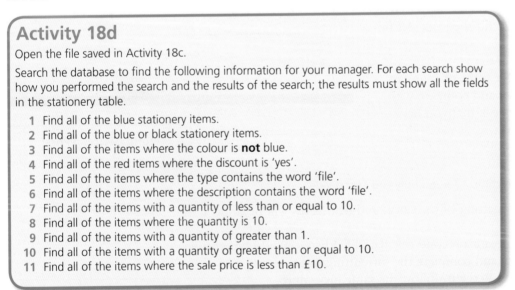

Activity 18d

Open the file saved in Activity 18c.

Search the database to find the following information for your manager. For each search show
how you performed the search and the results of the search; the results must show all the fields
in the stationery table.

1. Find all of the blue stationery items.
2. Find all of the blue or black stationery items.
3. Find all of the items where the colour is **not** blue.
4. Find all of the red items where the discount is 'yes'.
5. Find all of the items where the type contains the word 'file'.
6. Find all of the items where the description contains the word 'file'.
7. Find all of the items with a quantity of less than or equal to 10.
8. Find all of the items where the quantity is 10.
9. Find all of the items with a quantity of greater than 1.
10. Find all of the items with a quantity of greater than or equal to 10.
11. Find all of the items where the sale price is less than £10.

18.2.2 Use formulae in queries

You are sometimes asked to perform calculations at run time. This could be done
in one of two ways. The first method is by creating a calculated field, so that each
record has a calculation performed on it and the results are stored in a query. The
other method is to calculate on all (or a selection of) the records, for example to
add (sum) the data from a number of records.

Task 18o

Open the file saved in Task 18m.

Produce a new extract from all the data that:

- contains a new field called **Profit** which is calculated at run time. This field will subtract the purchase price from the sale price
- contains a new field called **Percent** to calculate the percentage profit for each car at run time. This field will divide the profit by the sale price.

To create a field that is calculated at run time, you must first open a query. For this task the query will not be used to search for data but to perform the calculation. Select the CREATE tab, then click in the New Queries section on the Query Wizard icon; select the Simple Query Wizard. In the Tables/Queries box select the table **tblCars** as the source of the data. Select all fields using the double arrow key. Click on [Next >] twice, name the query Profit calculation, select the radio button for Modify the query design, then click on [Finish].

In the Design View of the query, use the bottom scroll bar to scroll to the right and find the first blank field like this.

Move the cursor into the Field row for the first blank field. Enter the name Profit that you wish to give this calculated field followed by a colon. The colon tells *Access* that the next section is a calculation. Within the calculation, you must place square brackets around each field name so that *Access* looks up the data from the relevant field.

For this task, you need to subtract the purchase price from the sale price. The finished calculation will appear like this.

In the View section, select the Datasheet View. Calculate the profit for three or four cars by hand or using a calculator and compare with the results in the query to check that you have entered the formula correctly.

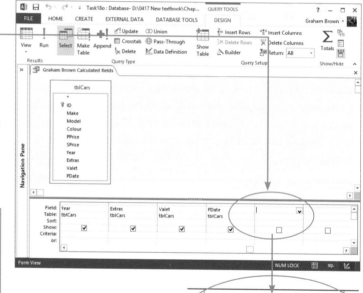

Profit: [SPrice]-[PPrice]

Advice

Use + for addition, − for subtraction, * for multiply and / for divide.

Do not worry about the formatting of the calculated field. This will be done at a later stage.

The task requires you to create a second calculated field so it would be sensible to include the new field now and complete the formatting later.

To create a new field called Percent, follow the same procedure, this time adding a formula to divide the profit by the purchase price. Again, check the calculations with a calculator to ensure that you have not made an error when entering the formula. When you have calculated this field and view the query in Datasheet View, you may see the values displayed as #####. This means the column is too narrow to see all the data. Drag the column to the right so that the data is fully visible. Save the database and close the query.

Profit: [SPrice]-[PPrice]	Percent: [Profit]/[PPrice]
☑	☑

Activity 18e

Open the file saved in Activity 18d.

Produce a new extract from all the data in the stationery table that:

- contains a new field called **Profit** which is calculated at run time. This field will subtract the purchase price from the sale price
- contains a new field called **Percent** to calculate the percentage profit for each car at run time. This field will divide the profit by the sale price
- contains a new field called **UnitProfit**. This field will divide the profit by the quantity.

For each calculated field show how you performed the calculation and the results of the calculation.

18.2.3 Present summary data in queries

Task 18p

Open the file saved in Task 18o.

Select only the cars made by Audi, BMW or Mercedes. Produce a new extract from all the data which, for the each of these makes of car, calculates:

- the sum of the sale price
- the average sale price
- the number of cars in stock.

Sort this data into descending order of average sale price.

This task requires the use of summary data. Open the file and, from the CREATE tab, select the **Query Wizard**, then the **Simple Query Wizard** followed by OK . In the Tables/Queries box select **tblCars** and from this table select only the **Make** and **SPrice** fields before clicking on Next > . Click the radio button for **Summary** data, then select the **Summary Options...** button.

This opens the **Summary Options** window.

To calculate the sum of the sale prices, tick the check box for **Sum**. For the average sale price tick the check box for **Avg**. For the number of cars in stock tick the check box for **Count records** in tblCars, followed by OK .

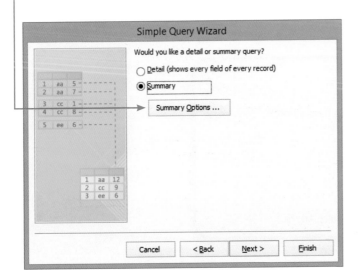

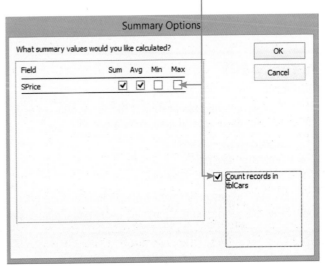

Click on [Next >]. Add a new title for the query. Select the radio button for Modify the query design, then click on [Finish] to enter Design View. Enter Audi or BMW or Mercedes in the Criteria: row of the Make column. The selection will look like this.

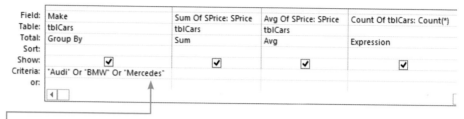

Field:	Make	Sum Of SPrice: SPrice	Avg Of SPrice: SPrice	Count Of tblCars: Count(*)
Table:	tblCars	tblCars	tblCars	
Total:	Group By	Sum	Avg	Expression
Sort:				
Show:	☑	☑	☑	☑
Criteria:	"Audi" Or "BMW" Or "Mercedes"			
or:				

The query results look like this.

Graham Brown Summary data on SPrice field			
Make	Sum Of SPrice	Avg Of SPrice	Count Of tblCars
udi	£52,635.00	£17,545.00	3
MW	£38,525.00	£12,841.67	3
lercedes	£53,630.00	£13,407.50	4

Save the database as task18p.

18.2.4 Sort data in queries

This data is sorted into ascending order of Make, but the question told you to sort this data into descending order of average sale price. Select the HOME tab, then click on the column heading for Avg of SPrice. This will highlight this column like this.

In the Sort & Filter section, select the descending sort icon.

FILE	HOME	CREATE	EXTERNAL DATA	DATABASE TOOL

Views | Clipboard | Sort & Filter

Graham Brown Summary data on SPrice field			
Make	Sum Of SPri	Avg Of SPric	Count Of tbl
Audi	£52,635.00	£17,545.00	3
BMW	£38,525.00	£12,841.67	3
Mercedes	£53,630.00	£13,407.50	4

The query results will now be sorted to look like this.

Graham Brown Summary data on SPrice field			
Make	Sum Of SPrice	Avg Of SPrice	Count Of tblCars
Audi	£52,635.00	£17,545.00	3
Mercedes	£53,630.00	£13,407.50	4
BMW	£38,525.00	£12,841.67	3

More complex sorting will be looked at in Section 18.3.7 as this is much easier using the report wizard, than in the queries.

Activity 18f

Open the file saved in Activity 18e.

Select all Type of items, except for any Binder. Produce a new extract from all of the stationery data which, for each Type of item, calculates:

- the average purchase price
- the average sale price
- the number of items in stock.

Sort this data into descending order of average purchase price.

Show how you performed the summary query and the results of the calculations.

18.3 Present data

18.3.1 Produce reports

The word 'report' can be quite confusing. A dictionary definition is 'a document that gives information about an investigation or a piece of research'. For our purposes, a report has this generic meaning: 'a document that gives information'. This is often confused with a report created in *Access*. The report created in *Access* will often be the most suitable report for a task, but sometimes it may be better to produce a report in a word processor, copying and pasting information into a document. For each task you will need to decide which method is the most suitable.

Task 18q

Open the database that you saved at the end of Task 18p.

Produce a report that:

- shows all of the cars made by Ford
- displays only the **Make**, **Model**, **Colour**, **SPrice**, **Extras** and **Valet** fields within the width of a landscape page
- has the text 'Report by' and your name on the left in the header of each page
- has a title 'All Ford cars in stock' centre aligned at the top of the first page
- has a subtitle 'request for Mr David Watson' right aligned at the top of the first page.

Open the database saved in Task 18p. Select the CREATE tab and find the Reports section. Click on the Report Wizard icon to open the Report Wizard window.

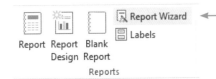

Advice

You **must** create the query first and then base the report on the query.

In the Tables/Queries box you need to select the correct query. For this task the report will be based on the query to select only the Fords (you created this query in Task18h). Use the arrow buttons to move the correct fields from Available Fields: into the Selected Fields: box like this, then click on [Next >]. Grouping is not needed at this level, so click on [Next >] again. You have not been asked to sort the report for this task (this is covered later in the chapter), so click on [Next >] again to get the Report Wizard window shown at the top of page 294.

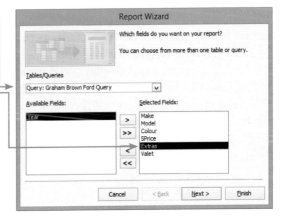

Use the Layout section to choose how the page will be laid out; in this case a Tabular format has been selected.

The task asked you to select a single landscape page. The page orientation is chosen using the Orientation radio buttons. Select Landscape then click on Next >.

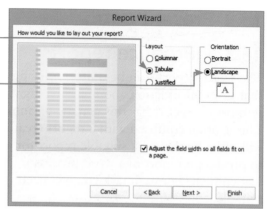

Change the report name so that it reads 'All Ford cars in stock' (which is the title from the task). As you still need to add the subtitle and ensure that the layout is correct, select the Modify the report's design radio button and click on Finish. The Design View of the report will look similar to this.

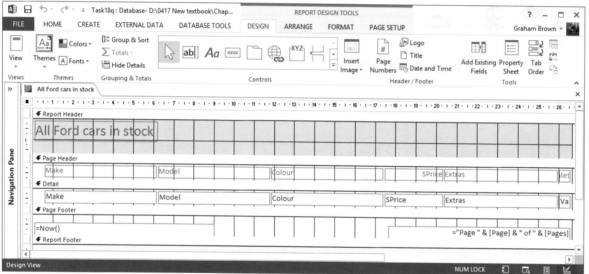

Each section of the report is shown with a light grey bar. The top section is the Report Header. Anything that you place in this section appears only once at the start of the document. Anything that you place in the Page Header is shown at the top of each page, in this case the field names. Similarly, information in the Page Footer is shown at the bottom of each page. The Report Footer appears at the very end of a report, although in this example the Report Footer is empty (it is not shown in white) and therefore will not be shown in this document. The Detail section is the most important, as this single row is where the data is shown for each car. This single row will appear as many rows (as many as there are Ford cars in the database) and display the details of each record.

The task asks you to place your name on the left in the header of each page. Move the cursor to the top of the light grey bar showing the Detail row; click on this so that the cursor changes into an arrow like this.

Hold the left mouse button down and drag the top of the Detail row down about 8 mm. Select all of the controls (objects) in the Page Header by dragging (and holding) the left mouse button. Move all of these controls down the page about 8 mm, so that they look like this.

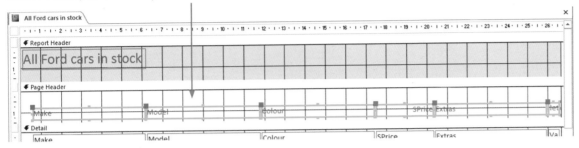

The **DESIGN** tab should already be selected. Find the **Controls** section and click on the **Label** icon. ───┐

Drag (to draw) a new control into the **Page Header** and type the text 'Report by' followed by your name into this control. This label needs editing so that the text is visible and right aligned. Select the control (the label you have just created) and, in the **DESIGN** tab, from the **Tools** section of the toolbar, click on the **Property Sheet** icon. ─────┐

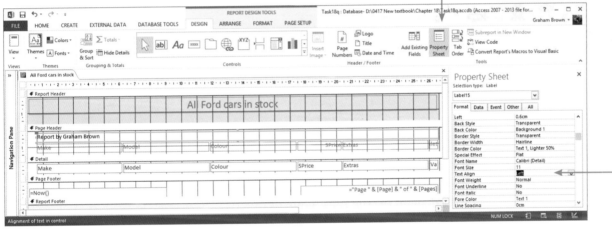

Select the **Fore Color** section and change the colour of the text to black; move to the **Text Align** section and use the drop-down menu to set the alignment to **Left**. ───┘

To see what the report will look like at any time, find the **View** section of the **DESIGN** tab and select the **Report View**. Use this section to change back to the **Design View** at any time.

The title 'All Ford cars in stock' needs to be centre aligned. Click on the control containing this label and use the drag handle to stretch the control to 26.5 cm (almost the edge of the page). You may need to close the **Property Sheet** to see this. If you stretch the control further to the right it will add another page width to the final printout, wasting paper when it is printed and no longer fitting to a single page wide. Once the control fits the page width, move to the **Property Sheet** and use the **Text Align** section to centre align the label.

To add the subtitle, drag the light grey bar for the **Page Header** down about 8 mm. Add a new label, the full width of the page, in the **Report Header** just below the title. Type the text 'request for Mr David Watson' into this control. Set the **Fore color** to white as before and right align this subtitle using the **Align Text Right** icon or in the **Property Sheet** change the **Text Align** to **Right**.

The Design View of the report looks like this.

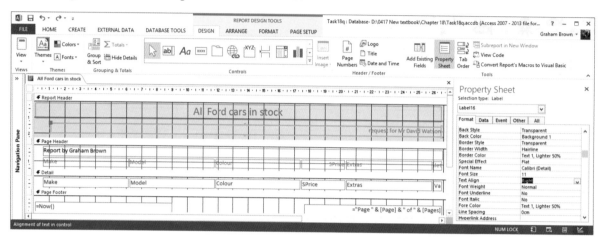

Move to the HOME tab and, in the View section, select Layout View. You can see that not all of the data within the report is fully visible.

Hold down the <Ctrl> key and click on both the control containing the field name Make and on the control containing the first car in the Detail row. Click the left mouse button again on the right edge of one of these controls. Use the drag arrow to narrow the space for these controls, making sure all the names are visible, like this.

Repeat this process to move the Model field closer to the Make field and resize it to fit the data.

Repeat this process for each field until the report looks like this.

Save the database as task18q.

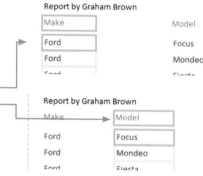

		All Ford cars in stock			
					request for Mr David Watson
Report by Graham Brown					
Make	Model	Colour	SPrice	Extras	Valet
Ford	Focus	Dark blue	£3,135.00	Alloy Wheels	No
Ford	Mondeo	White	£21,125.00		No
Ford	Fiesta	Blue	£8,975.00	Central Locking Air Conditioning	Yes
Ford	Mondeo	Silver	£3,795.00	Air Conditioning Alloy Wheels	No
Ford	Galaxy	Dark blue	£6,875.00	Air Conditioning	No
Ford	Mondeo	Black	£5.995.00	Central Locking Leather Seats Alloy Wheels	No

Activity 18g

Open the database that you saved at the end of Activity 18f.

Produce a report that:

- displays all the data in the stationery table within the width of a landscape page
- has your name on the right in the header of each page
- has a title 'All stationery in stock' centre aligned at the top of the first page
- has a subtitle 'request for the manager' right aligned at the top of the first page.

Task 18r

Open the database that you saved at the end of Task 18q.

Produce a report that:

- displays all the data for the **Make**, **Model**, **Colour**, **SPrice**, **Year** and **Extras** fields for all the cars with alloy wheels from Task 18l, within the width of a portrait page
- has your name in the report header followed by 'Cars with alloy wheels'.

Open the file task18q. Select the CREATE tab and, in the Reports section, click on the Report Wizard icon. In the Report Wizard window, select the query for alloy wheels (that you created in Task 18l) in the Tables/Queries box. As the task says 'display all the data', and specifies the fields, use the arrow buttons to move only these fields from Available Fields: to the Selected Fields: box. Go through the wizard as you did for the previous task, making sure that you set the page Orientation to Portrait. When the wizard has finished, the report is created and looks similar to this.

Graham Brown Alloy wheels

Make	Model	Colour	SPrice	Year	Extras
TVR	Tuscan	Black	£20,305.00	2012	Alloy Wheels Air Condit
BMW	Z3	Metallic black	£5,635.00	2006	Alloy Wheels
Toyota	Celica	Red	£24,695.00	2014	Air Conditioning Alloy
Audi	TT	Black	£17,545.00	2013	Central Locking Leather

You can see that *Access* has attempted to make all the fields fit across the page, but this has not been successful as not all of the data is fully visible. You must show all of the required data in full. Use the methods you used in Task 18l to make most of the data fit into the available space. Using both the Design View and Layout View will make this easier. In Design View you can see that the Valet field is only just visible.

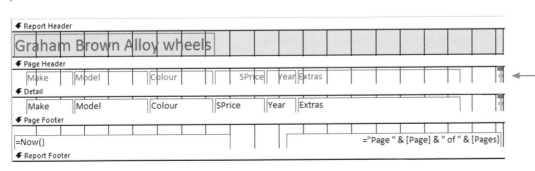

Reduce the width of the Extras field (and its label) and enlarge the Valet field
so that all its data can be seen. _____

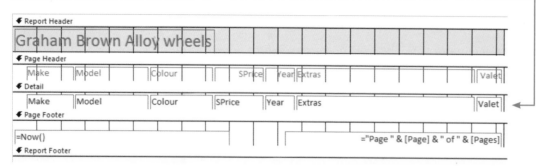

Change to Report View and check that all the data and labels fit within the
width of a single page. Other than the Extras field (which holds the most data),
all fields are now fully visible.

Make	Model	Colour	SPrice	Year	Extras	Valet
					Graham Brown Alloy wheels	
TVR	Tuscan	Black	£20,305.00	2012	Alloy Wheels Air Conditioning	No
BMW	Z3	Metallic black	£5,635.00	2006	Alloy Wheels	No
Toyota	Celica	Red	£24,695.00	2014	Air Conditioning Alloy Wheels	Yes
Audi	TT	Black	£17,545.00	2013	Central Locking Leather Seats Alloy Wheel:	No
Ford	Focus	Dark blue	£3,135.00	2009	Alloy Wheels	No

We can enlarge the Extras field by making the control for that field twice as deep.
Change to Design View and click the cursor on the top edge of the Page Footer.
Drag this down about 8 mm. In the Detail row, click the cursor on the lower
edge of the Extras control. Drag this down to double the height of this control.

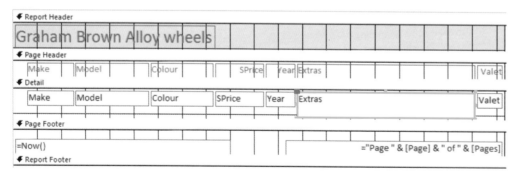

Change to Report View and check that all the data and labels fit within the width
of a single page, like this. Save the database as task18r.

Make	Model	Colour	SPrice	Year	Extras	Valet
					Graham Brown Alloy wheels	
TVR	Tuscan	Black	£20,305.00	2012	Alloy Wheels Air Conditioning	No
BMW	Z3	Metallic black	£5,635.00	2006	Alloy Wheels	No
Toyota	Celica	Red	£24,695.00	2014	Air Conditioning Alloy Wheels	Yes
Audi	TT	Black	£17,545.00	2013	Central Locking Leather Seats Alloy Wheels	No
Ford	Focus	Dark blue	£3,135.00	2009	Alloy Wheels	No

Activity 18h

Open the database that you saved at the end of Activity 18g.

Produce a report that:

- displays the data for all the items where the quantity is greater than or equal to 10, selected in Activity 18d, within the width of a portrait page
- has your name in the header of each page
- has a title 'Quantity >=10' centre aligned at the top of the first page.

Advice

The **Discount** field can appear as Yes/No, True/False or as a tick box. All of these would be correct for this activity.

18.3.2 Export data

Sometimes whole reports, queries or the data within them need to be exported into other packages to be manipulated as part of a report for someone, or to create a graph or chart.

Task 18s

Export the report saved in Task 18r into rich text format so it can be included in a word-processed document.

In the **Navigation** pane, find the report that you saved in Task 18r and right click the mouse button on the report name to get the drop-down menu.

Select the option to **Export**. This will open another drop-down menu. You need to export into .rtf format, so select **Word RTF File**. This opens the **Export – RTF File** window.

Click on the [Browse...] button to select a folder to save the document into. You will need to use this file for another task, so select the tick box for **Open the destination file after the export operation is complete**, then click on [OK]. The exported file will appear. Close the **Export – RTF File** window.

Advice

If you need to export the report without any formatting, select the **Text File** option.

Advice

If you need to export the data into .csv format (comma separated values), export it first into *Excel*, then save it in .csv format from *Excel*.

The same technique can be used in *Office 2013* for exporting to create graphs in *Excel*. In previous versions of *Office* you had to export the query rather than the report, but the latest version allows you to export either. To do so, change from **Word RTF File** format into *Excel* format in the export stage.

Activity 18i

Export the report saved in Activity 18h into:

- rich text format
- a format that can be used to produce a graph
- comma separated value format.

18.3.3 Hide data in a report

There are times when information in a report needs to be hidden in some way. In real applications a single report would be created for more than one task and some data would be hidden. This process is often done automatically using a created report and a programming language. Although that is beyond the scope of this book, the ability to hide fields within a report is useful. An example of this is when an invoice is produced for a customer and the same document is used as a delivery note, so that it shows the details of the items ordered but the costs are hidden. In *Access* this can be done in one of two ways: the first is to make a control invisible; the second is to use a background colour that matches the text colour.

> ### Task 18t
>
> Create a new report showing all the data for all the cars in stock made by Audi, BMW or Mercedes.
>
> Hide all the labels and data for the ID, Valet and PDate fields from the report. Hide the PPrice data (but not the title) by setting a black background.

Using the methods used so far in this chapter, create a new query from tblCars to select the three makes of car. Create a new report set in landscape format to display all fields for these cars, like this.

Audi or BMW or Mercedes

ID	Make	Model	Colour	PPrice	SPrice	Year	Extras	Valet	PDate
2	Mercedes	C200	Silver	£4,995.00	£5,995.00	2009	Air Conditioning	No	
4	BMW	Z3	Metallic black	£4,665.00	£5,635.00	2006	Alloy Wheels	No	
6	Audi	TT	Black	£15,495.00	£17,545.00	2013	Central Locking Leather Seats Alloy Wheels	No	
7	Mercedes	E320	Silver	£11,450.00	£13,095.00	2013	Air Conditioning	No	
26	Audi	TT	Green	£10,995.00	£12,595.00	2011	Air Conditioning Alloy Wheels	Yes	
41	Audi	TT	Blue	£19,995.00	£22,495.00	2013	Central Locking Leather Seats Alloy Wheels	No	
43	Mercedes	M class	Black	£16,995.00	£19,195.00	2011	Air Conditioning Alloy Wheels	No	
44	BMW	318i	Yellow	£15,995.00	£18,095.00	2013	Central Locking Leather Seats Alloy Wheels	No	
48	BMW	318i	Blue	£12,995.00	£14,795.00	2012	Central Locking Leather Seats Alloy Wheels	No	
50	Mercedes	Clk 320 Elegance	White	£13,495.00	£15,345.00	2010	Alloy Wheels Alarm	No	

Go into the Design View of the report; holding down the <Ctrl> key select all the controls for the ID, Valet and PDate fields. Open the Property Sheet and, in the Visible section, change the setting from Yes to No, which will hide these controls.

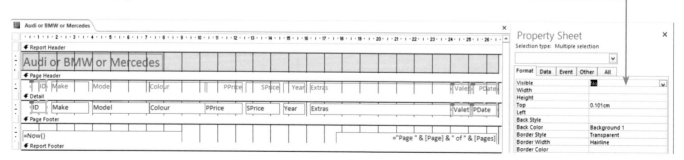

To set a black background for the PPrice data, in the Detail row of the report select the control for PPrice. Move the cursor into the Property Sheet, selecting the Format tab. Find the Back Color section and use the [...] icon to select the colour palette.

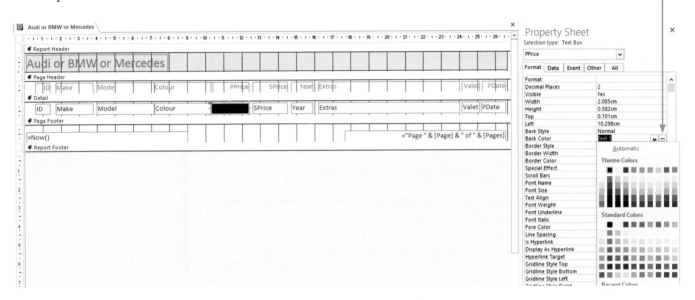

Select the black colour rather than the white background. Set the Fore Color to black in the same way. Change from Design View into Report View to see the changes.

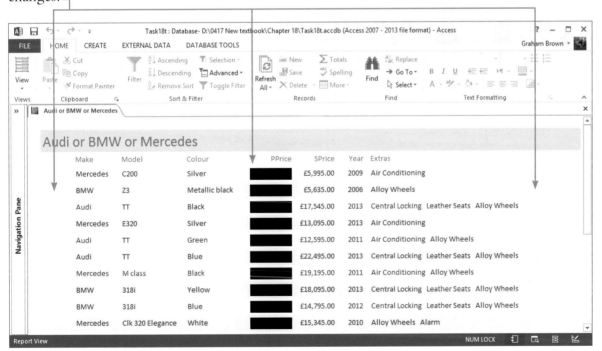

Save the changes to the report and close it.

Advice

Open the file you saved in Activity 21h. Move to All Access Objects and Reports. Use copy and paste to make a copy of the report for the quantity is greater than or equal to 10, before starting Activity 18j.

Activity 18j

Open the report created in Activity 18h.

Hide the label and data for the **Discount** field in the report and hide only the data in the **PPrice** field by setting a black background.

18.3.4 Produce labels

You may be required to produce other forms of output from your database, for example producing labels to advertise a product or address labels for mailing letters to customers.

Task 18u

Open the file that you saved at the end of Task 18t.

Find all the cars with a sale price of less than £4000 and, for these cars, produce labels that:

- have a page orientation of portrait
- fit two side by side on the page
- have a 16 point, centre aligned heading 'Special Offer' at the top of each label
- show only the fields **Make**, **Model**, **Colour**, **SPrice**, **Year** and **Extras**, sorted into make and model order
- have your name at the bottom right of each label.

Design a new query to extract only the cars with a sale price of less than £4000, selecting only the **Make**, **Model**, **Colour**, **SPrice**, **Year** and **Extras** fields from the table as you step through the **Simple Query Wizard**. When you have selected these cars, close the query and click the left mouse button on the query so that it is highlighted like this.

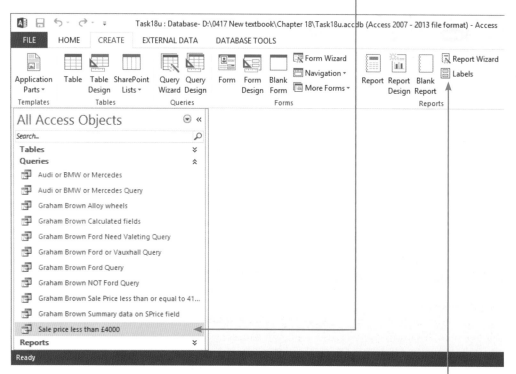

From the **CREATE** tab, find the **Reports** section and click on the **Labels** icon.

Advice

If you wish to change the display formats of any field, this can also be done in the **Property Sheet** pane using the **Format** tab. However, it is better to set the formatting for the fields in the **Design View** of the table as changing the display properties will not change the way that the data is stored, and this could lead to errors if fields are used for calculations.

This opens the Label Wizard. Select any label format that contains two labels across the page; in this case, use the Avery J8166 labels as they are slightly larger than some of the other labels (and it is therefore easier to fit all the data and labels on to each label). Click on Next > .

The next screen asks for the font size and colour of the text on the label. Leave this set to a small size (it is easier to enlarge this later, if needed, than to reduce it), such as 8 points high. Click on Next > .

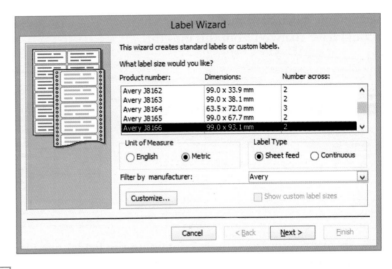

Type the text 'Special Offer' in the grey area as the top row of the label. Press <Enter> to move down to the second row. In Available fields: double click on the Make field. Press <Enter> to move to the next line. Add each field in the same way, entering the new line then the field. When all of the fields have been moved across, add a final row with your name, then click on Next > .

Move the Make, then Model fields across into the right to sort the labels by make and model as specified in the task, then click on Next > .

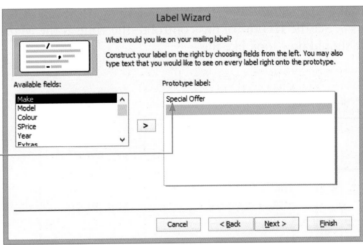

Give the labels an appropriate name and select the radio button for Modify the label design. Click on Finish .

Select all the controls except the one containing the text 'Special Offer'. Drag these down about 8 mm. Move the lower control down the label about 8 mm. Select the middle six controls and move the left edge to the right about 25 mm.

Select the control containing the text 'Special Offer' and stretch it down to give it more space. Open the Property Sheet and set the Font Size to 16 and the Text Align to Center. Stretch the Extras field down to give it more space, so that all the data should be visible. This will need checking when the labels are produced and edited again if necessary. Your name at the bottom of the label should also be right aligned by setting the Text Align to Right. Check the labels' layout from the HOME tab, using Print Preview to see all the labels set out on the sheet or Report View to

see a single label. Save the labels, which should have changed from this into this.

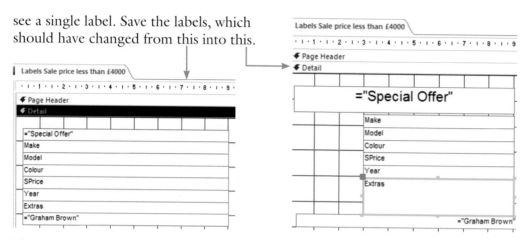

The six middle controls (those containing the fields) need labels. Click on the DESIGN tab and select the label box. Drag the label box out to the left of the Make field, enter the text 'Make' and, in the Property Sheet, set the Font Size to 8. Set the Height of this control to the same as the Make field control. It should now look like this.

Copy this control, paste it five times and move the new labels to the left of each field. Edit the text so that each shows what the field is. The label has changed to look like this.

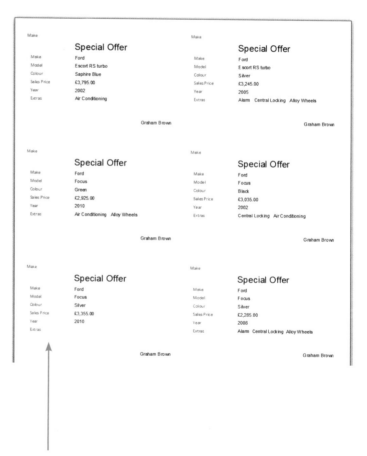

Check the labels' layout from the HOME tab using Print Preview to see all the labels set out on the sheet. If need be, make any adjustments to the controls. Save the labels.

Activity 18k

Open the database that you saved at the end of Activity 18j.

Find all the stationery items where the discount is 'Yes' and the sale price more than £30. For these items produce labels that:

- have a page orientation of portrait and fit two side by side on the page
- have a 20 point, right aligned heading 'Discount Offers' at the top of each label
- show only the fields **Type**, **Description**, **Colour** and **SPrice**, sorted into colour order
- have your name centre aligned at the bottom of each label.

18.3.5 Format reports

Task 18v

Open the file saved in Task 18u. Using the extract that contains the calculated fields Profit and Percent, produce a new report from all the data that:

- has the **PPrice**, **SPrice** and **Profit** fields formatted as Euro with two decimal places
- has the **Percent** field formatted as a percentage value with no decimal places.

Open the file saved in Task 18u. Create a new report from all the data in the extract using the Report Wizard. In the Tables/Queries box select the profit calculation query as the source of the data. Select all fields using the double arrow key. Click on [**Next >**] three times. Set the page Orientation to Landscape then click on [**Next >**]. Use Profit calculation as the report title. Select the radio button for Modify the report's design, then click on [**Finish**]. Adjust all the field widths so that all the data fits on the page.

Move to the Detail row of the report. Hold down the <Ctrl> key and select the PPrice, SPrice and Profit field controls. In the Property Sheet select the Format tab and use the drop-down menu in the Format section to select Euro.

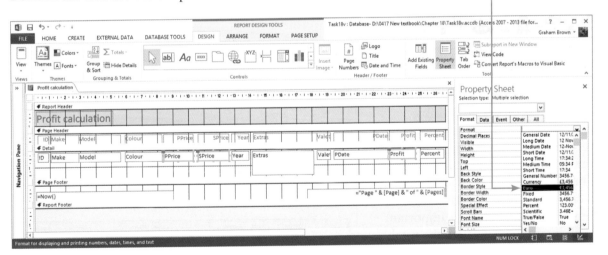

Move to the Decimal Places section and select 2. Click on the View icon to go into Report View and check that the formatting for these fields is in Euro and contains two decimal places.

Repeat this process for the Percent field, left mouse click on the control for Percent in the Detail row of the report. Select the Format tab and use the drop-down menu in the Format section to select Percent from the drop-down list.

Move to the Decimal Places section and select 0. Go into Report View to check that the formatting for this field is now correct and contains no decimal places. This is fine, but some field widths may need readjusting so that all data and labels are fully visible. Adjust these before saving the completed report.

Advice

If a question asks for a currency not held in this drop-down menu, select a Currency format.

Activity 18l

Open the file saved in Activity 18k.

Using the extract that contains the calculated fields Profit, Percent and UnitProfit, produce a new report. Apply appropriate formatting to this report. All currency values must be in Euro with two decimal places. All percentage values must be set to one decimal place.

18.3.6 Use formulae in reports

Other calculations may be needed on the data selected. These include calculating the sum (total), average, maximum or minimum values of selected data, or counting the number of items present in the selected data. All of these functions can be produced within a report in *Access*.

Task 18w

Open the file saved in Task 18v.

Produce a new report from all the data that:

- displays at the bottom of the report the total profit if all the cars were sold
- displays at the bottom of the report the maximum, minimum and average profit values
- displays the number of cars in this report.

You can use the Profit calculation report from Task 18v to help you with this task. Close this report (if it is open) and right mouse click on it once in the Navigation pane so that you get the drop-down menu. Select Copy, then Paste a new version into the pane with a name that relates it to Task 18w. Open this report in Design View.

Click the left mouse button on the bottom edge of the Report Footer and drag this down about 2 cm, so that this footer is now visible. Select the DESIGN tab, move to the Controls section and select the Text Box icon.

Move down into the Report Footer, click the left mouse button and drag to place a new control, in this case a text box, directly below the Profit column. This positioning is important as this control will be used to calculate the total profit for the data in this report.

If the Properties pane is not showing, right click the mouse button on the text box that you have just created then select Properties from the drop-down menu. In the Property Sheet select the All tab, find the Control Source section and

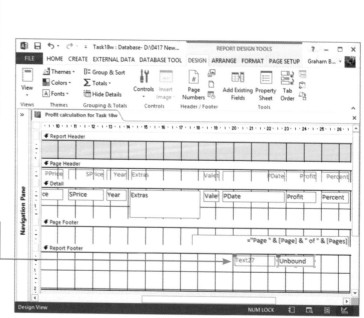

type the formula **=SUM([Profit])** into this row. The Property Sheet will change to this.

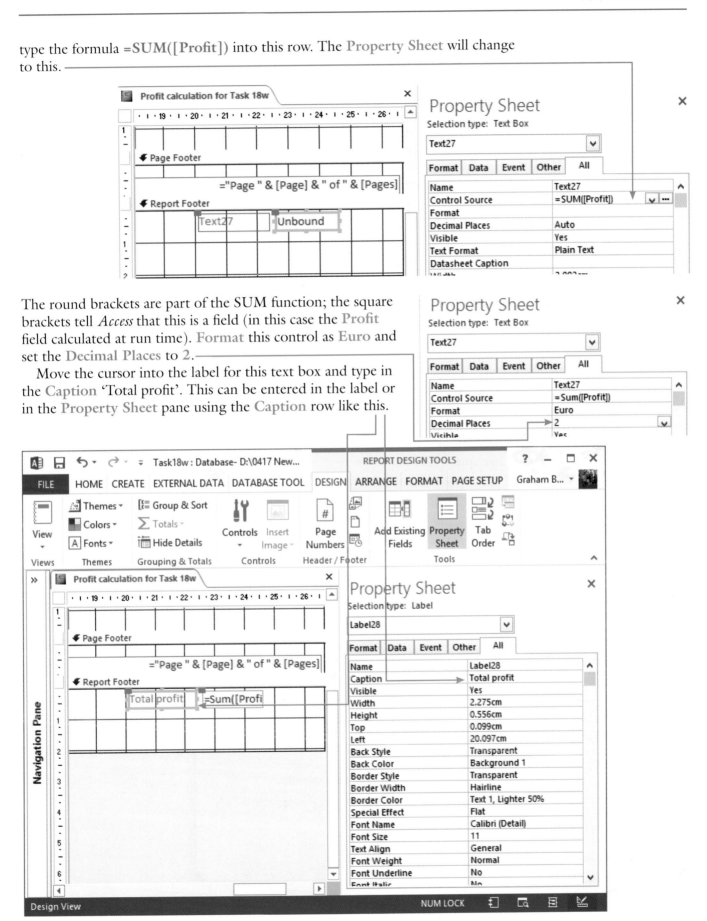

The round brackets are part of the SUM function; the square brackets tell *Access* that this is a field (in this case the Profit field calculated at run time). Format this control as Euro and set the Decimal Places to 2.

Move the cursor into the label for this text box and type in the Caption 'Total profit'. This can be entered in the label or in the Property Sheet pane using the Caption row like this.

Change to Report View and make sure that the control is in the correct place and appears to give the right answer (it is not too large or too small).

Rather than repeating this process four more times, it will be quicker to copy and paste these controls and edit each one to give the required results. Use the lasso tool to highlight both the Text Box and its Label. Use <Ctrl> and <C> to copy, then use <Ctrl> and <V> to paste the copies of these controls. Using <Ctrl> and <V> pastes the new controls directly under the existing ones and you do not need to reorganise the controls. It also extends the bottom of the Report Footer as needed. If you right mouse click and use Paste from the drop-down menu, this pastes the controls in the top left-hand corner of the Report Footer and you then have to drag and position each set of controls. Repeat <Ctrl> and <V> until you have five sets of controls like this. ——————————————

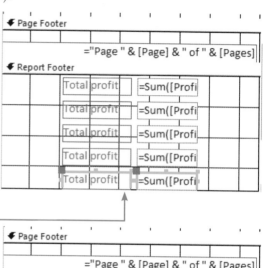

In the last four controls containing labels, change the Captions to 'Maximum profit', 'Minimum profit', 'Average profit' and 'Number of cars'. Select the second Text Box (for the maximum profit) and change the formula so that it becomes =MAX([Profit]). Change the formulae for the minimum profit so that it becomes =MIN([Profit]) and for the average profit so that it becomes =AVG([Profit]). In the final control to count the number of cars, change the formula so that it becomes =COUNT([Profit]). The controls should now look like this. ——————————————

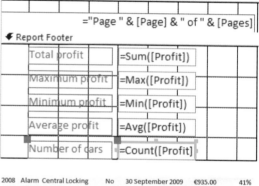

In the Property Sheet pane for the final Text Box, change the Format back from Currency to General Number. Set the Decimal Places for this control to 0. Check the layout and calculations in Report View. The completed calculations look like this.————————————————

Save the report. If you need to show evidence of the formulae that you used, use screen shot evidence of the calculated controls.

| 2008 | Alarm Central Locking Alloy Wheels | No | 30 September 2009 | €935.00 | 41% |

Total profit	€86,920.00
Maximum profit	€2,705.00
Minimum profit	€600.00
Average profit	€1,278.24
Number of cars	68

Advice

If you are using screen shot evidence of calculated controls, make sure that each control is wide enough to show all of the formulae in full. If you do not show all the formulae, marks will not be awarded.

Activity 18m

Open the file saved in Activity 18l.

Copy and edit the report which contains the calculated fields to produce one that:

- displays at the bottom of the report the maximum and minimum percentage profit for all the stationery items in stock
- displays at the bottom of the report the average profit per item
- displays the number of items in stock
- uses appropriate formatting for all data.

18.3.7 Sort data in reports

Although *Access* has the ability to sort data in both tables and queries, it is easier to save the sorting until the data is produced in an *Access* report.

Task 18x

Open the database that you saved at the end of Task 18w.

Produce a report that:

- displays all the data for the cars made by Ford or Vauxhall
- fits within the width of a single page
- is sorted into ascending order of make and model, then into descending order of sale price
- has your name in the report header followed by 'Ford or Vauxhall'.

You created the query in Task 18j. To produce this report, select the CREATE tab and click on the Report Wizard icon. In the Tables/Queries box select the Ford or Vauxhall query. Select all fields using the double arrow key and then click on Next > twice to obtain this view.

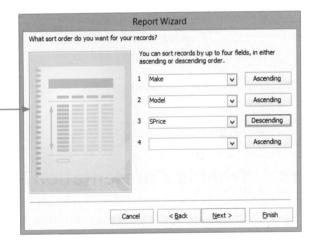

Use the drop-down lists to select the Make field, then the Model field and, finally, the SPrice field. For the SPrice field, click on Ascending to the right of this field and it will toggle (change) to Descending . When the fields have been set as shown, click on Next > . Set the Orientation to Landscape and run through the final stages of the wizard, giving this report a suitable name. This process is the same for other data types such as dates.

Activity 18n

Open the file saved in Activity 18m.

Produce a new report from all the data that:

- displays all the blue or black stationery items
- fits within the width of a single page
- is sorted into ascending order of colour and type, and then into descending order of description
- has your name in the report header followed by 'Blue or black stationery items'.

19 Presentations

In this chapter you will learn:

- what a presentation is
- why consistency in your presentation is important
- how to open a source file
- how to use a master slide to place objects
- how to create presentation slides
- how to add and edit text
- how to insert an image
- how to create and add a chart to a slide
- how to insert other graphical features to a slide
- how to use transitions between slides
- how to animate objects on a slide
- how to display a presentation
- how to save and print a presentation.

For this chapter you will need these source files from the CD:

- html.rtf
- powerpoint.rtf
- pressound.mp3
- presvideo.avi
- slogan.jpg
- website.jpg.

19.1 What is a presentation?

A presentation is a series of slides used to give information to an audience. A presentation can be used in many different ways: to teach or inform as a visual aid in a lecture, or as a constant on-screen carousel giving information or advertising, for example in a shopping centre or mall.

The media for delivery and type of presentation developed will depend on the purpose of the presentation and the target audience. For example, you would design a presentation on road safety to a class of five-year-old children to be short (for a short attention span); have only a few simple words (as they cannot read fluently); and contain bright, colourful, moving images (to keep their attention). The medium for the delivery of this presentation would be a multimedia projector and large screen.

It is important to understand all of this information before starting to design and develop a presentation, as different media will require different screen/page sizes. Most presentations will require a consistent colour scheme and consistently applied styles to all slides. You will be given details of these colour schemes and styles.

Consistency is really important in the development of your presentations; simple themes and colour schemes using one or two fonts save presentations from being messy and disorganised. A well-structured and organised presentation usually says to the audience 'I am a well-organised and reliable person'. One way of doing this is to use a master slide.

19.2 Open a source file

If you are given a source file that contains the slide contents, in older versions of *PowerPoint* the slide master/s had to be created first and the slide contents imported. In more recent versions the slide contents have to be opened and the master slide created after the contents. If new slides or slide contents are to be added by hand, then setting up the master slide would be a good starting point.

Task 19a

Open the file **powerpoint.rtf**, which will be used to create a short presentation for IGCSE students telling them how to use *PowerPoint*. The medium for delivery will be a multimedia projector with a 4:3 aspect ratio.

Open *PowerPoint* and double click the left mouse button on **Blank Presentation**. Select the **FILE** tab followed by **Open**. Find the source file using the **Computer** option, which opens the **Open** window. Select the correct directory and change the file type box from All *PowerPoint* Presentations to **All Files**.

The source files will be supplied as either text files (in .txt format) or rich text files (in .rtf format). The difference between the two is that .rtf files hold some formatting and styles (like text size and fonts) while .txt files only contain the characters and no formatting or styles.

Double click the left mouse button on the file **powerpoint.rtf**.

The file opens like this.

Save this as a presentation with the filename task19a.

Before changing any of the slides, you will now create and edit the master slide.

19.3 Use a master slide to place objects

A master slide allows you to design the layout of your slides before you start adding objects (such as text or images) to the slides. It holds the information on colours, fonts, effects and the positioning of objects on the slides.

Open the file saved in Task 19a and select the **View** tab. Find the **Master Views** section and click on the **Slide Master** icon.

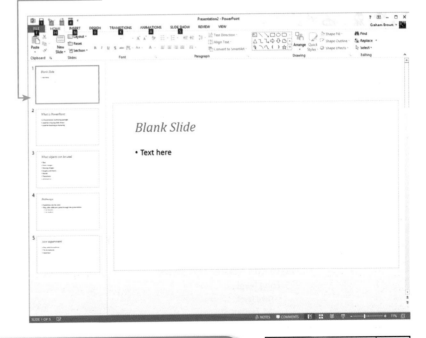

Task 19b

Open the file saved in Task 19a.

Create a master slide with a pale yellow background on the right-hand side (about a quarter of the width) with one vertical dark blue stripe as a border for the yellow background and two horizontal dark blue stripes. Each stripe should be 4 points wide. It should look like this.

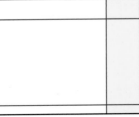

The display will change to this. ⎯⎯⎯⎯⎯⎯⎯⎯⎯⎯⎯⎯⎯

The layout of a presentation will depend on the medium for its delivery. In this task you are told that the medium for delivery will be a multimedia projector with a 4:3 aspect ratio. If you are not told the aspect ratio in the question, assume that it is 4:3 for multimedia projectors and 16:9 for presentations using a monitor. To change the slide size, go to the size section of the toolbar, click on the Slide Size icon and select the correct aspect ratio. ⎯⎯⎯⎯⎯⎯⎯⎯⎯

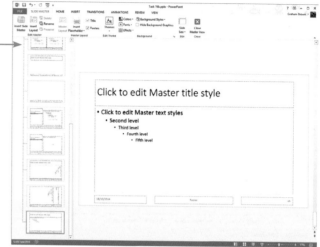

Because the slide contents have been opened and the default setting for *PowerPoint* on my computer is an aspect ratio of 16:9, I get this pop-up window. ⎯⎯⎯⎯⎯⎯⎯⎯⎯⎯⎯⎯⎯

If you get this message, select the Maximize button.

Use the scroll bar on the left of the window to scroll to the top and select the Primary Master Slide (the top one). This master slide is copied by all the other sub-types that are listed below it. ⎯⎯⎯⎯⎯⎯⎯⎯⎯⎯⎯

For this task the master slide has to contain a number of lines and one filled area. You should start with the filled area. This will be created by placing a filled rectangle in the right place. However, this rectangle will cover some of the objects already on the slide, so these objects to be resized or moved out of the way first.

Select the title text placeholder and use the drag handle to resize this text box.

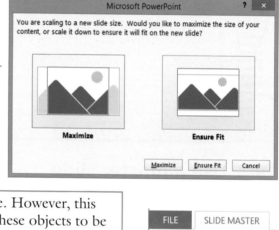

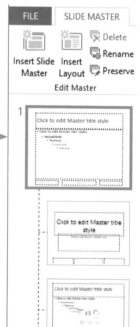

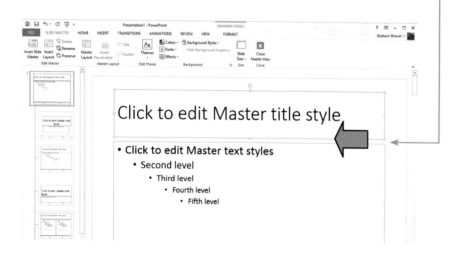

Repeat this for the body text placeholder on the master slide. This box has also been made less deep using the lower drag handle to create space to move the slide numbering.

The text box containing the slide numbering is too small to resize, so this will need to be moved from the right-hand side. Drag the entire text box into the space created below the body text box.

The page layout should now look like this.

Select the **INSERT** tab and find the **Illustrations** section. Click on the **Shapes** icon and select the **Rectangle** option from the drop-down menu.

Use the drag tool to drag a new rectangle that fills about a quarter of the right-hand side of the slide. Make sure that this rectangle fits to the top, bottom and right edges of the slide and leaves no white space.

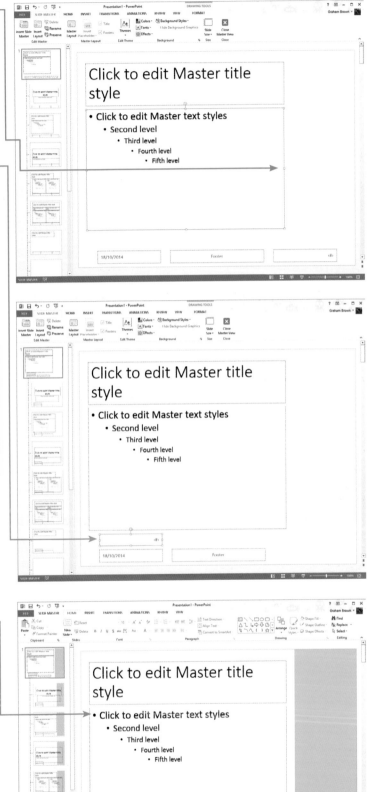

Advice

Many shapes, such as the rectangle, can also be found in the **Drawing** section of the **HOME** tab.

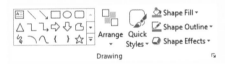

You now need to edit the appearance of the rectangle. Select the **HOME** tab and find the **Drawing** section. Use the **Shape Fill** icon to select the fill colour and click on the **Shape Outline** icon, followed by **No Outline** from the sub-menu, to remove the border from the

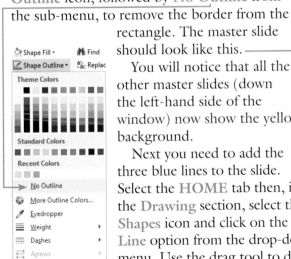

rectangle. The master slide should look like this.

You will notice that all the other master slides (down the left-hand side of the window) now show the yellow background.

Next you need to add the three blue lines to the slide. Select the **HOME** tab then, in the **Drawing** section, select the **Shapes** icon and click on the **Line** option from the drop-down menu. Use the drag tool to draw a vertical line on the border between the yellow and white areas.

Advice

Holding down the <Shift> key while placing the line forces it to be either vertical, horizontal or at 45 degrees.

Use the Shape Outline icon to change the line colour to dark blue. The Shape Outline icon can also be used to change the line thickness. Select Weight and, from the sub-menu, select the line weight. For this task the line weight should be 4 points. This option is not available from this menu so select the nearest weight available, in this case 4½ points.

Right mouse click on the line and select Format Shape… from the drop-down menu. From the Format Shape pane adjust the line Width: to 4 points.

Repeat this process to add the two horizontal lines to the master slide in the positions shown in the task.

Advice

You may find it easier to copy the first line and paste it twice; rotate the two new copies and resize and place them as required by the task.

Save the presentation with the filename task19b.

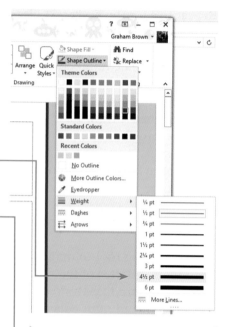

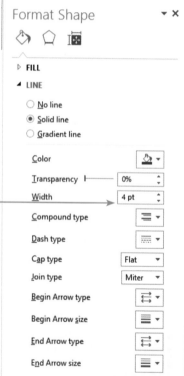

Task 19c

Open the presentation that you saved in Task 19b.

Include the heading 'Using *PowerPoint*', left aligned in a dark blue, 60 point serif font above the blue line at the top of the master slide. Include an automated slide number in the bottom left of the footer.

Enter your name, centre aligned, in the white area at the bottom of the master slide. Use a black, 14 point, serif font.

Place a clip art image of a computer or peripheral in the right-hand area. Crop and/or resize the image so that it fits within the yellow area and will not overlay the dark blue lines. Do not distort the image. Make sure that the image fills more than 50% of the available space.

Save your presentation.

To include the heading, add a new text box in the top left section of the slide. This text box will replace the title text box, so move the title text box down the slide to below the blue line. Go to the INSERT tab and click on the Text Box icon in the Text section. Drag out a new text box then select the HOME tab and find the Font section. Set the font size to 60 point and select a serif font, for example Times New Roman.

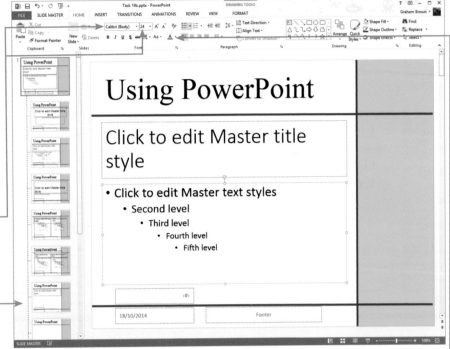

Enter the text 'Using PowerPoint' into this text box. You may need to move/resize the master text style to get this text box. The window should now look like this.

Highlight this text and set the font colour to dark blue, using the Font Color icon.

As the text is already left aligned, do not adjust the alignment. Notice how the text box has been aligned with the other objects on the slide so it can be checked that the text is left aligned.

The automated slide number is in the object moved from the right side of the footer. The task asks for this to be placed on the left in the footer. Resize this object (as shown previously) and change its alignment to left aligned by clicking on the Align Text Left icon in the Paragraph section under the HOME tab. Drag the box into the bottom left corner. As the date is not required on all pages, this object can be deleted before moving the automated slide number.

Enlarge the automated footer so that it fills the width of the white space, as shown. Make sure that you enlarge the footer so that it overlaps the slide number, which will ensure that it can be seen that the object is centre aligned. Change the text and the slide number to a black, 14 point, serif font as described above. The finished footer area should look like this.

Although you have set the footer area of the master slide, you have not yet added your name to the footer, nor told *PowerPoint* to display the page numbers. To do this, select the INSERT tab then, in the Text section, click on the Header & Footer icon. This opens the Header and Footer window.

Tick the box for Slide number and the box for Footer. Move the cursor into the text box for Footer and type in your name. To set this on all slides, click on Apply to All.

Use the drag handle to enlarge the body text box on the master slide. Now move down into each of the other master slides and resize all text boxes to ensure that they fit within the white space; for example, from this to this.

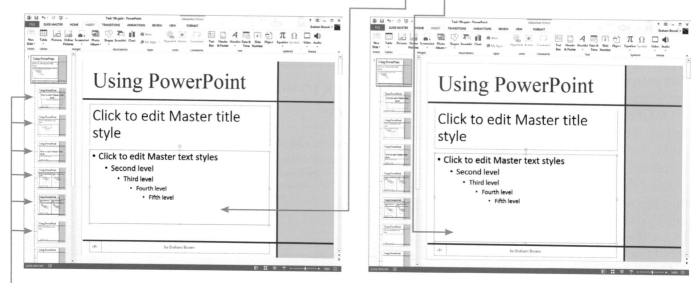

If the task requires particular font styles or sizes for each of these objects, these can also be set in these master slides as described earlier.

Depending on the presentation being created, the placeholders for the body text and title text will also need moving for some of the other master slide items. Move to each in turn and make sure that the text placeholders fit between the lines on the master slides. This will only need to be completed for the style of slides that you need for this presentation.

19.3.1 Clip art images

To insert a clip art image, return to the top Slide Master and select the INSERT tab. In the Images section click on the Online Pictures icon to open the Insert Pictures search pane.

For this task you need to find an image of a computer, so enter 'Computer' in the Office.com Clip Art box, then click on the search icon or press the return key.

This searches the online clip art library and finds pictures that may match what you are searching for. You can also browse your local drives for other images. Look through the images to find one that will fit well in the available space – remember that you can crop and resize the image but cannot distort it. When you have chosen the image, double click the left mouse button on it to download it. This places this clip art image on to the master slide. Move and resize it so that it fits into the correct area. To crop the image, select the image and click on the FORMAT tab. In the Size section, click on the Crop icon.

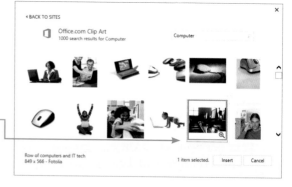

With the crop tool selected, use the drag handles of the image to crop the edges so that it changes from this to this.

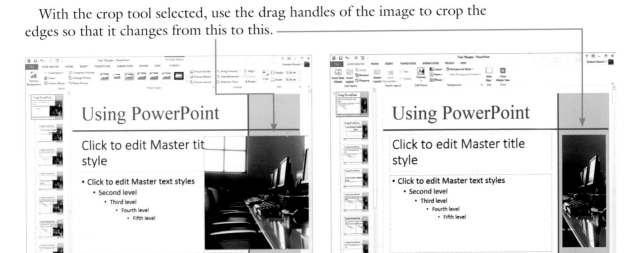

When the master slide is complete, select the VIEW tab and, in the Presentation Views section, click on the icon for Normal page layout.

Save your presentation as task19c.

19.4 Create presentation slides

One method of getting the text for the slides is to open an .rtf or .txt file (as you did in Task 19a). The second method used to create presentation slides is by inserting a new slide into an existing presentation and adding the text manually.

Task 19d

Add a new slide between slides 4 and 5 of the presentation that you saved in Task 19c. This slide will contain the heading 'Ease of use', a chart and this bulleted list:

- 86% of students found it easy to use
- 120 students in the sample.

Use this data to create a chart: Easy – 103, Difficult – 12, No response – 5. Show the percentage of students in each category.

On slide 1, add the heading 'Hints and tips', and add the subheading 'for IGCSE students'.

Set the following styles of text throughout the entire presentation:

- heading: dark blue, serif, left aligned, 40 point
- subheading: blue, sans-serif, centre aligned, 30 point
- bulleted list: black, sans-serif, left aligned, 24 point.

Save the presentation.

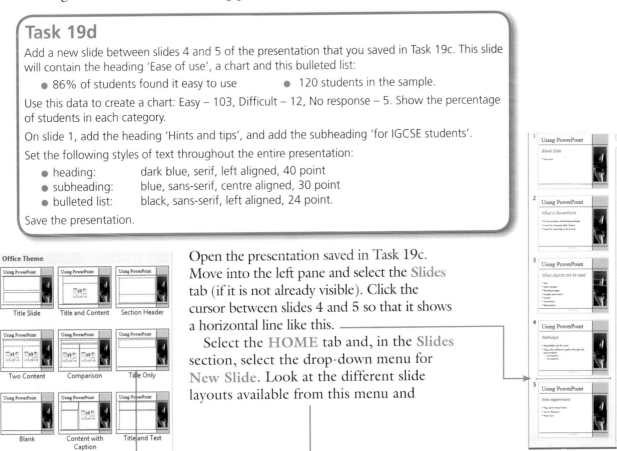

Open the presentation saved in Task 19c. Move into the left pane and select the Slides tab (if it is not already visible). Click the cursor between slides 4 and 5 so that it shows a horizontal line like this.

Select the HOME tab and, in the Slides section, select the drop-down menu for New Slide. Look at the different slide layouts available from this menu and select the layout that matches the slide you are going to produce. This slide needs a small bulleted list and a chart, so the most appropriate slide type will be **Comparison**. Although the option for 'Content with Caption' looks correct, it is more difficult to manipulate the caption box. Click once on this icon to get the new slide.

Delete both of the top text boxes that say 'Click to add text'. These are not needed in this slide. To do this click on the line for the text box and press the <Backspace> or <Delete> key. Use the drag handles to edit the two larger placeholders below them to make them fit the available space. The slide will change from this to this.

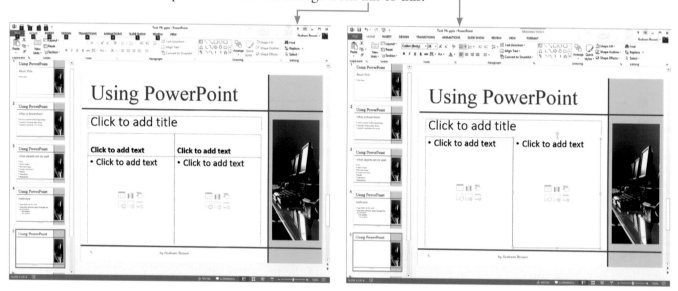

Click in the title placeholder and add the heading 'Ease of use'. Select the left object below the title. Click on the bulleted text 'Click to add text'. This will change this object into a text box. Type in the text '86% of students found it easy to use', <Return>, '120 students in the sample', so that it looks similar to this.

It is sensible to complete all the text parts of this task together and then add the chart at the end. Move on to slide 1. Replace the text 'Blank Slide' with the heading 'Hints and tips'. In the lower placeholder replace the text 'Text here' with 'for IGCSE students', so that slide 1 looks like this.

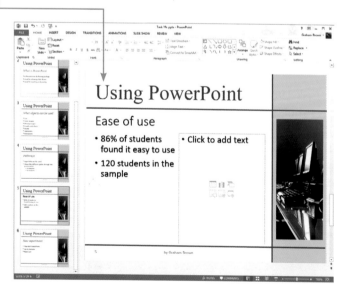
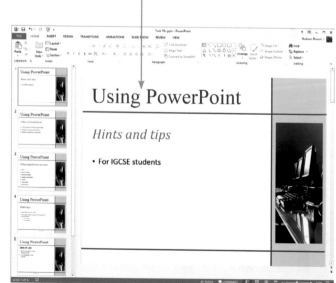

Some slides do not always import as you want them. This slide has imported as a bulleted list

rather than as a title slide. To change it to a title slide, right mouse click on the slide background and select Layout. Select Title Slide from the list of available options. The slide will change to look like this.

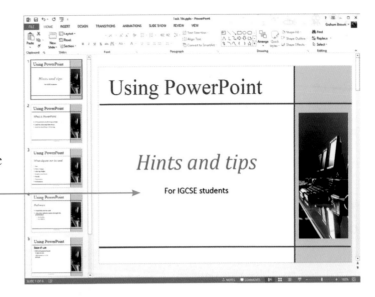

19.4.1 Set the styles for an existing presentation

Select the VIEW tab followed by Slide Master and select the Primary Master Slide (the top master slide). Highlight all the text in the heading (title) style placeholder and click the right mouse button to obtain a drop-down menu and miniature toolbar to allow you to edit the text style.

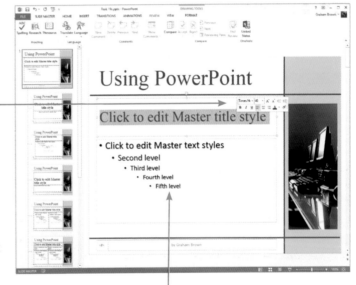

The heading style needs to be a dark blue, left aligned, serif font. Select a serif font, such as Times New Roman, using the font list. Use the Text Color icon to select a dark blue colour and (if need be) use the Align Text Left icon to change the text alignment. Use the drop-down list for the font size to change it to 40 point. The text box should now look like this.

Use a similar method to set the first level of the bulleted list to a black, sans-serif, left-aligned font (no changes are needed for these parts), 24 point high. Adjust the font sizes for the other levels of bullet points so that they are smaller relative to this one.

The subheading style is not visible in this master slide, so you need to move into the master slide for the Title Slide Layout (the first master slide down). Highlight the text for the Master subtitle style and set this to a blue, sans-serif, centre aligned, 30 point font. Use the same method as you did for the Master title style.

Move through each slide master in turn and edit any of the styles on other page layouts that need to be set.

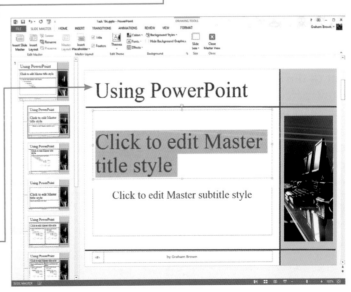

Select the VIEW tab and the Normal icon. Check each slide carefully to make sure that the styles that you have changed have been applied to each slide of the presentation.

Advice

You must open the data file into *PowerPoint* before setting up your master slides and styles. The instructions given in this task may not be in the easiest order within *PowerPoint*. It is sensible to read through the task before starting.

It is very important to make sure that all slides are consistent. Don't assume that the software itself will format the slides correctly and do check each slide carefully.

19.4.2 Create a chart in *PowerPoint*

Move on to slide 5. In the task you were instructed to: 'Use this data to create a chart: Easy – 103, Difficult – 12, No response – 5. Show the percentage of students in each category.'

Click on the chart icon in the unused object on this slide. This opens the Insert Chart window.

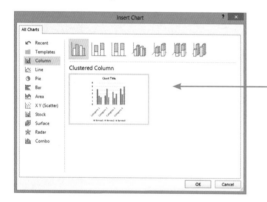

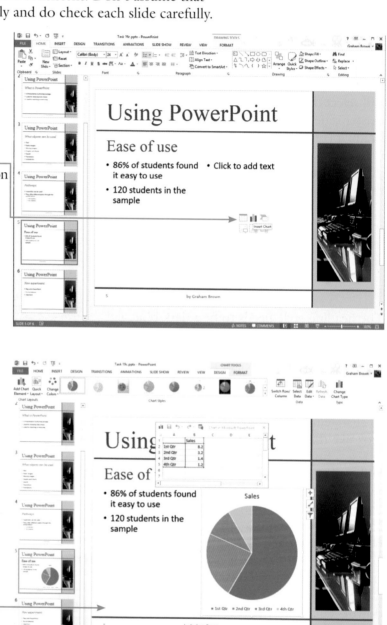

You must decide which type of chart is the most appropriate for the task. In this case, you are told to show the percentage of students in each category. There is a clue to the need for percentage values in the bullet points on the left of the slide. Because the chart needs to show percentage values (parts of a whole), a pie chart is the most appropriate type of chart. Select a simple pie chart from the available chart types and click on OK. This opens a default pie chart, but does not use the correct data. The slide should now look like this.

As you can see, the chart does not relate to the data for this task. Instead, it is about quarterly sales in a company. It may also open an *Excel* style spreadsheet like this that contains the data.

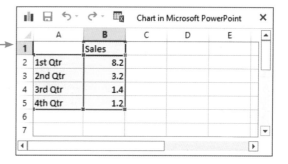

If this does not appear, select the DESIGN tab and under Chart Tools, find the Data section and click on the Edit Data icon.

Move into cell B1 and replace the label 'Sales' with the word 'Students'. In cell A2, enter the text 'Easy' so that it replaces the existing text, in A3 type 'Difficult' and, in A4, 'No response'. Replace the sales figures in B2 with 103, in B3 with 12 and, in B4, with 5. Delete the contents of cells A5 and B5. Drag the blue range marker using the drag handle so that it includes cells A1 to B4 only. It should now look like this.

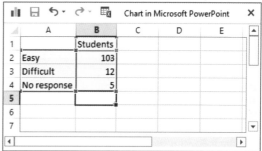

The slide now contains the chart. Close the spreadsheet containing the data. Save the presentation as task19d.

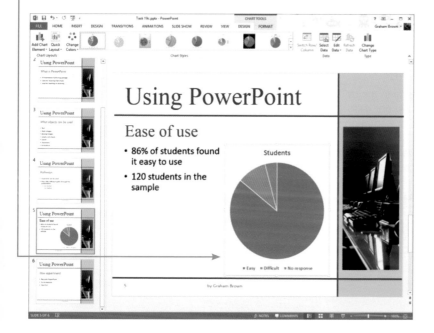

Advice

Charts may be created from contiguous or non-contiguous data and can have features such as titles, legends and labels for axes and segments. All the features that you studied in Chapter 16 can be applied to a graph or chart before it is cut and pasted into the slide.

19.4.3 Use charts imported from a spreadsheet

The latest versions of *Microsoft Office* have made the process of creating a chart in *Excel* almost identical to the creation of a chart within *PowerPoint*. In *Excel* select the INSERT tab and, in the Charts section, click on Pie Chart. For more detail of the production of the chart please refer to Chapter 16. When the chart has been created and fully labelled, copy the chart in *Excel* and paste it on to a slide in *PowerPoint*. Resize the chart to fit the available space.

Activity 19a

You are going to create a short presentation for IGCSE students giving them advice on website authoring. The medium for delivery will be a multimedia projector.

Create a master slide with a green background at the top (about $\frac{1}{8}$ of the height) and at the bottom of each slide (about $\frac{1}{16}$ of the height) with a dark green horizontal line as a border between the white and green backgrounds. Add two vertical dark green lines to the left of the slide. Each line should be 6 points wide. It should look like this.

Include the heading 'HTML', right aligned, in a black, 40 point, sans-serif font at the top of the master slide (as shown above). Include an automated slide number in the green area to the left of the two vertical lines. Make this a 14 point, black, sans-serif font. Include your name right aligned in the footer in the same style as the page numbering.

Set the following styles of text throughout the entire presentation:

- heading: black, sans-serif, left aligned, 40 point, within the green 'header' section
- subheading: red, serif, centre aligned, 40 point
- bulleted list: dark green, serif, left aligned, 32 point
- level 2 bulleted list: dark green, serif, left aligned, 24 point

Place a very small clip art image of a computer or peripheral in the bottom right corner of the white space. Crop and/or resize the image so that it fits. Do not distort the image.

Import the file **html.rtf**, placing the text as slides in your presentation software. On slide 1 add the heading 'Hints and tips' and the subheading 'for IGCSE and Level 2 students'.

Use this data to create a chart: Text editor – 42, FrontPage – 37, Dreamweaver – 31. Show the percentage of students in each category. Insert this chart into slide 4 with the heading 'Percentage of users from the survey'.

19.4.4 Audience and presenter notes

Delivery of a presentation with a multimedia projector may include the use of audience notes and/or presenter notes.

Audience notes

Audience notes are paper copies of the slides of a presentation that are given to the audience so that they can take them away and refer to them after the presentation. Sometimes people will want to write their own notes on their audience note printouts during a presentation. These can be printed in different formats, with several slides on a page, or just one slide with space for the person to add their own notes.

Presenter notes

Presenter notes are a single copy of the slides from a presentation, with prompts and/or key facts that need to be told to the audience by the person delivering the presentation. These notes are sometimes printed and not usually given to the audience.

Add presenter notes

Task 19e

Open the presentation that you saved in Task 19d. Add the following presenter notes to the slides:

- **Slide 1**: Welcome to this presentation giving you useful hints and tips on using *Microsoft PowerPoint* for your IGCSE practical examinations.
- **Slide 2**: The presentation that you are watching has been made using *PowerPoint*.
- **Slide 4**: Hyperlinks can be used to give different paths or to open external websites or documents.
- **Slide 5**: Graphs and charts can be added to enhance a presentation.

Open the presentation that you saved in Task 19d in **Normal** view. In the orange toolbar at the bottom of the slide is a NOTES icon. Click on this to show the presenter notes area of the page.

Move the cursor to the **Notes** area of the screen. Click the cursor into this box and type the presenter notes for slide 1. Use the **Slides** tab to select the next slide and continue with this process until all of the presenter notes have been entered. Not all of the slides have presenter notes. These notes will not appear on the slides when the presentation is run. You will learn how to print these so that the presenter can read from them later in the chapter.

Save the presentation as task19e.

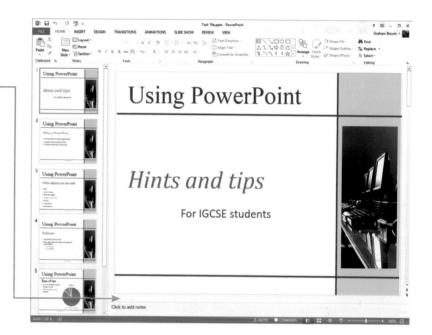

19.4.5 Use images and sound

Task 19f

Open the presentation that you saved in Task 19e.

Add the image **slogan.jpg** to the bottom of the final slide, above the blue line. Crop the image so that the red line and all contents below it are removed. Resize the image so that it fits about 1 cm from the left edge of the slide, 1 cm above the lower blue line and 1 cm to the left of the vertical blue line, maintaining its aspect ratio. Adjust the brightness and contrast of the image so that the background colour (pale yellow) is not visible.

In Task 19c you inserted a new image from clip art into the master slide. For this task you are going to insert an image given to you as a file.

Open the presentation saved in Task 19e and use the Slides tab to open slide 7. Select the INSERT tab and then click on the Pictures icon. This opens the Insert Picture window. Search through the files until you locate **slogan. jpg**, select the file and click on Insert to insert the image into the slide. Click the left mouse button on the image and from the FORMAT tab select click on the Crop tool icon.

Drag the lower handle up the screen above the red line, but below the red text, to crop the image.

Click the left mouse button off the image then back on it and drag the image down so that the left and bottom edges are in the correct place on the slide.

Grab the top right drag handle and drag this to resize the image to the correct position to the left of the vertical blue line. The image should now look like this.

To remove the pale yellow background colour from this image, you need to adjust the image brightness and contrast. Click the right mouse button on the image and select Format Picture... from the drop-down menu. This opens the Format Picture pane to the right of the slide. Select the Picture option from the right. Double click on the Picture Corrections option to open this menu.

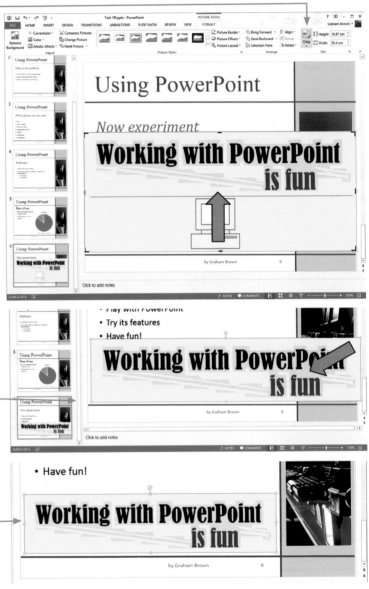

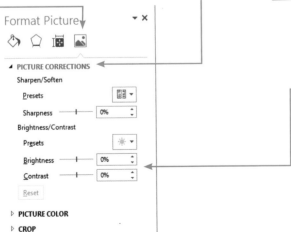

Move the sliders for the Brightness and Contrast, so that the pale yellow background disappears but the other colours remain unaffected. These figures are found using trial and error: both settings change from 0% to a brightness of around 35% and a contrast of around 75%.

When you have completed this, close the Format Picture pane. The slide should now look like this.

Notice how the red colour in the text has changed from its original dark red colour (see above) to this shade of red.

Save the presentation as task19f.

Add an animated image to a slide

To add an animated image (for example an animated gif file) to a slide, use the same method as adding a still image.

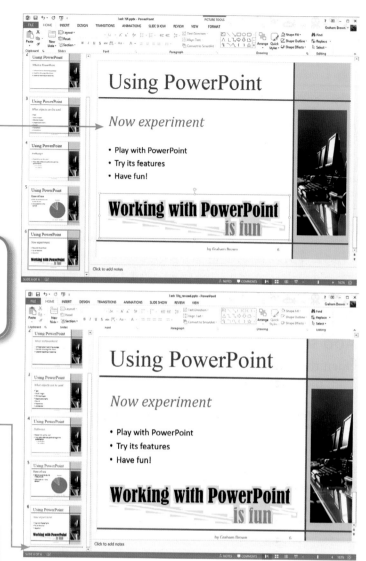

Task 19g

Open the presentation that you saved in Task 19f. Add a new slide at the end of the presentation into which you will place the video **presvideo.avi**. Make sure that this video plays when the slide is opened.

Add video to a slide

Open the presentation and scroll down to the end of the last slide. Click just below this slide to place the orange line at the bottom like this.

From the HOME tab select the New Slide icon then click on the Title and Content option. Add an appropriate title, such as 'Sample video', in the title placeholder. Look carefully in the centre of the content placeholder and choose the Insert Video icon. Use the From a file option to find the file **presvideo.avi**. in the Insert Video window, then click on the Insert button.

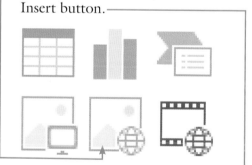

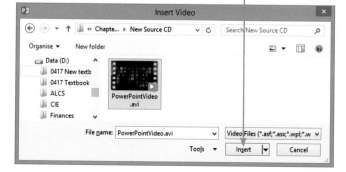

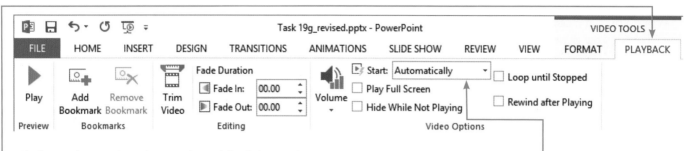

Click on the PLAYBACK tab and find the Video Options section. Set the Start setting to Automatically using the drop-down menu.

The video will now play when the slide is opened. Save the presentation as task19g.

Task 19h

Open the presentation that you saved in Task 19g. Add the sound clip **pressound.mp3** to slide 1. Play this sound track only once when the presentation is run.

Add sound to a slide

Open the presentation in slide 1. Select the INSERT tab, click on the Audio icon, then on Audio on My PC... from the drop-down menu.

From the Insert Audio window choose the file **pressound.mp3** and click on the Insert button.

The audio file (sometimes called a sound clip) is now on this slide. Move the cursor to the AUDIO TOOLS tab and double click the left mouse button to select Play in Background.

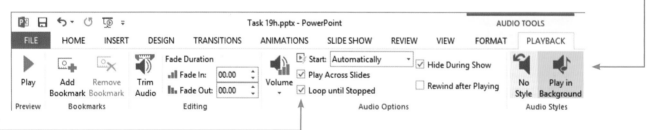

This will automatically change some of the other settings, for example the Start option changes from 'On Click' to 'Automatically' and the 'Play Across Slides' and 'Loop until Stopped' check boxes have been ticked. As the question asks for the sound track to be played only once, remove these two ticks. Test the presentation to check that it works. Save the presentation as task19h.

> **Task 19i**
>
> Open the presentation that you saved in Task 19h. Add:
>
> - an arrow on slide 5 pointing from the first bullet point to the largest segment of the pie chart
> - a callout box on slide 6 telling the reader that the image of a computer is placed on the master slide
> - the text '© Microsoft' at the end of the first bullet point on slide 6 in a in a black, 12 point, sans-serif font
> - a 6 point, horizontal, red line on slide 6, above the image you inserted in Task 19f.

Open the presentation and select slide 5 using the Slides tab. Select the INSERT tab and click on the Shapes icon. A drop-down menu of available shapes will appear.

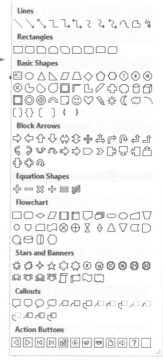

Select an arrow to be included on the slide. Click the left mouse button where you want the arrow to start and drag the point of the arrow to the position that you want it to finish. The finished slide should look like this.

To place the callout box on slide 6, select slide 6 and again select the INSERT tab and Shapes icon. This time select a callout box from the Callouts section of the drop-down menu. Click on the slide and drag the callout box to draw it. It is easier if you make the box too large and reduce the size later. When you have placed the box, grab and drag the yellow handle to move the point of the callout box so that it points to the image.

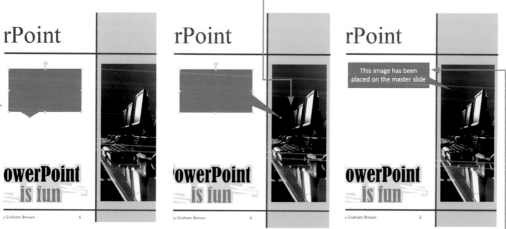

Type the text that you require into the callout box (you cannot see the cursor as you can with a text box) and then resize the callout box using the drag handles. It may look similar to this.

To insert the copyright symbol, click the left mouse button to place the cursor after the 't' at the end of the first bullet point. Select the INSERT tab and click on the Symbol icon.

This opens the Symbol window. Scroll through the available list of symbols until you find the '©' symbol.

Click on this symbol and then click on `Insert ▼` followed by `Close`. Add the text 'Microsoft' after the symbol and highlight both the symbol and the new text. Set this to a black, 12 point, sans-serif font using the methods learnt earlier in the chapter.

To insert the red line, select the INSERT tab, then click on the Shapes icon and select a line. Drag the line horizontally across the page. Click the right mouse button on the line to open the Format Shape window. Use the Line outline and Line style sections to change the colour and thickness of the line. The completed slide should look similar to this.

Save the presentation as task19i.

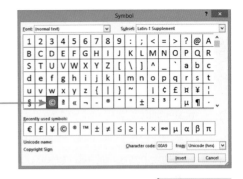

Task 19j

Open the presentation that you saved in Task 19i. Apply transitions between all slides in your presentation. Animate all the bullets on slide 3 so that they appear one at a time.

Using PowerPoint

Now experiment

> This image has been placed on the master slide

- Play with PowerPoint©Microsoft
- Try its features
- Have fun!

Working with PowerPoint is fun

by Graham Brown   6

19.4.6 Transitions between slides

Transitions between slides are the methods used to introduce a new slide. This can be simply replacing the existing slide with a new slide or using a number of different features to change from one to another. All transitions are located in the TRANSITIONS tab.

Open the presentation. Select the TRANSITIONS tab and find the Transition to This Slide section. Click the left mouse button to apply a transition and see the effect that it uses. There are more transitions available; you can use the scroll bar to see them.

Click on the icon to select the transition that you wish to use and then click on the Apply To All icon to apply the same transition to all slides.

Advice

Always use the same transition effect between slides and the same animation effect throughout the whole presentation. Consistency in these areas is just as important as using consistent styles and colour schemes.

19.4.7 Animation effects

Select slide 3 and highlight **only** the first item in the bulleted list. Select the ANIMATIONS tab and find the Animation section. Click the left mouse button to apply an animation and its effect. There are more animations available; you can use the scroll bar to see them.

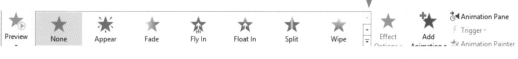

Click on the icon to select the animation that you wish to use. To set each bullet to be individually animated, select them one at a time to apply the animation to each individually. To change when the bullets appear, use the Start and Delay options.

Opening the Animation Pane allows you to see the timings and to edit these by dragging the slide bars for timing (as shown) or by clicking the right mouse button on each animation.

The task instructed you to 'animate all the bullets so that they appear one at a time', so select Fade, Wipe or Float In for each bullet point. This sets the animation. The timings are set as shown above, so there is a small delay between each bullet; in this case the chosen delay was 2 seconds, but this has only been applied to the first bullets.

It is a good idea to have the Animation Pane open so that, when you need to show evidence of your animation effects, these can be seen. To test the animations, highlight those you wish to test in the Animation Pane and click on ▶ Play Selected . Save the presentation as task19j.

19.5 Display a presentation

The easiest way to display a presentation is to press the <F5> key, which runs the presentation from the start. An alternative is to select the SLIDE SHOW tab and choose from the options to start from the beginning, from the current slide, or to present online and allow others to download and run your presentation. To stop a presentation that is running press the <Escape> key.

19.5.1 Set up the slide show

To set up the slide show, select the SLIDE SHOW tab then click on the icon for Set Up Slide Show. This opens the Set Up Show window, which will allow you to set the show up in the way you want to deliver it. If the show is to be used as an on-screen carousel, perhaps to show messages around a building or to visitors in a foyer, it is usual to loop the show continuously. This is selected by ticking this box.

Other options for showing the presentation manually, with or without the animations running, can also be selected from this window. When you have made your choices select the OK button.

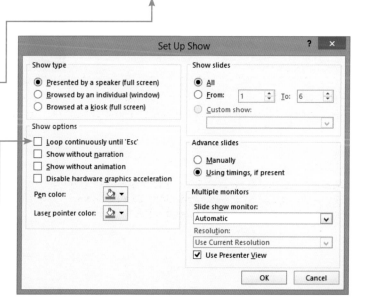

19.5.2 Save a presentation

As with all your work, make sure that you save your presentations regularly using FILE and Save.

19.5.3 Print a presentation

To print evidence of your work, you must identify what types of printouts are required. Sometimes you will be expected to print only the slides, but more often you will need to print audience or presenter notes; for these printouts you will need to select FILE and Print. Screen shots are the best way to show evidence of transitions and animations.

Task 19k

Open the presentation that you saved in Task 19j. Print your presentation showing:

- only the slides
- presenter notes
- audience notes with three slides per page and space for the audience to make notes
- evidence of the transitions between slides
- evidence of the animations used on slide 3.

Print slides

Select FILE and Print to open the Print window. In the Settings section, select Print All Slides if all slides are required. To print only the slide/s content with no additional notes or space, select Full Page Slides.

An example of the printed material (in this case slide 1) is shown here.

To send to the printer click on Print.

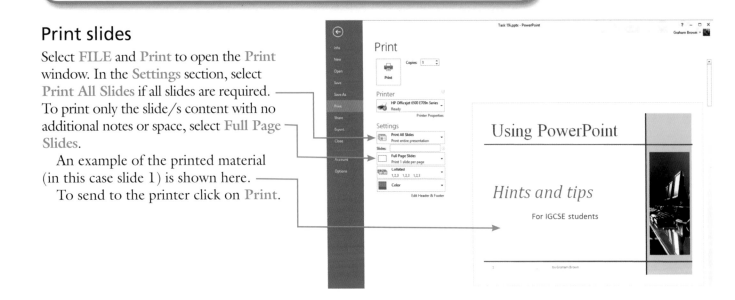

Print presenter notes

In the **Settings** section, select **Notes Pages**, which will produce a view of the slide with the presenter notes that you placed with each slide printed below the slide. Click the **Print** button.

Print audience notes

As you can see in the screen shot, the drop-down menu for the type of printing offers a wide range of options. If you require space for the audience to make their own notes, then **3 Slides** per page is the best option. This matches the printout required for the third part of Task 19k.

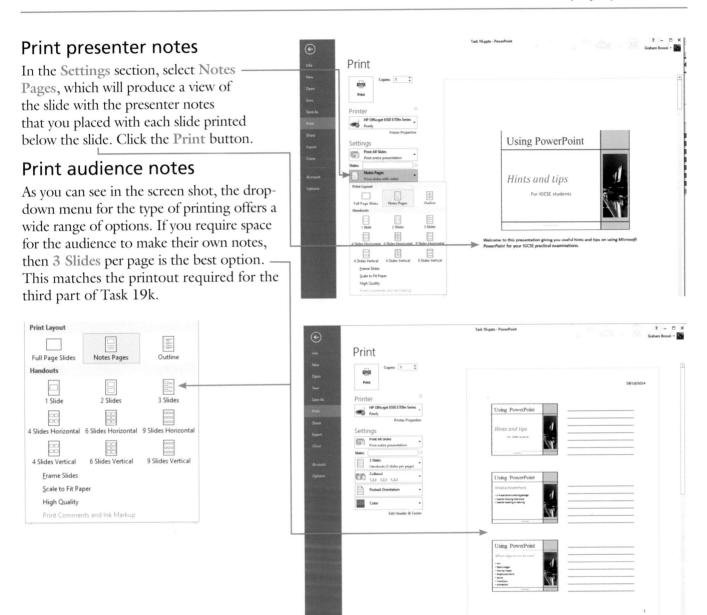

Print evidence of slide transitions

Select the **VIEW** tab and click on the icon for Slide Sorter view. Use the <Print Screen> key on your keyboard to copy this into the clipboard and paste the image into a word-processed document so that you can add your name and other details before sending it to the printer.

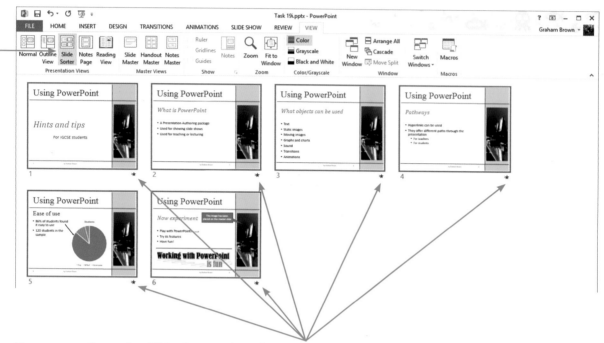

You can see from the Slide Sorter view the evidence that transitions have been added to each slide.

Print evidence of animations

Select the **VIEW** tab and click on the Normal icon to return to the Normal view of the slides. Select slide 3. Make sure that the Animation Pane is visible to the right of the slide. Use the <Print Screen> key on your keyboard to copy this into the clipboard. Paste the image into a word-processed document so that you can add your name and other details before sending it to the printer.

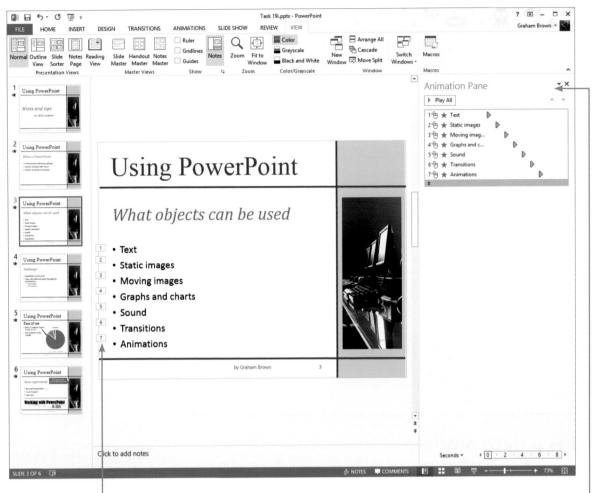

The numbering next to each bullet point shows that each bullet is animated separately from the others. Further detail about the animation of the bullets can be seen in the Animation Pane.

Activity 19b

Open the presentation that you saved in Activity 19a.

Add the following presenter notes to the slides:

- **Slide 1**: Welcome to my presentation giving tips about website authoring using HTML.
- **Slide 4**: An intranet is internal within an organisation and is managed. The internet is global and is not managed.
- **Slide 6**: There are many other websites that can offer you help.

Place the image **website.jpg** on the right side of slide 6. Crop this image so that only the crest and name are visible as shown below.

Add a red arrow, 3 points wide, from the text 'Cambridge website' to point to this image.

Apply transitions between all the slides in your presentation.

In slide 3 animate all the bullets so that they appear one at a time, in the order that they are in the list.

Print the presentation showing:

- presenter notes
- audience notes with six slides per page
- evidence of the transitions between slides
- evidence of the animations used on slide 3.

In this chapter you will learn how to:

- create the layout for a spreadsheet model
- enter text and numeric data into a spreadsheet
- use editing functions, such as cut, copy and paste
- enter formulae and simple functions into a spreadsheet
- replicate formulae and functions in the spreadsheet
- test the data model
- select subsets of data within a spreadsheet
- sort data within a spreadsheet
- change the display and format of cells within a spreadsheet
- change the size of rows and columns within a spreadsheet
- adjust the page orientation
- save a spreadsheet
- print a spreadsheet displaying formulae or values.

For this chapter you will need these source files from the CD:

- classlist.csv
- client.csv
- clubs.csv
- costs.csv
- items.csv
- jobs.csv
- operators.csv
- project.csv
- rooms.csv
- salary.csv
- sales.csv
- staff.csv
- tasks.csv
- teachers.csv
- tuckshop.csv
- tutors.csv.

20.1 What is a data model?

For data analysis, you will use a **spreadsheet model** to explore different possible answers. These models are often financial, mathematical or scientific. It is sometimes called using a 'what if' scenario or 'what if' modelling. It lets you change data in the spreadsheet to see what will happen to the results. In a practical examination you may be asked to build a simple spreadsheet model and edit (change) the data within the model, or even change the model itself, to produce different results.

20.1.1 Spreadsheet basics

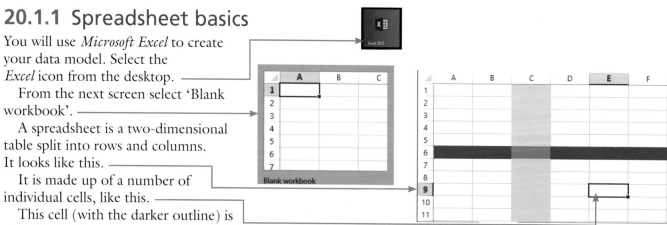

You will use *Microsoft Excel* to create your data model. Select the *Excel* icon from the desktop.

From the next screen select 'Blank workbook'.

A spreadsheet is a two-dimensional table split into rows and columns. It looks like this.

It is made up of a number of individual cells, like this.

This cell (with the darker outline) is the cell that has the cursor within it. To help us to use individual cells in a spreadsheet, each cell has an address. In this example the cell with the cursor in it is called cell E9 and the cell that has been coloured red is called cell C6. The red cell and all of the yellow cells are in column C, and the red cell and all of the blue cells are in row 6. A spreadsheet is sometimes called a sheet or even a worksheet. Many sheets can be held within a single workbook in *Excel*.

Insert cells, rows and columns

To insert a cell into a spreadsheet, **right** mouse click on the spreadsheet where you wish to insert the cell. From the drop-down menu select Insert... which opens the Insert window.

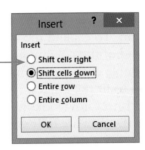

This will allow you to insert a cell (by selecting one of the top two options, which creates the space for the cell by moving all other cells to the right or down, depending on your choice) or allow you to insert a row or a column.

Delete cells, rows and columns

To delete a cell from a spreadsheet **right** mouse click on the cell you wish to delete. From the drop-down menu select Delete... which opens the Delete window.

This will allow you to delete a cell (by selecting one of the top two options, which removes the cell by moving all other cells to the left or up) or allow you to delete a row or a column.

Advice

Remember that a column holds up the roof and you can see a row of houses.

Task 20a

Create a spreadsheet to multiply any two numbers together and display the result.

The contents of a spreadsheet cell can be:

- a number
- text, which is called a label
- a formula, which always starts with an = sign.

Move the cursor into cell A1 and click the left mouse button. Type in the label 'Multiplying two numbers'. Move the cursor down into cell A2 and enter a number. Repeat this for cell A3. In cell A4, enter the formula =A2*A3 so that the spreadsheet looks like this.

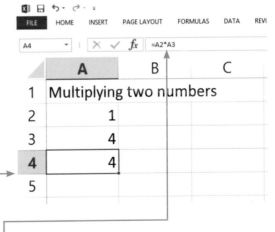

You will see that the formula is not visible in the sheet and that the cell A4 only contains the answer to the calculation within this cell. The formula for the cell containing the cursor can be seen in the formula bar.

If you have created the spreadsheet as shown, you should be able to change the contents of cells A2 and A3 to multiply any two numbers together. The changing of cells to see the results is called modelling.

If you enter large numbers into cells A2 and A3, the result in cell A4 may not appear as you expect it to. It may look like this.

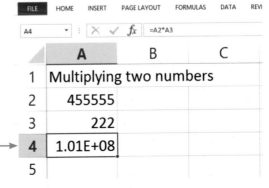

This tells you that the number is too large to fit into the column. To expand the width of the column, move the cursor to the end of the column heading for column A like this.

Double click the left mouse button to expand the column width to fit the longest item stored in this column. The spreadsheet now looks like this. You can see how the label and all of the data are fully visible.

Save your work in your Task20a folder.

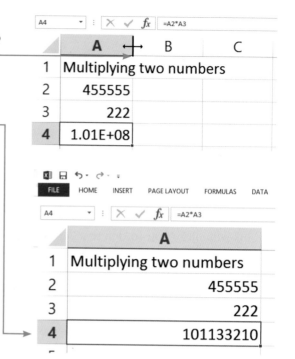

Advice

You **must** show the contents of all cells fully in your spreadsheet printouts so that your method and results can be seen.

20.2 Create a data model

Task 20b

Create a spreadsheet to display the times table for any number you choose to enter. Print your spreadsheet, showing values and formulae.

For this task, you need to design and create the data model to calculate and display the times table for any number that you choose. You must therefore have a single cell that contains the number to use for all the calculations. In this model you can place a simple number, such as 2, in cell A1, so that you can easily tell if you have made a mistake with your formulae later on. Type the label 'Times Table' in cell A2.

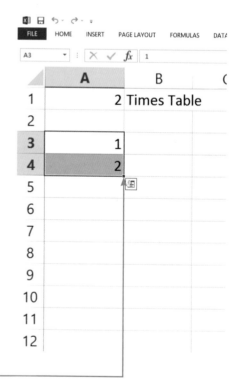

You are going to create the times table in cells A3 to B12. The cells in column A hold the number to multiply by and the cells in column B hold formulae to calculate the answer. Move the cursor into cell A3 and enter the number 1, then move into cell A4 and enter the number 2. Rather than repeating this process another eight times for the numbers 3 to 10, highlight cells A3 and A4, as shown here. Move the cursor to the drag handle in the bottom right corner of these cells.

Click and hold the left mouse button on the drag handle, dragging it down to the bottom right corner of cell A12. This replicates (copies) the cell contents. *Excel* realises that the numbers in cells A3 and A4 increase by one, so uses this pattern as it replicates the cells down.

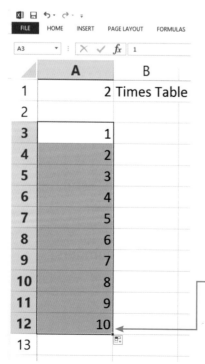

Move the cursor into cell B3 and enter the formula =A3*$A$1. The $ symbols in the reference to cell A1 will be used by *Excel* to keep that cell reference the same when this cell is replicated into cells B4 to B12. Use the drag handle in cell B3 to replicate this formula into the cells down to B12. The results should look like this.

Without checking the formulae, you can see that this has produced the correct results for the two times table. Change cell A1 to another number to check that the formula works correctly. Print this values view of the spreadsheet using the FILE tab, followed by Print and then the Print button.

	A	B
1		2 Times Table
2		
3	1	2
4	2	4
5	3	6
6	4	8
7	5	10
8	6	12
9	7	14
10	8	16
11	9	18
12	10	20

20.2.1 Display formulae

To display (and then print) the formulae used in the spreadsheet, select the FORMULAS tab and find the Formula Auditing section. Click on the Show Formulas icon. The spreadsheet now looks like this.

Each of these formulae contains both absolute and relative referencing. In cell B3, the reference to cell A1 (with the $ symbols) is an **absolute reference** and the reference to cell A3 is a *relative reference*. You can see from this view that the reference in cell B3 to cell A3 has been changed as the cell has been replicated, as it uses relative referencing, but the reference to cell A1 has not been changed during the replication, because absolute referencing has been used.

To return to the view of the spreadsheet that shows the values, click on the Show Formulas icon again.

20.2.2 More editing tools

Other standard *Windows* editing tools can be used in *Excel*, such as cut, copy and paste. These can be used to copy the contents of one cell into another cell. An alternative method of replicating cell B3 into cells B4 to B12 is to enter the formula in cell B3, right mouse click on this cell and select Copy from the drop-down menu. Highlight cells B4 to B12 and right mouse click, selecting Paste from the drop-down menu. This will paste the formulae, adjusting the cell references for A3 as this is a relative reference but keeping the absolute reference for A1. The results are identical.

	A	B
1	2	Times Table
2		
3	1	=A3*$A$1
4	2	=A4*$A$1
5	3	=A5*$A$1
6	4	=A6*$A$1
7	5	=A7*$A$1
8	6	=A8*$A$1
9	7	=A9*$A$1
10	8	=A10*$A$1
11	9	=A11*$A$1
12	10	=A12*$A$1

20.2.3 Accuracy of data entry

When you are asked to 'create a data model that looks like this', make sure that you copy the model in the question exactly as shown. Do not try to make improvements or use other features (such as colour and formatting) unless asked to do so. This is very important. Do not insert rows or columns, or remove rows or columns containing blank spaces, unless instructed to do so.

When you type data into a spreadsheet (or any other form of document) you must make sure that the data that you have entered is identical to the original source document or question. Do not rush the data entry and check carefully that it has been entered with 100 per cent accuracy. This is even more important when working in a spreadsheet because one error, for example a mistyped number or decimal point in the wrong place, could cause all of the data in the spreadsheet to be incorrect. Care must also be taken when entering a formula, as one small error is likely to stop the spreadsheet working as it is expected to.

20.2.4 Use formulae

Simple mathematical operators can be used to add, subtract, multiply, divide and calculate indices (powers) of a number. Each mathematical operator is placed in a formula, as you did in Tasks 20a and 20b.

- For addition use the + symbol.
- For subtraction use the − symbol.
- For multiplication use the * symbol.
- For division use the / symbol.

Indices are calculated using the ^ symbol, so the contents of cell A2 squared (x^2) would be typed as =A2^2.

Task 20c

Open the file **operators.csv**.

Choose two numbers. Place these in cells B1 and B2. Calculate in cell:

- B4, the sum of the two numbers
- B5, the difference between the two numbers
- B6, the product of the two numbers
- B7, the contents of cell B1 divided by the contents of cell B2
- B8, the contents of cell B1 to the power of the contents of cell B2.

Check that the formulae have worked before printing your spreadsheet showing the values and again showing the formulae used.

Open the file operators.csv in *Excel*. Extend the width of column A so that all the labels are fully visible (see Task 20a). Move the cursor into cell B1 and enter the number 4, then into cell B2 and enter the number 2. These numbers have been chosen so that you can easily check your calculations. It is wise to perform all calculations by hand before entering the formulae. This will make sure that you understand the formulae that you are using and you will be able to see the results of the calculation before the computer has shown you its results. These calculations may look like this.

Number X	4
Number Y	2

X+Y	4+2=6
X-Y	4-2=2
X*Y	4*2=8
X/Y	4/2=2
X^Y	4^2=16

- **Addition**: move the cursor into cell B4. The sum of the two numbers is needed in this cell, which means to add the contents of the two cells together. There are two ways of doing this: one method uses the + operator and the second uses a function. You will be shown how to use the SUM function later in this chapter, but the formula to enter in this cell for the + operator is =B1+B2. This can be typed in followed by the <Enter> key, or you can type the = sign, click the cursor into cell B1, type + and click in cell B2 before pressing the <Enter> key.
- **Subtraction**: move the cursor into cell B5. The difference between two numbers is needed in this cell. Enter (using either of the methods described in the addition section above) the formula =B1−B2, followed by the <Enter> key.
- **Multiplication**: move the cursor into cell B6. The product of two numbers means to multiply the two numbers together; you need to enter the formula =B1*B2, followed by the <Enter> key.

- **Division**: move the cursor into cell B7. This cell needs a calculation to divide the contents of cell B1 by the contents of cell B2 using the formula **=B1/B2**, followed by the <Enter> key.
- **Indices**: Move the cursor into cell B8. This cell needs to calculate the contents of cell B1 to the power of the contents of cell B2 using the formula **=B1^B2**, followed by the <Enter> key.

Advice

The ^ symbol is often found using <Shift> and <6>.

To check that the formulae are correct, compare your original paper-based calculations with the values in the spreadsheet.

You will notice that the values chosen earlier in this task were carefully selected to make the maths easy. The more difficult calculations are likely to be the division and indices. These numbers were selected so that the 4 divided by 2 gives an easy result; 4 to the power of 2 is also reasonably easy (4×4).

Print the values, making sure that your name is fully visible on the printout. Select the FORMULAS tab, then click on the Show Formulas icon to change the display to show the formulae, which should appear like this.

Save and print the spreadsheet.

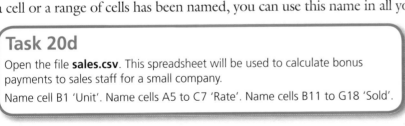

	A	B
1	First number - X	4
2	Second number - Y	2
3		
4	Sum of X and Y	6
5	Difference between X and Y	2
6	Product of X and Y	8
7	X divided by Y	2
8	X to the power of Y	16

	A	B
1	First number - X	4
2	Second number - Y	2
3		
4	Sum of X and Y	=B1+B2
5	Difference between X and Y	=B1-B2
6	Product of X and Y	=B1*B2
7	X divided by Y	=B1/B2
8	X to the power of Y	=B1^B2

20.2.5 Named cells and ranges

When an individual cell or an area of a spreadsheet is going to be used a number of times within the formulae of a spreadsheet, it is often a good idea to give it a name. This name should be short and meaningful. In the case of a large spreadsheet, it is easier to remember the name of a cell, for example VAT or AveMiles, rather than trying to remember the cell reference, for example AC456 or X232. Once a cell or a range of cells has been named, you can use this name in all your formulae.

Task 20d

Open the file **sales.csv**. This spreadsheet will be used to calculate bonus payments to sales staff for a small company.

Name cell B1 'Unit'. Name cells A5 to C7 'Rate'. Name cells B11 to G18 'Sold'.

Open the file and find cell B1. You will name this cell 'Unit'. Right click on the mouse in this cell to get the drop-down menu. Select the option to Define Name… which will open the New Name window. In the Name: box, *Excel* will suggest a name for the range. It uses the layout of your spreadsheet to do this. For practical examinations, ignore this suggestion (in this case the name that it suggests is too long to be used) and overtype it with the word Unit, as instructed in the question. Add suitable text in the Comment box so that the window looks like this.

To name the range click on OK.

When you move the cursor into cell B1, you will see in the Name Box that it is now called Unit.

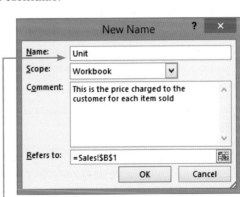

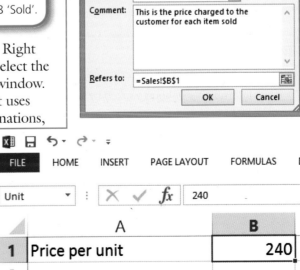

To create the named range for the rate, you must highlight the cells between A5 and C7. Do this by clicking on cell A5 and, while holding down the left mouse button, dragging the cursor to cell C7. Click the right mouse button within the highlighted range to get the drop-down menu. Change the contents of the Name: box to Rate. Check that the New Name window looks like this before clicking on OK. The name of the range is only visible in the Name Box when just the cells in the range are highlighted.

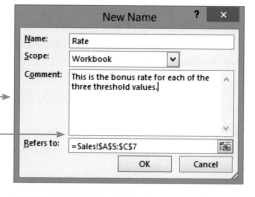

The final named range can be created in a similar way. Highlight cells B11 to G18, then name this range Sold. Each of these named cells and ranges will be used in other tasks.

Save this spreadsheet as Task_20d as an *Excel* workbook, **not** in .csv format.

20.2.6 Formulae and functions

A formula in *Excel* starts with an = sign. It could be a simple formula using mathematical operators, such as **=B1+B2**, a complex formula using nested statements (this will be explained later in this chapter) or a formula including functions. A function has a predefined name such as **SUM** or **AVERAGE**, to perform a particular calculation. It is an operation built into the spreadsheet. There are many of these functions in *Excel*, many of which are beyond the scope of this book, but each has a reserved function name. If a question asks you to choose your own name for a cell or range, you can not use these function names.

This section covers some of the more simple functions available in *Excel*, but does not describe all of the functions available or all those that may be used in examinations.

SUM

The **SUM** function adds two or more numbers together. In Task 20c, you used the mathematical operator + and the formula **=B1+B2** to add the contents of two cells together. As there were only two cells to be added, this was the most efficient way of doing this. If there had been more figures to add, particularly if they were grouped together in the spreadsheet, it would have been more efficient to use the **SUM** function.

Task 20e

Copy this spreadsheet model and calculate:

- the total number of hours worked by all of these five people
- the average number of hours worked per person
- the maximum number of hours worked by any of these five people
- the minimum number of hours worked by any of these five people.

	A	B
1	**Rate of pay**	£12.80
2		
3	**Name**	**Hours**
4	David Watson	26
5	Graham Brown	20
6	John Reeves	17
7	Brian Sargent	4
8	Dan Bray	13
9	**Total**	
10	**Average**	
11	**Maximum**	
12	**Minimum**	

Open a new sheet and copy the labels and values exactly as shown in the table. Select the HOME tab and use the **B** (bold) icon to embolden the cells shown. To find the total number of hours worked you will need to click the cursor into cell B9 and use SUM to add up the list of numbers. Enter the formula =SUM(B4:B8). This should give the value 80.

An alternative way to use this function without typing it into cell B9 is for you to use AutoSum. Move the cursor into cell B9, select the HOME tab and find the Editing section. Click on the AutoSum icon.

Advice

An alternative method is to enter =SUM(then drag the cursor to highlight cells B4 to B8, then type) and press the <Enter> key.

This will place the SUM function into cell B9 and attempt to work out which cells you wish to add up (by looking at the layout of your spreadsheet). It does not always get this range correct, so check carefully. If the range is correct (as it is in this case) press the <Enter> key to accept the AutoSum. If it is not correct, you can highlight the cells to be added before pressing the <Enter> key.

There are many ways of using the SUM function, some of which are shown in Table 20.1.

	A	B
1	**Rate of pay**	12.8
2		
3	**Name**	**Hours**
4	David Watson	26
5	Graham Brown	20
6	John Reeves	17
7	Brian Sargent	4
8	Dan Bray	13
9	**Total**	=SUM(B4:B8)
10	**Average**	

Table 20.1 Ways of using the SUM function

Function	Equivalent formula	What it does
=SUM(B4:B8)	=B4+B5+B6+B7+B8	Adds up the contents of all the cells in the range B4 to B8
=SUM(D3,D8,D12)	=D3+D8+D12	Adds up the contents of cells D3, D8 and D12
=SUM(D5:D8,F2)	=D5+D6+D7+D8+F2	Adds up the contents of the cells in the range D5 to D8 and the contents of cell F2
=SUM(MyRange)	None	Adds up the contents of all the cells within a named range called MyRange; this can be used with any named range

As you can see, the range of cells selected within these functions can include a number of individual cells, ranges of cells, named ranges, named cells or a combination of these. The AVERAGE, MAX (maximum), MIN (minimum), and COUNT functions also work like this.

AVERAGE

To find the average (mean) number of hours worked, click the cursor into cell B10 and use AVERAGE to calculate the mean (average) of a list of numbers. Enter the formula =AVERAGE(B4:B8).This should give the value 16. There are many ways of using the AVERAGE function, some of which are shown in Table 20.2.

Table 20.2 Ways of using the AVERAGE function

Function	Equivalent formula	What it does
=AVERAGE(B4:B8)	=(B4+B5+B6+B7+B8)/5	Calculates the mean of the cells in the range B4 to B8
=AVERAGE(D3,D8,D12)	=(D3+D8+D12)/3	Calculates the mean of the cells D3, D8 and D12
=AVERAGE(D5:D8,F2)	=(D5+D6+D7+D8+F2)/5	Calculates the mean of the cells in the range D5 to D8 and cell F2
=AVERAGE(MyRange)	None	Calculates the mean of the cells in a named range called MyRange

MAX

To find the person who worked the most hours, click the cursor into cell B11 and use **MAX** to select the largest (maximum) figure within the list of numbers. Enter the formula **=MAX(B4:B8)**. This should give the value 26.

MIN

To find the person who worked the least number of hours, click the cursor into cell B12 and use **MIN** to select the smallest (minimum) figure from the list. Enter the formula **=MIN(B4:B8)**. This should give the value 4.

The finished spreadsheet should look like this. ——————→
Save this spreadsheet as task20e.

	A	B
1	Rate of pay	£12.80
2		
3	Name	Hours
4	David Watson	26
5	Graham Brown	20
6	John Reeves	17
7	Brian Sargent	4
8	Dan Bray	13
9	Total	80
10	Average	16
11	Maximum	26
12	Minimum	4

Activity 20a

Open the file **tuckshop.csv**.

In cells B14 to B17, calculate the total number of days that all the students worked in the school shop, the average number of days worked, and the maximum and minimum values.

Place your name on the spreadsheet. Print your spreadsheet showing the values, then print your spreadsheet showing the formulae used.

Task 20f

John Reeves did an extra four hours work. Change the spreadsheet that you created in Task 20e to show the new figures. The manager wants to see the average number of hours worked displayed as:

- an integer value
- rounded to the nearest whole hour.

Print two copies of the spreadsheet showing these values.

Advice

Setting a cell as an integer value will remove the decimal/fraction part of the number. This is not the same as formatting a cell to 0 decimal places, which stops the decimal/fraction part from being displayed but will still be used in a calculation.

Open the file task20e. Change the contents of cell B6 to 21 to add the four extra hours that he worked. This gives an average value of 16.8 hours. Move the cursor into cell C9 and enter the text 'Integer', then move into cell D9 and enter the text 'Rounding'. To get the first value requested by the manager, we have to set cell B10 to hold an integer value.

INT

In mathematics, an integer is the word used to describe a whole number (with no decimals or fractions). In *Excel*, the **INT** function takes the whole number part of a number and ignores all digits after the decimal point. Move the cursor into cell C10 and enter the formula **=INT(B10)**. This should give the value 16.

ROUND

Move the cursor into cell D10 and enter the formula **=ROUND(B10,0)**. This uses the **ROUND** function, which takes the content of cell B10 and rounds the number to 0 decimal places: if the first digit after the decimal point is five or more the number in cell D10 will be increased by one. For example, in cell

B10 the value is 16.8, so the content of D10 is 17, as it has rounded the value to the nearest whole number. The spreadsheet should look like this.

Rounding can be used with any number of decimal places, for example using rounding for currencies with two decimal places can avoid calculation errors.

Table 20.3 shows more examples of how you can use the ROUND function, using cell A1, which contains the number **62.5512**.

	A	B	C	D
1	Rate of pay	£12.80		
2				
3	Name	Hours		
4	David Watson	26		
5	Graham Brown	20		
6	John Reeves	17		
7	Brian Sargent	4		
8	Dan Bray	13		
9	Total	80	Integer	Round
10	Average	16	16	17
11	Maximum	26		
12	Minimum	4		

Table 20.3 Ways of using the ROUND function

Function	Result of rounding	What it does
=ROUND(A1,2)	62.55	Rounds the contents of A1 to two decimal places
=ROUND(A1,1)	62.6	Rounds the contents of A1 to one decimal place. Note that the second figure 5 in 62.5512 has forced the previous figure to be rounded up
=ROUND(A1,0)	63	Rounds the contents of A1 to 0 decimal places. Note that the first figure 5 in 62.5512 has forced the previous figure to be rounded up
=ROUND(A1,–1)	60	Rounds the contents of A1 to the nearest 10. The negative value for decimal places allows this function to round numbers in tens, hundreds, etc.
=ROUND(A1,–2)	100	Rounds the contents of A1 to the nearest 100. Note that the figure 6 has forced the previous figure to be rounded up from 0 to 1

Save and print a copy of the spreadsheet showing the average number of hours worked displayed as an integer value. Print a copy of the spreadsheet showing the average number of hours worked rounded to the nearest whole hour.

Activity 20b

Create a new spreadsheet model to calculate:

- the whole number part of 375.56411
- 375.56411 rounded to two decimal places
- 375.56411 rounded to the nearest whole number
- 375.56411 rounded to the nearest ten
- 375.56411 rounded to the nearest hundred
- 375.56411 rounded to the nearest thousand.

Task 20g

Open the file **project.csv**. This file lists some workers and below each worker is the number of jobs they have still to finish for a project.

Place a formula in cell A22 to count the number of jobs that still have to be finished for the project. Place a formula in cell A24 to count the number of workers on the project.

COUNT

For this task you will need to use functions that count different values. It is possible to count the number of numeric (number) values in a list using the COUNT function. Open the file, place the cursor in cell A22 and enter the formula **=COUNT(A2:A19)**. This will look at the range A2 to A19 (notice that you have not counted cell A1, which contains the title, nor cell A20, which may be used for something else later) and count only the cells with numbers in them. It will not count any blank spaces and should give the value 7.

COUNTA

The **COUNTA** function works in a similar way to the **COUNT** function. Rather than counting just the number of numeric values, this function counts the number of numeric or text values displayed in the cells. It will not count any blank cells within the range. There is no count function for just text values in *Excel*, so the **COUNTA** and **COUNT** functions will both be used to calculate the number of workers on the project. Place the cursor in cell A24 and enter the formula **=COUNTA(A2:A19)–COUNT(A2:A19)**. This will look at the range A2 to A19 and count the cells with text or numbers in them, then subtract the number of cells with numbers in to leave only the cells with text in them, in other words the names of the employees. It should give the value 9 and look like this.

	A
1	Project 142
2	Laila Aboli
3	4
4	Sri Paryanti
5	7
6	David Watson
7	2
8	Graham Brown
9	12
10	John Reeves
11	
12	Brian Sargent
13	6
14	Dan Bray
15	
16	Thirumalar Asokmani
17	3
18	Lea Cabusbusan
19	2
20	
21	Number of workers who have not finished
22	7
23	Number of workers on the project
24	9

21	Number of workers who have not finished
22	=COUNT(A2:A19)
23	Number of workers on the project
24	=COUNTA(A2:A19)-COUNT(A2:A19)

Activity 20c

Open the file **classlist.csv**. This spreadsheet lists all the students in a class. If a student has attended any clubs during the year, the number of times they have attended is recorded in the cell below their name.

Place a formula in cell A71 to count the number of students in the class. Place a formula in cell A74 to count the number of students who have attended extra clubs this year.

Task 20h

Open the file **staff.csv**. This file lists some workers on another project and lists each worker's job.

Place formulae in cells B24 to B28 to count how many of each type of worker are employed on the project. Place a formula in cell B31 to count the number of employees with less than five years' experience.
Place a formula in cell B32 to count the number of employees with ten or more years' experience.

COUNTIF

For this task, you need to count how many people have each type of job. Open the file and place the cursor in cell B24. The function needed for this task is **COUNTIF**, which looks at the cells within a given range and counts the number of cells in that range that meet a given condition. The condition is placed in the function and can be a number, text, an inequality or a cell reference. There are a number of ways the COUNTIF function can be used: any of the formulae given in Table 20.4 can be entered in cell B24 and will give the correct result.

Table 20.4 Alternative formulae using the COUNTIF function

Function	What it does
=COUNTIF($B$3:$B$21,"Director")	Counts the number of cells in the range B3 to B21 that contain the word 'Director'
=COUNTIF(Job,"Director")	Counts the number of cells in the named range Job (B3 to B21) that contain the word 'Director'. This only works if cells B3 to B21 have been named 'Job'
=COUNTIF($B$3:$B$21,A24)	Counts the number of cells in the range B3 to B21 that contain the same text as the contents of cell A24
=COUNTIF(Job,A24)	Counts the number of cells in the named range Job (B3 to B21) that contain the same text as the contents of cell A24. This only works if cells B3 to B21 have been named 'Job'

Advice

Note in examples one and three in Table 20.4 that the range $B$3:$B$21 has been set as an absolute reference so that this range is always in the same place if the formula is replicated. Also note that examples three and four have cell A24 set as a relative reference so that it will look for the next job title when the formula is replicated. Named ranges are absolute references, but you must show screen shot evidence that you have named the range correctly in practical examinations.

Replicate the function in cell B24 into cells B25 to B28. As these cells are to be replicated, methods three and four in Table 20.4 are the most efficient, as you do not have to edit each formula with a different name for each row. If a question asks you to show evidence of absolute and relative referencing, then method three would be the most appropriate. If named ranges are required, or absolute and relative referencing are not asked for in the question, method four is the most efficient.

To count the number of employees with less than five years' experience, place the cursor in cell B31 and enter the formula =**COUNTIF($C$3:$C$21,"<5")**. This will look at the range C3 to C21 and count the cells with a number value of less than 5. The speech marks around the <5 are needed to tell *Excel* that it is dealing with another formula (in this case an inequality), rather than searching for the symbols <5. The spreadsheet should show the value 7.

To count the number of employees with ten or more years' experience, place the cursor in cell B32 and enter the formula =**COUNTIF($C$3:$C$21,">=10")**. The value calculated should be 5.

Save your spreadsheet as task20h.

Activity 20d

Open the file that you saved in Activity 20c. This spreadsheet lists all the students in a class. Next to each student's name is the colour of the house that they are in.

Place formulae in cells E2 to E5 that use both absolute and relative referencing to count the number of students in each house.

Place a formula in cell E7 to count the number of students with less than five clubs.

Place a formula in cell E8 to count the number of students with 12 or more clubs.

IF

An **IF** function contains a pair of brackets and, within the brackets, three parts, each separated by a comma. An example of an **IF** function is =**IF(A1=5,A2*0.05,"No discount")**. The first part is a condition; in this example, it is testing to see if cell A1 contains the number 5. The other two parts are what to do if the condition is met, and what to do if it is not met. If the condition is met a number or label could be placed in the cell, or a reference to another cell, or even a calculation that needs to be performed. The same range of options applies if a condition is not met. In this example, if the condition is met, the result of multiplying the contents of cell A2 by the figure 0.05 is displayed in this cell. If the condition is not met this cell will display the text 'No discount'.

Task 20i

Open the file that you saved in Task 20h.

Add a new label 'Category' into cell D2.

Place formulae in cells D3 to D21 to display 'Very experienced' for employees with ten or more years' experience, otherwise to display 'Not experienced'.

Open the file and place the cursor in cell D2. Enter the label 'Category'. Place the cursor in cell D3 and enter the formula **=IF(C3>=10,"Very experienced","Not experienced")**. The reason that C3>=10 is used rather than C3>9 (which in many circumstances would be a more efficient formula), is because one employee has 0.2 years' experience. As the data does not only contain whole numbers, there could be an employee with 9.5 years' experience so C3>9 would not work for all data. Do not use absolute referencing in this formula as the reference to cell C3 needs to change when you replicate the formula. Replicate this formula so it is copied into cells D4 to D21. Your spreadsheet should look similar to this. ——————

Save your spreadsheet as task20i.

	A	B	C	D
1	Project 153			
2	Name	Job	Years exp	Category
3	Laila Aboli	Programmer	3	Not experienced
4	Greg Mina	Programmer	2	Not experienced
5	Sri Paryanti	Analyst	12	Very experienced
6	Bishen Patel	Sales	5	Not experienced
7	Rupinder Singh	Engineer	7	Not experienced
8	Sergio Gonzalez	Programmer	5	Not experienced
9	Rupinder Vas	Sales	6	Not experienced
10	Henri Ramos	Sales	10	Very experienced
11	John Mortlock	Programmer	14	Very experienced
12	Cameron Garnham	Analyst	7	Not experienced
13	Brian Guthrie	Director	3	Not experienced
14	Julia Frobisher	Engineer	6	Not experienced
15	Dan McNevin	Programmer	9	Not experienced
16	Patrick O'Malley	Engineer	11	Very experienced
17	Thirumalar Asokmani	Sales	10	Very experienced
18	Sean O'Byrne	Programmer	2	Not experienced
19	Lea Cabusbusan	Programmer	1	Not experienced
20	Brian O'Driscoll	Programmer	0.2	Not experienced
21	Wim Van Hoffmann	Engineer	2	Not experienced
22				

Activity 20e

Open the file that you saved in Activity 20d.
Add a new label 'New students' into cell F1.
Place formulae in cells F2 to F6 to display 'Add to this house' if the number of students in this house is less than 6 or to display 'Full' if the number is 6 or more.

20.2.7 Nested formulae and functions

A nested formula or function is having one formula or function inside another one. Sometimes nested formulae could contain several formulae nested within each other. If the nested functions include a number of **IF** statements, be careful to work in a logical order. Work from smallest to largest or vice versa (depending on the question). Do **not** start with middle values; this will give incorrect results.

Task 20j

Open the file that you saved in Task 20i.
Change the formulae in cells D3 to D21 to display 'Not experienced' if they have less than five years' experience, 'Experienced' if they have five or more years' experience and 'Very experienced' for employees with ten or more years' experience.

For this task, three conditions exist. If the value for experience is:

- >=10 then display 'Very experienced'
- >=5 then display 'Experienced'
- <5 then display 'Not experienced'.

Place the cursor into cell D3 and change the formula so that it becomes **=IF(C3>=10,"Very experienced",IF(C3>=5,"Experienced","Not experienced"))**

Advice

Note that as the conditions are all 'greater than', they have been placed in reverse order. For example, if the value for experience was 40 and the condition <5 was first, then >=5 next and then >=10: the first condition <5 would be not true, so it would go to the next condition; >=5 would be true, so the result displayed would be 'Experienced'; it would never get as far as the test for >=10.

Notice how the second part of the formula (highlighted in yellow) has been placed as a 'No' condition within the first formula. Be very careful to get the brackets correct: each condition has one open and one close bracket. When you work through this formula, it checks whether the value is greater than or equal to 10 first; if so, it displays the correct text. Then, if it was not true, it would check if the value is greater than or equal to 5 next; if so, it displays the correct text. As there are no other conditions that could occur, rather than having another nested statement the resulting text has been placed.

Replicate this formula into cells D4 to D21. Your spreadsheet should look similar to this.

Save your spreadsheet as task20j.

	A	B	C	D
1	Project 153			
2	Name	Job	Years exp	Category
3	Laila Aboli	Programmer	3	Not experienced
4	Greg Mina	Programmer	2	Not experienced
5	Sri Paryanti	Analyst	12	Very experienced
6	Bishen Patel	Sales	5	Experienced
7	Rupinder Singh	Engineer	7	Experienced
8	Sergio Gonzalez	Programmer	5	Experienced
9	Rupinder Vas	Sales	6	Experienced
10	Henri Ramos	Sales	10	Very experienced
11	John Mortlock	Programmer	14	Very experienced
12	Cameron Garnham	Analyst	7	Experienced
13	Brian Guthrie	Director	3	Not experienced
14	Julia Frobisher	Engineer	6	Experienced
15	Dan McNevin	Programmer	9	Experienced
16	Patrick O'Malley	Engineer	11	Very experienced
17	Thirumalar Asokmani	Sales	10	Very experienced
18	Sean O'Byrne	Programmer	2	Not experienced
19	Lea Cabusbusan	Programmer	1	Not experienced
20	Brian O'Driscoll	Programmer	0.2	Not experienced
21	Wim Van Hoffmann	Engineer	2	Not experienced
22				

Activity 20f

Open the file that you saved in Activity 20e.
Change the formulae in cells F2 to F6 to display 'Add to this house' if the number of students in this house is less than six, 'Ideal number' if there are between six and ten students, or to display 'Full' if the number is more than ten.

Task 20k

Open the file that you saved in Task 20j.
Insert the label 'Total experience for:' in cell A34, the label 'Programmer' in cell A35 and 'Engineer' in cell A36.
Insert a formula in cell B35 that uses both absolute and relative referencing to calculate the number of years' experience for the programmers.
Insert a formula in cell B36 that uses both absolute and relative referencing to calculate the number of years' experience for the engineers.

SUMIF

SUMIF works in a similar way to COUNTIF. It compares each value in a range of cells and, if the value matches the given condition, it adds the value in another related cell to form a running total.

Add the labels as required by the task into cells A34, A35 and A36. Move the cursor into cell B35 and enter the formula =SUMIF($B$3:$B$21,A35, $C$3:$C$21). The total for this cell starts at 0. This looks at the contents of each row in the range B3 to B21 and compares the value in each cell to the contents of cell A35 (which contains the text 'Programmer'). If these two items are identical it adds the value from the same row within the range C3 to C21 to the total. When all rows in this range have been checked the total is displayed in this cell. This happens within a fraction of a second as you press the <Enter> key or change any value within these ranges.

To calculate the number of years' experience for the engineers, place in cell B36 the formula =SUMIF($B$3:$B$21,A36,$C$3:$C$21). The results of these formulae should look like this.

Save the spreadsheet as task20k.

Advice

You could use named ranges rather than absolute referencing for cells B3 to B21 and C3 to C21. One alternative formula in cell B35, which uses the named range 'Job' created earlier in the chapter, is =SUMIF(Job,A35,$C$3:$C$21).

	A	B
34	Total experience for:	
35	Programmer	36.2
36	Engineer	26

Activity 20g

Open the file **clubs.csv**.
Insert a formula in cell B37 that uses both absolute and relative referencing to calculate the number of clubs attended by students in red house.
Replicate this formula in cells B38 to B40 for each house colour.

20.2.8 Use lookups

The term 'look up', as used in practical examinations, means to look up from a list. It does not mean that you should use the LOOKUP function, as there are three variations of the LOOKUP function that can be used within *Excel*. These are: LOOKUP, HLOOKUP and VLOOKUP.

LOOKUP

LOOKUP is used to look up a value using data in the first row or the first column of a range of cells and returns a relative value. For our purposes, this is probably the least useful of the three formulae.

HLOOKUP

HLOOKUP is a function that performs a horizontal look up of data. This should be used when the values that you wish to compare your data with are stored in a single **row**. The values to be looked up are stored in the rows below these cells.

Task 20l

Open the file **jobs.csv**.
Insert formulae in the Description column to look up and display the JobTitle using the JobCode as the look-up value.

Open the file jobs.csv and click the left mouse button to place the cursor in cell C6. Enter the formula =HLOOKUP(B6,$B$2:$H$3,2) into this cell. This formula will look up and compare the contents of cell B6 with the contents of each cell in the top (horizontal) row of the range B2 to H3. When it finds a match, it will take the value or label stored in the second row, which is directly under the matched cell. The '2' at the end of the formula tells *Excel* to look in the second row of the given range. Replicate this formula into cells C7 to C27. The results should look similar to this.

Save the spreadsheet as task20l.

	A	B	C	D
1	Project 160			
2	JobCode	1	2	3
3	JobTitle	Director	Engineer	Analyst
4				
5	Name	JobCode	Description	
6	Laila Aboli		5 Programmer	
7	Greg Mina		5 Programmer	
8	Sri Paryanti		3 Analyst	
9	Bishen Patel		4 Sales	
10	Rupinder Singh		2 Engineer	
11	Sergio Gonzalez		5 Programmer	
12				

VLOOKUP

VLOOKUP is a function that performs a vertical look up of data. This should be used when the values that you wish to compare your data with are stored in a single **column**. The values to be looked up are stored in the columns to the right of these cells. The look up data can be stored either in the same file or in a different file.

Task 20m

Open the file **tasks.csv**.
Insert formulae in the CurrentTask column to look up the client, using the TaskCode for the look up value and the file **client.csv**. Make sure that you use both absolute and relative referencing within your function.

Open the file tasks.csv and click the left mouse button to place the cursor in cell C3. The task instructs you to use the file **client.csv** for the look up. Open this file in a new spreadsheet. Examine the layout of this file to decide which type of look up formula to use. **client.csv** looks like this.

	A	B
1	TaskCode	Client
2	1	Rootrainer
3	2	Quattichem
4	3	Hothouse Design
5	4	Avricom
6	5	Binnaccount
7	6	LGY
8	7	Rock ICT

Because it is stored with the look up data in vertical columns, a VLOOKUP is the most appropriate formula to use. Enter the formula **=VLOOKUP(B3,Client.csv!$A$2:$B$8,2,FALSE)** into this cell. This formula will look up and compare the contents of cell B3 with the contents of each cell in the left (vertical) column of the range A2 to B8 within the file **client.csv**. When entering this formula, you can add the yellow highlighted section of the formula by moving the cursor into this file and dragging it to highlight all of the cells in both columns, so it includes the look up value and the result. The number '2' in the formula tells *Excel* to look in the second column of this range. The 'False' condition in the formula tells *Excel* to only display the match if it is an exact match. If you set this to 'True' it will find the nearest approximate match. When it finds a match, it will take the value or label in the second column of the range A2:B8, which is to the right of the matched cell. Replicate this formula into cells C4 to C24.

The first few results should look similar to this.

Save the spreadsheet as task20m.

	A	B	C
1	Current client list		
2	Name	TaskCode	CurrentTask
3	Laila Aboli		6 LGY
4	Greg Mina		4 Avricom
5	Sri Paryanti		6 LGY
6	Bishen Patel		6 LGY
7	Rupinder Singh		3 Hothouse Design
8	Sergio Gonzalez		5 Binnaccount
9	Rupinder Vas		1 Rootrainer
10	Bryan Revell		1 Rootrainer
11	Henri Ramos		7 Rock ICT

Advice

Experiment with these settings. Change the value in cell B24 to 5.2. See the result of this change. Now change the exact match condition from False to True in cell C24. See the result of this change. Try other numbers, like 5.9 in B24, to see what happens.

Activity 20h

Open the file **tutors.csv**. This lists a number of students and the initials for their personal tutor.
Insert formulae in the Tutor Name column to look up the tutor's name using the file **teachers.csv**.
Insert formulae in the Room Number column to look up the room number using the file **rooms.csv**.
Make sure that you use both absolute and relative referencing within all of your functions.
Save your spreadsheet.

20.3 **Test the data model**

Designing a test plan and choosing your test data are the most important parts of testing the data model. If you test every formulae of the spreadsheet thoroughly the number of possible errors is reduced when you use the spreadsheet with real data. Choose data that will test every part of a condition. If you are testing calculations, use simple numbers that make it easier for you to check the calculations. Be careful to test each part of the spreadsheet with **normal** data that you would expect to work with your formulae, with **extreme** data to test the boundaries, and with **abnormal** data that you would not expect to be accepted. Carefully check that each formula and function works as you expect it to by using simple test data.

For example, to test the look up used in Task 20m:

- make sure that each number between 1 and 7 (**normal** data) is used in the TaskCode
- use 0 and 8, and other **abnormal** data
- use decimal values between 1 and 7.

Write down each number and the expected results before trying each number in the TaskCode column. Check that the actual result matches the expected result for every entry. If not, change the formula before starting the whole test process again. A test plan for this formula would be similar to that shown in Table 20.5.

Table 20.5 Sample test plan for Task 20m

Data entry in B3	Data type	Expected result	Actual result
1	Extreme/Normal	Rootrainer	
2	Normal	Quattichem	
3	Normal	Hothouse Design	
4	Normal	Avricom	
5	Normal	Binnaccount	
6	Normal	LGY	
7	Extreme/Normal	Rock ICT	
0	Abnormal	Error – value not available	
8	Abnormal	Error – value not available	
1.3	Abnormal	Error – value not available	
5.6	Abnormal	Error – value not available	
7.2	Abnormal	Error – value not available	
94	Abnormal	Error – value not available	

It is very important to check carefully ranges within formulae and functions. Check that all formulae and functions work before using real data in your model. If you find an error during testing, correct it, and then perform all of the tests again as one change to a spreadsheet can affect lots of different cells.

20.4 **Manipulate data**

Selecting a subset of data means getting *Excel* to search through data held in a spreadsheet to extract only rows where the data matches your search criteria.

20.4.1 Search using text filters

Task 20n

Open the file that you saved in Task 20m.
Select from all the data only the employees who are currently working on jobs for Binnaccount.

Open the file that you saved in Task 20m and highlight cells A2 to C24. Select the DATA tab and find the Sort & Filter section. Click on the Filter icon to display an arrow in the top right corner of each column, like this.

For this task, you need to use this arrow to select the people working on the Binnaccount task. When you click on the CurrentTask arrow, a small drop-down menu appears like this.

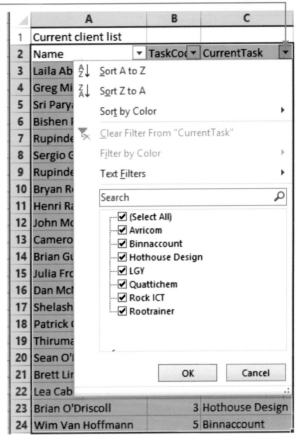

	A	B	C
1	Current client list		
2	Name	TaskCode	CurrentTask
3	Laila Aboli	6	LGY
4	Greg Mina	4	Avricom
5	Sri Paryanti	6	LGY
6	Bishen Patel	6	LGY
7	Rupinder Singh	3	Hothouse Design
8	Sergio Gonzalez	5	Binnaccount
9	Rupinder Vas	1	Rootrainer
10	Bryan Revell	1	Rootrainer
11	Henri Ramos	7	Rock ICT
12	John Mortlock	2	Quattichem
13	Cameron Garnham	2	Quattichem
14	Brian Guthrie	1	Rootrainer
15	Julia Frobisher	5	Binnaccount
16	Dan McNevin	1	Rootrainer
17	Shelash O'Leary	1	Rootrainer
18	Patrick O'Malley	5	Binnaccount
19	Thirumalar Asokmani	5	Binnaccount
20	Sean O'Byrne	3	Hothouse Design
21	Brett Ling	2	Quattichem
22	Lea Cabusbusan	7	Rock ICT
23	Brian O'Driscoll	3	Hothouse Design
24	Wim Van Hoffmann	5	Binnaccount

In the Text Filters section of the menu, click on the tick box for (Select All) which will remove all of the ticks from every box. Find, then tick only the Binnaccount box, before clicking on OK. This will display only the five selected rows like this.

	A	B	C
1	Current client list		
2	Name	TaskCode	CurrentTask
8	Sergio Gonzalez	5	Binnaccount
15	Julia Frobisher	5	Binnaccount
18	Patrick O'Malley	5	Binnaccount
19	Thirumalar Asokmani	5	Binnaccount
24	Wim Van Hoffmann	5	Binnaccount

The same method can be use to select more than one company from the list. By selecting different drop-down menu options, searches can be made using different criteria in different columns. Save the spreadsheet as task20n.

20.4.2 Search using number filters

Task 20o

Open the file that you saved in Task 20m.
Select from all the data only the employees where the task code is between 3 and 6 inclusive.

Advice

To remove the AutoFilter, either click on the tick box for (Select All) or use select Clear Filter in the drop-down list.

Open the file and set the AutoFilter arrows for cells A2 to C24 as in the previous task. This time the search will be performed on the TaskCode column. Select the drop-down menu for this column using the arrow followed by Number Filters to get a sub-menu, it should look like this.

Select Custom Filter… to get the Custom AutoFilter window.

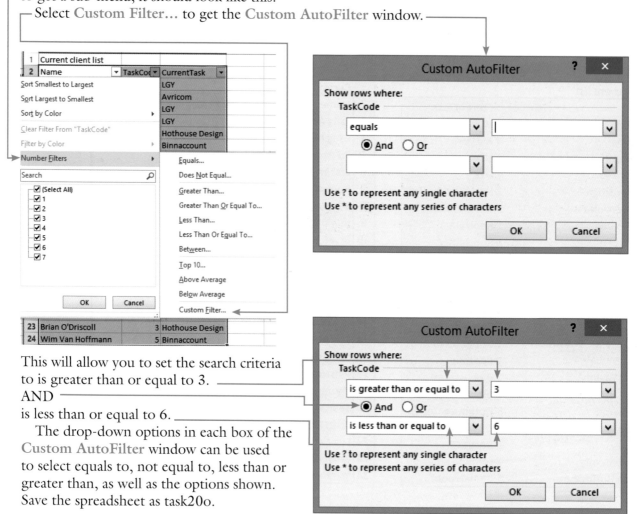

This will allow you to set the search criteria to is greater than or equal to 3.
AND
is less than or equal to 6.

The drop-down options in each box of the Custom AutoFilter window can be used to select equals to, not equal to, less than or greater than, as well as the options shown. Save the spreadsheet as task20o.

Advice

The method shown here is an alternative to selecting only the boxes for 3, 4, 5 and 6. Even though it may seem easier to click on the tick boxes for this question, you will need to use the Custom AutoFilter window when a number of options are required. The Custom AutoFilter window also allows you to select Is not equal to and to perform wildcard searches.

20.4.3 Search using more than one criteria

Task 20p

Open the file that you saved in Task 20m.
Select from the data all the employees who are currently working on jobs for Quattichem or Hothouse Design, except John Mortlock and Sean O'Byrne.

Open the file and set the **AutoFilter** arrows for cells A2 to C24 as in the previous task. This time the search will be performed on both the Name and CurrentTask columns. Select the drop-down arrow for the Name column, **Text Filters** and then select **Does not equal** from the sub-menu. This opens the **Custom AutoFilter** window; enter the initial letter 'J' in the right box (this speeds up the search). When you click on the arrow for the drop-down list it will show you all the Names starting with 'J', so select 'John Mortlock' from the list.

Select the AND operator and repeat the process for Sean O'Byrne, selecting **Does not equal** in the left box and typing 'S' to find Sean O'Byrne, selecting his name from the list in the right box. Click on OK.

Select the search arrow for the CurrentTask column. Select from this menu only the two tick boxes for 'Hothouse Design' and 'Quattichem', or select **Text Filters** and set up the OR search like this.

The results of this task should look like this.

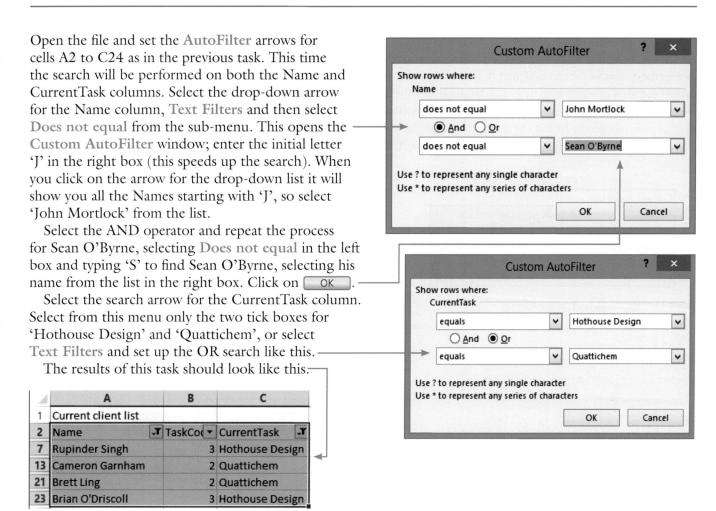

Save the spreadsheet as task20p.

Activity 20i

Open the file that you saved in Task 20h. Select from all the data:

- all the students with a tutor called Chris Scott
- all the students who will be using rooms numbered between 22 and 74 inclusive
- all the students except Kiah and Hartati with a tutor called Kate Morrissey or Mike Arnott.

20.4.4 Search using wildcards

A wildcard is a character that is used as a substitute for other characters. The * (asterisk) character is often used to show a number of characters (including 0), while the ? (question mark) is often used to show a single character. *Excel* uses these wildcard characters but **AutoFilter** also contains other features that simplify some of these searches.

Task 20q

Open the file that you saved in Task 20m.
Select from all the data only the employees who have a name that starts with the letter 'S'.

Open the file and set the **AutoFilter** arrows for the cells A2 to C24 as in the previous task. This time the search will be performed on the Name column. Click on the drop-down arrow for this column and select **Text Filters** followed by **Begins with…** from the sub-menu. This opens the **Custom AutoFilter** window. Enter the initial **S** in the right box like this and click on [OK]. You should find these four rows.

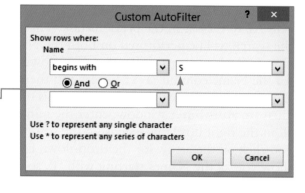

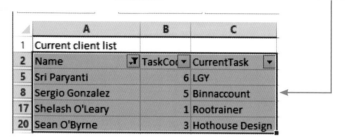

	A	B	C
1	Current client list		
2	Name	TaskCod	CurrentTask
5	Sri Paryanti	6	LGY
8	Sergio Gonzalez	5	Binnaccount
17	Shelash O'Leary	1	Rootrainer
20	Sean O'Byrne	3	Hothouse Design

Save the spreadsheet as task20q.

Task 20r

Open the file that you saved in Task 20m.
Select from all the data only the employees who have a name that ends with the letter 'a'.

This is a similar process to the previous task. Use the same process, this time selecting the **Text Filters** from the menu, then the **Ends with…** option to obtain the **Custom AutoFilter** window. Enter the letter **a** in the right box like this and click on [OK]. You should find this single row.

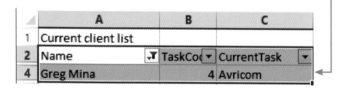

	A	B	C
1	Current client list		
2	Name	TaskCod	CurrentTask
4	Greg Mina	4	Avricom

Save the spreadsheet as task20r.

Advice

The method shown here is an alternative to selecting **Text Filters**, then **Equals** and entering **S*** before clicking on [OK].

Advice

The method shown here is an alternative to selecting **Text Filters**, then **Equals** and entering ***a** before clicking on [OK].

Task 20s

Open the file that you saved in Task 20m.
Select from all the data only the employees who have a name that contains the two characters O'.

Again, select the **Text Filters** from the drop-down menu in the Name column. This time select the **Contains…** option, enter the letter **O** followed by an apostrophe to the right box and click on [OK].

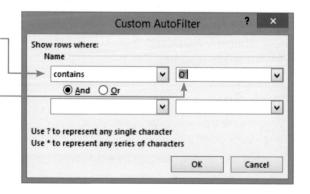

You should find these four rows.
    Save the spreadsheet as task20s.

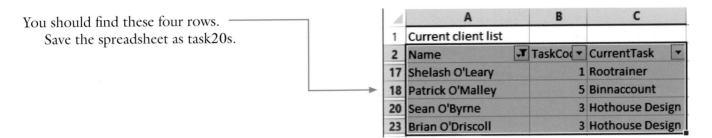

	A	B	C
1	Current client list		
2	Name	TaskCo...	CurrentTask
17	Shelash O'Leary	1	Rootrainer
18	Patrick O'Malley	5	Binnaccount
20	Sean O'Byrne	3	Hothouse Design
23	Brian O'Driscoll	3	Hothouse Design

Task 20t

Open the file that you saved in Task 20m.
Select from all the data only the employees who have a first name that has the second and third letters 'ea'.

Advice

The method shown here is an alternative to selecting Text Filters, then Equals and entering *O'* before clicking on ⟨ OK ⟩.

Using the same methods as the previous searches, select the Text Filter from the drop-down menu in the Name column. This time select the Begins with… option and add the characters ?ea to the right box before clicking on ⟨ OK ⟩.
    This tells *Excel* that the first letter can contain any character. Then there must be the letters 'ea' followed by any other characters. You should find these two rows.

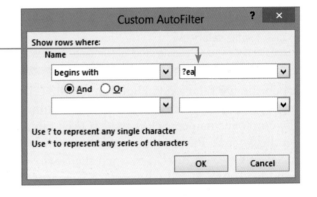

	A	B	C
1	Current client list		
2	Name	TaskCode	CurrentTask
20	Sean O'Byrne	3	Hothouse Design
22	Lea Cabusbusan	7	Rock ICT

Advice

The method shown here is an alternative to selecting Text Filters, then Equals and entering ?ea* then clicking on ⟨ OK ⟩.

Save the spreadsheet as task 20t.

Activity 20j

Open the file that you saved in Activity 20h. Select from the data:

- all the students with a forename that starts or ends with the letter 'R'
- all the students with a forename that contains the letters 'eth'
- all the students with a forename that contains the letters 'Jam' and who have a tutor who uses room 60.

20.4.5 Sort data

Before you try to sort any data, make sure that you select all of the data for each item to be sorted. One common error is to select and sort on a single column. If you were to do this, the integrity of the data would be lost. Table 20.6 gives an example showing correct and incorrect sorting on the student's name for a spreadsheet containing test results in Maths and English. The yellow shaded cells show the areas selected for the sort. Note how the results for each person have been changed when sorting without highlighting all the data.

Table 20.6 Correct and incorrect data selection for sorting

Original data		
Name	Maths	English
Sheila	72	75
Marcos	64	34
Vikram	61	44
Karla	52	75

Sorted correctly with all data selected		
Name	Maths	English
Karla	52	75
Marcos	64	34
Sheila	72	75
Vikram	61	44

Sorted with only the name column selected (this is an example of data integrity–the correct test scores no longer match the students)		
Name	Maths	English
Karla	72	75
Marcos	64	34
Sheila	61	44
Vikram	52	75

Task 20u

Open the file **salary.csv**.
Sort the data into ascending order of surname, then ascending order of forename.

Open the file salary.csv. Highlight all the cells in the range A2 to C43. Do not highlight row 1 because if you do the column headings will also be sorted within the employee names. Select the HOME tab and find the Editing section. Click on the Sort & Filter icon to obtain the drop-down menu.

Select Custom Sort… to open the Sort window. In the Sort by box select Surname from the drop-down list. This will be the primary sort for this task. Make sure that the Order box contains A to Z to sort the data into ascending order.

To add the secondary sort to this data you need to add a second level to the Sort window. Click on Add Level to add the second sort level. In the Then by box select Forename from the drop-down list. Again, make sure that the Order box contains A to Z to sort the data into ascending order. Click on OK to perform the sort.

The data should look like this.
Save the spreadsheet as task20v.

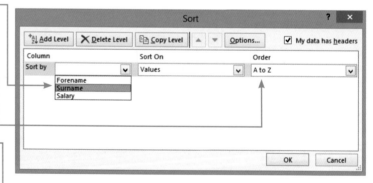

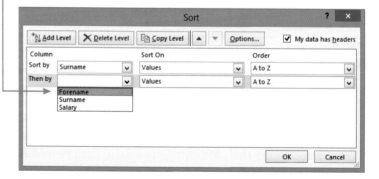

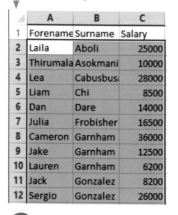

	A	B	C
1	Forename	Surname	Salary
2	Laila	Aboli	25000
3	Thirumala	Asokmani	10000
4	Lea	Cabusbus	28000
5	Liam	Chi	8500
6	Dan	Dare	14000
7	Julia	Frobisher	16500
8	Cameron	Garnham	36000
9	Jake	Garnham	12500
10	Lauren	Garnham	6200
11	Jack	Gonzalez	8200
12	Sergio	Gonzalez	26000

Advice

You can sort into descending order rather than ascending order by selecting Z to A rather than A to Z in the Order box.

Activity 20k

Open the file that you saved in Activity 20h.
Sort the data into descending order of tutor name, then ascending order of forename.

20.5 Present data

Many of the features described in this section can be applied to an individual cell, a range of cells, to one or more rows or columns, or to the entire spreadsheet. To apply the feature to the entire spreadsheet, click in the top left-hand corner of the sheet.

To select a row or rows, click on the number or numbers to the left of the row and it will select all the cells in that row.

To select a column or columns, click on the column letter or letters to select all the cells in the column or columns.

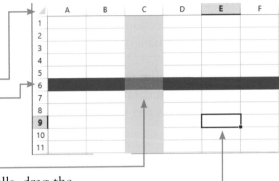

To select a single cell, click in that cell. To select a range of cells, drag the cursor to highlight a range of cells. If you need to select different cells or ranges from different parts of the sheet at the same time, hold down the <Ctrl> key while making your selections.

20.5.1 Enhance data

To enhance data, first select the data to be enhanced. All of the enhancement features are located using the HOME tab. The Font section contains icons that allow you to set the cell contents to underlined, *italic* (sloping) or **bold**.

The font size of a cell can be changed by either typing a new size in the point size box or using the drop-down menu to select a suitable size.

Cells can also be enhanced using different colours for the background of the cell. Again, highlight the area to be coloured and select the drop-down menu from the Fill Color icon. The drop-down menu looks like this.

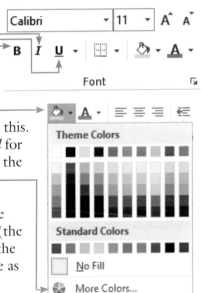

There are a number of standard colours as well as colours selected by *Excel* for the current colour schemes. If the colour that you want is not there, click on the colour palette icon.

When you are selecting colours, ensure that the foreground and background colours contrast and can be seen easily when printed. Do not use green and red to help people who are colour blind. The text colour of a cell (the font colour) can be selected in the Font section. The Font Color icon is to the right of the Fill Color icon. The drop-down menu from this icon is the same as the menu for the background colour.

If you wish to use cell shading (or other pattern fill) instead of a solid colour select the font settings arrow to open the Format cells window.

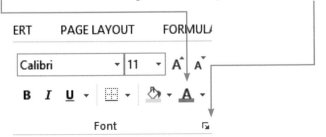

Choose the **Fill** tab along the top: this gives more options than the **Fill Color** icon. By using the **Pattern Style:** drop-down box you can select the style of shading required.

The **Format cells** window is useful for many other enhancements. After highlighting the cell/s to be formatted, selecting the **Alignment** tab will let you change the way the text fits into a cell/s, either by rotating the text direction (by dragging the red handle in the **Orientation** panel), merging cells or wrapping text within a cell.

Sometimes wrapping text in the cells will be needed to make sure that all data is fully visible without making the columns too wide. Try this for yourself, for example:

Before wrapping:

This text is far t	This is shorter.	
This text is far too long to fit in a single cell, but wraps well like this.		

After wrapping:

This text is far too long to fit in a single cell, but wraps well like this.	This is shorter.
This text is far too long to fit in a single cell, but wraps well like this.	

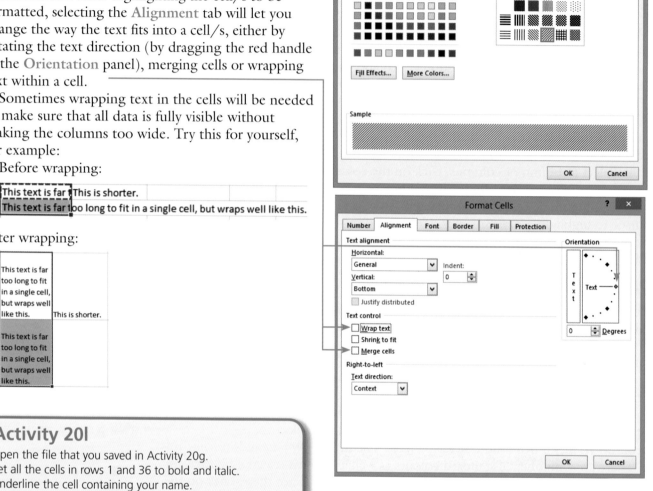

Activity 20l

Open the file that you saved in Activity 20g.
Set all the cells in rows 1 and 36 to bold and italic.
Underline the cell containing your name.
Set cells A1 to C1 to have white text on a black background.
Set the background colour for each of the cells in the range A37 to A40 to match the colour of each house.

20.5.2 Format cells

Formatting cells containing numbers changes the way a cell is displayed but does not change the values held within it.

Task 20v

Create a spreadsheet model that looks like this. Place a formula in cell C2 that multiplies the contents of cell A2 by the contents of cell B2. Format cell A2 as an integer.

	A	B	C
1	First	Second	Product
2	1.2	5	

Create the spreadsheet as shown. In cell C2 enter the formula **=A2*B2**. The spreadsheet will look like this.

	A	B	C
1	First	Second	Product
2	1.2	5	6

To format cell A2 as an integer, place the cursor in this cell and select the **HOME** tab. In the **Number** section, click on the arrow in the bottom-right corner to open the **Format Cells** window.

When this window opens, it should have the **Number** tab selected. The **Format Cells** window will allow you to format cells in different currencies, into percentages or even as dates or times.

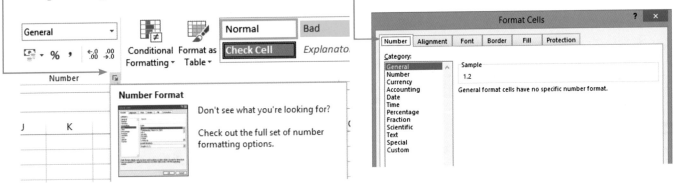

For this task, you need to format this cell as a number. Select the **Number** option in the **Category:** section. Change the cell formatting to 0 **Decimal places:** so that the window looks like this.

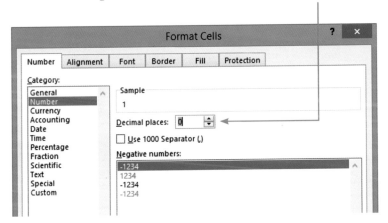

	A	B	C
1	First	Second	Product
2	1	5	6

Click on **OK** to set the formatting. The spreadsheet will now look like this.

If you compare the two views of the spreadsheet, you can see that cell A2 has changed. The contents still remains 1.2 but in the second view the answer for the product appears to be incorrect.

Use the **INT** or **ROUND** function to force a cell to contain whole numbers. Formatting a cell does not always appear to give the correct answer.

Original

	A	B	C
1	First	Second	Product
2	1.2	5	6

Formatted

	A	B	C
1	First	Second	Product
2	1	5	6

Task 20w

Open the file **costs.csv**.

Format cells A1, D1, D3 and G3 so that the font is bold and 14 point.

Format all numeric cells in row 2 into their respective currencies to 3 decimal places.

Format all numeric cells in columns C and D into pounds sterling with 2 decimal places.

Format the cells E5 to E15 into Euros with 2 decimal places.

Format the cells F5 to F15 into Japanese Yen with 0 decimal places.

Format all cells between G5 and G15 into percentage values with no decimal places.

Open the file costs.csv. Click in cell A1. Select the HOME tab, find the Font section, then use the drop-down list to change the size of this cell to 14 point.

Click the mouse on the Bold icon to set this cell to bold.

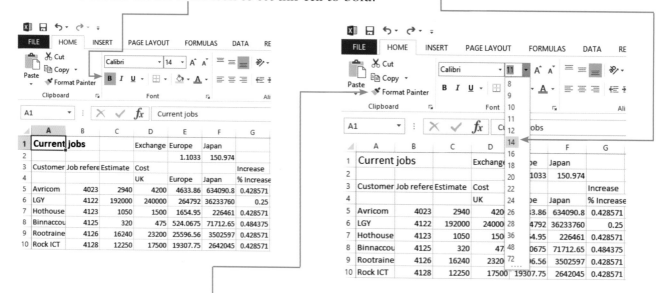

Click on the Format Painter icon and then click in cell D1. Click on the Format Painter again and then click in cell D3, then Format Painter again and click in cell G3. This process should copy the formatting from cell A1 into these other three cells.

Move the cursor into cell E2. In the Number section, click on the arrow in the bottom-right corner to open the Format Cells window in the Number tab. In the Category: section, select Currency.

Set the number of decimal places to 3. Although this is not the correct number of decimal places for Euro, it was specified in the task.

In the Symbol: section, select an appropriate Euro format from the list. You may need to scroll down the list of available currencies to find it. The Sample area will show you what the formatting of the cell will look like when you click on ⬚OK⬚. When you have checked this formatting, click on ⬚OK⬚.

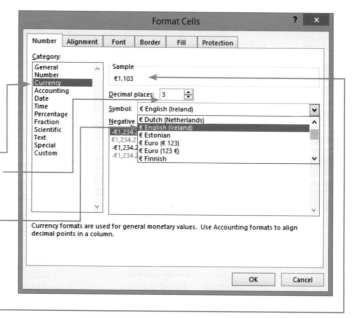

Repeat this process for cell F2, but this time selecting Japanese Yen. Some currencies, such as the Japanese Yen, have no decimal places (so would normally need to be formatted to zero decimal places) but in this task you were told to set this cell to 3 decimal places. The Format Cells window should look like this. ——————

Click on [OK].

To format all the numeric cells in columns C and D, highlight all cells in the range C5 to D15. Then open the Format Cells window and set the Category: to Currency, the number of Decimal places: to 2 and the Symbol: to pounds sterling (£). Repeat this process for cells E5 to E15, selecting Euro with 2 decimal places, and for cells F5 to F15 with Japanese Yen set to no decimal places (which are the appropriate formats for both of these currencies).

To format all cells between G5 and G15 into percentage values, highlight this range then, in the Format Cells window, set the Category: to Percentage. Set the number of Decimal places: to 0. Resize columns as necessary. The finished spreadsheet should look like this. ——————

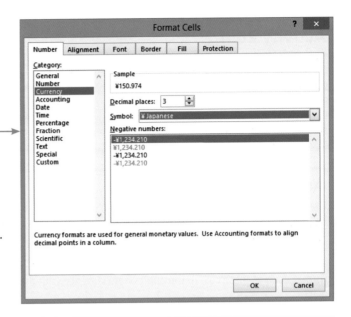

Advice

If the currency symbol that you are looking for (for example, ¥) does not appear in the drop-down list, there are a number of text options available. In this case you can select JPY, which is the international standard code for Japanese Yen.

	A	B	C	D	E	F	G
1	**Current jobs**			**Exchange**	Europe	Japan	
2					€1.103	¥150.974	
3	Customer	Job reference	Estimate	**Cost**			**Increase**
4				UK	Europe	Japan	% Increase
5	Avricom	4023	£2,940.00	£4,200.00	€4,633.86	¥634,091	43%
6	LGY	4122	£192,000.00	£240,000.00	€264,792.00	¥36,233,760	25%
7	Hothouse Design	4123	£1,050.00	£1,500.00	€1,654.95	¥226,461	43%
8	Binnaccount	4125	£320.00	£475.00	€524.07	¥71,713	48%
9	Rootrainer	4126	£16,240.00	£23,200.00	€25,596.56	¥3,502,597	43%
10	Rock ICT	4128	£12,250.00	£17,500.00	€19,307.75	¥2,642,045	43%
11	Quattichem	4129	£1,400.00	£2,000.00	€2,206.60	¥301,948	43%
12	LGY	4130	£10,800.00	£12,000.00	€13,239.60	¥1,811,688	11%
13	Hothouse Design	4131	£720.00	£720.00	€794.38	¥108,701	0%
14	Binnaccount	4132	£1,680.00	£2,400.00	€2,647.92	¥362,338	43%
15	Hothouse Design	4133	£4,500.00	£5,000.00	€5,516.50	¥754,870	11%

Advice

An alternative to this for percentage values with no decimal places is to highlight the cell/s, select the HOME tab and click the Percent Style icon in the Number section.

Activity 20m

Open the file that you saved in Activity 20g.
In cell A41, place the label 'Total'.
In cell B41, add the total number of times clubs were attended by people in all four houses.
In cell C36, add the label 'Percent'.
In cells C37 to C40, calculate, using absolute and relative referencing, the percentage of students in each house. Format these cells as a percentage with 1 decimal place.

Activity 20n

Open the file **items.csv**.
Format cells A4 and A5 so that the font is bold, italic and 20 point.
In cells C3 to F3, place current exchange rates for each currency shown. Use the internet (or exchange rates supplied by your teacher) to do this. Do not format these cells as currency.
For each cell in the range C8 to F22, calculate the price of each item in the correct currency. Format each of these cells in the appropriate currency with the appropriate number of decimal places.

20.5.3 Adjust rows and columns

Earlier you learnt how to expand column widths using the drag handle to make sure that all data in the spreadsheet is visible. Row heights can be adjusted in exactly the same way.

The settings for row heights can also be changed by right clicking the mouse button on the row number on the left to obtain this drop-down menu.

The row can be hidden from view by selecting the Hide option, or can have a different row height set using the Row Height... option.

This option opens the Row Height window, where you can adjust the height setting before clicking on OK.

The column width can be hidden or adjusted in a similar way. To get the drop-down menu click the right mouse button on the column heading at the top of the column.

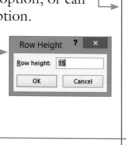

Advice

To unhide a row or column, select the rows/columns on both sides of the hidden one/s. Right mouse click on the selection and choose the Unhide option.

20.5.4 Conditional formatting

Conditional formatting is used to change the display format (usually the font or background colour within a cell), depending on the contents of the cell. There are many different methods for completing this: using rules that you apply (rather than the spreadsheet's default settings) is the recommended method and will enable you to attempt anything that may be asked at IGCSE level.

Task 20x

Open the file that you saved in Task 20k. Format the cells in column D so that:

- if they contain the text 'Not experienced' they are coloured with a red background
- if they contain 'Experienced' add an amber (orange) background
- if they contain 'Very experienced' add a green background.

Apply appropriate foreground colours to this text.

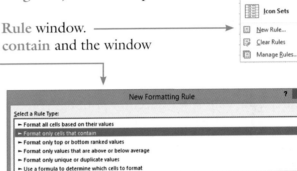

Open the file task 20k.

In previous tasks we have highlighted the range of cells to be formatted (in this case D3 to D21). This question has asked for column D, so click on the column heading (the letter D) to highlight the entire column. Select the HOME tab, find the Styles section, then select the Conditional Formatting icon, which will open this drop-down menu.

Choose New Rule... to open the New Formatting Rule window.

Select the second option for Format only cells that contain and the window will change to look like this.

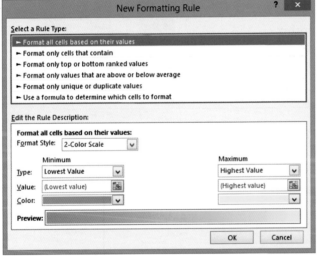

Using the drop-down box on the left, choose Specific text (as the cells all contain labels). In the right dialogue box enter the text 'Not experienced'. Click on the Format button, select the Fill tab and a red background colour, then OK, then the Font tab and an appropriate foreground colour, then OK. You can see what the font will look like at each stage. In this case we have chosen a white font as this gives good contrast.

When you are happy that this looks good, click OK. Repeat this process for the other two items of text. Be careful with the Experienced one – it must start with 'Experienced', not just contain it, or all cells will become amber. This section of the completed sheet looks like this.

20.5.5 Adjust page orientation

You may need to change the page orientation from portrait to landscape, especially when displaying the formulae that you have used. To change this select the PAGE LAYOUT tab and find the Page Setup section. Click on the Orientation icon, then select either Portrait or Landscape from the drop-down menu.

> ### Activity 20o
>
> Open the file that you saved in Activity 20m.
> Add coloured backgrounds to show the colour of each house that are dependent on the cell contents. Apply appropriate foreground colours to this text.
> Print your spreadsheet showing the values. Take screen shot evidence of the rules used to apply this formatting.

Project 153			
Name	Job	Years experience	Category
Laila Aboli	Programmer	3	Not experienced
Greg Mina	Programmer	2	Not experienced
Sri Paryanti	Analyst	12	Very experienced
Bishen Patel	Sales	5	Experienced
Rupinder Singh	Engineer	7	Experienced
Sergio Gonzalez	Programmer	5	Experienced
Rupinder Vas	Sales	6	Experienced
Henri Ramos	Sales	10	Very experienced
John Mortlock	Programmer	14	Very experienced
Cameron Garnham	Analyst	7	Experienced
Brian Guthrie	Director	3	Not experienced
Julia Frobisher	Engineer	6	Experienced
Dan McNevin	Programmer	9	Experienced
Patrick O'Malley	Engineer	11	Very experienced
Thirumalar Asokmani	Sales	10	Very experienced
Sean O'Byrne	Programmer	2	Not experienced
Lea Cabusbusan	Programmer	1	Not experienced
Brian O'Driscoll	Programmer	0.2	Not experienced
Wim Van Hoffmann	Engineer	2	Not experienced

20.5.6 Prepare to print

When preparing your spreadsheet for printing, you can adjust the layout of the spreadsheet on the printed page/s before you print. To do this, select the FILE tab and then Print from the drop-down menu. The print preview will be shown to you along with options to change the Page Setup and Printer Properties.

If you need to make adjustments most can be made using the Page Setup link, which allows you to change the number of pages wide or tall in the

Advice

This window can be used as another way of changing the page orientation.

printout. Use the **Fit to:** radio button in the Scaling section and select the number of pages.

If you set a printout to a single page wide, ensure that that all the formulae/values and labels can be seen clearly. If the font size is so small that it is not clearly readable, you may not be awarded the marks for that section. When you have changed the page settings, click on ⬚OK⬚. If the question asks for two pages wide and does not say how many pages tall, just set the width and clear the tall box. Do not set this manually to one as, if this is a formulae print, the font is likely to be so small it would be unreadable.

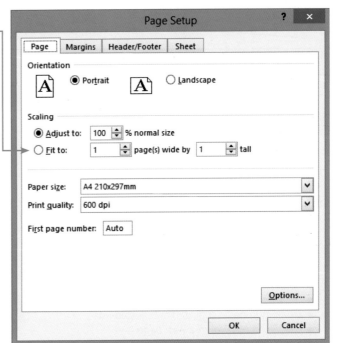

Save and print data

Save your work regularly. As recommended before, it is a good idea to save different versions, at all times each with a different version number. If you make a mistake and corrupt a file, you can always go back and redo a small part of the task without losing too much time.

When printing your spreadsheets, make sure that you have adjusted all column widths and row heights to ensure that your printouts show all:

- labels in full
- formulae in full
- data in full.

Don't forget to submit printouts showing the formulae used; check that you have worked through the section on displaying formulae near the start of the chapter. You can use screen shots to show how you achieved your results. Make sure that all printouts contain your name, candidate and Centre number.

To print, select the FILE tab followed by Print from the menu. Check your work to make sure that all the all data/formulae are fully visible before you select the Print button.

You may be required to export your spreadsheet data into different formats. In *Excel*, this is done by selecting the FILE tab followed by Export. If you select Change File Type it will allow you to export the data into common text formats like .txt (text format) and .csv (comma separated values). Although other export features exist, these should be sufficient.

21 Website authoring

In this chapter you will learn how to:

- describe the three layers used in web page creation
- use the content layer to create the web page structure
- use the presentation layer to define styles
- define and use HTML tags within the content layer
- use a text editor to create the content layer of a web page
- annotate your markup with comments
- display your web pages in a web browser
- format text using predefined styles
- design and create page layout using tables
- create, resize and format tables, including headers, footers and body sections
- embed CSS styles into an HTML page
- insert, place and manipulate an image within a web page
- manipulate an image in a graphics package
- insert animated images, videos and audio files into a web page
- apply colour to text and backgrounds
- use colour names and hexadecimal colour codes
- create numbered, bulleted and nested lists
- use hyperlinks within a web page
- use hyperlinks to external pages and to send email
- open a web page in a new window
- create a hyperlink from an image
- describe what is meant by the term cascading stylesheet
- describe the hierarchy of multiple attached stylesheets and in-line styles
- define and use CSS elements within the presentation layer
- create, edit and attach a cascading stylesheet
- add comments to a stylesheet
- format, align and enhance text using the presentation layer
- create styles using specific and generic font families
- set font sizes using absolute and relative values
- set background colours and images using the presentation layer
- use classes within a stylesheet
- create table formatting using the presentation layer
- upload and publish the content of a website using ftp
- create a test plan to test a website
- test that web page elements work when published
- test navigation within/from a web page using a test plan
- justify your test plan choices.

For this chapter you will need these source files from the CD:

- brick.css
- brick.png
- bricknblocktopia.htm
- class1.css
- colourcodes.htm
- htmltips.htm
- ptct.jpg
- remora.htm
- remora.jpg
- style1.css
- style2.css
- subscript.htm
- sun.png
- task21ai.png
- turtle.jpg
- turtlelogo.gif
- wall.png
- webpage1.htm
- webpage2.htm
- webpage3.htm
- webpage4.htm
- webpage5.htm
- webpage6.htm
- webpage7.htm
- whale.mp3
- wreck.mp4.

21.1 Web development layers

21.1.1 What is a website?

A **website** is a collection of individual but related **web pages** that are often stored together and hosted by a web server. Web pages can include different objects such as text, sound, video and still images. A web page is created using three layers:

- the **content layer** (sometimes called the structure layer)
- the **presentation layer**
- the behaviour layer (which often involves script languages, but we will not cover the practical programming of this at Cambridge IGCSE level).

You develop the content/structure layer of your web pages in a language called **HTML** and the presentation layer of your web pages in **CSS**.

21.1.2 What is HTML?

HTML is an abbreviation for HyperText Markup Language. It is a text-based language used to develop the content layer of websites. Files are written in HTML using a simple **text editor** (or **web-authoring package** such as *Macromedia Dreamweaver*, *Microsoft Visual Studio* or *Expression Web*). Files are written in text format and are usually saved with an .htm (or .html) file extension. These files are recognised by **web browsers** such as *Microsoft Internet Explorer*, *Google Chrome* or *Mozilla Firefox* as web pages. You are going to develop your own web pages using a simple **text editor**.

21.1.3 What is CSS?

CSS is an abbreviation for cascading stylesheet, a different text-based language. Styles are created and added to web pages. CSS can be written (embedded) into HTML but it is usually created in a separate file saved with a .css file extension. The stylesheet is then attached to a web page. Many websites have one or more common stylesheets attached to every page in the website. This makes all the pages have a similar appearance, with the same font styles and colour schemes, etc. You will also develop your own stylesheets using a simple **text editor**.

21.1.4 Getting started

A good technique for working on web pages is to tile four windows on the screen at the same time: this means to fit them side by side like tiles. Whenever you do any work in HTML and CSS, it is recommended that you open two copies of a text editor, a web browser and a list of your files in their storage folder.

Move the cursor to the top right corner of the screen to select the Windows 8 charm bar.

Advice

To select the charm bar with the keyboard, press the **Windows** and **C** keys together.

Select the **Search** charm then select the **Everywhere** search. Enter the text **Notepad** into the search box. The result should look similar to this.

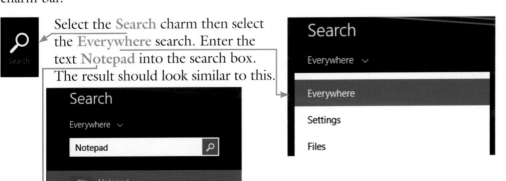

Click the right mouse button on the Notepad icon to open the App bar, which appears at the bottom of the screen and looks similar to this.

Click on Open in new window. Place this window in the top left of the screen. Resize the window so that it fills about a quarter of the screen. Open a second copy of *Notepad* using this method. Place and resize it to fill the lower left quarter of the screen. These text editors will be where we create the content layer (the HTML markup) and the presentation layer (the Cascading Stylesheet) for each web page.

Open the File Explorer window by pressing the Windows and E keys together. Place the File Explorer window in the lower right corner of the screen and resize it to fill about half the width and a quarter of the height of the screen.

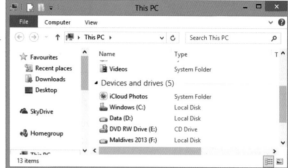

Click the left mouse button to select the drive that you will use as your work area. Then click on the New folder icon and name this folder Chapter 21.

The location of this will depend on the structure of the system you are using. Go into this folder and create new subfolders for each task in this chapter. Call these folders Task21a to Task21z, and Task21aa to Task21am. You must save all the files for each task in this chapter in the correct folder.

Make sure you are in the folder Task21a. This is where all the work from the first part of this chapter will be stored. The window should look similar to this.

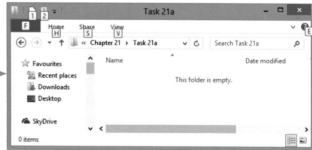

Open your web browser and resize this window so that it fills the remaining area of your screen. Make sure that the windows fit together and do not overlap. The screen will look similar to this.

Although many people refer to HTML as a programming language, that is not strictly true. It is a markup language that uses a set of markup tags to describe a web page to the browser. HTML tags are shown using angle brackets around them like this:

```
<html>
```

The angle brackets tell the browser that this is a markup tag and not text to be placed on the web page. The browser does not display the HTML tags but uses them to display the content of the page. Most HTML commands have two tags: one to open the command and one to close it. Each tag has a pair of angle brackets around it.

Web browser – webpage viewed in here

HTML created in here for the content layer

CSS created in here for the presentation layer

File Explorer – files saved in here

21.2 Create a web page

All HTML web pages start with a <!DOCTYPE html> declaration and, although it has angle brackets, it is not an HTML tag. This is always the first thing in your markup. The <!DOCTYPE html> declaration is an instruction to the browser to tell it that the page is written in HTML rather than another markup language. The first tag that will usually appear in any web page will be <html>. This tag tells the browser that the markup following this tag will be written in hypertext markup language. The tag </html> tells the browser that this is the end

Advice

Note that **all** text in HTML tags should be in lower case.

of this markup language and appears at the end of the markup. The forward slash shows that it is a closing tag. All other HTML tags will appear between these tags.

Each web page will have two clearly defined sections: the **head** and the **body**. The head section starts with <head> and closes with </head> and objects between these tags are not usually displayed by the web browser. Only a few tags are universally accepted within the head section of a web page; these are: <base>, <link>, <meta>, <title>, <style> and <script>. The head section should always contain a title. This is the name displayed in the browser toolbar. It is the page title used if a page is added to your 'favorites' in your browser and is the title displayed in search engine results. The body section starts with <body> and closes with </body> and objects between these tags will be displayed in the web page. The basic structure of any web page should therefore include these tags.

Insert tags for the head section here. ———

Insert objects to be displayed by the browser in the body section here. ———

```
<!DOCTYPE html>
<html>
  <head>
    <title>Web page name</title>
  </head>
  <body>
  </body>
<!-- This is a comment -->
</html>
```

21.2.1 Add comments to your HTML markup

Comments can be added to your markup if there are notes that you wish to make but not display on the web page. This is very useful for making sure that your name, Centre number and candidate number are on every web page, even if you are not instructed to display them. Comments start with <!-- and end with -->. As the comments do not affect the markup, they can be placed before or after any tags. Comments look similar to this. ———

21.2.2 The use of preset HTML styles in the content layer

Text is organised into paragraphs, with the paragraph style applied. Headings usually have different styles to the paragraph style. All text added to a web page should have a tag telling the browser what the text style should look like. There are a number of predefined styles available for use in a web page. The normal paragraph style is obtained using <p> and ended with </p>. Likewise, six heading styles are available and are defined with the style names <h1> to <h6>. Each item in a bulleted or numbered list can be defined with the <li> tag and finished with </li>; there are more details on lists later in this chapter.

Task 21a
Create and save a new web page showing paragraph and heading styles.

Click the cursor into the top text editor. Type the following markup into the editor, replacing *MY NAME HERE* with your name. Always remember to add your name, Centre number and candidate number to all of your printouts.

```
<!DOCTYPE html>
<html>
  <!-- Markup created on 06/01/2015 -->
  <head>
    <title>Task 21a</title>
  </head>
  <body>
    <p>My first web page by MY NAME HERE</p>
    <h1>This is style h1, the largest heading style</h1>
    <h2>This is style h2</h2>
    <h3>This is style h3</h3>
```

Advice

It is essential that the text is typed exactly as shown here. One typing error may cause the web page not to function as expected.

Advice

It is acceptable to use capital letters in the text that is displayed on the page, but **not** in the HTML tags.

```
    <h4>This is style h4</h4>
    <h5>This is style h5</h5>
    <h6>This is style h6, the smallest heading style</h6>
    <p>This is style p, the paragraph style</p>
  </body>
</html>
```

When this has been entered and carefully verified (by checking this original document with your typed copy), you must select **File** followed by **Save As…**, which will open the **Save As** window.

Click on the folder names until you find the Task21a folder created earlier in this chapter.

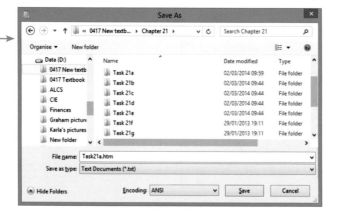

You need to enter a filename for the web page. This filename **must** be saved with an .htm extension. If you do not use a .htm file extension, this will operate as a text file rather than as a web page. Enter the filename task21a.htm and click on Save . The file should appear in the **File Explorer** window and may look similar to this. If the file cannot be seen, move into the Task21a folder.

Make sure that the file displays the browser (usually the, 🅮 🅮 or 🅮) symbol to show that this is a web page and not a text document with a 🗎 symbol. The text document symbol only appears if you forget to add the .htm extension to the filename.

Select the file task21a.htm from the **File Explorer** window and drag this file (holding the left mouse button down) into the browser window. The screen should now look similar to this.

The browser view now contains your first web page.

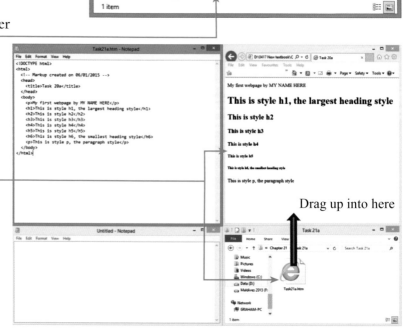

21.2.3 Open existing web pages and enhance text

To open an existing web page in both the text editor and the web browser you must find the web page in the File Explorer window. For all web page files, it is advisable to copy the files into a subfolder of your HTML directory before starting.

Task 21b

Open the file **webpage1.htm** and view this web page in both the text editor and browser.

Improve this web page by emboldening the word 'bold', setting the word 'italic' to an italic font, setting the '3' in x3 as superscript and setting the '2' in H₂ as subscript.

Copy the file **webpage1.htm** into your Task21b folder. Drag this file from the File Explorer window into the top text editor. Drag another copy of this file from the File Explorer window into your browser.

The screen should look like this.

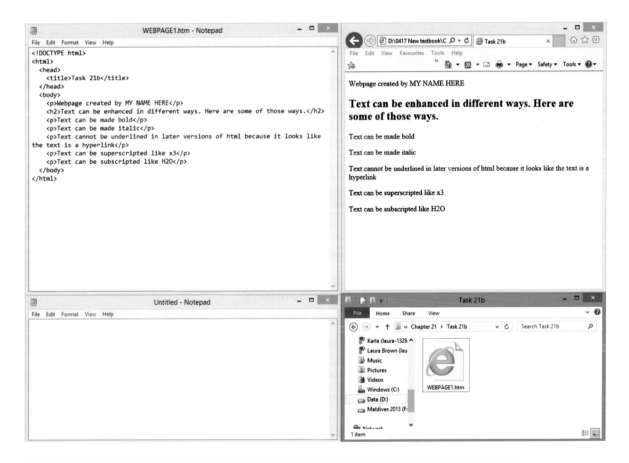

Move the cursor into the text editor window and make the following changes to the markup:

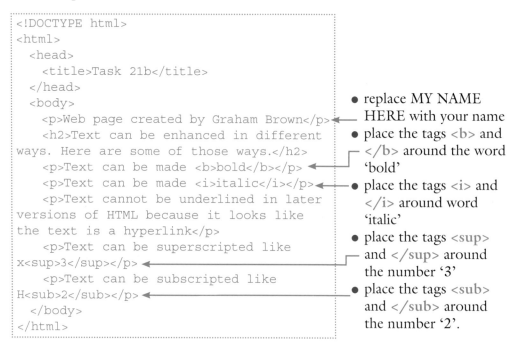

```
<!DOCTYPE html>
<html>
  <head>
    <title>Task 21b</title>
  </head>
  <body>
    <p>Web page created by Graham Brown</p>
    <h2>Text can be enhanced in different
ways. Here are some of those ways.</h2>
    <p>Text can be made <b>bold</b></p>
    <p>Text can be made <i>italic</i></p>
    <p>Text cannot be underlined in later
versions of HTML because it looks like
the text is a hyperlink</p>
    <p>Text can be superscripted like
x<sup>3</sup></p>
    <p>Text can be subscripted like
H<sub>2</sub></p>
  </body>
</html>
```

- replace MY NAME HERE with your name
- place the tags <b> and </b> around the word 'bold'
- place the tags <i> and </i> around word 'italic'
- place the tags ^{and} around the number '3'
- place the tags _{and} around the number '2'.

When you have made all these changes to the web page, save the page by selecting the text editor, followed by **File, Save As…**, selecting the **Task21b** folder and entering the filename **task21b.htm** before clicking on [Save]. Test the web page works by dragging this new filename from the **Documents** window into the browser window.

The new browser view should look like this.

Advice

If you prefer you can click the mouse on the browser window and then press the function key <f5> to refresh the browser view each time you have saved the file.

21.2.4 Print web pages

From time to time, you will be required to print different views of your web pages. You must ensure that your name is included on the web page before it is sent to the printer, in whichever view is specified. Printing the HTML view is often required. Even if you are using a WYSIWYG (what you see is what you get) package, like *Macromedia Dreamweaver* or *Microsoft Expression Web*, you will need to open the web page in a text editor to print the HTML.

If you are printing from a web browser, make sure that your name and candidate details are fully visible on the printout. If you are using a WYSIWYG package, make sure that you test the web page in a browser and not just within the package. Some products will display what appears to be the browser view but it is only a development tool and does not

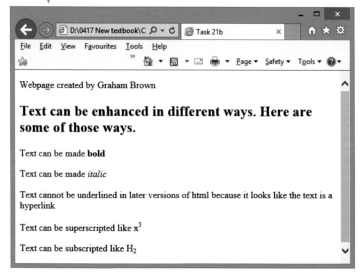

necessarily display the page as it will be seen. Use screen shots of your pages, taken using the <Print Screen> button on your keyboard, to copy the screen contents into the clipboard. Then paste the clipboard into another package (often a word processor) to present evidence of your work.

Activity 21a

Open the file **subscript.htm** and view this web page in both the text editor and browser.

Replace the text MY NAME HERE with your name. Improve this website by emboldening the word 'emboldened', setting the word 'italic' to an italic font, and the word 'underlined' to an underlined font.

Set the '2' in 10 m^2 and the '3' in 500 cm^3 as superscript, and set the '2' in CO_2 as subscript. Set the text 'Enhancing Text' into style h1. Print your web page as HTML and as it is viewed in your browser.

21.2.5 Tables in the content layer

Tables are used to create the basic structure of many web pages. They are used to organise page layout and are often used in web pages even though the borders may not be visible. If you need to create a table within a web page, it is always worth planning it on paper before starting to create the markup.

Advice

This planning stage will often be given to you in the question.

Task 21c

Create a new web page that looks like this and has the caption 'Colours':

Red	36%
Green	23%
Blue	41%

Advice

It will be much easier to use **WYSIWYG** software to create your tables. This section is designed to ensure that you understand how to create and edit tables. You will need to understand the markup used to define tables. To begin with, this may be difficult for you if you decide to use a WYSIWYG package to develop your tables.

Basic table structure

Tables in HTML always start with a <table> tag and end with </table>. Start by adding these tags in the body section of the markup. Make sure you replace the text 'your name' with your own name. It should look similar to this.

Everything between these tags will be included in the table, except for the caption. This is added using the <caption> and </caption> tags, which allows you to display a caption (usually centre aligned) above the table. If a caption is used it **must** be the first HTML tag after the <table> tag.

Each table is split into rows.

Row 1	Red	36%
Row 2	Green	23%
Row 3	Blue	41%

```
<!DOCTYPE html>
<html>
    <!-- Task 21c by your name -->
  <head>
    <title>Task 21c</title>
  </head>
  <body>
    <table>
    </table>
  </body>
</html>
```

```
<body>
  <table>
    <caption>Colours</caption>
    <tr>
    </tr>
    <tr>
    </tr>
    <tr>
    </tr>
  </table>
</body>
```

For this task, the table you need to create has three table rows. The tag for a table row is <tr>. Create the three blank rows between the caption and the end of the table like this.

Each table row will contain two cells of table data. The tag for table data is <td>. A row can have one or more <td> tags. Between each <tr> and </tr> tag, place start table data <td> and end table data </td> tags like this. This table row has two pieces of table data. A table cell can contain text, images, other tables, lists, paragraphs, forms, horizontal rules, and so on.

Advice

It is sometimes quicker to create one complete table row first with the table data cells included, then copy this row a number of times using copy and paste.

The data can now be added to each cell like this. Your table will look similar to this.

Colours

Red   36%

Green 23%

Blue   41%

Table borders

This table has been created but does not have a visible border. The word 'border' is an attribute. To show the table gridlines you must add a border **attribute** with a value of "1". Attributes should be in lower case and attribute values should always be enclosed in quotes. Change your markup like this.

```
<body>
  <table border="1">
    <caption>Colours</caption>
```

The only valid border values in HTML5 are "1" and "":

- "1" makes the border visible
- "" hides the table border, yet allows the table to control the structure of the page.

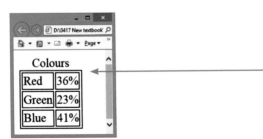

Save this web page as task21c.htm in your Task21c folder.

```
<body>
<table>
  <caption>Colours</caption>
  <tr>
    <td>
    </td>
    <td>
    </td>
  </tr>
  <tr>
    <td>
    </td>
    <td>
    </td>
  </tr>
  <tr>
    <td>
    </td>
    <td>
    </td>
  </tr>
</table>
</body>
```

```
<body>
  <table>
    <caption>Colours</caption>
    <tr>
      <td>Red
      </td>
      <td>36%
      </td>
    </tr>
    <tr>
      <td>Green
      </td>
      <td>23%
      </td>
    </tr>
    <tr>
      <td>Blue
      </td>
      <td>41%
      </td>
    </tr>
  </table>
</body>
```

Advice

This is different from earlier versions of HTML where "0" hid the border.

Headers and footers in tables

Tables can have three sections: a header, a body section and a footer. These are defined using the <thead>, <tbody> and <tfoot> tags, and closed with </thead>, </tbody> and </tfoot> respectively. Notice how these all begin with t (for table).

Task 21d

Create a new web page that looks like this and has the caption 'Fruit sales'.

Fruit	Price
Apple	$1230
Orange	$780
Pear	$240
Banana	$4235
Lemon	$75
Total	$6560

To create this web page you need to first create the open table and close table tags within the body section of the markup. Place the caption tags between these in the same way that you did when you completed Task 21c. The initial markup for this section should look like this. ——————————→

```
<body>
  <table border="1">
    <caption>Fruit sales</caption>
  </table>
</body>
```

Before continuing with the markup it is worth planning the table using a hand-drawn sketch similar to this.

This will help you work out the structure needed for the markup. For this table, you will need three sections to the table.

These three sections need creating next within the markup. The header section is created using the table head tags, with <thead> to start the section and </thead> to finish the section. The footer section uses the tags <tfoot> and </tfoot>, and the body is defined with <tbody> and </tbody>. In HTML you must define the table header, footer and then body (in that order) if all three sections are to be included. Create the three sections within the table of your markup like this. ————————→

Within each section add the correct number of table rows, using the notes you made on your sketch to help you.

You can add the table data sections to the footer and body of the table using the tags <td> and </td>. Do not use these tags in the table header. At each stage, save your web page and check that the markup that you have written gives you the results that you expected.

In the table header, create heading cells (which are bold and centre aligned) using the tags <th> and </th> rather than the table data tags. These will set the column headings in heading style. Heading cells can be used inside the table body and table

Caption

Fruit	Price
Apple	$1230
Orange	$780
Pear	$240
Banana	$4235
Lemon	$75
Total	$6560

Table Header — 1 table row with 2 table header cells.

Table Body — 5 table rows, each with 2 cells of table data.

Table Footer — 1 table row with 2 cells of table data.

```
<body>
  <table border="1">
    <caption>Fruit sales</caption>
    <thead>
    </thead>
    <tfoot>
    </tfoot>
    <tbody>
    </tbody>
  </table>
</body>
```

footer sections and are useful in the left column of a table if row headings are required. Don't forget to replace the text 'your name' with your own name.

Place the contents (in this case text) of the header section in the header cells and place the contents of the body and footer sections in the relevant cells. The finished markup and resulting web page should look like this. ⟶

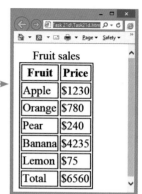

```
<!DOCTYPE html>
<html>
<!-- Task 21d by your name -->
<head>
  <title>Task 21d</title>
</head>
<body>
  <table border="1">
    <caption>Fruit sales</caption>
    <thead>
      <tr>
        <th>Fruit</th>
        <th>Price</th>
      </tr>
    </thead>
    <tfoot>
      <tr>
        <td>Total</td>
        <td>$6560</td>
      </tr>
    </tfoot>
    <tbody>
      <tr>
        <td>Apple</td>
        <td>$1230</td>
      </tr>
      <tr>
        <td>Orange</td>
        <td>$780</td>
      </tr>
      <tr>
        <td>Pear</td>
        <td>$240</td>
      </tr>
      <tr>
        <td>Banana</td>
        <td>$4235</td>
      </tr>
      <tr>
        <td>Lemon</td>
        <td>$75</td>
      </tr>
    </tbody>
  </table>
</body>
</html>
```

Save this web page as task21d.htm in your Task21d folder. Save copies of this page as task21e.htm in your Task21e folder, as task21f.htm in your Task21f folder, and as task21i.htm in your Task21i folder.

Activity 21b

Create a new web page with a table that looks like this and has the caption 'Hours of sunshine last week'. Make sure the top row of the table is in the header section and the bottom row is in the footer section. Print your web page as HTML and as it is viewed in your browser.

Day	Hours
Monday	6
Tuesday	4.5
Wednesday	8
Thursday	7
Friday	3.5
Saturday	5
Sunday	6
Weekly total	40

21.2.6 Use embedded CSS in HTML

Although this section introduces the use of styles into your web page, this will not be covered in detail until Section 21.3.

Styles can be applied to tables and other HTML elements by placing CSS instructions in a **style** attribute within the HTML tag. This is called embedded CSS.

Task 21e

Open the file task21e.htm. Set the table to be 400 pixels wide and each row to be 50 pixels high. Set the left column to be 280 pixels wide.

Resize a table

Open the file task21e.htm. You have seen that each table grows to fit the data in each cell. In order to avoid this, each table, as well as each row/column within the table, can be set to a fixed width or a width related to the size of the browser window. For this task an attribute is added to either the table <table>, table row <tr> or table data <td> tags. This attribute is an embedded CSS **style** attribute. In the **table** tag add a second attribute named **style** with the embedded CSS property value **width:400px**, like this.

```
<body>
  <table border="1" style="width:400px">
    <caption>Fruit sales</caption>
    <thead>
```

The width of the table will now be fixed to 400 pixels. If the browser window is resized, this table size will not change; if the window is made smaller than 400 pixels the browser will display scroll bars.

Advice

Use px for pixels and **do not** put a space between the digits and px.

Advice

The syntax for CSS elements is the property name, colon, the value to be applied, e.g., name:value

If more than one property is to be applied these are separated with semi-colons, e.g, name1:value; name2:value

Use similar style attributes in all seven table row tags to set the row height like this. ─

In the first table header cell add a similar attribute to set the CSS **width** property to 280 pixels like this. ─

```
<thead>
  <tr style="height:50px">
    <th style="width:280px">Fruit</th>
    <th>Price</th>
```

377

These two style attributes only need applying once; all other cells in the row/column will match the attribute set. The finished table looks like this. ———

Save this web page as task21e.htm in your Task21e folder.

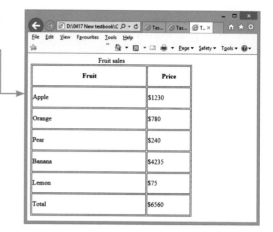

Task 21f

Open the file task21f.htm. Set the table to fit to 80% of the browser window and the left column to be 75% of the width of the table. Set the top row to be 60 pixels high and the bottom row to be 40 pixels high. Align the table in the centre of the browser window. Set the names of the fruit to be centre aligned and the prices in the right column to be right aligned.

Open this web page. Set a style attribute for the table tag with the width property and a value of 80%. Use a similar 75% property for the **style** attribute in any table data (or table header) tag in the left column, like this. ———→

Centre align a table in a window

To centre align the table within the window, two more **style** properties must be used with the **table** tag. These are to set the margin to the left to automatic and the margin to the right to automatic. In CSS, if more than one property is used, the semi-colon (;) is used between one property and value and the next. The extra properties for the **table style** attribute will look like this. ———

```
<body>
  <table border="1" style="width:80%">
  <caption>Fruit sales</caption>
  <thead>
    <tr>
      <th style="width:75%">Fruit</th>
      <th>Price</th>
```

```
<body>
  <table border="1" style="width:80%; margin-left:auto; margin-right:auto;"> ◄—
    <caption>Fruit sales</caption>
```

The table is now centre aligned inside the browser. If the browser is resized the table still has the same size and alignment like this. ———

Set the row height of the table header (the first row) to 60 pixels and the bottom row to 40 pixels. Use `<tr style="height: 60px">` and `<tr style="height: 40px">` to do this.

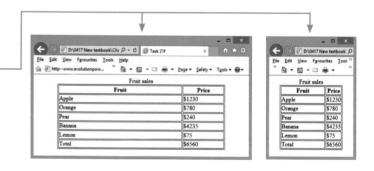

Horizontally align cell contents

To align the text to the centre in the left column, add the **style** attribute to each table data tag in the table footer and table body, so that the style has the property and value "**text-align:center**".

To align the text to the right in the right column, add the **style** attribute to the table data for each cell in this column (except the table header) so that the style has the property and value "**text-align:right**". The web page will now look like this. ———

Advice

Note the American spelling of 'center' rather than the English spelling 'centre'.

Save this web page as task21f.htm in your Task21f folder. Save copies of this page as task21g.htm in your Task21g folder and task21o.htm in your Task21o folder.

Advice

Colgroup tags to align cell elements are no longer supported in HTML5.

Activity 21c

Create a new web page with a table that looks like this and has the caption 'SupaHols visitors 2016'.

Country	Visitors
Egypt	440
India	2000
Jamaica	140
United Arab Emirates	420
Total visitors	3000

Make the company name, SupaHols, bold. Make sure the top row of the table is in the header section and the bottom row is in the footer section. Set the table to fit to 70% of the browser window and the left column to be 100 pixels wide. Set the top row to be 60 pixels high. Align the table in the centre of the browser window. Set the contents of row 1 and the names of the countries to be centre aligned and the number of visitors to be right aligned. Print your web page as HTML and as it is viewed in your browser.

Table borders

You have already studied how to set the table borders on or off with a border attribute for the table tag. To set table borders to appear as we want them we can change the border settings in the whole table or parts of the table. You will notice that all of the tables that we have created so far have a double border because the table and the table header/table data parts have separate borders.

Create a single table border

Task 21g

Open the file task21g.htm. Display the table with a single, solid border 4 pixels wide, and with internal gridlines 2 pixels wide.

Open this web page in *Notepad*. Set a style attribute for the table tag with the border-collapse property and a value collapse, like this.

```
<body>
  <table border="1" style="width:80%; margin-left:auto; margin-
  right:auto; border-collapse:collapse;">
    <caption>Fruit sales</caption>
```

The table will now look like this. ──────────────────────────→

Set table border widths

Table borders can be set using embedded CSS with the **style** attribute with the **border** property and values.

To set the outside border of a table the **style** attribute is added to the **table** tag. The values assigned to this tag must set the **border** to **solid** and to **4px**. To set internal gridlines style, attributes are added to the **<th>** and **<td>** tags; each of these tags must have the style attribute with **border:solid 2px**.

Advice

Table border settings in CSS are different from the border attribute for the table, which is only used to show if borders are visible or invisible.

```
<!DOCTYPE html>
<html>
<!-- Task 21g by your name -->
<head>
  <title>Task 21g</title>
</head>
<body>
  <table border="1" style="width:80%; margin-left:auto; margin-right:auto; border-collapse:collapse; border:solid 4px;">
    <caption>Fruit sales</caption>
    <thead>
      <tr style="height:60px">
        <th style="border:solid 2px; width:75%;">Fruit</th>
        <th style="border:solid 2px;">Price</th>
      </tr>
    </thead>
    <tfoot>
      <tr style="height:40px">
        <td style="border:solid 2px; text-align:center;">Total</td>
        <td style="border:solid 2px; text-align:right;">$6560</td>
      </tr>
    </tfoot>
    <tbody>
      <tr>
        <td style="border:solid 2px; text-align:center;">Apple</td>
        <td style="border:solid 2px; text-align:right;">$1230</td>
      </tr>
      <tr>
        <td style="border:solid 2px; text-align:center;">Orange</td>
        <td style="border:solid 2px; text-align:right";>$780</td>
      </tr>
      <tr>
        <td style="border:solid 2px; text-align:center;">Pear</td>
        <td style="border:solid 2px; text-align:right;">$240</td>
      </tr>
      <tr>
        <td style="border:solid 2px; text-align:center;">Banana</td>
        <td style="border:solid 2px; text-align:right;">$4235</td>
      </tr>
      <tr>
        <td style="border:solid 2px; text-align:center;">Lemon</td>
        <td style="border:solid 2px; text-align:right;">$75</td>
      </tr>
    </tbody>
  </table>
</body>
</html>
```

The finished table will look like this.

Later in this chapter you will learn how to fix styles for all table cells without repeatedly entering the same style attribute for each tag.

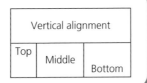

Activity 21d

Edit the web page you created for Activity 21c so that the: table has a single border of 6 pixels, the table header and footer 4 pixels, and the table data 2 pixels. Print your web page as HTML and as it is viewed in your browser.

Vertically align table cell contents

Data held in table cells can be vertically aligned with embedded CSS so that it fits in the top, middle or bottom of the cell. The style attribute is added to the <td> tag with a property of vertical-align and a value of top, middle or bottom.

Task 21h

Create a new web page that looks like this. Set both row heights to 60 pixels. Centre align the contents of all cells. Vertically align to the top, centre and bottom of the cell as shown.

Vertical alignment		
Top	Middle	
		Bottom

Advice

In some questions you may be instructed to vertically align to the centre of the cell; if so, always set the property value to middle.

Create a new web page that has a table with two rows. In the top row include one piece of table data and, in the second row, include three pieces of table data. Save this in your Task21h folder. It should look like this.

Find the three table data <td> tags in the second row and add the following attributes to them.

```
<tr style="height:60px; text-align:center;">
  <td style="vertical-align:top">Top</td>
  <td style="vertical-align:middle">Middle</td>
  <td style="vertical-align:bottom">Bottom</td>
</tr>
```

The text will now align in the table like this.

Extend (merge) cells

To create a single cell that spans across all three columns in the top row of the table, you need to add a colspan attribute to the table data <td> tag for this row.

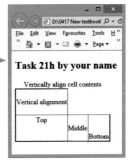

```
<tr style="height:60px; text-align:center;">
  <td colspan=3>Vertical alignment</td>
</tr>
```

Save your web page as task21h.htm in your Task21h folder.

The completed table should look like this.

To merge cells vertically use the rowspan attribute in the same way.

Activity 21e

Create a new web page to look like this. Table and header borders must be 6 pixels and all other gridlines must be 3 pixels. The right column must be 50% of the width of the table.

Class 11A Exam Results		
Amir	96	Students who have performed extremely well.
Belle	96	
Cai	94	
Denise	92	
Eric	66	Must do better.
Fiona	23	

Cell padding

Cell padding is the space between the cell contents and the border of the cell.

Task 21i

Open the file task21i.htm. Copy the table so that there are three tables, one above the other, on the page. Change the captions from 'Fruit Sales' to 'No padding' for the top table, 'Padding set to 25pixels' for the middle table and 'Variable padding' for the lower table. Set the cell padding of the middle table to 25 pixels and the padding of the lower table to have a top padding of 25 pixels, bottom padding of 20 pixels and left and right padding of 15 pixels.

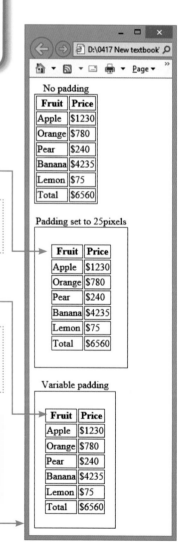

Open the file task21i.htm. Copy the table and paste it twice. Place a `<br>` tag between each table to set a line break. The `<br>` tag does not have a close tag. Add an ID attribute to each table so we can identify them: they will be called top, middle and bottom. In the `<table>` tag for the middle table, add the single CSS style padding property with a value of 25 pixels like this.

```
<br>
<table border="1" id="middle" style="padding:25px">
  <caption>Padding set to 25 pixels</caption>
```

For the bottom table we can set the different padding by stating all four values, starting at the top and rotating clockwise like this.

```
<br>
<table border="1" id="bottom" style="padding:25px 15px 20px 15px;">
  <caption>Variable padding</caption>
```

Advice

This is a shortened version of the CSS padding properties. Where padding should be specified in full, for each side it will look like this.

```
padding-top:25px;
padding-bottom:20px;
padding-right:15px;
padding-left:15px;
```

The web page now looks like this.

This has only set the padding for the table borders. To change each cell the same style attributes, properties and values will need copying and pasting into every <th> and <td> tag. This will change the tables to look like this. ————

Save your web page as task21i.htm in your Task21i folder, and a copy of your page as task21j.htm in your Task21j folder.

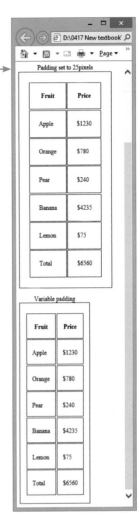

Task 21j

Open the file task21j.htm. Set the top table to have a horizontal border spacing of 20 pixels and a vertical border spacing of 10 pixels.

Border spacing

The spacing between the borders of individual cells is set in the <table> tag. The style attribute is used with the border-spacing property. Two values can be passed to this property: the horizontal spacing first, then the vertical spacing, like this. ————

```
<body>
  <table border="1" id="top" style="border-spacing:20px 10px;">
    <caption>No padding</caption>
```

The top table of the web page will look like this. ————

Advice

If the horizontal and vertical border spacing are the same, you can use a single value.

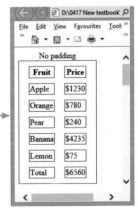

Activity 21f

Open your finished web page from Activity 21b. For each table cell, set the padding to have a top value of 8 pixels, bottom of 12 pixels, a left value of 20 pixels and a right value of 16 pixels. Set internal and external border spacing for the table to 20 pixels.

Task 21k

Create a new web page with a table that looks like this and has the caption 'Sales team'. The image that you require is called **turtle.jpg**.

	Expenses		
	Lee	Amir	Maxine
Travel	$162.20	$285.75	$150.00
Hotel	$240.00	$182.40	$322.00
Food	$146.50	$102.10	$104.50

Plan the table using a hand-drawn sketch similar to this.

Caption

		1 cell three columns wide		
Table Header	Image here 1 cell 2 rows deep	Lee	Amir	Maxine
Table Body	Travel	$162.20	$285.75	$150
	Hotel	$240	$182.40	$322
	Food	$46.50	$62.10	$64.50

2 table rows with 4 columns, 2 cells in first row merged, 3 cells in second row merged, 3 table heading cells.

3 table rows, each with 1 heading cell and 3 table data cells.

Shading shows cells with a heading format rather than table data format.

Create the basic markup as you did with the earlier tasks, starting with the table tags, the table attributes to show the borders, the caption, the header and body sections of the table, then insert the table rows. The markup so far will look like this.

```
<body>
  <table border="1" style="border-collapse:collapse; border:solid 1px;">
    <caption>Sales team</caption>
    <thead>
      <tr>
      </tr>
      <tr>
      </tr>
    </thead>
    <tbody>
      <tr>
      </tr>
      <tr>
      </tr>
      <tr>
      </tr>
    </tbody>
  </table>
</body>
```

The top row of the table header has only two cells. The first of these is a cell that covers two rows. For this you use a rowspan attribute to tell the browser this cell is going to span the first two rows. The markup for this section will look like this.

The second cell in the top row is a cell that covers three columns. Use the colspan attribute to tell the browser that this cell is going to span three columns. This cell was identified in the sketch as a being a heading cell, so the colspan attribute is used within the table heading tag. The markup will look like this.

Advice

When creating a new table like this, it is wise to add a single letter as the contents of the cell when you create it. In this case a single letter 'A' has been added to the top left cell, the letter 'B' to the next cell and so on. This is because some web browsers do not display a table cell if it is empty. By adding these single letters it allows you to test the table as you are creating it.

```
<thead>
  <tr>
    <td rowspan="2">A</td>
    <th colspan="3">B</th>
  </tr>
```

Using the sketch to work from, add the cells to each row of the table. In the body of the table, set the first cell of each row as a table heading and the next three cells as table data. This section of the table will look like this. ─────

The table structure should now look like this. ─────

Enter all the text and currency values into the correct cells in the table. The web page should look like this.

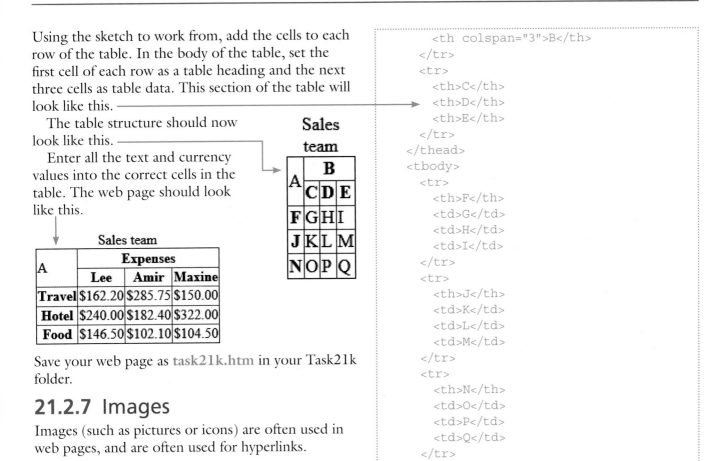

Sales team

A	Expenses		
	Lee	**Amir**	**Maxine**
Travel	$162.20	$285.75	$150.00
Hotel	$240.00	$182.40	$322.00
Food	$146.50	$102.10	$104.50

```
          <th colspan="3">B</th>
        </tr>
        <tr>
          <th>C</th>
          <th>D</th>
          <th>E</th>
        </tr>
      </thead>
      <tbody>
        <tr>
          <th>F</th>
          <td>G</td>
          <td>H</td>
          <td>I</td>
        </tr>
        <tr>
          <th>J</th>
          <td>K</td>
          <td>L</td>
          <td>M</td>
        </tr>
        <tr>
          <th>N</th>
          <td>O</td>
          <td>P</td>
          <td>Q</td>
        </tr>
      </tbody>
    </table>
  </body>
</html>
```

Save your web page as task21k.htm in your Task21k folder.

21.2.7 Images

Images (such as pictures or icons) are often used in web pages, and are often used for hyperlinks.

Insert an image

To complete the web page for Task 21k, you need to replace the letter 'A' in the top left cell of the table with the image **turtle.jpg**. To do this you have to tell the web browser the name of the image source, which should be stored in the same folder as your web page. Make sure that you have copied the file **turtle.jpg** into your Task21k folder. Add the following to the markup. As some browsers may not display the image, you can tell the browser to replace the image with alternative text. This usually describes the image so that the user can still understand what is being shown even though they cannot see the image. The markup will look like this.

```
<thead>
  <tr>
    <td rowspan="2"><img src="turtle.jpg" alt="Company Logo"></td>
    <th colspan="3">Expenses</th>
  </tr>
```

Where to store an image

Images must be stored in the same folder as the web page. This is called the current folder. Notice in the markup shown above how the filename **turtle.jpg** is given as the image source. This does not contain any reference to which folder the image is stored. Because there is no absolute reference to a folder, the browser automatically looks in the current folder for the image. This means that if this web page is opened on another computer, as long as the image is stored in the same folder as the web page, it will work properly.

If an absolute reference had been used for a file, for example:

```
<img src="C:/My websites/My pictures/turtle.jpg" alt="Company
Logo"></td>
```
X

This would prevent the file being found unless the folders in all the computers were structured in this way. If the file **turtle.jpg** is not in the current folder, the web page will look like this. The image has been replaced by the text 'Company Logo' to tell the user what the missing image should be.

If the image file is stored in the current folder, this will be displayed.

Save the web page as task21k.htm in your Task21k folder and save a copy as task21m.htm in your Task21m folder.

Advice

A common mistake made by students is to use absolute pathways for files, such as images, stylesheets, etc.

Sales team

Company Logo	Expenses		
	Lee	Amir	Maxine
Travel	$162.20	$285.75	$150.00
Hotel	$240.00	$182.40	$322.00
Food	$146.50	$102.10	$104.50

File types for images

There are three common file types for images used in websites. These are JPEG files, GIF files or PNG files. You can use a graphics package such as *Adobe Photoshop* to change images from one format to another by opening them and using Save As… to change the file format for the new image.

Advice

Image files added to web pages are usually in bitmap graphics formats such as .jpg, .gif or .png format. Many other image formats, for example vector graphics such as .tif, will not work in a web page.

Sales team

Turtle Travel	Expenses		
	Lee	Amir	Maxine
Travel	$162.20	$285.75	$150.00
Hotel	$240.00	$182.40	$322.00
Food	$146.50	$102.10	$104.50

Activity 21g

Create a new web page with a table that looks like this and has the caption 'Last week'. The image that you require is called **ptct.jpg**. Print your web page as HTML and as it is viewed in your browser.

PTC Travel	Expenses			
	Anne	Dan	Lisa	Udoka
Petrol	$182.20	$185.75	$260.00	$322.00
Food	$80.00	$62.40	$54.00	$40.00
Hotel	$420.00	$382.10	$104.50	$260.00

Resize an image

Images can be resized using two methods:

- The first method is to change the size of the displayed image in the markup. This is the easier of the two methods but often uses large image files, which are slower to upload and can delay the display of a completed web page.
- The second method is to physically resize the image in a graphics package. You did this in Task 11b. This method has the advantage of being able to

reduce the file size of an image so that a web page will be displayed more quickly. It has the disadvantage of using low-resolution images, which can appear pixelated, particularly if you wish to enlarge them.

Task 21l

Open the file **webpage2.htm**. Use both methods to resize this image to 80 pixels wide and compare the relative file sizes of the two images. Save both versions of your web page.

Resize an image in the markup

Copy the web page and supporting files **remora.htm**, **remora.jpg** and **turtle.jpg** into your Task21l folder. To change the size of an image in the markup use either the width or height attributes within the image tag. For this question the width needs setting to 80 pixels. If you change the width of the image to 80 pixels and do not specify a height for the image, it will maintain its **aspect ratio**. This means that it will keep the same proportions. Sometimes you may be asked to distort an image to give a different effect within a web page. This is done by specifying both width and height but not keeping the aspect ratio of the original image. Find the markup for the image **remora.jpg**, in the file **webpage2.htm**, which looks like this.

```
<tr>
  <td rowspan="3"><img src="remora.jpg" alt="Remora"></td>
  <td colspan="3"><h1>Image alignment</h1></td>
```

Add a new attribute to the image tag to specify the new width of the image, like this.

```
<tr>
  <td rowspan="3"><img src="remora.jpg" alt="Remora" style="width:80px" >
  </td>
```

Save the web page which will change from this to this.

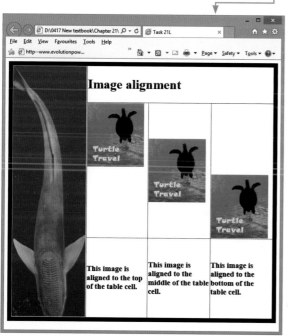
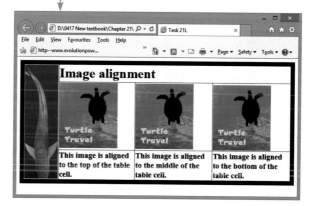

Although the vertical alignment of all three turtle images has not been changed in the markup, the effect is to make the images appear to have the same vertical alignment. This is because the row height has been reduced to fit with the new row height for the image of the remora.

Resize an image in an external package

You have already completed this in Task 11b. Copy the image that you resized and called **remora1.jpg** from your Task11b folder into your Task21l folder.

When using this technique it is useful to have a small, low-resolution image (called a thumbnail) on a web page. If the user wants to see more detail they can click on the image and a new window will open containing a high-resolution version of the same image. The web page needs to be amended so that the width attribute is no longer present, and the source attribute within the image tag points to the new filename.

```
<tr>
  <td rowspan="3"><img src="remora.jpg" alt="Remora"></td>
  <td colspan="3"><h1>Image alignment</h1></td>
```

Save your amended web page with the filename **task21l.htm**.

Comparing the two methods

Open the File Explorer window and navigate to the Task21l folder.

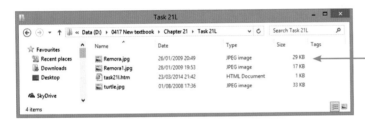

This folder contains the two image files and shows you the difference in file sizes between the two methods. Your image sizes may vary from this depending on the resolution you selected when you saved the file. As can be seen here, in this case the new image should load in less than 60% of the time the original will take.

Insert an animated image

There are two different methods used to place an animated image on a web page. If the file is an animated GIF, the method is the same as inserting a still image.

Task 21m

Edit the web page saved in Task 21k to replace the image with the moving image **turtlelogo.gif**.

Open the file **task21k.htm** in *Notepad*. Copy this file and **turtlelogo.gif** into your Task21m folder. Change the image source from turtle.jpg to **turtlelogo.gif**, like this.

```
<td rowspan="2"><img src="turtlelogo.gif" alt="Animated Company Logo"></td>
```

Save the web page as task21m.htm in your Task21m folder.
The resulting web page will look like this. ──────────►

Sales team			
Turtle Travel	Expenses		
	Lee	Amir	Maxine
Travel	$162.20	$285.75	$150.00
Hotel	$240.00	$182.40	$322.00
Food	$146.50	$102.10	$104.50

Insert a video file

Videos can be placed in a web page using the <video> and
</video> tags. You must include width and height attributes within
the <video> tag, so that the correct space is saved on the page for the
video. The controls attribute shows the video controls and allows the
user to control (start/pause/maximise/adjust volume, etc) the video.

The video source is different from other HTML elements as it uses
a <source> tag as well as the src attribute. In the <source> tag the
type attribute tells the browser the file type of the video to be shown.

You must include text between the <video> and </video> tags for
browsers that do not support HTML5 or videos of this type.

Advice

Accepted video formats
are .MP4, .webm and
.Ogg. Many other video
formats, such as .wmv, will
not work with the <video>
tag.

Task 21n

Open the file **webpage3.htm** and save this as task21n.htm. Replace the text *Place video here*
with the video **wreck.mp4**. Replace the text *Place audio here* with the sound **whale.mp3**.

Copy the files **wreck.mp4** and **whale.mp3** into your Task21n folder. Open
webpage3.htm in *Notepad*. Replace the text *Place video here* with this HTML.

```
<video width="300" height="224" controls>
Your browser does not support this type of video.
<source src="wreck.mp4" type="video/mp4">
</video>
```

Save the web page as task21n.htm in your Task21n folder.
The resulting web page will look like this. ──────────►

Advice

The controls on the video are only shown when the cursor
moves over them.

Insert an audio file (sound clip)

Audio clips can be placed in a web page using the <audio> and
</audio> tags. The controls attribute works in a similar way to the
video controls. It allows the user to control the sound clip.

The audio source works in a similar way to the video source. In the
<source> tag the type attribute tells the browser the file type of the
audio to be played.

You must include text between the <audio> and </audio>
tags for browsers that do not support HTML5 or files of this type.

Replace the text *Place audio here* with this HTML.

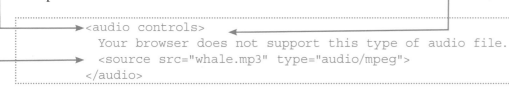

```
<audio controls>
   Your browser does not support this type of audio file.
<source src="whale.mp3" type="audio/mpeg">
</audio>
```

Save and test the web page. It should look like this.

21.2.8 Colour – Part 1

Colour is always defined in CSS, either embedded in the HTML or within an attached stylesheet (which you will meet later in the chapter). One method is to use colour names as the property values, such as red, green and blue within the HTML code. There are currently only 16 colour names accepted as web standards in CSS and by the World Wide Web Consortium (known as W3C). These are: aqua, black, blue, fuchsia, gray (note the American spelling), green, lime, maroon, navy, olive, purple, red, silver, teal, white and yellow. Other colour names are, however, accepted by some browsers (a table showing these colours and their names is included on the CD).This can be found on the web page called colourcodes. You can open this web page and use these colours in your own stylesheets attached to your web pages.

It is not always easy to remember the names of the colours, and many web designers prefer to use hexadecimal codes (often referred to as hex codes) to define the colour of text, backgrounds or objects. Hexadecimal is a counting system where counting is done in 16s (rather than in the tens used in the decimal system). Because we do not have 16 different characters for numbers, we use letters and numbers as shown in Table 21.1.

Table 21.1 The hexadecimal counting system

Decimal	1	2	3	4	5	6	7	8	9	10	11	12	13	14	15	16	17	18	19	20	21	22	23	24	25	26	27	…
Hexadecimal	1	2	3	4	5	6	7	8	9	A	B	C	D	E	F	10	11	12	13	14	15	16	17	18	19	1A	1B	…

Decimal	…	152	153	154	155	156	157	158	159	160	161	162	163	164	165	166	167	168	169	170	171	172	…
Hexadecimal	…	98	99	9A	9B	9C	9D	9E	9F	A0	A1	A2	A3	A4	A5	A6	A7	A8	A9	AA	AB	AC	…

Advice
Check this table to help you work out which hex codes are useful.

The largest number that can be stored in a single byte (8 bits) of information is the decimal number 255, which is FF in hexadecimal.

Each pixel (dot) on a monitor or projected on to a screen is made up of three different colours. The primary colours when using light (which is very different from the primary colours used in painting) are Red, Green and Blue. You will notice that the initial letters are RGB, hence RGB monitors. Each of these colours can be off, partially on or fully on. In hexadecimal, if a colour is off it is set to 00 and if it is fully on it is set to FF. To create the colour for any pixel you must tell the computer how much red, green and blue light to show. This means that all colour codes have six characters, the first two being red, the next two green and the final two blue. This example uses the hex code for red, as the red component is fully on (FF), the green component is off (00) and the blue component is also off (00).

```
<h1 style="color:#ff0000">This is red</h1>
```

Advice
Note the American spelling of 'color', rather than the English 'colour'.

Advice
The hash symbol (#) tells the browser that the number is in hexadecimal.

All of the different combinations of red, green and blue allow more than 16 million different colours to be used.

Table 21.2 Using hex codes to create different colours

Amount of light (colour)	Hex code	Example (red only)	Colour
Fully on	FF	FF0000	
¾ on	C0	C00000	
½ on	80	800000	
¼ on	40	400000	
Off	00	000000	

The web page **colourcodes.htm** contains the hex codes (as well as the names) for the most popular colours. It is interesting to note that, working with light, mixing red and green gives yellow, green and blue gives cyan, and mixing red and blue gives magenta. If all three colours are fully on, the result is white. If no colour is on, the result is black.

Set the background colour
You must set the background colour using the CSS property background-color.

Task 21o
Open the file task21o.htm. Edit the web page to look like this. The colour codes you will need are #32879B for the header, #92CDDC for the footer and #B6DDE8 for the table body.

Fruit	Price
Apple	$1230
Orange	$780
Pear	$240
Banana	$4235
Lemon	$75
Total	$6560

Open the file task21o.htm in *Notepad*. Add a style attribute to the <thead> tag like this.

```
<thead style="background-color:#32879b">
```

Add a style attribute to the <tfoot> tag like this.

```
<tfoot style="background-color:#92cddc">
```

Add a style attribute to the <tbody> tag like this.

```
<tbody style="background-color:#b6dde8">
```

Save your web page.

Hexadecimal colour codes can be used with background and foreground colours, for example: in CSS text colours can be changed using the style attribute with a color property.

21.2.9 Lists

You can include on a web page either a numbered list, which is an **ordered list**, or a bulleted list, which is an **unordered list**. Bulleted (unordered) lists can also be nested (placed one inside the other) to give you more flexibility in the design of your web pages. Items to be placed in a list start with the markup `<li>` and close with `</li>`. These are used in the same way as the style definitions for headings (styles h1 to h6) and paragraph styles. Each item in the list must have the list tags around it. The way each of these lists is displayed can be changed using CSS. An example of an item placed in a list would look like this.

```
<li>This is one item from a bulleted or numbered list</li>
```

Numbered lists

Numbered lists are ordered lists in HTML because they are in number order. Place the tag `<ol>` at the start of the numbered list and the tag `</ol>` at the end.

> ### Task 21p
> Create a web page containing the heading 'Fruit' and a numbered list for the following items: Apple, Orange, Pear, Banana and Lemon.

Enter this markup into your text editor.
 Save the web page, as **task21p** in your Task21p folder, which should look like this in your browser.

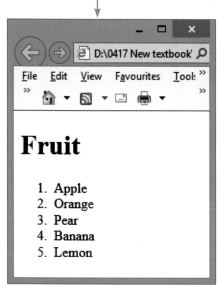

```
<!DOCTYPE html>
<html>
<!-- Task 21p by your name -->
<head>
  <title>Task 21p</title>
</head>
<body>
  <h1>Fruit</h1>
    <ol>
      <li>Apple</li>
      <li>Orange</li>
      <li>Pear</li>
      <li>Banana</li>
      <li>Lemon</li>
    </ol>
</body>
</html>
```

Bulleted lists

Bulleted lists are called unordered lists in HTML. Place the tag `<ul>` at the start of the numbered list and the tag `</ul>` at the end.

> ### Task 21q
> Create a web page containing the heading 'Colours' and a bulleted list for the following items: Red, Yellow, Blue, Green and Cyan.

Enter this markup into your text editor.

Save the web page, which should look like this in your browser.

```
<!DOCTYPE html>
<html>
<!-- Task 21q by your name -->
<head>
  <title>Task 21q</title>
</head>
<body>
  <h1>Colours</h1>
    <ul>
      <li>Red</li>
      <li>Yellow</li>
      <li>Blue</li>
      <li>Green</li>
      <li>Cyan</li>
    </ul>
</body>
</html>
```

Nested lists

Task 21r

Create a web page containing the names of two resorts as a bulleted list. These resorts are Ellmau in Austria and Sharm El Sheikh in Egypt. For each resort, list the main activities.

Bulleted lists can be nested by having sub-lists. These are created by placing one unordered list within another list.

Enter this markup into your text editor to create the primary list.

```
<!DOCTYPE html>
<html>
<!-- Task 21r by your name -->
<head>
  <title>Task 21r</title>
</head>
<body>
  <ul>
    <li>Ellmau</li>
    <li>Sharm El Sheikh</li>
  </ul>
</body>
</html>
```

After each resort, enter a new sub-list that contains the activities offered in each of these places. Note that the sub-list fits between the list item name and the close tag for that item. The finished markup will look like this.

```
<!DOCTYPE html>
<html>
<!-- Task 21r by your name -->
<head>
  <title>Task 21r</title>
</head>
<body>
  <ul>
    <li>Ellmau</li>
      <ul>
        <li>Skiing</li>
        <li>Snowboarding</li>
        <li>Sledging</li>
        <li>Mountaineering</li>
      </ul>
    <li>Sharm El Sheikh</li>
      <ul>
        <li>Scuba diving</li>
        <li>Snorkelling</li>
      </ul>
  </ul>
</body>
</html>
```

Save the web page, as task21r in your Task21r folder, which should look like this in your browser.

> ## Activity 21h
>
> Create a new web page containing the heading 'Winter sports', a brief introduction and an unordered list of the following winter sports: skiing, tobogganing and snowboarding. For each winter sport, make a sub-list of the items of clothing required. Set these sub-lists as unordered lists. Print the web page as viewed in your browser and as HTML.
> Change these sub-lists to ordered lists. Again, print the web page as viewed in your browser and as HTML.

21.2.10 Hyperlinks

A **hyperlink** is a method of accessing another document or resource from your current application. Hyperlinks do not just relate to web pages: other applications software can also use them. Hyperlinks are often used to create menu options with web pages, using either text or images. When you select a hyperlink (usually by clicking the left mouse button), the hyperlink will perform an action. It may move your position within a page, open another page either locally or on the internet, or open your email editor so that you can send an email to a specified place or company.

Anchors and divisions

A division is a point of reference within a web page. It is similar to a bookmark when using word-processing or desktop publishing software. If you create a web page that will not fit in a single window, it is useful to use one division for each section of the web page (or document), so the user can move to any section without having to scroll through the whole document. An anchor is used to set a hyperlink to allow you to navigate within the page or navigate to an external page. An anchor starts with an <a> tag and closes with an </a> tag.

Division tags

The <div> tag is short for a division or section of an HTML document or page. These can be used for many functions within a webpage, but at this level are used to give an identity (ID) to a part of a webpage. In previous versions of html anchors were used to hold the ID of a placeholder to define places like the top of a page. These have been replaced in HTML5 <div> and </div> tags to define an ID for the hyperlink. This placeholder often has an ID called 'top' or 'start'. To create a <div> placeholder called 'top' enter this markup in the body section of the page. This anchor will work without any text between the open and close tags.

```
<div id="top">Any content could appear here</div>
```

The text *Any content could appear here* will be visible in the browser but the division will not be visible.

Advice

If the division name is visible in the browser view of the page it often means you have made a syntax error (an error in the structure of the markup).

Hyperlinks within a web page

> ## Task 21s
>
> Edit the web page **webpage4.htm** so that each new section contains an anchor. Use these anchors to create hyperlinks from the appropriate text in the first paragraph. Make the word 'top' in the last line a hyperlink to the top of the page. Make the words 'CIE website' a hyperlink to the website www.cie.org.uk, and the words 'W3C website' a link to www.w3.org.

Copy the file **webpage4.htm** into your Task21s folder. Open the web page in your text editor and in your web browser. Each section needs a placeholder with a different name. You should always choose short yet meaningful names for each ID. For this web page you will give each division an ID (identifier). These will be called top, 21a, 21b, 21c, 21d, 21e and 21f, as these relate directly to the sections within the web page. It is sensible to place all the division names into the document before creating the hyperlinks to each division name. Each division name is created like this.

```
<h1><div id="top"></div>Chapter 21</h1>
```

You can see that the division tags are inside the tags defining the style for the text. The initial division tag contains the division **id**, which is placed in speech marks. This ID will be used in all hyperlinks to navigate this point. Add the other anchors to the markup, one for each section of the document, like this.

```
<hr>
<h2><div id="21a"></div>21a Understand what HTML is</h2>
<p>Many students sit the practical examinations without…
```

```
<hr>
<h2><div id="21b"></div>21b Problems with WYSIWYGs</h2>
<p>There are many well designed WYSIWYG packages on the…
```

```
<hr>
<h2><div id="21c"></div>21c Use the correct terms</h2>
<p>Over the past few years, as the practical examinations…
```

Add divisions for 21d, 21e and 21f with similar markup. In the final sentence, find the word 'top'. This will be used to create a hyperlink to the division with the name 'top' that you created earlier. The hyperlink is created using an anchor. The two anchor tags are placed each side of the word 'top'. The markup includes a hyperlink reference (the markup attribute for this is **href**) and the name of the destination anchor. This anchor name is always inside speech marks and preceded by the # symbol, like this.

```
<p>Back to the <a href="#top">top</a></p>
```

In the first paragraph find the text 'what is HTML?' Edit the markup for this text so that it creates a hyperlink to the anchor with the ID 21a. It will look like this.

```
<h3>Here is advice to try to help you succeed; if you follow this you are likely to
create better web pages. First you need to know, <a href="#21a"> what is HTML? </a> Once
you have a sound understanding of HTML, it is worth considering the use of WYSIWYGs
and the potential problems of using these packages…
```

```
<h1>Advice for practical web page creation</h1>
<h3>Here is advice to try to help you succeed; if you follow this, you are
likely to create better web pages. First you need to know <a href="#21a">
what is HTML?</a> Once you have a sound understanding of HTML, it is
worth considering the use of <a href="#21b">WYSIWYGs</a> and the potential
problems of using these packages. Make sure that you <a href="#21c">
use the right terms</a> to describe what you have done, are doing or could
be asked to do. Learn how to <a href="#21d">create and attach stylesheets
</a> to your web pages. Make sure that you can <a href="#21e">work with tables</a>.
These provide a fundamental structure to web pages and seem to be replacing frames in
many areas. There are other methods of formatting layout including the use of DIVs,
but these are currently beyond the scope of this book. Look for <a href="#21f">other
resources</a> to help you prepare for the practical examinations.</h3>
```

Now that the hyperlinks have been created, each one needs testing. Save the web page and refresh your browser, then try each hyperlink in turn and make sure that it directs you to the correct place in the web page. If the name that you have used in the hyperlink reference does not exist, your browser will go to the top of the page and the browser does not show you that there is an error.

Hyperlinks to other web pages

Hyperlinks can be created to another web page stored locally, usually in the same folder as the current web page, or to an external website on the internet. The markup for both of these links has the same syntax (structure). The only difference is the address of the web page that the hyperlink is to go to.

To complete Task 21s, two hyperlinks need adding to external web addresses. These follow a similar format, with the URL for the web address appearing as the hyperlink. The markup for these two hyperlinks is shown here.

```
<h2><a id="21f"></a>21f Other useful links</h2>
  <p>There are other places that can be used to gain valuable information that
may help. These include the <a href="http://www.cie.org.uk">CIE website</a> and the
<a href="http://www.w3.org">W3C website</a>.</p>
  <p>Back to the <a href="#top">top</a></p>
```

Add these hyperlinks to the last section of your markup and save your web page as **task21s.htm** in your Task21s folder, and as **task21t.htm** in your Task21t folder. Test the hyperlinks to make sure they work as you expected.

References to pages stored in the same folder as your web page just have an address without the URL. To link to a local file called 'next_page.htm', you would include a hyperlink reference like this.

```
<p><a name="next_page.htm">Click here for the next page</a>.</p>
```

Advice

Make sure that you do not put an absolute address in a hyperlink reference (for example, <a href ="C:my documents/my folder/html/next_page.htm">) as this is only likely to work on your computer. Other computers are unlikely to have the same folder structure and filename.

Activity 21i

Open the web page **htmltips.htm** and replace the text *YOUR NAME* with your name.

Edit the web page so that each new section contains an anchor. Use these anchors to create hyperlinks from the appropriate text in the first section. Make the word 'top' in the last line a hyperlink to the top of the page.

Make the word 'CIE' a hyperlink to the website www.cie.org.uk, the words 'Hodder Education' a hyperlink to the website www.hoddereducation.co.uk and the text 'W3C' a hyperlink to www.w3.org.

Print the HTML view of this web page.

Open a web page in a new browser window

When a web page is opened, it may open in the current window or it may open in a new window. This is set using the target attribute. An attribute is something that is added to one of the markup commands to give further information/instructions to the browser. This attribute is part of the anchor and tells the browser which window to use for the web page that you are going to open. The target attribute can either be set as a default setting in the head section of the markup or as an individual setting for a hyperlink within the body section. If the target attribute is not used, the browser will decide where to open a web page.

To set a target window for a single hyperlink, add the target attribute to the first anchor. Some target attributes have specific functions. If a target name of _blank is applied, this will open in a new target window. If _self is applied it will open in the current window. Other target names, such as _parent and _top, are reserved and perform different functions with frames, which are beyond the scope of this book. Any other target name that you use will open the specified web page in a window with that target name, if it exists, or open it in a new window with that target name.

Task 21t

Using your web page task21t.htm, make the hyperlink you created to the W3C website open in the same window and the hyperlink to the CIE website open in a new window called _cie.

Open the web page task21t.htm in your text editor and in your web browser. Edit the markup for the last two hyperlinks to include the target attributes like this.

```
<p>There are other places that can be used to gain valuable
information that may help. These include the
<a href=http://www.cie.org.uk target=" _cie"> CIE website</a> and
the <a href="http://www.w3.org" target="_self"> W3C website</a>.
</p><p>Back to the <a href="#top">top</a></p>
```

Save your website and test the hyperlinks to make sure that they work as you expected, checking the tabs at the top of the browser to see if a new target window has been opened.

Use a hyperlink to send an email message

Hyperlinks from web pages, other applications packages or documents can be used to open an email editor and prepare a message to be sent to another person or company. This is very useful in a website where you can set up your email address and subject line within the markup and instruct the browser to open the email editor and insert these details into a new message when the hyperlink is selected.

The format for this is very similar to the hyperlinks shown earlier in this section. In place of the URL or path of a web page that is placed within the hyperlink reference of the anchor, the **mailto:** instruction is used. This is followed by the email address of the recipient. To include the subject line for the message, this is included by specifying **subject=** followed by the text for the subject line. The whole hyperlink reference is enclosed within speech marks.

Task 21u

Create a new web page that contains a hyperlink to prepare an email message to be sent to graham.a.brown@hotmail.co.uk with the subject line 'IGCSE Book'.

For this task you need to prepare a new markup in your text editor that contains this line.

```
<p><a href="mailto:graham.a.brown@hotmail.co.uk?subject=IGCSE%20Book">
Click here to contact us page</a></p>
```

Save this in your Task21u folder and try it in your browser. When you click on the hyperlink it will open your email editor; place the address in the **To:** section and the text 'IGCSE Book' in the **Subject: line**.

Note how the space in the text 'IGCSE Book' has been replaced in the markup with **%20**. This is the hex value for the ascii character 32, which represents a space. There are no spaces inside the speech marks for the hyperlink reference.

Advice

Body text could also be added by adding '&body=Add%20the%20body%20text' as an extra value at the end of the mailto property.

Hyperlinks from images

Task 21v

Open the file task21v.htm. Make the image in this web page a hyperlink to the web page **remora.htm**.

Copy all the files from your Task21l folder to your Task21v folder. Rename task21l.htm as task21v.htm. Open the file task21v.htm in *Notepad*.

Images can be used as hyperlinks in the same way as text. To create a hyperlink to the web page **remora.htm**, add this anchor tag with its **href** attribute and value so that it surrounds the image tab like this.

```
<tr>
  <td rowspan="3">
    <a href="remora.htm"><img src="REMORA.JPG" alt="Remora">
</a></td>
  <td colspan="3"><h1>Image alignment</h1></td>
```

This hyperlink will open the partially constructed web page called **remora.htm**. Test the hyperlink and save the web page.

Activity 21j

Edit the web page that you saved for Activity 21g. Set the border, the cell padding and cell spacing to four pixels. Print your web page as HTML and as it is viewed in your browser.

	Expenses			
PTC Travel	**Anne**	**Dan**	**Lisa**	**Udoka**
Petrol	$182.20	$185.75	$260.00	$322.00
Food	$80.00	$62.40	$54.00	$40.00
Hotel	$420.00	$382.10	$104.50	$260.00

The background colour code that you will need is #FFFF00. Make the image a hyperlink to send an email message to ptc_travel@outlook.com with the subject line 'Expenses' and the body text 'Please send me updated expenses details.' Print your web page as HTML and as it is viewed in your browser.

21.3 Use stylesheets

Using styles in your web pages helps you to be consistent in the way the pages look. Using styles is much quicker and easier than applying individual settings – such as font face, font size, text alignment and font colours – to every piece of text in each web page that you create.

You have already met the heading styles, h1 to h6, and the paragraph style, p, earlier in the chapter. When you used these styles the web browser did not find any of these style definitions in your HTML markup so used its own default settings. However, you can set your own definitions for each style and the web browser will attempt to apply these styles to the page.

Styles are set with HTML tags but the styles are defined in the presentation layer of the web page in CSS format. You have already embedded some presentation layer elements in the HTML using the style attribute. Styles are not only set for text, but can also be used to define page layout, colour schemes and default settings for other objects and links on the page. Using a consistent style is often important to give a 'corporate feel' to a website. Particular elements, such as colour schemes, table presentation, logos and font faces, are often used to aid recognition of well-known companies or brands.

Styles are always defined in the head section of a web page. They may be defined in each web page or defined in an external stylesheet. If stylesheets are used, the stylesheet is attached to the web page in the head section of the markup. As we have already seen, styles can be applied individually to each page, but it is more efficient to write, edit and attach one or more common stylesheet/s to all the pages in a website.

Styles are often gathered together and held in a stylesheet. This is a collection of styles saved in a different file in cascading stylesheet (.css) format.

21.3.1 What is a cascading stylesheet?

A cascading stylesheet is a simple way of adding style (for example, fonts, colours, spacing) to web pages.

One or more of these cascading stylesheets can be attached to a web page, and the styles in the stylesheet will be applied to this page. Where more than one web page is used, the styles only have to be defined once and attached to all the web pages. In-line styles usually over-ride styles attached from an external stylesheet. This allows companies to develop different stylesheets for specific items such as colour schemes, text styles and styles for a particular document or set of documents.

If more than one stylesheet is attached to a web page at the same time, those attached later in the markup have priority over earlier ones. If a style has more than one declaration of the same property, the last value is used for the property.

21.3.2 What is CSS format?

CSS rules have a selector and a declaration block like this.

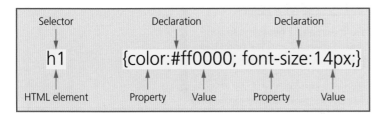

- Each element has one or more declarations, each separated by a semicolon.
- Each declaration has a property name and a value, separated by a colon.
- Each declaration block is surrounded by curly brackets.

To make the CSS easier to read, you can put one declaration on each line, like this.

```
h1      {color:#ff0000;
        font-size:14px;}
```

Task 21w

Open a copy of the web page that you saved in Task 21g. Add an external stylesheet to this page to define the table header and table data so that they each have a solid border 4 pixels wide.

Open the web page task21g.htm in *Notepad*. Save it as task21w.htm in your Task21w folder. Copy one line of the embedded CSS from the table header and paste it in your second *Notepad* window (for the stylesheet) like this.

```
td style="border:solid 2px;
```

Edit this so the stylesheet looks like this.

```
td,th    {border:solid 4px;}
```

The element name/s, in this case td and th, are followed by curly brackets {}. In this example: you have set each piece of table data and each table header so that its border property has a solid border that is four pixels thick. By defining the two elements td and th at the same time, you have saved yourself extra work. Save this file using the filename tablestyle.css in the same folder as your web page. The saved file should look like this when viewed in File Explorer. ⟶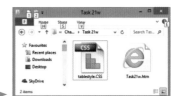

Advice

Make sure that you use the .css file extension and **not** .htm or .txt.

Go back to the *Notepad* window for the HTML of task21w.htm and remove all the border properties and values from each of the style tags in the table header and the table body, like this.

```
<thead>
  <tr style="height:60px">
  <th style="width:75%;">Fruit</th>
  <th>Price</th>
```

Attach an external stylesheet to a web page

Add this line of text below the title tags in the head section of the markup.

```
<link rel="stylesheet" type="text/css" href="tablestyle.css">
```

Advice

Make sure that you do not put an absolute address in a hyperlink reference (for example, `<link rel="stylesheet" type="text/css" href ="C:/my documents/my folder/css/tablestyle.css">`) as this is only likely to work on your computer. Other computers are unlikely to have the same folder structure and filename.

This defines the relationship of this link as a stylesheet, in cascading stylesheet format, and searches for the file tablestyle.css and applies this to the page. The filename in this line of markup **must** match the name of the CSS file that you saved.

The new markup should start like this.

```
<!DOCTYPE html>
<html>
<!-- Task 21w by your name -->
<head>
  <title>Task 21w</title>
<link rel="stylesheet" type="text/css" href="tablestyle.css">
</head>
```

Save this web page. View this web page in your browser; it should have changed from this to this.

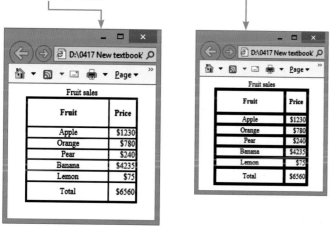

Advice

Using external stylesheets saves you lots of time. One stylesheet can be attached to many web pages and one style can be attached to every element on those pages with little effort.

Activity 21k

Edit the web page that you saved for Activity 21j so that the styles in the head section are removed and edited to become a new external stylesheet called 21kstyles. Change all references for 21j to 21k. Attach this stylesheet to your web page. Print your stylesheet, and your web page, both as HTML and as it is viewed in your browser.

When you mark Activity 21k, check the answers carefully. Although both of the answers shown (in text format and as a screen shot) meet the requirements of the question, you may not be credited with this work. Why?

Answer: your name, Centre number and candidate details are not visible on the print out.

Add comments to a stylesheet

Although you will often be told to place your name and candidate details as text on the web page, this is not as easy in a stylesheet. Text placed in a stylesheet will often stop the styles from working. Any text must have /* before it and */ after it, so that the browser knows to ignore it.

Task 21x

Open a copy of the web page and stylesheet that you saved in Task 21w. Add your name and a brief description of the stylesheet as comments to the stylesheet.

Edit the stylesheet so that it looks like this. ——→

You can see that the comments can be on a single line or on more than one line. Only one /* and */ are required for each comment. Check that the stylesheet still works with the web page.

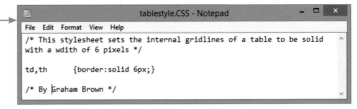

```
/* This stylesheet sets the internal gridlines of a table to be solid
with a wdith of 6 pixels */

td,th        {border:solid 6px;}

/* By Graham Brown */
```

Advice

Whenever you edit a stylesheet, save it and refresh the browser view of the web page to make sure that the changes you have made work.

Task 21y

Open a copy of the web page that you saved in Task 21a. Change the title of this page to Task 21y. Apply the stylesheet **style1.css** to this page and save this web page. Change the attached stylesheet to **style2.css** and save this with a new filename.

Select the folder called Task21y in your Documents window. Copy the file task21a.htm into this folder. Rename this file as task21y.htm. Open this file in your text editor and in your web browser. Copy the files **style1.css** and **style2.css** into this folder.

Change the title of the web page to Task 21y. To apply the styles from the stylesheet **style1.css**, you must attach it to the web page. Move the cursor to the text editor containing the HTML and add this line of text below the title tags in the head section of the markup, like this.

```
<html>
<head>
  <title>Task 21y</title>
  <link rel="stylesheet" type="text/css" href="style1.css">
</head>
<body>
  <p>My first web page by MY NAME HERE</p>
  <h1>This is style h1, the largest heading style</h1>
  <h2>This is style h2</h2>
  <h3>This is style h3</h3>
  <h4>This is style h4</h4>
  <h5>This is style h5</h5>
  <h6>This is style h6, the smallest heading style</h6>
  <p>This is style p, the paragraph style</p>
</body>
</html>
```

Save this web page. View this web page in your browser. You will notice that your web page has changed from this to this.

Advice

Your browser settings may show you different fonts to those shown here.

The page content has not changed but the styles applied to the page are very different. Notice that the font face, sizes, colours and alignment have all been specified in the stylesheet. This stylesheet is a poor example because it contains too many variations. If you change the markup to attach **style2.css** to the page rather than **style1.css**, you should see something like this.

This is the same web page again but with the slightly improved stylesheet **style2.css**, which has a background colour defined in the stylesheet. You will discover how to create and amend these stylesheets later.

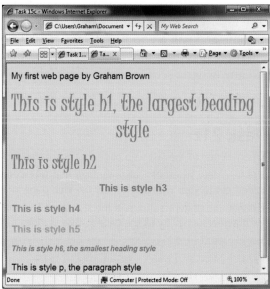

21.3.3 CSS text

It is very easy to create a cascading stylesheet in your text editor. The structure of a .css file has a few very simple rules. Stylesheets do not have tags in them as they are not a markup language. Each style has a style name which is called a selector. The selector is followed by curly brackets {}. Inside these curly brackets are the property for the style, followed by a colon, then the property's value. For example, if you want to set the text in style h1 to be centre aligned, it would appear like this.

```
h1      {text-align: center}
```

Note the American spelling of 'center'.

Each style can have a number of properties and values. If there is more than one property then each property is followed by a semi-colon. For example, if you want to set the text in style h1 to be centre aligned, 16 point high and bold, it would appear like this.

```
h1      {text-align: center;
         font-size: 16pt;
         font-weight: bold}
```

If a value within a style contains more than one word, it must be placed in speech marks like this.

```
h2      {font-family: "Times New Roman", serif}
```

Stylesheets are saved with a .css format (in a similar way to saving in .htm format) from the text editor.

Font families

Individual fonts can be specified but these are not always available in all browsers, so there are a number of **generic font families**, including **serif** and **sans-serif** fonts, which can also be used. These include 'serif', 'sans-serif', 'cursive', 'fantasy' and 'monospace', which has proportional spacing.

The generic font family must always be listed after the other preferred font/s. The **font-family** property must contain a hyphen. In the example above, the font-family is set so that the browser will look at the list of fonts installed in the machine and will try to find Times New Roman first (it is in speech marks in the stylesheet because there are spaces in the font name); if it cannot find it, it will find any generic serif font that is available.

Advice

A serif font is one that has small lines or strokes (called serifs) at the ends of characters, like this:

A font that does not contain serifs is known as a sans-serif font.

Task 21z

Open a copy of the last web page that you saved in Task 21y.

Create a new stylesheet called serif.css that sets all the styles as generic serif fonts. Apply this stylesheet to your web page. View the web page in your browser.

Change the generic settings in the stylesheet to a different generic font style. Save the stylesheet with a new name. Try all the generic style settings to see what each one looks like.

Copy the last web page you saved in your Task21y folder into your Task21z folder and rename it task21z.htm. Open this file in your text editor and in your web browser. Edit the title of the web page so it becomes Task 21z. To attach the stylesheet to the web page, you must edit the link line in the head section of the markup so that it becomes:

```
<link rel="stylesheet" type="text/css" href="serif.css">
```

Save the web page. You are going to create the stylesheet by opening a second copy of the text editor. Enter the following style definitions into it.

```
h1      {font-family: serif}
h2      {font-family: serif}
h3      {font-family: serif}
h4      {font-family: serif}
h5      {font-family: serif}
h6      {font-family: serif}
p       {font-family: serif}
```

Carefully verify your stylesheet by checking this original document with your typed copy. Save the file using the filename serif.css. Refresh your browser so that you can see the effect that this has on the web page.

Group style definitions

As all the styles have the same values for the font-family property, you can group all of the styles together and change the value only once. This stylesheet can be simplified to this single line.

```
h1,h2,h3,h4,h5,h6,p     {font-family: serif}
```

Advice

This technique could save you time, which can be invaluable in a practical examination.

Edit it and save it so that it replaces the old version. Refresh the browser to check that it still works.

Edit this stylesheet so that it sets the font-family to 'sans-serif'. Save this file using the filename sans-serif.css. Change the markup in the HTML to link to this file and save this web page. Repeat this process for each of the other generic font families.

Font size

The font-size property must contain a hyphen and can be followed by absolute heights, by setting values relative to each other, or a mixture of both.

Absolute values can be used to set the number of **points** or **picas**, or the number of **pixels** high, for each character. If point sizes are used, there are 72 points to an inch, so a 28-point font will be about 1 cm tall. This will not be affected by the size or resolution of the monitor. The sizes specified are set as numbers with 'pt' to show it is in points, for example an 18-point font is written as 18pt. Some web pages are created using the measurement in picas, which is abbreviated as 'pc' and is the equivalent of 12 points, so a two-pica font size is the same as a 24-point font. A pixel is one dot on a computer monitor. This means that pages will appear differently depending on the size and resolution of the monitor used. For older style monitors, one pixel was often about the same size as one point, but high-definition (HD) monitors now mean that characters appear much smaller on these devices. The abbreviation for pixels is 'px'.

Other absolute values include 'in' to show the measurement in inches, 'cm' for centimetres or 'mm' for millimetres. Do not place a space between the number and the abbreviation: 24px sets a 24 pixel height, but 24 px will not set the value to pixels.

> ## Task 21aa
>
> Open a copy of the web page and stylesheet that you saved in Task 21z.
>
> Edit this stylesheet so that style h1 is 36 point, h2 is 24 point, h3 18 point, h4 16 point, h5 14 point, h6 12 point and the paragraph style is 12 point.
>
> Change these settings to try and get similar results using the settings for pixels (the number will depend on your monitor display settings), picas, inches centimetres and millimetres.

Because all of the font settings are different in this case, it is more sensible to keep all of the settings for each style together. It is possible to produce a stylesheet giving these results like this.

```
h1,h2,h3,h4,h5,h6,p    {font-family: serif}
h1                     {font-size: 36pt}
h2                     {font-size: 24pt}
h3                     {font-size: 18pt}
h4                     {font-size: 16pt}
h5                     {font-size: 14pt}
h6                     {font-size: 12pt}
p                      {font-size: 10pt}
```

Although this works, I would recommend the method below as it is easier to edit if all of the settings for each style definition were together like this.

```
h1    {font-family: serif; font-size: 36pt}
h2    {font-family: serif; font-size: 24pt}
h3    {font-family: serif; font-size: 18pt}
h4    {font-family: serif; font-size: 16pt}
h5    {font-family: serif; font-size: 14pt}
h6    {font-family: serif; font-size: 12pt}
p     {font-family: serif; font-size: 10pt}
```

Amend the markup for the web page to link to the new stylesheet **size.css**. Save this in your Task21aa folder. Save the new stylesheet as **size.css** in the same folder. Refresh your browser so that you can see the effect that this has on the web page. It should change from this to this. ⎯⎯⎯⎯⎯⎯⎯

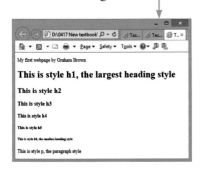

Try different absolute font sizes to see what they look like in different fonts.

Relative values are often based on previously defined values for the fonts, as defined by the default browser settings. Two values are shown using the abbreviations 'em' and 'ex': One em is the same as the current font size; two em is twice the current font size, etc; one ex is about half the height of the current font size and is the measured height of the letter 'x'. This can be useful as it automatically selects the default fonts set by the user in other stylesheets or by the browser.

> ## Task 21ab
>
> Open a copy of the web page and stylesheet that you saved in Task 21aa.
>
> Edit the stylesheet so that the paragraph style is 16 point. Set style h1 so that it is 3 em, h2 is 2 em, h3 is 1.5 em, h4 is 3 ex, h5 is 2 ex and h6 so that it is 1.5 ex.

Open the web page saved in Task 21aa and edit this to attach the stylesheet **size2.css** to it. Save this as task21ab.htm in the Task21ab folder. Open the stylesheet **size.css** and edit it so that it changes the font sizes like this.

```
p     {font-family: serif; font-size: 16pt}
h1    {font-family: serif; font-size: 3em}
h2    {font-family: serif; font-size: 2em}
h3    {font-family: serif; font-size: 1.5em}
h4    {font-family: serif; font-size: 3ex}
h5    {font-family: serif; font-size: 2ex}
h6    {font-family: serif; font-size: 1.5ex}
```

Save this stylesheet as **size2.css** in the task21ab folder. View the web page with this stylesheet attached. Notice the difference in the em and ex sizes.

Other relative values frequently used in cascading stylesheets are **percentage** values, for example setting the font size to 200% would force the font to be twice the size of the current paragraph style.

There is also a set of predefined relative sizes that can be used. These are: 'xx-small', 'x-small', 'small', 'medium', 'large', 'x-large' and 'xx-large'. Other acceptable relative values are 'smaller' and 'larger', which can be very useful if defining different classes within a style.

> ## Task 21ac
>
> Open a copy of the web page and stylesheet that you saved in Task 21ab.
>
> Edit this stylesheet so that style h1 is xx-large, h2 is x-large, h3 is large, h4 is medium, h5 is small, h6 is x-small and the paragraph style is xx-small.

Open the web page saved in Task 21ab and edit this so that the stylesheet **size3.css** is attached to it. Save this as task21ac.htm in the Task21ac folder. Open the stylesheet **size2.css** and edit this so that it changes the font sizes like this.

```
h1    {font-family: serif; font-size: xx-large}
h2    {font-family: serif; font-size: x-large}
h3    {font-family: serif; font-size: large}
h4    {font-family: serif; font-size: medium}
h5    {font-family: serif; font-size: small}
h6    {font-family: serif; font-size: x-small}
p     {font-family: serif; font-size: xx-small}
```

Save this stylesheet as **size3.css** in the Task21ac folder. View the web page with this stylesheet attached.

Align text

A font style (or class within a style) can be aligned in one of four different ways. You can use the text-align property to format text so that it is left aligned, centre aligned, right aligned or fully justified, as shown in this sample stylesheet. The text-align property must contain a hyphen.

```
h1      {text-align: left}
h2      {text-align: center}
h3      {text-align: right}
h4      {text-align: justify}
```

Advice

For centre aligned text, note the American spelling for center.

Task 21ad

Open the file you saved in Task 21b. At the top of the page add a new title 'Aligning text' in style h1. Set the heading style h1 to be centre aligned. Set style h2 to be right aligned. Set style p to be left aligned.

Open the web page saved in Task 21b and edit this by attaching a new stylesheet called **align.css**.

```
<link rel="stylesheet" type="text/css" href="align.css">
```

Add the title 'Aligning text' in style h1. Save this as task21ad.htm in your Task21ad folder. Create a new stylesheet like this.

```
h1      {text-align: center}
h2      {text-align: right}
p       {text-align: left}
```

Save this stylesheet as **align.css** in the Task21ad folder. Check that this works and that the styles have been applied correctly like this.

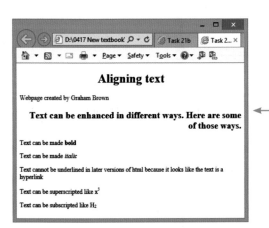

Advice

Carriage returns within the HTML have no effect on the layout of the web page.

Enhance text within a stylesheet

You are going to use some similar techniques to those used for Task 21b. This time the enhancements will apply to the whole style (or class of style as you will see later in this chapter). Each of the enhancements uses a different property setting. The default value for all three enhancements is normal.

To get bold text, set the font-weight property to 'bold', like this.

To italicise text, set the font-style property to 'italic', like this.

To underline text, set the text-decoration property to 'underline', like this.

```
h1    {font-weight: bold;
       font-style: italic;
       text-decoration: underline}
```

Advice

Although the underline command is no longer part of HTML, it can still be used by setting it within a style in the stylesheet.

Task 21ae

Create a new stylesheet called **mystyle1.css** and attach this to the web page called **webpage5.htm**. This stylesheet will set style h1 to a bold, italic, 18 point font. If 'Times New Roman' is available the browser will use that, otherwise it will choose 'Times', but if this is not available the browser's default serif font will be used. Make this text centre aligned.

Copy the file **webpage5.htm** into your Task21ae folder. Open this file in your web browser and text editor. Enter the following CSS and save it as a new stylesheet called **mystyle1.css** in the Task21ae folder. Refresh this file in your web browser.

```
h1    {font-family: "Times New Roman",Times,serif;
       font-size: 18pt;
       text-align: center;
       font-weight: bold;
       font-style: italic}
```

Advice

Notice that each property and its value/s are on a new line. This makes it easier to read and check for mistakes.

Activity 21l

Create a new stylesheet called **mystyle2.css** and attach this to the web page called **webpage6.htm**. This stylesheet will set style:

- h1 as an italic, centre aligned, 24-point font. If 'Helvetica' is available the browser will use that, otherwise it will choose 'Arial Narrow' but, if this is not available, the browser's default sans-serif font will be used
- h2 as a bold, right aligned, 16-point font. If 'Courier Narrow' is available the browser will use that, otherwise it will choose 'Courier' but, if this is not available, the browser's default proportional spaced font will be used
- h3 as an underlined, left aligned, 16-point font. If 'Courier Narrow' is available the browser will use that, otherwise it will choose 'Courier' but, if this is not available, the browser's default proportional spaced font will be used
- p as a 14-point, left aligned, serif font.

Print evidence of your stylesheet, the HTML source and the browser view of the web page with the stylesheet attached.

21.3.4 Colour – Part 2

Text colour

You can use the color property to change the colour of text within a style. Earlier in the chapter you changed text colour with an embedded CSS color property in the HTML (see Section 21.2.8). As mentioned earlier it is usual to work with hex colour codes. These are always preceded by a hash (#) symbol.

> **Task 21af**
>
> Edit your files for Task 21ae so that style h1 is red.

Copy both files from your Task21ae folder into the Task21af folder. Open the stylesheet **mystyle1.css** in the text editor. Edit the stylesheet to add a new color declaration with the value #ff0000, like this.

```
h1     {font-family: "Times New Roman",Times,serif;
        font-size: 18pt;
        text-align: center;
        font-weight: bold;
        font-style: italic;
        color:#ff0000;}
```

The first two characters (ff) are red, 00 for green and 00 for blue. Save the stylesheet and refresh the browser to test it.

> **Task 21ag**
>
> Edit your files for Task 21af so that style h1 is contains the following colour hexadecimal components: red 0, blue ff and green 00.

Copy both files from your Task21af folder into the Task21ag folder. Open the stylesheet **mystyle1.css** in the text editor. Edit the color declaration to have a new value like this.

```
color:#0000ff;}
```

The value #0000ff is correct: the single 0 for the red component has been turned into 00, and the colours have been placed in the correct RGB (red-green-blue) order. Save the stylesheet and refresh the browser to test it.

Activity 21m

Copy the files saved in Activity 21l. Edit the stylesheet so that each style has the following colours. All values are in hexadecimal, and only hexadecimal codes should be used in your stylesheet:

- h1 is blue
- h2 has a full red component, green is 45 and blue is 0
- h3 has 8B blue, 3-D green and 48 red
- h4 has 8B for red and blue, and 0 green
- p is half red and no other colour.

Print evidence of your stylesheet and the browser view of the web page with the stylesheet attached.

CSS background colour

In Task 21o you set the background colour of a table using an in-line (embedded) CSS style. It is possible to do this for each element but is much easier to define once to be applied to all pages and for all elements on the page.

Task 21ah

Edit your files for Task 21ag so that the web page has a khaki (f0e68c) background colour.

Copy both files from your Task21ag folder into the Task21ah folder. Open the stylesheet **mystyle1.css** in the text editor. Add a new selector to define the body section of the web page. Use the background-color declaration to have a new value like this.

```
body     {background-color:#f0e68c;}
```

The background-color property must contain a hyphen. Save the stylesheet and refresh the browser to test it.

The background colour can be applied to the whole page (like this), or to tables, table rows, headers or footers with a single definition in the stylesheet.

Advice

The background-color declaration can also be used with other styles to give different effects. Try defining the defining the CSS or different styles like this.

```
h1    {background-color:#0000ff;}
```

Activity 21n

Copy the files saved in Activity 21m. Edit the stylesheet so that the web page has a background colour with a red component of f2, a blue component of 8e, and e8 green. All values are in hexadecimal, and only hexadecimal codes should be used in your stylesheet. Print evidence of your stylesheet and the browser view of the web page with the stylesheet attached.

21.3.5 Background images

Background images can be applied to the body section of a web page using the background-image declaration with a value containing the Uniform Resource Locator (which is often shortened to URL) followed by the image's address or filename. This can be used to place either a single background image in the centre of the page or can be repeated to place lots of copies of an image tiled to make the background.

Task 21ai

Edit your files for Task 21ah so that the web page has the file **task21ai.png** as a single background image placed in the top right of the window.

Copy both files from your Task21ah folder into the Task21ai folder. Copy the file **task21ai.png** into your Task21ai folder.

Add to the body section of the stylesheet **mystyle1.css** new background-image and background-repeat declarations with these values.

```
body    {background-color:#f0e68c;
         background-image:
         url("task21ai.png");
         background-repeat: no-repeat;
```

Each of these properties must contain a hyphen. Save the stylesheet and refresh the browser to test it. The page will look like this.

Tiled background images

Try changing the value for the background-repeat declaration to this.

```
background-repeat: repeat;
```

Save the stylesheet. Test the following section in your browser, maximised to fill the entire screen. What do you notice?

Also test out the values repeat-x and repeat-y with the background-repeat declaration to see what effects these have. Change the background-repeat declaration so that the image is no longer tiled. Save your web page and stylesheet in your Task21ai folder.

Advice

In later browsers, more than one background-image declaration can be placed in a window at the same time.

Position a background image

A single background image can be positioned within the browser window. Add a new background-position declaration like this to the body style in **task21ai.css**.

```
background-position: right top;}
```

Although this positions the image into the top right corner of the window, some of the text overwrites the background image. In some cases this effect can be very useful (for example, a watermark) but in this case it is difficult to read all of the text, as shown here.

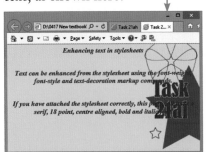 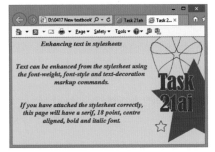

By adding a margin-right definition like this, you can force the contents away from the image so that the page now looks like this.

```
background-position: right top;
margin-right: 200px;}
```

Save and test the stylesheet.

Activity 21o

Open the stylesheet **brick.css** and the web page **bricknblocktopia.htm**. Edit the stylesheet so that the web page has a tiled background image using the file **brick.png**. Print evidence of your stylesheet and the browser view of the web page with the stylesheet attached.

Activity 21p

Copy the files saved in Activity 21o. Replace the background image with the file **wall.png**. Repeat this image down the left side of the web page only. Do not allow any of the text to overlap these images.

21.3.6 Use classes within a CSS

You can define different classes, which are subtypes within an element, in a stylesheet. You can define a class in the stylesheet by using the dot or full stop (.) symbol. These are very useful for adding to or changing styles without defining completely new styles. For example, this stylesheet defines the style h1 in the normal way. It also defines a class that can be used with any style to change the colour and alignment of the style that it is applied to.

```
h1       {text... ....left}
.right   {color: #0000ff;
          text-align: right}
```

Task 21aj

Open the stylesheet called **class1.css** and add a new class within this stylesheet that changes the default style to be right aligned and blue. Open the web page called **webpage7.htm** and apply this class to each line of text that starts with the word 'This'.

Copy the files **class1.css** and **webpage7.htm** into your Task21aj folder. Open these files in your text editor and in your web browser. Add the following markup to the stylesheet and save this in cascading stylesheet (.css) format.

```
.right   {color: #0000ff;
          text-align: right}
```

Enter the highlighted markup to the web page to add a class subtype to each line starting with the word 'This'. It should look like this.

```
<!DOCTYPE html>
<html>
<head>
  <title>Task 21aj</title>
  <link rel="stylesheet" type="text/css" href="class1.css">
</head>
<body>
  <h1>Task 21aj</h1>
  <h1>Style h1 is a sans-serif, 20 point, centre aligned font.</h1>
  <h1 class="right">This is the subtype of h1 called .right</h1>
  <h2>Style h2 is a sans-serif, 14 point, left aligned font.</h2>
  <h2 class="right">This is the subtype of h2 called .right</h2>
  <h3>Style h3 is a sans-serif, 12 point, left aligned, italic
font.</h3>
  <h3 class="right">This is the subtype of h3 called .right</h3>
  <p>Style p is a serif, 10 point, left aligned font.</p>
  <p class="right">This is the subtype of p called .right</p>
  <p>Last edited by YOUR NAME</p>
</body>
</html>
```

The screen should now look similar to this.

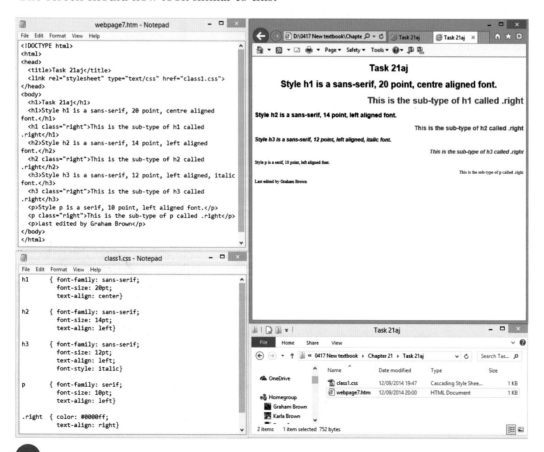

You can see from this printout that the original style definitions (except for the text alignment) have all been applied to the page. The text alignment and colour have been added to the styles using a class called 'right'.

21.3.7 CSS tables

Table definitions can be set in external stylesheets. The selector can be set for the whole table or for elements, such as the table header, table footer, table rows and individual cells of table data.

Task 21ak

Add an external stylesheet to your answer to Task 21d to set the following styles:

Selector	Property	Value
Web page	Background colour	#90ee90
Table	Background colour	#0000ff
Table cells	Background colour	#2eb757
Table header	Background colour	#cfcf00

All values are in hexadecimal. Show evidence of your method.

Copy the web page from your Task21d folder into your Task21ak folder. Open this file in your text editor. Add a new line to the head section to attach an external stylesheet to this web page, like this.

```
<link rel="stylesheet" type="text/css" href="table1.css">
```

In your second text editor window create in your Task21ak folder a new stylesheet called **table1.css**. For the first style the selector says the whole web page. This is the same as the body section, so create a style definition like this.

```
body  {background-color: #8fbc8f;
```

Save the web page and the stylesheet and test that this has worked. At to the stylesheet the background colour for all of the table like this.

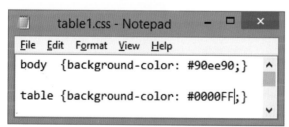

Save the stylesheet and test the web page, which should now look similar to this.

To change the table cells, add the td selector and a background-color property with a value of #2eb757 like this.

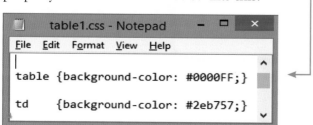

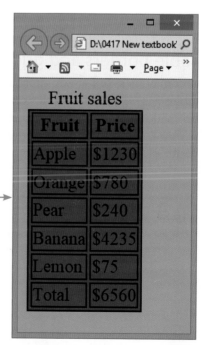

Save the stylesheet and test the web page, which should look similar to this.

You will see that the table background is still visible between the cells with the table data, but the table data is now a green colour.

Now add the thead selector and a background-color property with a value of #cfcf00 like this.

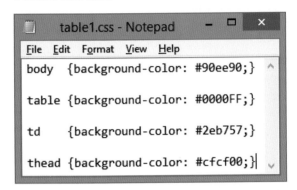

When you have saved the stylesheet and tested it in the browser your web page should look similar to this.

Advice

The technique used in this task – to do one small part, test it, correct it and test again (if need be) before going on to the next part – is ideal for any web development (or programming) and is very useful in practical examinations.

Activity 21q

Copy the files saved in Activity 21b. Attach an external stylesheet to this web page that defines the web page with a background of ff8c00 and a table with a background colour of ff4500. The table header should have a background with ffd700 and all other cells in the table should have a background with ffff00. All values are in hexadecimal. Place a single image of a sun (using the file **sun.png**) in the top right corner of the web page and make sure no other elements on the page could overwrite this. Print evidence of your method.

Table borders and gridlines

You may be asked to set internal gridlines and/or external table borders for tables. As you created tables earlier in the chapter, you will now be able to set the cell padding and spacing within a stylesheet as well as define table and cell borders within it. To set the border width of internal gridlines you must adjust the border width of the table data (or table header); for the external borders set the border for the table.

Task 21al

Edit the external stylesheet for your answer to Task 21ak so that the table has single external borders 4 pixels wide and internal gridlines 2 pixels wide.

Copy the files from your Task21ak folder into your Task21al folder. Open the stylesheet in your text editor. For the external borders add these three lines to table section of the CSS.

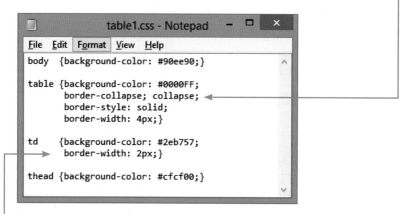

Save the stylesheet and test the web page, which should change from this to this.

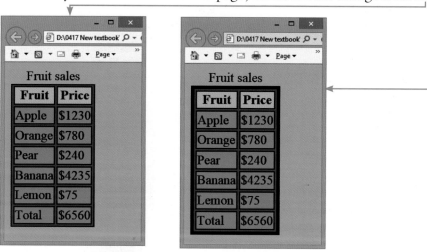

For the internal gridline width add this extra line to the table data section of the stylesheet.

    Again save and test to see the gridlines have reduced in width. ————————

    Experiment with other values for the border-style such as dashed, dotted or double.

Activity 21r

Copy the files saved in Activity 21q. Edit this stylesheet so that the table has a solid red border 4 pixels wide and cell padding of 10 pixels. Align all text in the table to the centre of each cell. All values must be in hexadecimal. Print evidence of your method.

21.4 Test and publish a website

Every web page that you have created has been stored in a single folder. This is to make sure that all the page elements are kept together for uploading a website to the internet. There are many ways of creating and uploading a website and its elements to the internet. It can be hosted on your computer, but this is rarely done as few of us have the hardware and enough bandwidth on our internet connection to do this. Many people use hosting companies in order to do this and upload a website into their hosting space.

21.4.1 Publish a website

All websites have a **domain name**, such as www.hodder.co.uk, which is used to find the site. To publish your website you must register the domain name you wish to use. You will use **FTP**, which means file transfer protocol, to upload your files to your web hosting space. To move the files you will need to install FTP client software on to your computer. In the screen shot below, I have used a free client package called Filezilla that will operate with both *Microsoft Windows* and *Apple Mac* platforms.

You need to upload:

- all the files in one folder
- an FTP client
- login details to a web hosting server that includes the name of the FTP host and the port used, and the username and password for the FTP.

Once you have logged on to the FTP host server you upload the files – in this case by dragging and dropping them from your folder into your web hosting space, like this.

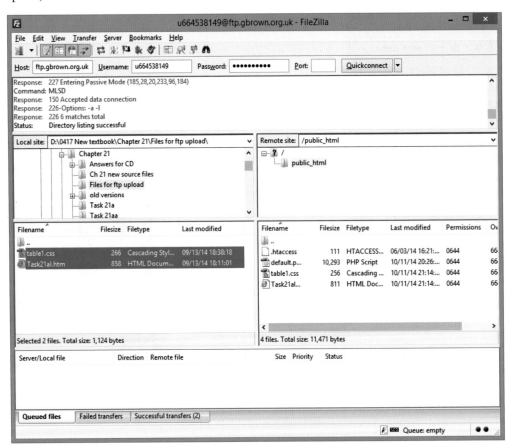

This will publish your website and it should appear when you open your browser and type in your domain name.

21.4.2 Test a website

Before testing takes place it is important to understand the purpose of the website and web page, and the target audience for the page. As much as possible, every element of a website should be tested before it is uploaded to the web server.

A test plan should be developed to make sure that you do not miss anything. Testing consists of two phases: functional testing and user testing. For the purposes of this book, you will use a simplified test plan.

Functional testing

All page elements must be checked to ensure that they appear as you expected. This will include for each web page:

- Is the table structure correct?
- Do all images appear as planned?
- Are all objects that are not supposed to be visible hidden from the user?
- Do all internal hyperlinks work?

For the entire website test:

- Can each page be found from the expected URL?
- Do all links between pages work as expected?
- Do all external hyperlinks open the correct web pages?

Table 21.3 gives an example of part of a test plan for a web page.

Table 21.3 Test plan for a web page

Test	Expected outcome	Actual outcome	Remedial action
Is table stylesheet attached?	Table format as in design specs	Yes	
Is font stylesheet attached?	Fonts as in design specs	No	Edit h4 to be #ff0000 rather than #f800000 Then retest.
Table structure 2 × 7	2 × 7	Yes	
Table borders hidden	Hidden	Visible	Set table attribute to border=" " Then retest.
Image XX995.jpg visible	Visible	Visible	
Image XX995.jpg 400 × 250	400 × 250	Yes	
Image XX995.jpg alt attribute set to "Image of 2nd edition of the textbook"	Yes	Yes	
Hyperlink from **Click here** goes to the top of page	Returns to top	Yes	
Hyperlink from **Home** icon goes to home page	Returns to home page	Yes	
Hyperlink from **Publisher** goes to www.hodder.co.uk	Opens Hodder home page	Yes	

User testing

The plan:

1 Decide what needs to be tested.
2 Find a suitable test audience of between two and five users or potential users. If a website is not designed for a specialist audience, select a variety of different users. **Do not** use IT specialists unless that is who the site is designed for.
3 Tell the users it is the website being tested not them, and that you value their thoughts and opinions.
4 Ask the users to speak their thoughts as they work but **do not** respond.
5 Observe the test so that difficulties can be noted (**do not** help in any way).

The test may include:

- tasks to complete using the site
- questions to answer
- navigation to the page to be tested from the home page.

Here is an example of some user test questions.

Let the user view the web page for 15 seconds, then ask:

1 What are your first impressions of the web page?

Give the user sufficient time to read the web page content, then ask:

2 What is the purpose of the web page?
3 Was this purpose clear from the beginning?
4 How easy is it to read and understand?
5 It there too much or little information?
6 What did you like about the web page?
7 What did you dislike about the web page?
8 Did you experience any difficulties on the web page?
9 What was the overall quality of your experience?
10 What could be done to improve the web page content or presentation?
11 Do you have any other comments or suggestions?

Justify the choice of test plan

You must be able to identify which elements of the test plan are functional testing and which are user testing. You must be able to make decisions on why and how you might test some elements of a web page.

Task 21am

Create one element of a functional test plan and one part of a user test plan for this website. Each text item is a hyperlink to a new page and a stylesheet, **rockstyle.css**, has been used. For each element justify your choices.

Starting with the functional plan, you are told each text item is a hyperlink to a new page, so look at the image provided and identify two words that need to be hyperlinked. Answers for this task might include:

Advice

If you are asked to do something and justify it, make it clear **why** you have made your choices and not made other choices.

Functional test: The hyperlink from 'News' goes to the News page. I must test that this link works so that I can navigate through to this web page; if the link is broken the page will not work. The original page may have contained a reference including a drive letter and path that may not appear on another computer.

User test: I would select a range of test users from the target audience who are aged between 14 and 40. I would select these test users because they are more likely to want to listen to rock music than young children or older people.

Index